THE COMPLETE POEMS OF KENNETH REXROTH

The COMPLETE POEMS *of* KENNETH REXROTH

EDITED BY SAM HAMILL &
BRADFORD MORROW

COPPER CANYON PRESS

詩

Published by arrangement with New Directions Publishing Corporation.

Printed in the United States of America

COVER ART: *Relic*, 1963. Gouache with gauze collage on Chinese paper, by Leo Kenney, collection of Mary Randlett, Olympia, Washington. Photograph by Rob Vinnedge. Grateful acknowledgment to Mary Randlett and William Merchant Pease for making it possible to use Mr. Kenney's art.

Copper Canyon Press is in residence at Fort Worden State Park in Port Townsend, Washington under the auspices of the Centrum Foundation. Centrum is a gathering place for artists and creative thinkers from around the world, students of all ages and backgrounds, and audiences seeking extraordinary cultural enrichment.

LIBRARY OF CONGRESS CATALOGING-IN-PUBLICATION DATA

Rexroth, Kenneth 1905–1982
[Poems]
The complete poems of Kenneth Rexroth / edited by Sam Hamill and Bradford Morrow
p. cm.
ISBN 1-55659-164-0
ISBN 1-55659-217-5 (pbk.)
I. Hamill, Sam. II. Morrow, Bradford. [date] III. Title.
PS3535.E923 A17 2002
811'.52 – dc21
2002001706

9 8 7 6 5 4 3

COPPER CANYON PRESS
Post Office Box 271
Port Townsend, Washington 98368
www.coppercanyonpress.org

ACKNOWLEDGMENTS FOR UNCOLLECTED POEMS
"Noretorp-Noretsyh" appeared in *Evergreen Review*, Vol. I, No. 2, 1957; "Untitled" appeared in *Ark III*, San Francisco, Winter, 1957; "140 Syllables" was previously published in *Ark II, Moby I*, San Francisco, 1956–57; and "The Working Day" appeared in *Our San Francisco*, Garden City, N.Y., Diablo Press, 1964. Our gratitude to the editors and publishers.

CONTENTS

THE HOMESTEAD CALLED DAMASCUS (1920–1925)

THE ART OF WORLDLY WISDOM (1920–1930)

A PROLEGOMENON TO A THEODICY (1925–1927)

IN WHAT HOUR (1940)

THE PHOENIX AND THE TORTOISE (1944)

THE SIGNATURE OF ALL THINGS (1949)

THE DRAGON AND THE UNICORN (1952)

IN DEFENSE OF THE EARTH (1956)

NATURAL NUMBERS (1964)

GÖDEL'S PROOF (1965)

THE HEART'S GARDEN, THE GARDEN'S HEART (1967)

LOVE IS AN ART OF TIME (1974)

THE MORNING STAR (1979)

> *We have preferred the power that apes greatness – Alexander first of all, and then the Roman conquerors, whom our school history books, in an incomparable vulgarity of soul, teach us to admire. We have conquered in our turn…our reason has swept everything away. Alone at last, we build our empire upon a desert. How then could we conceive that higher balance in which nature balanced history, beauty, and goodness, and which brought the music of numbers even into the tragedy of blood? We turn our back on nature, we are ashamed of beauty. Our miserable tragedies have the smell of an office, and their blood is the color of dirty ink.*
>
> – Albert Camus

The year was 1948. Camus's relationships with André Breton and Jean-Paul Sartre had begun to feel the strain that would eventually lead him to disavow all ties with the existentialists. In North America, the official policies of the Cold War were under way. Senator Joseph McCarthy had recruited young politicos like Robert Kennedy and Richard Nixon to help him "purge the United States Government of communist infiltrators." School children were drilled in preparation for "atom bombs." And American poetry was divided between the conservative New Critics, for whom T.S. Eliot was a standard-bearer, and those who followed William Carlos Williams's insistence upon "American idiom" and measure for poetry. The Bollingen Prize Committee meeting in 1948 included Eliot himself as well as elements from both camps (Conrad Aiken, W.H. Auden, Louise Bogan, Robert Lowell, Allen Tate, Karl Shapiro, and Léonie Adams) and was timed to coincide with Eliot's visit to the United States that fall. When they awarded the prize to Ezra Pound for his *Pisan Cantos*, a furor ensued. Pound was locked up in St. Elizabeth's Hospital for the insane – charged (but untried) with treason for his infamous radio broadcasts from Rome during World War II – writing his great poem and translating Confucius. The "runner-up" was *Paterson* (*Book Two*), by Williams. It had been the stated ambition of Pound and Williams to "break the back of the iamb," to liberate

American poetry. Williams admired some of Eliot's poetry but despised his influence.

In San Francisco, the forty-three-year-old Kenneth Rexroth must have watched with interest. He had connections with many of those involved. Reading Ezra Pound's *Cathay*, translations from the eighth-century poet Li Po, had first opened Rexroth's eyes to Chinese poetry while he was still a teenager. It was a huge awakening. In the early 1930s, he corresponded with Pound, who provided insights into French and Chinese poetry especially, and who introduced him to James Laughlin, publisher of New Directions and Rexroth's enduring friend and patron. The Pound/Rexroth letters conclude in political hostility and mutual animosity. Rexroth was then involved with the Wobblies and many left-wing causes and despised "Pound's virulent, anti-Semitic doggerel." Pound was immersed in the economic theories of Major Douglas and Social Credit, and actively supported Mussolini. When Rexroth objected to including an Ezra Pound rant in *An "Objectivists" Anthology*, Pound responded that he would have nothing to do with the project if "dot Chew Bolschevick Rexwrothsky" was included.

Also in the thirties, Rexroth explored cubist art and poetry, eventually resolving his own differences with Tristan Tzara and Breton in a "cubist" poem, "Fundamental Disagreement with Two Contemporaries" (from *The Art of Worldly Wisdom*, 1949). The exact nature of their disagreement remains for speculation. His experiments with cubist poetry were short-lived, although he would say years later that he gave them up only because so few people understood what he was doing. He returned to the spare style he had been evolving since his first poems.

Politically, he was a pacifist, like Lowell, William Stafford, and several other poets of the time. But Rexroth's has been an almost solitary voice for pacificism throughout all the world's violence since World War I. Before the end of World War II, he wrote in his note to *The Phoenix and the Tortoise*, "If the shorter poems might well be dedicated to [D.H.] Lawrence, 'The Phoenix and the Tortoise' might well be dedicated to Albert Schweitzer, the man who in our time pre-eminently has realized the dream of Leonardo da Vinci. Leonardo died impotent and broken, all his projects half done. He proved that the human will is too small a door for the person to force through into universality. Schweitzer is an outstanding example of a man who found that door which is straight, and smaller than a needle's eye, but through which the universalization of the human soul, the creation of the true person, comes freely, as a guest."

One thing is clear: Rexroth, already a citizen of the world, believed that the "universalization of the human soul, the creation of the true person," may come freely, but only after enormous struggle to find that "door which is straight, and smaller than a needle's eye." The awakening he sought would lie in a poetry of increasing limpidity and deceptive simplicity. His search for that door would lead him through the history of philosophy, comparative religion, and the history of ideas. Like Pound, he was a neoclassicist engaged in the avant-garde. He was a master of juxtaposition and polyphony. Along with the Greek and Latin translations in *The Phoenix and the Tortoise* are three poems by the T'ang dynasty poet Tu Fu, whom Rexroth would come to revere. He translated about forty of Tu Fu's poems over the years, calling him "the greatest non-epic, non-dramatic poet in history."

In the long title poem, "The Phoenix and the Tortoise," Rexroth incorporates paraphrases and translations of Japanese tanka from Gotoku Daiji, *Hyakunin Isshu*, Lady Akazome Emon, Emperor Sanjo, and many others. By 1948, his course and methodology were set. He adopted something similar to what has since been labeled the "ideogrammic method" advocated by Pound. All being becomes contemporary in his hands. He borrows, he layers, he juxtaposes, holding his poems together lyrically through the effective use of a roughly seven-syllable line. Echoes and paraphrases and translations of ancient classics of the East and West become an integral part of the poem in progress, rewarding the reader with evocative and associative resonances. This practice also elevates the poetry out of the realm of the merely personal lyric or monologue, creating a historical context. Rexroth the poet is the contemporary of Sophocles and Sappho, Tu Fu and Pierre Reverdy, and literature is the bread of their communion.

Another clear example of Rexroth's craft is "When We with Sappho," which begins with a direct translation of the Sapphic fragment "about the cool water / the wind sounds..." but suddenly becomes an intensely personal love poem, a meditation that runs nearly four pages. Sappho becomes a presence opening the mind of the poet. A door. Rexroth's poetry incorporates the past as a presence in daily reality and evolving consciousness. What he reads is an essential element of mundane reality. Donald Gutierrez, in his study *"The Holiness of the Real": The Short Verse of Kenneth Rexroth*, has written of this poem, "Rexroth's verse sounds like an exalted experience undergone through words that have been rendered so plain, so 'artless,' and 'right' as to take on a transparency revealing the heart of the poem's life itself."

William Carlos Williams, reviewing *The Phoenix and the Tortoise* in *The Quarterly Review of Literature*, would say almost nothing about translation. And of Rexroth's philosophy he wrote, "I know nothing of mysticism... I'm going to try to take out the poetry, appraise it as best I can and leave the mysticism, as far as I can, intact. But first let me say that this is one of the most completely realized arguments I have encountered in a book of verse in my time." The title poem is rich in what Williams called mysticism. It begins with the geologic past of the California Coast Range, moving quickly and surely into "The falling light of the Spartan / Heroes of the late Hellenic dusk," while considering various ideas of Aquinas, early Chinese philosophers, some ancient Greeks, and far too many other references and accretions to quote out of context. The net is cast wide. This "ideogrammic" style is common in Asian literature, and Rexroth knew it via Japanese *honkadori*.* The "dance of the intellect among the ten thousand things," as Tu Fu would say.

Rexroth received a Guggenheim Fellowship in 1948 and traveled in Europe, working on his long poem "The Dragon and

* the common practice of paraphrasing classics.

the Unicorn." Also in 1948, he added the finishing strokes to one of the most beautifully conceived and executed volumes of poetry since Pound's *Cathay*, *The Signature of All Things*. Most of the poems and poems-in-translation were composed to be sung, their melodies an essential part of the composition. Among these poems, two elegies stand out: "Delia Rexroth," a poem addressed to the poet's mother, who died in 1916 when he was eleven; and "Andrée Rexroth," an elegy for the woman to whom he was married for thirteen years and who died in 1940 following years of struggle with an inherited brain disease.

There is also a remarkable homage, "A Letter to William Carlos Williams," in which Rexroth observes, "And you're 'pure,' too, / A real classic, though not loud / About it – a whole lot like / The girls of the Anthology. / Not like strident Sappho, who / For all her grandeur, must have / Had endometriosis, / But like Anyte, who says / Just enough, softly, for all / The thousands of years to remember." The poem illuminates the "sacramental relationships" that he had come to understand as essential to poetry, and does so at least in part by praising Williams's optimism. Rexroth held on to hope despite devastating personal and social losses and a struggle with deep-seated paranoia. But he was no wide-eyed optimist. He believed that love is the sacramental expression of hope and responsibility. Williams would claim later that the events described in the poem never actually took place, but what does that matter? The poem creates its own occasion.

BETWEEN TWO WARS

Remember that breakfast one November –
Cold black grapes smelling faintly
Of the cork they were packed in,
Hard rolls with hot, white flesh,
And thick, honey sweetened chocolate?
And the parties at night; the gin and the tangos?
The torn hair nets, the lost cuff links?
Where have they all gone to,

The beautiful girls, the abandoned hours?
They said we were lost, mad and immoral,
And interfered with the plans of the management.
And today, millions and millions, shut alive
In the coffins of circumstance,
Beat on the buried lids,
Huddle in the cellars of ruins, and quarrel
Over their own fragmented flesh.

"They have hope," Thales said, "who have nothing else." By age forty-three, Rexroth had survived the deaths of his mother and first wife; he had roamed the west during the Depression and written trail guides for the WPA; he worked as camp cook and roustabout in the Cascades and hiked through the Sierras. During World War II, he was a conscientious objector who worked in a hospital and personally provided sanctuary for Japanese Americans. Upon the incarceration of thousands of Japanese Americans at the outset of World War II, he declared his "disaffiliation from the American capitalist state" complete – and for the remaining years of his life, he would act in American letters and history not as a disaffiliated passive bystander recollecting in tranquillity or in bitterness, but as an alienated activist-poet, a devoted social commentator and agitator. He wrote literary journalism, "for money or for log-rolling for one's friends." He was one of the great essayists of his age, and some of his best were simply dictated, then transcribed from tape.

Rexroth's poems reflect an increasingly breathtaking sweep of understanding – of the languages and cultures he studied, of naturalism, and of the poetries of preliterate peoples. He delved into Kabbalah and Gnosticism. Reading the *Encyclopædia Britannica* inspired his poem, "Gic to Har." He read it, he said, "Straight through. Like a novel." He translated poems by Neruda and Lorca, Heine, classical Chinese poetry, Japanese classics, the French poems of O.V. Milosz and Reverdy; he studied Bakunin and the Anarchists, Buddhist and Taoist classics, the *Bhagavad Gita* and the Greeks of the *Anthology*; he wrote reviews on jazz, newspaper columns, and he composed a libretto for a ballet, *Original Sin*, that was performed in San Francisco with music composed and led by John Lewis of the Modern Jazz Quartet. He edited an anthology of new young English poets, one of whom, Denise Levertov, he praised and promoted tirelessly even though they had never met. He also persuaded New Directions to publish Levertov and William Everson, who would later don the robes of Dominican Catholicism and publish as Brother Antoninus.

By 1958, the American political scenario had changed. Suburbia was spreading everywhere. Eisenhower warned of the growing threat of the "military-industrial complex," and much of the country enjoyed a feeling of well-being, but for the escalating Cold War. Poetry was the province of New Critics and the poetry establishment was firmly ensconced within the walls of academia. There were very few women poets and even fewer minority poets being published. But there were little coffeehouses beginning to spring up in various cities where the hip crowd would read poetry aloud in public.

And the San Francisco Renaissance was in full swing. Rexroth promoted poets on the airwaves at KPFA, including Lawrence Ferlinghetti, the surrealist Philip Lamantia, the young Gary Snyder, Philip Whalen, Levertov, Brother Antoninus, LeRoi Jones (Amiri Baraka), Diane di Prima, Bob Kaufman, and many more. He helped found the Poetry Center at San Francisco State University and wrote his "Classics Revisited" columns surveying the literature of the world for *Saturday Review*, and later collected them in two volumes. Then Jack Kerouac's prose swept through a generation like a brush fire. Rexroth, although praising Kerouac's *On the Road*, would later claim (in a letter to Morgan Gibson) that he'd never read *The Dharma Bums*, in which he is unflatteringly portrayed. And he bristled at being labeled "father of the Beats." He and Kerouac didn't like each other.

Nevertheless, the publication and obscenity trial of Allen Ginsberg's "Howl" was the result of a poetry reading on October 13, 1955, at the Six Gallery in San Francisco, organized in part and emceed by Kenneth Rexroth. Although the audience was tiny, given the venue was a whitewashed 20-by-25-foot stall, the reading shook American poetry – indeed the poetry of most of the world – to its very core. The readers included Gary Snyder, Philip Whalen, Michael McClure, Philip Lamantia, and Ginsberg, who read "Howl" for the first time, ending in tears to wild applause. When Lawrence Ferlinghetti published Ginsberg's book at City Lights, one of this country's great literary legal battles followed. Called to testify in court, Rexroth confounded the prosecution by placing Ginsberg's poem directly "in the long Jewish Old Testament tradition of testimonial poetry."

It has often been suggested that the major inspiration for the poem probably was not as much Walt Whitman's model as Rexroth's lament on the death of Dylan Thomas, "Thou Shalt Not Kill," written in 1953, with its heavy cadences and charged imagery.

They are murdering all the young men.
For half a century now, every day,
They have hunted them down and killed them.
They are killing them now,
At this minute, all over the world,
They are killing the young men.
They know ten thousand ways to kill them.
Every year they invent new ones.
In the jungles of Africa,
In the marshes of Asia,
In the deserts of Asia,
In the slave pens of Siberia,
In the slums of Europe,
In the nightclubs of America,
The murderers are at work.
....
You killed him,
Benign Lady on the postage stamp.
He was found dead at a Liberal Weekly luncheon.

He was found dead on the cutting room floor.
He was found dead at a *Time* policy conference.
Henry Luce killed him with a telegram to the Pope.
Mademoiselle strangled him with a padded brassiere.
Old Possum sprinkled him with a tea ball.
After the wolves were done, the vaticides
Crawled off with his bowels to their classrooms and
    quarterlies.

....

The Gulf Stream smells of blood
As it breaks on the sand of Iona
And the blue rocks of Canarvon.
And all the birds of the deep sea rise up
Over the luxury liners and scream,
"You killed him! You killed him.
In your God damned Brooks Brothers suit,
You son of a bitch."

It is interesting to note that "Possum" – Eliot – ruling deity of the poetry establishment, appears among Rexroth's list of murderers of poetry. Both Ginsberg and Rexroth are on record, however, denying that Rexroth's poem influenced "Howl." Ginsberg's poem achieved acclaim and notoriety unlike any other poem of its time. Whether Rexroth liked it or not, his name would be associated with the Beats for the rest of his life. And public poetry readings would play a major role in making American poetry in the twentieth century a true revolution.

But Kenneth Rexroth would not be caught in a "coffin of circumstance." His house had become a weekly meetingplace for existentialist poets, free-love advocates, anarchists, artists, and literary hangers-on. He would later say of those years that, if nothing else, he finally had some readers he didn't know on a first-name basis. In the early days, these gatherings had been vital and exciting, but by the time Snyder and Whalen had left for Japan, Duncan for Mallorca, and Brother Antoninus for a Dominican retreat, Rexroth was about out of patience with strung-out "Beatniks" who arrived with their imitations of *On the Road*. He charged them with being "mere examples of a veneer, a gastro-pharmaceutical change rather than of a profound spiritual awakening." Most of his closest friends in San Francisco were "Beat poets." Was he? "An entomologist," he declared, "is not a bug." He disliked what he saw on the San Francisco horizon as his marriage fell apart and America began building for war in southeast Asia.

He had married a third time, to Marthe Larsen, and was the father of two girls when this marriage collapsed in 1955. By the late fifties, his personal life was chaos. He was poverty-stricken and suffered severe attacks of paranoia. He wrote newspaper columns. He withdrew. A gourmet who insisted that today's groceries be purchased today and who always wore a jacket to his well-set table, he lived from hand to mouth, insisting, "In America, being poor is no excuse for not eating well." Devastated by another failed marriage and dispirited by a string of lovers, alienated from many of his old friends, he sought refuge in lecture and reading tours. His performances were legendary. He read to jazz and to koto music, alone or with friends invited to join. But his last years in San Francisco were mostly difficult and lonely, and finally, after forty-one years there, he decided to leave.

He moved to Santa Barbara in 1968 and several years later married his longtime assistant, Carol Tinker. He taught two courses at the University of California: a poetry-and-music class designed for a dozen or so students, but which drew over 400 students during the protests against American involvement in Vietnam; and a weekly "evening-with-Kenneth" modeled on the salon he'd orchestrated in the city. He reveled in the company of young people eager to learn from a scholar out of office. Friends and students gathered at his little house in Montecito with wine and cheese, and Rexroth would install himself in a huge easy chair in a corner of the tiny living room and read in French, Japanese, Greek, Latin, or Spanish, giving spontaneous translations of the poems along with capsule biographies of the poets under discussion. Everything led into his great web. He was happiest in this element. One could hardly be expected to understand Georg Trakl without understanding German expressionism, traditional taboos pertaining to incest, pre–World War I economic conditions in Europe, the history of German rebellion against the Catholic church, the peculiarly German approach to anarchism in Trakl's milieu, and of course the poet's troubled mind. Rexroth believed poetry embodied a great history of ideas and could become a path to enlightenment. His appetite for knowledge was insatiable and he had almost perfect recall.

He was a unique polyglot iconoclast, a pacifist who loved tweaking the nose of bourgeois complacency and pretension, but whose bouts of paranoia sometimes left friends utterly confounded. He believed the embodiment of justice could not be separate from the physical and emotional expression of compassion, and could still declare, "You killed him.... You son of a bitch." His poetry reflects an increasing interest in Shingon Buddhism while he loudly objected to what he perceived to be the abuse of power by Buddhist teachers in America.

The Buddhist bodhisattva of compassion, Kuan Shih Yin (Chinese for, "who-listens-to-the-world's-cries"), in Japanese Kannon, figures prominently in his later books. She is the embodiment of Buddhist compassion for the suffering of all sentient beings, a figure of eternal mercy who "pours the morning dew."

SUCHNESS

In the theosophy of light,
The logical universal
Ceases to be anything more
Than the dead body of an angel.
What is substance? Our substance
Is whatever we feed our angel.
The perfect incense for worship
Is camphor, whose flames leave no ashes.

Rexroth brings an essentially Catholic attitude to his sacramental practice, but the equation, the realization is fundamentally Buddhist. In his sacrament he finds Buddhist emptiness, the essence of the "dead body of an angel." Buddhism has no angels. The flame without ash is the light of coming to comprehend the essential emptiness or thusness at the heart of Zen practice.

Toward the end of his life, his poems achieved a grand simplicity that should not be mistaken for lack of consequence. Incense and sacrament are rituals preparing one for the door that is straight and smaller than the needle's eye. Like his favorite poet, Tu Fu, he was a deeply spiritual and political poet who included rather than excluded the world's religions. Unlike Tu Fu, he was a poet of erotic love without peer in his lifetime, perhaps without peer in the American language, as Eliot Weinberger has written. "Erotic love," Rexroth was fond of saying, "is one of the highest forms of contemplation." Spirituality and erotic love could not be separated in his poetry, except mockingly, ironically. This same spirituality earlier produces:

THE ADVANTAGES OF LEARNING

I am a man with no ambitions
And few friends, wholly incapable
Of making a living, growing no
Younger, fugitive from some just doom.
Lonely, ill-clothed, what does it matter?
At midnight I make myself a jug
Of hot white wine and cardamon seeds.
In a torn grey robe and old beret,
I sit in the cold writing poems,
Drawing nudes on the crooked margins,
Copulating with sixteen year old
Nymphomaniacs of my imagination.

Does he mock himself or is he tweaking noses? The poem draws heavily from Greek and Latin traditions and even more from the classical Chinese. It achieves tragic proportion through self-mockery, and boldly reveals its poetic tradition. It could almost pass as a version of Catullus or of Li Po. His humor is often double-edged. He delighted in the scandalous, both in his behavior and in his writing, for years telling his audiences, "I write poetry to seduce women and to overthrow the capitalist system… In that order." And yet he was a feminist who did more to encourage young women poets (and women in general) than any writer of his generation. No artist can do more than contribute to a tradition and leave a legacy. Rexroth was our Catullus, our Li Po, shocking his audience with laughter, his tradition one of celebratory eroticism and social protest and his legacy a devotion to learning.

Nor can the erotic be separated from the scientific. Rexroth combined the study of science with personal experience and philosophy like no poet before him. He was among the first American poets to recognize the complex utter interdependence of things in the ecology of the imagination as in biological reality. Reading Lyell's nineteenth-century study of geology, he composes "Lyell's Hypothesis Again" (another poem for Marie Kass Rexroth, his second wife), which looks hard at the "ego, bound by personal / Tragedy and the vast / Impersonal vindictiveness / Of the ruined and ruining world…" and concludes:

> We have escaped the bitterness
> Of love, and love lost, and love
> Betrayed. And what might have been,
> And what might be, fall equally,
> Away with what is, and leave
> Only these ideograms
> Printed on the immortal
> Hydrocarbons of flesh and stone.

Ultimately, he finds his tenderness in stone and in time. His mystical transcendence is as rooted in modern science as in traditional wisdom-teaching. The later books are the culmination of a lifetime's struggle toward a true spiritual awakening. The erotic and the scientific become one while time is seen in multiple contexts ranging from the momentary to the geologic.

Each of his longer poems, he notes, ends at a point of transcendent experience. The same is often enough true of his shorter poems, especially his erotic poetry. "It's one thing to write a love poem at twenty," he would laugh, "and quite another at seventy."

CONFUSION OF THE SENSES

Moonlight fills the laurels
Like music. The moonlit
Air does not move. Your white
Face moves towards my face.
Voluptuous sorrow
Holds us like a cobweb
Like a song, a perfume, the moonlight.
Your hair falls and holds our faces.
Your lips curl into mine.
Your tongue enters my mouth.
A bat flies through the moonlight.
The moonlight fills your eyes
They have neither iris nor pupil
They are only globes of cold fire
Like the deers' eyes that go by us
Through the empty forest.
Your slender body quivers
And smells of seaweed.
We lie together listening
To each other breathing in the moonlight.
Do you hear? We are breathing. We are alive.

We live in an age in which the poetry of mature erotic love is out of fashion. Our poets and critics tend to prefer the cool cerebral play of Stevens to the naked jig of Dr. Williams. Much of our poetry takes no political or emotional risks. Rexroth was fond of quoting Yvor Winters, "Emotion in any situation must be as far as possible eliminated," following it with a pregnant pause and a great guffaw. What he claimed for the poetry of Lawrence may be claimed equally for his own poems, for "behind the machinery is an intense, direct, personal, mystical apprehension of reality" that is informed by his acceptance of responsibility in the cruelest century. For Rexroth, love is the ultimate expression of that responsibility. Like Camus, whom he admired, he engaged philosophy for the sake of clarity of commitment. "Practical philosophy," he often told his students, "has a test: If your mother or father or closest friend suddenly died, would you turn first to your Philosophy professor for understanding?" Unlike Camus, he sought a "personal, mystical apprehension of reality" that was fundamentally Buddhist.

To some, Rexroth is a quintessential erotic poet; to others, a great nature poet; to others still, a political, literary, or spiritual master; and to still others, the great translator of classical Chinese and Japanese poetry at midcentury. Often, all or most of these aspects congeal within a single poem, just as the whole body of his poetry reveals a universe. In few other poets has sixty years of prolific writing so consistently followed and expanded the themes of the earliest work.

In his note to *The Collected Longer Poems*, he wrote, "all the sections of this book now seem to me almost as much one long poem as do *The Cantos* or *Paterson*." He also wrote, "Most poets resemble Whitman in one regard – they write only one book and that an interior autobiography." Rexroth's poetry is vast and contains multitudes. The longer poems may indeed be read as a single poem. Or they may be read as they turn up among the shorter poems. And sometimes shorter poems are revealed again within the longer ones, changing their context. Like Pound and Williams, he built with many blocks. If his life is to be found and known through the poetry, it is only in moments of awakening to a transcendent insight, whether in poems informed by years of hiking and camping in the California mountains, or by spiritual and philosophical inquiry.

*

His last years were remarkably productive. In 1967, he visited Japan for the first time and wrote "The Heart's Garden, the Garden's Heart," one of his most accomplished suites of poems. There was a Fulbright Fellowship to Kyoto in 1974, and some significant literary recognition that included a Guggenheim Fellowship and the Copernicus Award for his lifetime's achievement. He made several other visits to Japan, and established a modest Kenneth Rexroth Award for Young Women in 1975. He used his influence at Seabury Press to have published the first volumes of Czesław Miłosz and Homero Aridjis, among others, in American English. Remembering Rexroth's generosity, Milosz has written, "For me, however, he was above all a splendid poet and a splendid translator of Chinese and Japanese poetry."

There is a particular sweetness, a depth of love, in the later poems that is probably a result of the poet's "feminization." During his last years he produced, in collaboration with Ling Chung, the remarkable *Complete Poems of Li Ch'ing-chao*, one of China's greatest poets and a woman who also wrote a deeply personal poetry, and *The Orchid Boat* (later retitled *Women Poets of China* for its paperback release); produced, in collaboration with Ikuko Atsumi, *The Burning Heart* (retitled *Women Poets of Japan* for the paper edition); edited *Seasons of Sacred Lust*, selected poems of Kazuko Shiraishi; and, in one of the most remarkable of feats, pulled off the invention of "a contemporary young woman" poet from Japan, Marichiko, whose love poems are explicit.

VII

Making love with you
Is like drinking sea water.
The more I drink
The thirstier I become,
Until nothing can slake my thirst
But to drink the entire sea.

XXV

Your tongue thrums and moves
Into me, and I become
Hollow and blaze with
Whirling light, like the inside
Of a vast expanding pearl.

He calls her a follower of Marichi, an avatar of the Shakti of Shiva, and "A great Indian prostitute / Who was really an incarnate / Bodhisattva. The girl herself [Marichikvo] / Turned out to be a Communist." His persona was so convincing that a number of Japanese scholars went in search of Marichiko.

Critics and biographers have spent much more ink on Rexroth's personality and his stormy relationships with wives, lovers, and friends than on his work. Born in 1905 in Indiana, he was particularly close to his mother. She died, bedridden, with the young Kenneth at her side in 1916. Unable to care for a child, his father left him in Toledo, with his grandmother who routinely beat him with a cane. Eventually rescued by his father, he ended up in Chicago where he quit school and began his astonishing journeys. Although apparently incapable of monogamy, he nevertheless believed in marriage as the highest sacrament. Like many an inconoclastic genius, he was a mass of contradictions, but there is little doubt that at the root of his complex personality lay an orphaned, battered child, a man who overcompensated for deep self-doubts while struggling to embody profound spiritual awakening.

Millions of pearls in the mist
Of the waterfall added
Together make a rainbow.
Deep in the heart one pearl glows
With ten million rainbows.
....

XXXIII

Not by flesh, but by love, man
Comes into the world, lost in
The illimitable ocean
Of which there is no shore.

Of his last suites of poems, "The Heart's Garden, the Garden's Heart" (quoted above) and "On Flower Wreath Hill" are journey poems in which the search for love and its embodiment and the search for spiritual realization become completely integrated. But the nirvana that can be glimpsed is not the nirvana that can be realized; that is, nirvana cannot be reached through the desire to reach nirvana. The bodhisattva Kannon responds to the suffering of the world with infinite compassion as she pours the morning dew.

The promise of the vow of
The Bodhisattva is so
Powerful the stormy ocean of
Karma turns to an unruffled mirror.

And yet the poet finds that his own heart cannot achieve such calm transparency except in the eternal moment of the poem. "My heart is not a mirror. / I cannot see myself in it." He cannot fully embody the bodhisattva's vow to remain in the cycle of birth and death until the last sentient being becomes enlightened and enters nirvana. He cannot master the practice of infinite compassion, although he comprehends its possibility. Hell, to some, is seeing an image of unattainable paradise. But Rexroth never believed the bodhisattva vow to be unattainable. He simply could not quite get there before he died. The Midwestern boy who began life attending his mother's agonizing death and was beaten by his grandmother, began his last poetic journey, "On Flower Wreath Hill," with a search for the primally feminine in Kyoto:

An aging pilgrim on a
Darkening path walks through the

Fallen and falling leaves, through
A forest grown over the
Hilltop tumulus of a
Long dead princess, as the
Moonlight grows and the daylight
Fades and the Western Hills turn
Dim in the distance and the
Lights come on, pale green
In the streets of the hazy city.

A dead princess, whatever else she may be, is unattainable. The poet therefore eventually finds only himself in a world that is simultaneously ancient and contemporary, and where

The mist
Dissolves everything else, the
Living and the dead, except
This occult mathematics of light.

Ultimately, he realizes, "this / Transcendent architecture / Lost in the forest where no one passes / Is itself the Net of Indra." And in the "occult mathematics of light" within the poem, Rexroth brings the "music of numbers even into the tragedy of blood." The poem concludes on the note of a soundless flute resonating in the void.

The man who survives in these poems is a great man, wise beyond words, a poet polished by great loss and small glory. He has given in his work exactly what he sought in life: a sense of a compassionate moral center from which the possibility of ultimate awakening may be realized.

His death, on the anniversary of D-Day, in 1982, went almost unnoticed by the literary establishment. Newspaper obituaries were brief, noting only the passing of the "father of the Beat Generation." No doubt his vocal disdain for the "eastern literary establishment" and bourgeois taste-making in general kept his work from being more favorably and widely reviewed in the media. If he was sometimes paranoid, arrogant, or self-absorbed, he was much more often funny, generous, and compassionate. He played the *enfant terrible* to the end, even as a grand old man. He was the author of fifty-four books and an enormous unpublished anthology of poetry of preliterate peoples from around the world. Much of his archived work remains uncataloged two decades after his death.

Rexroth is buried in Santa Barbara on a bluff above the Pacific. All the other graves face the continent. Rexroth alone faces the ocean, the west that leads into the east. His epitaph: "The swan sings / In sleep / On the lake of the mind."

– SAM HAMILL

THE COMPLETE POEMS OF KENNETH REXROTH

EARLIEST AND UNCOLLECTED POEMS

SAINT JOHN

He loved you and you lay upon His breast,
And you were with Him there on Calvary,
And you saw Peter follow Him to rest
Upon another Cross beyond the sea;
Peter found peace head down in a far land
But you for love remained on Calvary;
Your heart was dark save for the spot that shone
In pain upon His cross eternally.

In all the simple daily things His hand
Had touched in the old house at Bethany
Was stain of blood and mark of agony.
A myriad deaths were yours to die alone,
Humblest of martyrs, thy humility
Kept thee for very love on Calvary.

A LANTERN AND A SHADOW

"IN THAT HOUR I HAVE SEEN"

I

In that hour I have seen
The long white gleaming throats of mountains
With faces lifted
To the moon.

II

The momentary angles
    of a shattered prism
    hold wraiths of
    iridescent mountains
    which were sorrow
    and pain is
    in a mirror of
    ice.

"I PASS YOUR HOME IN A SLOW VERMILION DAWN"

I pass your home in a slow vermilion dawn,
the blinds are drawn and a window is open,
the subtle breeze from the lake
is as your breath upon my cheek.

All day long I walk in an intermittent rainfall,
I pluck a vermilion tulip in the city gardens
tasting the delicate raindrops that cling to its petals –
four o'clock and it is a lone colour in the city.

I pass your home in a rainy evening,
your figure is a faint gesture amongst lighted walls.
Late into the night I sit before a white sheet of paper –
till a wet vermilion petal quivers on my hand.

"THE MINUTE FINGERS OF A TINY WIND"

The minute fingers of a tiny wind
    arrange a shadow tracery
    of leaf and hair about your face,
    our superficial conversation

strikes overtones amongst
nuances of the nonexistent,
downstream a group of working-men
posed in unaccustomed languor
catch insignificant fish,
a brown row of ducklings
jerks itself across the water
moving like cartridges
into a machine gun.
We shall arise presently,
having said nothing,
and hand in vibrant hand
walk back the way we came.

"THE ABSORBENT GLIMMER OF THE NIGHT"

the absorbent glimmer of the night
receives a solitary nighthawk cry
marshalls its naked housefronts
and waits

the lights of a passing yacht
hang momently in your hair
and the shadows of the Lombardy poplars
tilt – like planks on water
the crystalline sea breeze
offers a chaste caress
smelling faintly of hospitals

and down the cool perspectives of passion
great hills slide silently into the sea

"I DO NOT REMEMBER THE NUMBER"

I do not remember the number
 of our kisses
but I cannot forget the green
 blur of a falling star
upon your trembling eyelids.

YOU FAIL AN APPOINTMENT

Nervously my fingernails
 rattle against the paper knife,
 and the pale saffron rays
 of the smoky sun
 have come and gone upon
 the uncut pages
 of my book.

"SOMEONE HAS CAST AN UNWARY MATCH"

Someone has cast an unwary match –
 in the tamarack wood –
 a herd of silent swine
 watch the long flames
 blend into the sunset.

Midnight, and the fire is out,
 streamers of grey smoke
 drift like funeral barges
 amongst the fireflies of the marsh.

I shall not sleep well tonight
 and tomorrow
 three days shall have passed
 since I have heard your voice.

"ALL IS GONE NOW"

All is gone now...
    that month of pain and passion
    that lasted late
    into the August meteor swarms,
    September an eternity
    of loneliness,
    October filled with fleeing shadows,
    and half November;
today the fountain in the square
    leaps and disappears
    into the fog that crawls
    across my window,
    and the fallen leaves
    no longer rattle to passing feet,
    only in the early morning,
    white and furry against my shoes,
    they break silently
    into many pieces.

"THERE SHALL COME FAINT LIGHT"

I

There shall come faint light
    and a passage of little winds out of the west
    between the rose and lavender verticals of the city
    the uneasy souls of men arrange themselves
    on crowded street car platforms

Thought wanders like goose-crossed smoke.

II

I shall take me away to a place
of lonely birds
of hawk and heron
and of silent owls
hushed with the stillness
of black tarns
and marshes always twilit
for I am grown weary
of this procession
of faces from off Gothic tombs
and you will understand
for you must know
the mirrored image
of a grey woodland
that breaks with silver circles
spreading
from the one distended leg
of a meditative white crane.

"THE UNPEOPLED, CONVENTIONAL ROSE-GARDEN."

There are cannas now on the guarded lawns –
crimson and Chinese orange
with wine brown leaves,
there is dust on the green-black privet.

Colours of things gone dead
of dear moments lost in tragedy –
you pierce my heart and leave me
weeping, weak with memory.

I shall flee from you and walk
down long hedged paths

snapping the brittle privet leaves
between tremulous, tired fingers.

"NOVEMBER HAS HUNG THE LOCUST"

November has hung the locust
    with mummied fingers
        that claw my
            window.

"ET POUR EUX SEULS, LES PARADIS CHANTENT ENCORE"

There is a mist that moves off Acheron
    pushing heavily over the sunken gardens,
    laboriously over the autumn flowers
    and the dust-grey rose trees.

The drip, drip, drip of the fog
    from fragile, bloodless leaves, and the panting
    of the wings of death's wizened herons
    that follow forever the sourceless, mouthless river
    beat a slow monotone of pain –
    measure of my eternities.

TO ANOTHER

Let us sit now in the broad window
    that overlooks the teakwood balcony,
    the grey rain will be filled with soft doves
    and you will read in a faint voice

the frail, evasive things
dead Chinamen have said.

And then,
I shall tell you the legend of a delicious madness,
of the courtesan who believed
that it was her face, looking over his shoulder,
that Li Po saw in the drowned rushes.

"SPEAK NOT, LET NO WORD BREAK"

Speak not, let no word break
the silence of my sorrow and your weariness;
your steel-white fingers had the gold
of my life to carve. Keep silent,

Speak no word, I leave
with you a little heap of brittle coils
like the hair of a Roman Apollo –
the silence falls like stones.

They are many, the host of Acheron,
many dead men and dank, decaying gods –
through their shadows, beyond the shadowy waters,
I see the ivory gleam of your paleness

and your lips, weak
with the silence I have placed on them.

"THE FRAGRANCE OF THE TEAPOT"

The fragrance of the teapot
mingles with the odours of wet petals.

In the little stone pagoda
I play at solitaire
with counters of ebony and ivory
on a vermilion table.

I rest at ease
for the rain has stopped the sundial
and I no longer fear
that it may strike.

MISSISSIPPI RIVER

Autumn morning

These are the ghosts of tears
that drift along
lost, wandering streams where lonely men
have hidden their proud weeping,
and drifting past the sorrows of a nation,
find at last the mother river –
These mists that dwell upon its face,
seeking oblivion in its eternal flow,
turned back, refused the comradeship
of the world's purpose,
Creep up the muted canyon and stretch
lean fingers toward the crouching fox
and strangle the harpers
of the waterfall.

"SUCH WAS OUR GARDEN"

That is all, merely
a matter of poised
cups and fragile
wafers –

    the fallen
        flowers of the trumpet vine
        lie in fragments
        of bloody daggers
        about your feet,

    and the hollyhocks
        are like beribboned,
        aged virgins,
        sentimental
        with reservations

    as the architecture
        they complement,
        as a flirtation
        on a moonlit
        doorstep.
That is all –
    our lives are
    measured with tea
    and almond cakes in austere
    gardens,

and we
    shall strive to ignore
    the insistence
    of decaying
    crimson daggers –

        fleshy,
        and phallic.

PRUFROCK IN WONDERLAND

These sky-rocket etchings are my life
    and behind them lies the thing
    you fall through in your dreams,
    along derisive elevator shafts that meandering,
    lead to an overwhelming…
    white rabbit.

CHICAGO CABARET

    That was a strange game of chess
    she played in Uxmal
    a long time ago
                        a long time ago
    a strange game and her fingers moving
    faintly like thin clouds of gaseous gold
    her black lacquered eyes revealed nothing
    she was all a black surface

Her lips tingled
amongst the ribbons of my fantasy
that swayed to the passing
of an Apocalyptic thought
gone out over a great dark valley.
Her body wound away into the dance
sibilant with insinuation.

    "Funny," he said, "how many whores is
        called Fantine, and she
            ain't no shine
        pure Indian that kid
            and Some Jazz."

OLD STREET

I think these houses are the ghosts
    of dinosaur, and mammoth, and all
    the other giants now long dead,
    and that on lonely nights they take
    their ancient forms again.
    I see them shift and move ahead of me
    for elbow room,
    and as I pass they touch me here and there
    in puzzled awe,
    and then with lurching, evil step
    close in upon my heels.

REQUIEM

A thousand leaves slant down across the rain
    and, swirling, heap themselves where she at last
    has found the calm and comfort of a home.

Yet one, aquiver on the windowpane,
    waits tremulously till the gust is past
    then lends itself singly to the loam.

ENTRANCE

whether or not, it is no question now
    of time, or place, or even how...
    it is not time for questions now
    nor yet the place
    and the soft shadows of your face
    arrange themselves in memories
    of half a frown or half a smile

that flutters – so – and then is gone
and I stand hesitant
at the rug's edge
and you are reading
propped up in the window seat

"Whether or not" – it is no question now
and so I trace the fragile irony
of the pattern of our lives

"YOU DID NOT KNOW SHE WAS ETERNAL? THERE"

You did not know she was eternal? There
Her fingers stray amongst the pale tea rose,
That grass that smells of muck was once her hair,
Her eyes peep out where any violet grows,
And lily stalks are but an holy stair
For her slim feet, up which she singing goes
Toward paradise, and poised delicately
Her faint heart flowers, an anemone.

PORTRAIT OF A LADY

She was a symphony of silent smokes
And slender sails that up the smooth inclines
Of turquoise seas slide toward the Southern Cross;
And through her every movement breathed
A moonlit music of soft silks
And mandolines whose crystal strings
Tossed somnolent white fountains high
Against the fragile stars of Gothic gardens

Well schooled she was in all the simple grace

Of exquisite sophistications and the soft
Nuances of her yielding lips were what
A culture born of elegant
Velvet hung murders had named as most
To be desired of all life's offerings.

NORETORP-NORETSYH

Rainy, smoky Fall, clouds tower
In the brilliant Pacific sky.
In Golden Gate Park, the peacocks
Scream, wandering through falling leaves.
In clotting night, in smoking dark,
The Kronstadt sailors are marching
Through the streets of Budapest. The stones
Of the barricades rise up and shiver
Into form. They take the shapes
Of the peasant armies of Makhno.
The streets are lit with torches.
The gasoline drenched bodies
Of the Solovetsky anarchists
Burn at every street corner.
Kropotkin's starved corpse is borne
In state past the offices
Of the cowering bureaucrats.
In all the Politisolaters
Of Siberia the partisan dead are enlisting.
Berneri, Andreas Nin,
Are coming from Spain with a legion.
Carlo Tresca is crossing
The Atlantic with the Berkman Brigade.
Bukharin has joined the Emergency
Economic Council. Twenty million
Dead Ukrainian peasants are sending wheat.
Julia Poyntz is organizing American nurses.

Gorky has written a manifesto
"To the intellectuals of the World!"
Mayakofsky and Essenin
Have collaborated on an ode,
"Let *Them* Commit Suicide."
In the Hungarian night
All the dead are speaking with one voice,
As we bicycle through the green
And sunspotted Californian
November. I can hear that voice
Clearer than the cry of the peacocks,
In the falling afternoon.
Like painted wings, the color
Of all the leaves of Autumn,
The circular tie-dyed skirt
I made for you flares out in the wind,
Over your incomparable thighs.
Oh splendid butterfly of my imagination,
Flying into reality more real
Than all imagination, the evil
Of the world covets your living flesh.

UNTITLED

I am fifty-two years old.
I used to think that someday
I'd be rich and successful.
Well, now I am successful,
But I am still just a bum.
Nobody ever offered
Me a job cataloging
His collection. Nobody
Took me cruising on his yacht.
Only once a dangerous
Millionairess asked me over

For dinner. We instantly
Hated each other's guts. I
Have always led a clean life.
Still, I get along best with
Tramps, faggots, whores and hop heads.
I am ill at ease around
People who quote Cleanth Brooks.
I haven't read Henry James
In a long time. If my wife
Lost her job I doubt if we
Could feed the kids on my income.
I will never get back to
Aix-en-Provence. The second
Week of the next depression
The whole family will be
On relief. What kind of fame
Is this? Still, I never wrote
Letters like Baudelaire did
To his mother; D.H. Lawrence
Didn't get along with children
As well as I do; I take
Myself too seriously,
But not as bad as Goethe;
I never diddled Duchesses
And boasted about it in print;
I guess I really have no
Major vices; but I am
Awful cantankerous. My
Daughters are going to have
To grow up liking simple things.
It would be nice to take the
Family to Europe for
The summer, but maybe it
Is better not to be rich.

140 SYLLABLES

All my life I have wondered,
Why doesn't somebody write
A terrible poem that says
In so many words, this world
Is a fraud, the people who
Run it are murderous fools,
Everything ever printed
Is a lie, all their damn art
And literature is a fake,
Behind their gods and laws, and
Pee hole bandits, their science
Is just a fancy way to kill
Us and our girls and kids.
What I want to know is why
Somebody doesn't write it
All down in about twenty
Lines of seven syllables
Once and for all, and scare the shit
Out of all the dirty squares.

THE WORKING DAY

The hands of the clock go 'round.

Rose-gold flakes in the paling sky, dawn comes over the bay.

Rose and gold minute fires burn under the pale blue water,
    and then the sun steps fully clothed in brilliance out of the
        hills.

Delicate wrists of wind move lost single human figures
    through long morning shadows down empty streets.

Mid-morning – new scrubbed faces swarm the streets. Tiny
elastic silhouettes run girders in the sky.

Luncheon models teeter self-conscious amongst dice-
shooting Elks. Plans, options, deals. Underneath, work pauses
for salami.

Sun warms the tiring head, bright streets dazzle. A sudden
chill blasts through the alleys. Jade pieces in a dark, still shop.

Five o'clock faces swarm unscrubbed and vanish in endless
ribbons of blue haze.

Traffic stops. A small submarine window opens before a
million TV dinners. Muzak, wine, soft lights, pressed duck.
Jewels sparkle on the velvet bay.

The wind grows, waste paper whirls, desolate loiterers, jazz,
bare-bosoms, silky violins, hamburger joints glare at the dark.

A prowl car wanders, its spotlight poking into black
doorways.

The summer stars are far apart in the empty sky and a
broken moon plunges through blowing fog.

UNTITLED, 6 SEPTEMBER 1969

Dramatic light, gold and rose
Sculptured clouds, sky like deep blue water.
Far away on the eastern shore of the Pacific
I miss the skies of Venice, the most noble in the world.

THE HOMESTEAD CALLED DAMASCUS (1920–1925)

For
Leslie
Dorothy

THE HOMESTEAD CALLED DAMASCUS

I

Heaven is full of definite stars
And crowded with modest angels, robed
In tubular, neuter folds of pink and blue.
Their feet tread doubtless on that utter
Hollowness, with never a question
Of the "ineluctable modality"
Of the invisible; busy, orderly,
Content to ignore the coal pockets
In the galaxy, dark nebulae,
And black broken windows into space.
Youthful minds may fret infinity,
Moistly dishevelled, poking in odd
Corners for unsampled vocations
Of the spirit, while the flesh is strong.
Experience sinks its roots in space –
Euclidean, warped, or otherwise.
The will constructs rhomboids, nonagons,
And paragons in time to suit each taste.
Or, if not the will, then circumstance.
History demands satisfaction,
And never lacks, with or without help
From the subjects of its curious science.

Thomas Damascan and the mansion,
A rambling house with Doric columns
On the upper Hudson in the Catskills,
Called Damascus. We were walking there
Once in early Spring; his brother Sebastian
Said, staring into the underbrush,
"If you'll look close you'll see the panthers
In there eating the crocus." And Thomas said,
"Panthers are always getting into

The crocus. Every spring. There were too many
Panthers about the courts in my father's time."
They had an odd wry sort of family humor
That startled idle minds and plagued your
Memory for years afterwards.
We sat up late that night drinking wine,
Playing chess, arguing – Plato and Leibniz,
Einstein, Freud, and Marx, and woke at noon.
The next day was grey and rained till twilight,
And ice from somewhere in the Adirondacks
Drifted soggily down the river.
In the afternoon Sebastian read
The Golden Bough, and Thomas said
"Remember, in school, after we read Frazer,
I insisted on signing myself Tammuz,
To the horror of all our teachers?"
"And now," he said, "we're middle aged, wise,"
(They were very far from middle aged)
"And what we thought once was irony
Is simple fact, simple, sensuous,
And so forth. Fate is a poor scholar."
We said nothing, and the three of us
Watched the rain fall through the budding trees,
Until at last Thomas rose and took
A bow from the rack, sprung it, and said,
"I wish we could shoot these things in the rain."
Sebastian said, "I'd much rather shoot
In the sunshine, and besides it spoils
The arrows. I'm going for a hike."
So we went off through the hanging woods,
Scratched by thistles, in a thistle wind –
Last year's thistles, and a pungent wind.
Thomas said, "We've got to move the goats
Before they ruin all the pasture.
There'll be nothing but thistles next year."
Sebastian said, "Thistles or bluegrass,
Goats or cattle, what does it matter,
We'll have to die quick to be buried here."

The goats hurried ahead up the slope,
Stopped among the rocks and there gave us
Their clinical goatish regard.
We climbed to the top of the Pope's Nose
And stood looking out at the river,
Slaty in the rain, and the traffic
Wallowing on the muddy highway,
And beneath us in the closed hollow,
The swollen carp ponds, the black water
Flowing through the clattering rushes,
And, poised each on one cold leg, two herons,
Staring over their puckered shoulders
At a hieroglyph of crows in the distance.

"Leslie wants to see us," Thomas said.
"I think they are giving a party."
In the evening, after dinner, we
Took the canoe across the river,
Drifting downstream in the blue twilight.
Another columned house but with great
Windows full of the darkening sky.
Some people in bare shoulders and white shirtfronts
Were standing about in candlelight,
Listening to Leslie play the clavichord.
She looked very precious and British
In her thick braids and bronze green velvet.
While she sang Lawes' *Go, Lovely Rose*,
Sebastian watched an Autumn moth flown
Delicately from the garden to
Rest in pale sienna in his hand.
He saw her with her father's falcons,
Greensleeves and moth breasted birds, and pale
Braided hair, riding side saddle, dressed
In velvet. Daytimes she wore a chatelaine,
And this in twentieth century,
Upstate New York – Guardi and Longhi
On the walls. The moth, he noticed, had
Green eyes, a Horus head, antennae

Thrown over its wings like plumed eyebrows.
It titivated much like a fly.
Somebody had a flute – they were playing
Debussy's trio now – music for the moth.
There were two moths now, one rushing through
The candelabrum on the clavichord;
And from his hand the green eyed Horus
Lifted and took his undulant way
Towards the music, across the peopled room.

Sebastian stood alone in the hollow dark
And watched the long lift of resounding
Black water, the march and countermarch
Of the white wave crests. Alone in the spray
Filled rushing night he walked the shingle
Barefoot, with wet open lips, his nostrils
Flaring to the beating air. There were
Figures in the night, unseen but there,
Invisible journeys begun and
Ended there at the land's end amongst
The damp odorous sea litter.
Springing from such a shingle over
Such water went the perilous bridge
To the shining city, went the knight
Who did not come back and the red
Single star. Sebastian tires and turns,
Back to the sleeping village, back to
The dim lit station, the late slow train,
And the city of steel and concrete towers.
He will know many days of walks in
Little parks of dead leaves and sparrows,
Afternoons with fountains in the haze,
And the martyrdom of arrows.

The sheep are passing in the snow,
Their hooves aclatter on the frozen marsh.
Before them and behind them go

The wading shepherds, tall and bent.
And Thomas, with a narrow light,
Comes out and watches, by the gate;
And muses in the turgid night;
And goes into the house again.
The library is calm and prim.
The shepherds and the sheep have passed.
And Botticelli ladies, slim
And hyperthyroid, grace the walls.

The rose astonished Sebastian and
He was astonished that some day he
Would be irretrievably quite dead.
Beside the rose he placed a small worn
Stone that had been loved and tended by
Some undersea Brancusi. He thought
Of the electron and the nebula.
His mind was like a dark vault full of
Spider webs of light. He thought of Spring
And Thomas long ago expounding
The *Timaeus* in the rainy night –
Damascus in bygone Spring weather.
Now he pressed his thumb against the stone
And watched and waited expectantly.
Once he watched the hopeful young poplar
Day by day shivering up towards
Heaven. It seemed almost transparent
In the level afternoon sunlight
With here and there its artificial
Leaves pinned on like fine ground scales of jade.
Years before he had written a poem –
"Between slender trees a drowse of petals falls."

Suddenly he came on the footprint
Of a Picasso nude on the dull
Red sand beneath the grey heat of skies
Of some very different chemistry.

Her lips moved exactly as always,
Saying the same irrevocable,
Common things. Outside, winter evening
Lay blue and electric on the snow.
And in the room the asbestos glow
Came from the gas log efficiently.
He thought of all the things that had been
Fossilized safely so long ago.
He could not forget in César Franck
Or Haydn or the evening paper.
Somewhere there was still an old dry world
Of trouble and amazement filled with
Things of stone and meditation. Then,
Too, there was a humid garden where
In the lewd green dark a lewd white
Animal minced kneelessly away.
Somewhere far off the rigid granite
Flames revolved across the steppe and high eyes
Swung to the right and left horizon.

Sebastian dreamed and saw the room, marked
With the dwelling of her ordered hands,
Saw her favorite poems turned down
On the sewing table, and shadows
Curled like tabby cats around the pots,
Saw the chairs arranged as she liked them,
The broken chaise longue by the orchard
Window where the morning sun came in,
The same atmosphere of bosom calm.
Her fingers had just run through his hair.
He dreamed, "She is in another room
Or out shopping. She will be back soon."
And then into his sleep from waking
Hours came the memory that things
Had not been this way for many years.
Dreaming, Sebastian said, "That was a dream."
And slowly he awoke and said, half

Dreaming, "Bishop Berkeley's cherries are
Still weighted with me. I shall sit for
Many a day eating illusions,
And dream at night and in the morning
Wake to the same worn-out cruelty."

Sebastian said, "There is a coral
Garden path which ends at a statue
Of Priapus. In my mind a man
And woman walk along it and do
Not come back. The ooze of the sea floor
Red with rust of countless meteors
Covers the broken gold forgotten
There. I know a diver once went mad,
He said he'd seen Atlantis, the rooms
Of the courtesans bright with electric
Fish and octopus hanging from the
Ceilings of the temples. When I left
He said, 'I have seen that poor city.'"
Sebastian, sitting in Romany
Marie's one stormy evening, watching
The green distorted faces pass the
Street lamp, watching the distorted
Silhouettes on the drawn shades of the
Tenement across the street, listens
To gitanas on the phonograph
And drinks a glass of fermented milk.

Thomas remembered the panthers' soft
Cries, mating once in the underbrush,
As he climbed alone through the rafters,
Past the sleeping bells and hats and owls.
Here the devil came to play cribbage
With the sexton, here the prayers go past
On small bright twinkling metallic wings,
The ghosts of votive lamps in their beaks.
This dusky ascension is peopled

With more than horned and hairy shadows.
Here is the long comrade, the little
Brother of death with his chalk old skull,
This is the other with his mincing
Fellowship, and here is the man with
The vorpal blade, who is pale because of the
Surrounding darkness. Alone
In this prehistoric night, each naked
Marionette is dismayed at his
Own conduct and flees, leaving a spoor
Of scratches on the snow. Before this
He had remembered the brown darkness,
The trigonometry of the rafters,
The astronomy of the ladders,
Long before this, alone among the panthers.
Modred observed the static terror
Of the poised archaic archangels.
Lucifer gave fire, guided the Kabbalah
To chemistry and back again. Death
Where hinges fall, a land of crusts and
Rusted keys, the desert colored like
A lumpy fog, geologic ages
Of searing suns – consider that place.
Modred, the dark and crimson man, rose
And walked from the place called the Skull, walked
Far, and the Lamb beside him like a
Star, with feet of stars and flowers walked.
Dark Modred covertly from his bloody eyes
Beyond the tangled thicket and the thorns saw
Hakeldama, the potter's field
Full of dead strangers.

II THE AUTUMN OF MANY YEARS

In a ruddy light, in a craggy
Land, where at the turning of the paths,
Horrible stone figures slipped away

As they approached, Thomas descended
Slowly towards the empty city from which
Alternate noise and utter stillness
Came. Sebastian halted, waited at
The last hill crest and watched him go.
Beyond the place he stopped not a leaf
Or blade of grass appeared nor any
Warm- or cold-blooded moving thing. He
Waited. The dogs nuzzled his knees, and
Whined. It grew dark. He waited all night.

Forgotten, unknown, anonymous,
He threads his way through narrow places
Between the worn hills. He is alone
Where there are dim forms, fronds of sorrow
Spreading in the close dusk of rock and
Horizontal pines. His face is pale
In the dimness, and his pale hands part
The ever present leafy curtain,
Gently, wisely, as if he parted
The green velvet bodice and skirt
Of a weak girl. The green dimness grows.
He vanishes in the vegetable light.

"This is my scene, this part must I
Fulfill." So life turns back upon
Itself. Sebastian at last came to
An afternoon, a parcel of hours
In the Autumn of many years.
A time which he had always known,
A passing light in which he had
Always lived. A heart beat in the clock.
Stars, blue flowers and blue unicorns?
Perhaps Thomas's rutting panthers?
His own especial arc in time curved
And then went flat around him, moment
And century in which he lived life –

This bland forever, known forever,
An Autumn afternoon, Damascus
With the brown rock lunging from the elm,
The oak leaf scuff in the level light.

Webster one morning after breakfast
Knew, "Like diamonds we are cut with our
Own dust." Sebastian sat in the
Broken belvedere above the river
Playing chess with himself and drinking
Not wine, nor whiskey, but bitter tea,
Cold and steeped too long. The two knights moved
Reciprocally. One side was sure
To lose. Relatives came to visit
The instant. Every instant has them.
Sebastian thought, "I have no relatives.
I am like the little figure of
Daruma secreted in the last
Encapsuled Japanese box. I am
All alone at Christmas time somewhere
Like Durban, Bergen, or Singapore."
He unfolded the revolving knights.
The pattern seemed to be different now.
Sebastian finished the astringent tea.
"Like myself," he said, "this is getting
Nowhere," and went back to the house and
To a book he had turned down.

In the deep blue winter evening
The homeward crowd murmurs and hurries
And rearranges itself to the
Color of signal lights and shrilling
Whistles. Sebastian disengages
Himself and walks in the cold, smoky
Twilight of Central Park, spotted with
Week old dirty snow, and stands to watch
The skaters, skating there beneath the

Acrid revelation of forty
Floodlights. Northward many nightbound miles
Gathering the winter about it
Damascus keeps the long January
Darkness. Once in a long while, far off,
Men move, very small with very small
Bright lanterns, and the frosted breath of
Old dogs clouds their footsteps as they fall.
Foxes on the mountains go delicate
Across the snow on sly fox errands.

Something living passed this way, something
Alive and dreamed about. The steep bulge
Of the pale expansive hills arches
Gently over that other world. The moon
Is transparent as a soap bubble
And looks as likely to burst. Somewhere
A violin awakes and says, "A blonde."
The uneasy souls of men arrange
Themselves on streetcar platforms. Autumn,
Thought wanders like goose-crossed smoke. And all
The stone and ironic city turns
To smoke and glass, to verticals of
Rose and lavender. And then there comes
The blue and saffron moment, nighthawks
Cry and plunge above the roofs, and waste
Paper settles in the dirty courtyards,
And pigeons murmur and settle in
The cornices. Burnt fried potatoes,
Automobile smoke and one lonely
Rattling streetcar. Something living passed –
Invisible in the haze, but alive.

Haitian drums or African and horns
From New Orleans. She rolls her buttocks
Like kelp on the sea surge or taffy
In a churn. Rhinestones cover her bee-stung

Pussy and perch on each nipple. Drums
Roll as she rolls her belly and her eyes.
Grove or colonnade, porch or garden –
White, blue and silver garments and long
Carefully tended beards and hands.
Sebastian paints a Rousseau landscape
Of gnarled pine and giant dogwood, paths
Of pink coral and stone moon bridges
Over obese gold fish. "Figures by
Another hand." The School of Athens?
He waits for her act to end. She smiles
A warm domestic smile. The band explodes.
The rhinestones fall. A polar wind blows
Down South State Street under the Northern
Lights. The taxi bores into the Rousseau
Landscape of warm domesticity.
The figures are by another hand.

The Lotophagi with their silly hands
Haunt me in sleep, plucking at my sleeve;
Their gibbering laughter and blank eyes
Hide on the edge of the mind's vision
In dusty subways and crowded streets.
Late in August, asleep, Adonis
Appeared to me, frenzied and bleeding
And showed me, clutched in his hand, the plow
That broke the dream of Persephone.
The next day, regarding the scorched grass
In the wilting park, I became aware
That beneath me, beneath the gravel
And the hurrying ants, and the loam
And the subsoil, lay the glacial drift,
The Miocene jungles, the reptiles
Of the Jurassic, the cuttlefish
Of the Devonian, Cambrian
Worms, and the mysteries of the gneiss;
Their histories folded, docketed

In darkness; and deeper still the hot
Black core of iron, and once again
The inscrutable archaic rocks,
And the long geologic ladder,
And the living soil and the strange trees,
And the tangled bodies of lovers
Under the strange stars.
                                        And beside me,
A mad old man, plucking at my sleeve.

Persephone awaits him in the dim boudoir,
Waits him, for the hour is at hand.
She has arranged the things he likes
Near to his expected hand:
Herrick's poems, tobacco, the juice
Of pomegranates in a twisted glass.
She piles her drugged blonde hair
Above her candid forehead,
Touches up lips and eyelashes,
Selects her most naked robe.
On the stroke of the equinox he comes,
And smiles, and stretches his arms, and strokes
Her cheeks and childish shoulders, and kisses
The violet lids closed on the grey eyes.
Free of suggestive Aphrodite,
Free of the patronizing gods,
The cruel climate of Olympus,
They feed caramels to Cerberus
And warn him not to tell
The cuckold Plato of their adulteries,
Their mortal lechery in dispassionate Hell.

Nobody knows him, nobody cares.
He is alone in a foreign place.
He cannot understand their ways. He
Cannot appreciate the beauty
Of the landscape. "Here are his footprints,"

They say, "he went this way, through the woods,
Over the rocks and towards the desert."
They say, "There was nobody with him."
He and she, matching stride for stride, pace
The garden walks. It was very
Pleasant where they went. He chews his sun
Baked mustache. Her eyes are almost closed.
They say, "See, there are his footprints, still
Black in the early morning hoarfrost."

You can see through the level days
A long way, clear to the end of life,
Through the bars of pale gold level sunlight.
In the evening the blunt fingers
Of shadows stammer behind us,
Shadow forests, beams of chaos, collapse
Against the walls, gold and scarlet fire
Cities with avenues of copper
Explode at our feet in crashing earthquakes.
The lamp burns out. Outside in the cold,
Loneliness comes down from between
The far off mountains, like a black fog
Over the prairie. Fire and darkness
After the arid day, arms entwined,
We remember the confused racket
Of rapid water broken by stones.
Afloat again, the green canoe creeps
Slowly down the twisting green water.
Here there are miles of burnished barley,
Pine on the foothills, and the bare red
Ranges streaked with snow. How long ago
We fished in a narrow full river,
In a forest of damp broad leaves.

How short a time for a life to last.
So few years, so narrow a space, so
Slight a melody, a handful of

Notes. Most of it dreams and dreamless sleep.
And solitary walks in empty
Parks and foggy streets. Or all alone,
In the midst of nightstruck, excited
Crowds. Once in a while one of them
Spoke, or a face smiled, but not often.
One or two could recall the tune if asked.
Now she is gone. Hooded candles in
The Spring wind tilt and move down the
Narrow columned aisle. Incense plumes whirl.
Thuribles clink. The last smoke dissolves
Above the rain soaked hills, the black pines,
Broken by a flock of migrating birds.

Thomas climbed the ice and crossed the pass.
Coneys whistled in the shrill air. Ice
And rock and indigo sky – Enoch
Walked the hills and waged war on substance
In the vertical. Is it best to
Remember always the same memory,
To see the world always in the same hour?
Good Friday, incense and hooded candles.
Sebastian descends the wet hillside
Into the coiling river fog. He
Sinks from sight into the hidden world.
And on the mountain crest the tattered
Crows wheel like an apparition
In a fog as serpentine and cold,
And much more opaque, and unseen caw
And caw. This hour the sacramental
Man was broken on the height, in dark
Opacity rent with caw and caw.

Thomas, called Tammuz, the first
Of twins, "the beloved one," the one
Called Didymus in the upper room –
The involuntary active man –

Peers in the black wounds, hammers the frame
That squeezes the will. The arrow breaks.
He breaks the gold arrow in the gold
Light. The arrow breaks the brittle flesh,
Breaking upon it. Baldur in the
Autumn light, the level lawn.
Modred, Iscariot, Loki cross
Beyond the Catskills. Sebastian drinks
Cold astringent tea in the damp
Summerhouse above the hazy river.

III THE DOUBLE HELLAS

Claret enim claris quod clare concopulator

Before the ice the convulsions of
Thought sprawled baroque in baroque forests
Glutted with boa constrictor swamps,
Where green terror stalked the aborigine.
From the mountains where the ice lay waiting
The foggy sun fondled a landscape
Voluptuous and odorous as
Flesh and ambergris. Now high above
Mammoth and behemoth buried in
Immemorial ice the black starved
Procession winds to the tolling of
Black bells. The frozen saint is buried
In a shrill vault of glittering ice.
When the hills appeared again, soggy
And white, only the memories of
Being crept across their faces, only
The creeping shadows of life in the
Long red night beneath the dying sun.

A dry static tightness of pigment,
Aloofness to more accessible
Experience, the hand dry and white

In bygone porcelain drawing rooms,
Hot, dry, indoor wintry afternoons,
Crisp crinolines and bright figures of
Twisted glass. The children coming home
Through the grey green fog that prowled between
The grey stone and dark brick closed housefronts.
And later, the deep blue evenings,
The yellow lights, the humming tile stove,
Father with his silver flute,
Mother singing to the harmonium,
Thomas thought – My parents had that life,
And they in turn recognized themselves
In Henry James and would in Proust
If they had lived long enough, and now
We seem to be unable to escape
From our own ornate, wasted fictions.

There are cannas now on the guarded
Lawns, crimson and Chinese orange, with wine
Brown leaves. The privet hedges are black,
And grey with dust. The thick blood squeezes
In and out of the heart and falls like
Quicksilver down the arteries. The brain
Unrolls in its own vaults its own arid,
Endless frieze. Sebastian strolls along
The narrow privet lanes of the garden
Labyrinth. Ignorant, invisible,
The catechumens move along the wall.
Sebastian idles in the infant
Canyon of small leaves stiff with Autumn.
Floral vulvas of orange and crimson
Squirm inside his head, his fingers snap
The brittle privet leaves. The day sleeps.

The capon sits spatulate, Origen
Among the teacups, the lowering,
Not quite invisible genius of

The case at hand. Manipulations,
Especially ante-Steinach and
Unsure, do not suffice to still the Pauline,
Age-long battle. A puzzled fire
Still hovers. Tin plated words unfold
From her lips, glitter briefly before
Her scarcely moving, maidenly mouth –
Kore entertaining impotent
Hades. Her hands are never still, never
Hurried. The sun declines, the garden
Gives off its perfumes. The conversation
Builds bridges and arches to nowhere.
Cups and wafers move. The fallen flowers
Of the trumpet vine lie like red meat
Underfoot. The dusty hollyhocks
Defend the wall. Last night someone
Kissed her on the moonlit doorstep.
The phallic vermilion flowers rot.
His hands, like huge white grubs, hang dying
To his wrists. Hers build another bridge
And send a covey of words out on it.
The mellow mountains undulate
Down to the river through the blue haze.
The air smoulders with the beginning
Of Autumn. In the background vacant
Figures outlined with thin strokes of white
Move transparently across the landscape.

That was a strange game of chess she played
In Uxmal – a long time ago.
Her fingers move out from her body
And dissolve like faint wisps of gaseous
Gold. Her head jerks, the black lacquered eyes
Stay still. An impenetrable black
Surface falls from them, between her and
The musicians. The music is lost
In an illimitable nightbound

Valley. Her flesh unbraids itself like
A rope. The metal melts and flows away.
Brown, brown, brown is the color of my
True love's skin. Her lips are sweeter than
The full blown rose. Her eyes are sad where
Love has entered in. Graceful and wise
Before my eyes she goes. Her learned
Body and her childish ways possess
All my mind and all my days... Maxine...
Uxmal, Konarak, or Ajanta.
His walls have fallen, his painted
Beauties are yellow dust forever now.

The world is composed of a pair of
Broken pillars, a round sun in a
Rigid sky, a sea, and in the great
Distance, a red line of cliffs. The world
Is composed of a pair of broken
Pillars, of pillars, of a suave line
Conceived in a mind infinitely
Refined by edges infinitely
Sharp. The world is composed. There is a
Little boat upon the sea, a striped
Sail. They raise a net from the bright sea
And go away rowing with the wind.
Recently awe and precision hung
In this landscape, the keen edge of pride,
The suave line, the Doric mind. Voices
Of children come up the steep valley.
A blur of smoke smudges the skyline.
"Come back, baby, I miss your little
Brown body and your childish ways."
"Hush, Chloris, heed not the stars
Narcissistically parading
There above the mannered pools."
You can always find pity
And terror amongst the broken

Statuary. Whose profiles
Coin the wind? The Bactrian
Kings. Pisanello's courtesans.
The whole sky is made of gold.
The dancing master in a
Castled wig, Priapus in
The vines. The soft sliding eyes.
"Ah, Chloris, heed not the stars,
The smoky shattering fountains
In the teeming night."

My parents had their life, it was not
Your soft dark tragedy. It was not
Anything like it. Saffron twilights
Over the gaslit horse-drawn city.
Purple and gold above the desert.
When they were sad, they shut their mouths tight.
When God spoke to Job from the whirlwind
He refused to answer his questions –
On the advice of his attorney.
The rainbow mountains glitter in
The breaking prism. Within the mirror
Of ice, pain speaks to sorrow outside.
And now the sun has set and the strange
Blake-like forms fade from our memories.
The sky was deeper than a ruby.

The hoarfrost spreads over the marshes
Like a mandolin note over water.
Between the mountains a candle burned.
A narrow leaf of flame casting no
Light about it. The epic hero
Came, in full armor, making a huge
Clatter, and fell, struck down from behind,
And lay in the barren eternal
Dawn, geometrically prostrate,
As the clock ticks measured out his death –

As the spouting flame leaped from roof to
Roof and all the houses full of ticking
Clocks caught fire one after another.

Not rock, not mountains, not twisted pine,
No scar of twisted fire, but water,
The dominion of water, the sound
Of light wind and water in a place
Of watery light. In the turmoil
Of marketplace or war, in the
Stress of love or music, this place
Will tabernacle the heart. This place
Will be inviolate, the mind's home.
Luminous apple leaves animated
Into a soft glitter of sound. The
Voice of speaking leaves and lustral water.
Hands that moved like soft grave birds,
Tending the flowers in the garden.
At Crotona, soft grave eyes and large
Soft grave lips that hardly ever spoke.
She was a street walker, just brought out,
Twelve years old with naked breasts and gauze
Thighs, cuddled in the shadow of the
Golden man-headed bull at the gate
Of the Great King. His Greek companions
Said, "There is the goddess, not yet awake."
The Indians called her Marichi,
The Chinese were polite but afraid.
In less than a year, she spoke their language.
They sat before the mountain cottage
High above the great plain of China.
The philosophers, so polite, came
And offered their polite discourses.
She interpreted as best she could.
They lowered their eyes so politely.
His eyes were lambent, like a beast's eyes.
So many long years, usually

The avatars of the goddess are
Short lived. He said, "She had four lives to live.
Love, and wisdom, and sorrow, and joy –
Four fleshly emanations in one flesh."
Aristotle never heard of her.
Iamblichus knew she must have been and
Reinvented her. He called her Theano.

They have put a bust of Bach in the
Little park. Around him they have planted
The old time flowers small town grandmas
Still grow somewhere. Two nuns walk the new
White gravel path, spacing their rosaries
Between a Naiad fountain and the
Bust of Bach. Sebastian is alone.
She is asleep in her scented bed,
The shades drawn, the room warm and dark, her
Body dark and coiled in heavy sleep.
Sebastian reads Socrates on love.
"Putte him bye –." The current flows the other
Way. Or at the most oscillates like
The nuns and their tinkling rosaries.
Her sex sleeps like a dark wet mystic eye.

Sebastian said, "Is this my very creed?
Shall I embody the svelte engines
Of the present fact? Shall personal
Loneliness give way to the enduring
Geological isolation?
Shall the filaments strung to gusty
Brown Autumn roads snap? The tender
Trickles in the Spring woods dry quite up?
Somewhere quests a strange simplicity.
And oh, my music, when she walks
In beauty, through smoking traffic
Between the twilight skyscrapers
The verve undulance of the lonely

Heart. Are you my Narcissus pool?
Brilliant rockets of the sun dappled
Waterfall? Young and beautiful with
Old eyes and quick feet. Philosopher –
No hunk of this matter will receive
Any impression of the pure Idea."

"The book turned down." They left the long halls.
Death came in uncountable fashions.
Death when they passed beneath Caesar's yoke.
The clank and clang of swords and armor.
Beatrice, the aeon Beatrice.
The courtesan of the fiery stars.
The old town in mist and falling leaves.
How can you bear to watch me weeping?
How indeed? I wonder at myself.
The stairs collapse, the long halls fall down.
"If I live forever, I shall not
Forget that summer. He and I sat
Late in the hot August evenings
And talked endlessly of the panic
And of our hopes and fears and of my
Historical and economic
Theories, and so the summer wore
Away amidst an excitement verging
On a revolution." Death in Venice?

Thomas said, "This land is too well manured.
In fact it's nothing but dead flesh and rock.
The Thanksgiving turkey bones alone
Make an immense midden. The bedrooms
Mold with the sweat of bygone death beds.
The parlor is choked with meaningless
Bric-a-brac, the flotsam of India,
The China trade, and whaling round the poles.
And the bark cloth my great grandfather
Wore the night he bedded the princess."

Under the church is a crypt. There are
Bones there, but of a pterodactyl,
Not a man, and beneath the black crypt
A blacker catacomb, ceiling and walls
Painted with women copulating
With beasts and monsters. Before we cleaned them
They could not be seen for the smoke of
Assignations. Thomas said, "She's nice.
But the chirr of bracelets on her wrists,
The scorching hallucinations of
Her thighs, her buttocks rolling like two
Struggling slugs – these things are not for me.
I hear them echoing in the tunneled
Sepulcher, once more the underground
Hocus pocus of torches and cavern trysts.
Once more Aholah, and Aholibah.
My arteries and veins are my own.
Pass me the paper." A man alone
In a hazy autumnal garden,
A man alone in a hazy desert.
A man and a woman alone in bed.
Many dead men and women each alone.

I know this is an ambivalent
Vicarity – who stands for whom?
And this is the reality, then –
This flesh, the flesh of this arm and I
Know how this flesh lies on this bone
Of this arm, this is reality –
I know. I ask nothing more of it.
These things are beautiful, these are
My sacraments and I ask no more.
Did I dream about the same woman?
My fingers twine on themselves and twine
On the memory of a hand, long
After that hand. My being is her
Dream, she has dreamed that journey and dreamed
That cruel map, that strong manual

Of demands. I know I am her dream.
Now the new brick warehouse shouldering
Strong by the shore of the lake through soft
Smoke, rests in the sunset like the vast
Cheek of a peasant resting on the vast
Chest of her lover. Pied cattle come
Home down hills of young grass once more
In the beautiful hour. Once more
The bridges lift in the blue twilight.
White boats go out. I forgot this is
Undeniably reality.

I had forgotten. The movement of
The lotus horned barge is the symbol
And enunciation of the movement
Of the malachite water and the
Movement of the quartz and the silver
Veinings of the fishes, of the golden
Poinsettias of fishes breaking
Before the prow. Behind and below
The lotus horn and the coiled ocher
Of the girls' bare breasts and shoulders,
The young favorite of Ikhnaton
Reclines on a bed of rushes. In
The next picture he stands with wide arms.
His eagerness communicates to
And swells in the flying curve of death,
The throw stick. The pattern breaks into
Breaking birds, rises and shatters in
An interrupted arrow of herons.
In the hands of the girls javelins
Lie long and still. The nervous profile
Of the boy is a perfect example
Of the Tel-el-Amarna decadence.

On the sidewalk the shadows lie sharp
And inviolate in the lonely
Light of a Sunday, unblurred

By smoke in the sharper air. Figures
Paired upon the street – colored and black,
Lean feet to feet like folded fingers.
Heel taps are audible as at night.
Gold, scarlet, mitered, the Cardinal
Fluctuates across the steps between
Furry prisms of incense filled sunlight
And sings the Ite Missa Est closing
The Mystery of the Holy Ghost.
Parmenides was sure he had fixed
The eye fast to vision forever –
The duplication of the crystal cube.
Heraclitus said the world was made
Of the quick red tongue between her lips,
Or else from the honey that welled up
From the shady spring between her thighs.
At Oxford in the dreamy Autumn,
Charles Stuart, King and Martyr to be,
Often known as Shorty to his friends,
Raised his hand and bade the tide to stop.
Let the world stay frozen in a bird's eye –
Let the oak leaf freeze in the mid quiver
At Dodona, let the knife freeze fast
Above Iphigenia's red heart.
Let the long ships wait, let the thought wait,
Let the fleshy flame lick the crystal.

Like doors his thoughts snap shut one after
One with his steps. The tree, moon isolate
In moonless night, stiffens in an
Explosion of wind and rips off every
Leaf. The sky cuts like a cleaver at
His toes. He waits on phosphorescent
Ruts. The way is closed. There was a word.
Once there was some one sure Sesame.
In an immense twilit library
Book after book congeals beneath

The hands. The pages close. A lantern
Shuttles through a cold like wires. A far
Off farm. What was the word? Darkness
Searches the earth, a million valleys,
A million streets, moving a finger
Over and over its chart, nearer
And near, and near circles, stalks him,
Rims wine glass-wise his skull and whistles.

That morning above Metapontum,
Of such a green of storm marine the
Such a hand upon the such a granite,
The icy line of rhythm, aloof
And rigid, the cleaving hieratic
Gesture of all his known, all his owned
Universe. There in a time of level
Light, an air in which the motes of music
Suspend uninterrupted in the
Imagination, in the beams of
Blue and gold sound, in the announcement
The fall of guided lambent water,
Of the presence of learned instruments,
An atmosphere where substance becomes
A visible dance, where the gilded,
Spun and polished acrobat explores
The flying vectors of harmonic range,
Frail cascaded parallelograms,
Bladed gulls up over grey old seas,
Lipped winds risen in Orion's swift
Geometries, horizon mountains
Kissing the curving cheek secluded
In gardens dense with perfume, in those
Tangents of living masks like comets
Which never escape the centripetal
Architects of memory – this girl
Who said, "My life is bought and paid for,
So much pleasure for so much pain."

The unkempt boy who said, "My mind slips
Through my fingers like Crusoe's doubloons
On his desert island." The aging
Gent who sucked his yellow teeth and said,
"I want life visible only through
The delicate anastomosis
Of the little bright red nerves of sex."
In its very own Ten Towns of Troy,
The brain encapsulate like an onion jewel,
And Jason in his black ship in the
Phosphorescent coral sea under
The hidden moon, Jason or Gauguin,
Dun camels in the smoky desert,
The Pyramids gone crimson into time.
Things known are nice, worlds long remembered,
Ears attuned to catch from sliding thought
The slightest harmonies of ordered
Music of objects worn by careful hands.

So the slim loaf held in her bland hands,
Hair as blonde as mown rice, the simple
Newly domesticated flowers,
The lucent wine, olive oil, honey,
Figs, dry cheese, and fish, and pickled squid,
Accumulated in the movements
Of her wise body the pulse of China,
Of Ganges, and the painted Persian
Corridors, of all the long days danced
With military grace, and lived with
Caution and expectant beauty in
The Golden City at Crotona,
Milk of goat and cow and sheep, fruit and
Oil of the olive, honey and wheat,
White wool and dyes from the sea to dye
It, and fruit and juice of the grape.
These have entered her and garbed her, formed
The aura and measure of her movement.

Object by object, with poetic
Precision, recollection awakes
Note by memorable note of quiet
Song. So having broken bread beneath
The white pillars he rose and left the hill
To walk the seastrand of sculpt and colored stones and shells.

IV THE STIGMATA OF FACT

This calcined idiocy, the fool
Naked and white in the night, the chalk
Old skull breaks, and breaks into weeping.
Tears water the roots of the living,
The pale lewd beast, Death's little chum, breaks
Into tears, corrupt and obscure tears.
We discovered on the last morning
Of the dig, at the very bottom
Of the excavation, the record
Of disgrace and dismay. We knew he
Was only hiding, shattering tears
Over our heads like clattering steel.
The sky was like the blue belly of
A boiler. The sun went over it
With hammers. Everything was present.
It was only a horn protruding
From the alkali crust, a relic
Of the days when the bison were here.

No matter where the spirit goes or
Goes out, the flesh will stay here mixed with
This place. So many molecules, so
Many hairs in the head and mustache.
So many movements and no more, out
Of what might seem a most capacious
Infinitude. A piece of landscape
At Damascus. A smile in the
Gorgon's face rooted in only one

Instant as no mountain can ever
Be – gracious or anguished acceptance –
But rooted and fixed and no cavil.

One day as we were approaching one
Of the lesser islands, a barren
Place of burnt rock, which we all knew was
Uninhabited, we heard across
The water a great commotion like
A crowd of weeping women and then
A voice crying out, "Tammuz! Tammuz!"
There was a fellow on board called Thomas
And so for a joke he answered them,
"What do you want with me?" and the voice
Came back saying, "When you come to Crete,
Tell them there that the unknown god is dead."
It was a funny thing to happen
Nowadays on a dirty stinking
Tub like that. I never heard
What happened to the Thomas fellow
When we got to Crete, although I thought
I saw him once along the harbor,
His hat pulled over his eyes in an
Awful sun, watching a gang unloading goats.
A crumbling kingdom, a leper king,
Halls, banners, swords, and better plumbing
Than anything in Europe and silks
For all the women to wear all the time,
Up or in bed, impregnable forts
In the desert garrisoned by thieves,
Assassins everywhere, no street is safe,
In the country we travel only
With armed escort. Krak of Moab
Like a stone battleship in the desert.
"At last we have worn out our welcome."
Tammuz, the envoy of Alamut,
Smiles, sympathetic, reminiscent,

And noncommittal. Let the Graal pass.
Keep silence – the word is not worth giving.
The leper king lies in a bed all
Covered with purple and pall. Tammuz
Parts the arras, smiles again, farewell,
And goes across the drawbridge through the
Orchards, past the jousting and polo
Field, into the hazy hills dim with
Dust, his burnoose drawn across his face.

Dust – the turning years bring once again
In a hundred years exploring feet
To stir dust in one narrow sunbeam,
Dry choking dust, once each hundred years
A cough and sneeze, and then the thick dust
Settles once more on the disordered
Bones in their endless sleep, and the sand
Drifts against the doorway, nearer the
Lintel year by year. The law by which
We live is the law by which we die.
The rose breasted grosbeak obscured by
Flowering dogwood bloomed in the eye,
A sweet vertigo bloomed in the brain.
Her sex was moist, her mouth full of night.
At this point the peaks show best above
The valley through the trunks of the yellow pines.
Thomas looked at the pale blue snow peaks
And thought of the long crash of emirate
And corporation, the Caliph hiding
In some foetid desert tent, the ships
Of Royal Dutch Shell in the Malacca
Straits, or the others, the immortal
Element in an otherwise all
Dissolving corruption, the germ plasm
Of history. Here in this brilliant
Summer region, his painted landscape,
Thomas says, "There is no self subsistent

Microcosm." He thinks a while of
Chuang Tzu fishing with a straight pin and
Says, "There is no self subsistent
Macrocosm either."

The Old Man
Told Sebastian, "Everybody wants
To make that gruesome exploring trip
Sometime. The stone blocks are bigger than
A horse and every figure is life size
And plated with gold. Some of the galleries
Are like an aquarium, full of
Fish and octopuses, mostly though
It's bulls and naked women wiggling
In the torch light. The gold is as red
As blood in the torch light. It's quite a
Sight. A lot of fellows and girls
Come here from Athens on their honeymoons.
They are always shocked at the way our
Women paint and our men use perfume.
Some of them come back again and again.
Last week we had a couple on their
Golden wedding. Used to, you could hire
A guide, but they put a stop to that."

Sebastian said, "I am the master of the
Pattern of my life, freedom
Is the knowledge of necessity."
That evening when her act was over
She said, "My mother's sick. I've got to
Go see her." She sat in the cab
Calling her flesh back from the public,
Squeezing the orchestra out of it
And offering it to him. They bought
Some things to take. Self conscious for once,
Sebastian stood like a movie gent in the gas
Lit cubicle. The hamper on the

Single kitchen chair. A Sacred Heart
And an old calendar with "The Lone Wolf"
On the walls. The old Negress like a
Scrap of lumber under the thin cover.
Huge candy eyes wet with admiration.
The face like plum colored wood in the gas light.
She was obviously dying and
Going to be very hard to kill.
Circumstance had embalmed her long ago.
The most industrious worm would never
Penetrate her, no corruption take
Her dead as none could take her living.
Maxine fed her fried chicken and a
Hot peach fried pie and black eyed peas.
She was too weak to sit. Sebastian
Held her propped up, the one hard pillow
In his lap. They left her with a cup
Of steaming coffee laced with gin on
The chair beside her bed. "She's pretty
Sick," Sebastian said. "How long has she
Been this way?" Maxine said, "A couple
Years." They danced together, to the same
Band on the phonograph, in her flat.
She said, "I want to do my act just
For you, like I can never do it
In the club. I'll do it wonderful."

The five forerunners of cognition
Pause where the paths tangle in the wood.
They wait, naked and panting, startled.
Nothing moves along the forest trails.
The grass spreads over the meadows like
Green butter sprinkled with sequins.
Virgins came here with wicker baskets
To sing and pick the spangled flowers.
In the high mountain meadows wild goats
And mountain sheep bound over the rocks.

The bear ambles and the fox trots where
The light hangs like a high fog in the
Far off tree tops. Birds pulsate in the
Light. These athletes were cut by cleaner
Hands than Myron's. The man who did them
Is the man who sculpt the Minotaur.
Let no man to the hierosgamos
Of these minds admit impediment.

It might have been a gnarled dark rabbi
Sitting there, or an accident of
High tide and driftwood, down the beach there
In a whorl of sticks and feathers, bones
And dried-out seaweed. It huddled there.
The fog left, blowing in over the land.
The blind eye of the sea and the blind
Rabbi exchanged stares. Sebastian had
No question. Far down some men
Were poking at the sea. Nearby, birds
Scratched it as it ran away from them.
This was not the Argonauts' water
But it wasn't a great deal different.
Sebastian said, "Do I possess this?
Or do I repossess myself? Dead?
No, living with a limitless sterile
Kind of life." Sebastian lay naked,
Blind, salty, and relaxed on the edge
Of the blind sea alone with the blind rabbi.

Morphology repeats ontology.
Thomas drank all night and read John of the Cross.
He was drunk and forsaken before
Dawn. At daylight he went out through the
Lion Gate and bought a ticket for
Knossos, where the women paint their breasts
And the men use perfume and the girls
Mate with bulls. The crowd boiled around him,

Lonely as beasts in a slaughter house.
The period grew blackly backward
Across its sentence. Theseus died
At last in a vulgar brawl. The priests,
Stinking of perfume, got him ready.
Why these overstrained contortionist
Tricks? Archaeologists have proved
The Minotaur a lie, the labyrinth
A vast grocery store, Knossos so mild
It went unwalled. Even the Easter
Island anthropoliths were harmless
Statues of the royal kinfolks. Near
To us, nearer than the lamps that lit
The ceilings of Altamira and Dordogne,
The uncanny geomorphous companions wait –
Maybe, but today his theromorphs
Have outlasted every Pharaoh.

Saturday night, rain falls in the slums.
Rain veils the tired hurrying faces,
Sordid and beautiful in the rain.
Sebastian walks, puzzled, in the rain.
This is the macrocosm, on these
Materials it subsists. And the
Microcosm – This is the very thing.
There is no self that suffers rebirth.
Few trigliths of Stonehenge still stand there
In that immense windy nightbound plain.
It is cold after the summer rain.
"This is the place," she says, "let's eat here."
She turns against him, warm and firm, rain
On her brown cheeks and odorous hair.
When he got home his cheeks were bronze, too,
As though with fever rather than sun,
His beard grizzled, his hair thinner.
The old dog discovered him and died.
The evil rivals died. The web flew wide.

And this was the little brother, the
Holy comedian, offering
Him the password at which all rusted
Hinges fall. This is the place where knowledge
Was so close to poplars and to stones.

Thomas looks out over the valley.
Far off in the low mists and fireflies
The lights along the railroad track change.
Then the whistle comes as distant as
A star and finally the distant
Roar and like a diamond necklace falling
Through the long somber valley the lighted
Cars, pulsating and slipping away
And the headlight twisting into the
Dimness like a cold needle. All so
Far away, not like a toy train but
Like some bright micro organism,
The night train to Omaha goes by.
Then Thomas quiets the zebra dun,
Tends the bannock and the tea and turns
The bacon. Grey low shapes of night bulk
Slow and make their own horizon. White
Ash flakes fall from the heart of the fire.
Now far, now near, the chuck-will's-widows
Call. Thomas smokes and spits into the
Fire. Bats cry, the creaking of the hundred,
Tiny, closing doors of silence.

THE ART OF WORLDLY WISDOM (1920–1930)

THE EPITAPH AT CORINTH

This little book, dear Andrée,
is all the memorial of our
great love. I miss you always.
And I hope that you, when
you drank from the waters
of death with the new dead,
drank no forgetfulness of me.
– Anonymous

IN THE MEMORY OF ANDRÉE REXROTH

a

is a question of mutual being
a question of congruence or
proximity a question of
a sudden passage in air beyond
a window a long controlled fall
of music or is congruence
an infusion illumination have
you waited at places have
you seen places have
you said where have
you said adverbs now
air goes up and in glitter
out of mossy darkness memory
more real than anything
anything that ever was in all
the world and they shall
find at least these bodies broken against
no fact and no dream

b a lamb in the distance

On the reality of loss and tense
and the participation of loss and tense
where loss is an imagined real
and tense may break in case
i.e.: as aorist breaks in instrumentals
dative garment and ablative
informant. Distinguish that the problem is not
of being and the dilemma is
not scalar and it is not differences
but distinctions that matter for
there can be no avoirdupois

of location, nor metric of purpose except
as contingent to mensurand. As
death, an objective
and spasm.
Thus a present; the water-buckle and night
as a fist or from the local an express
        face pulls
away in the subway. There are
conversely, no rulers in instants,
for susceptibility to temporal position
is either habit or donation
and reveals primes,
gratuity and volition

c   *a time*

take one
from a pair a pair
from a quartet a quartet
from an
octet
the arrow through the octave
and the sun rising athwart
the ungloved thighs
the diamond refracted in honey
creep in thought
the minute spider creeps on the
eyeball the glass
rod swinging descends
ultimately to be
refracted in the pale
luminous solution
hair pulled by the wind
eyeballs flaked with light
the two princesses fall
from the ether of intensity
to the ether of irrevocables

and the yellow
animal climbs the cascade in the secret
interior of the highest
mountain

d

cause of a difficulty
trauma of the word
conflicts the eyes the clocks makes
morning pale makes artifacts
of cause so one a deep
so a single fact cool
one a person it was
then a time then and
a position not the same position
as formerly not the unknown
causes of slight cool being
not the cleave the borders
one pull the somatic anemone
or a person she interprets
this objectification as the interest
of a body being a place being
one a person a woman undertakes
this a thing an understood touched
artifact being more substantial
as having evolved out of
process and generality
not anticipated when
arrived not fully
understood

e

for an abrupt
conscious adjustment externalizes
shoulders instants and graces not

of a joy of being in one place and
then in another but of being
profoundly in one place thinking a
place internally
return to an irrevocable body
to the perpetuity of a death
to a gong in a dream
as there is a qualitative difference
between two stars, and a tightening
incline as result of thought
brilliant infinitesimals so now
undulant and cold this is displayed
as a field for a unique progress as a
quality of atmosphere measurable
and inescapable nothing can
foreclose this chrism nothing
can withstand for long memory
always awakens this usufruct
is held by a very old very endurable
meaning

THE THIN EDGE OF YOUR PRIDE

poems for Leslie Smith

I

Later when the gloated water
Burst with red lotus; when perfect green
Enameled grass and tree, "I most solitary,
Boating," rested thoughtful on the moated water;
Where the low sun spread crimson
Interstices in the glowing lotus; aware
Of the coming, deep in the years, of a time

When these lagoons and darkening trees,
This twilight sliding mirror where we have floated,
Would surge hugely out of memory
Into some distant, ordinary evening –
Hugely, in vertigo and awe.

II

Six months as timeless as dream,
As impotent…
You pause on the subway stairs,
Wave and smile and descend.
Was it an instant between waking
And waking,
That you smile and wave again,
Two blocks away on a smoky
Chicago boulevard?
How many dynasties decayed
Meanwhile, how many
Times did the second hand
Circumvent its dial?

III

Indigenes of furnished rooms,
Our best hours have been passed
At the taxpayers' expense
In the public parks of four cities.
It could be worse, the level
Well-nurtured lawns, the uplifted
Rhythmic arms of children,
A bright red ball following
A graph of laughter,
The dresses of the little girls
Blossoming like hyacinths
In early August, the fountains,
The tame squirrels, pigeons

And sparrows, and other
Infinitely memorable things.

IV

Chill and abandoned, the pavilion
In Jackson Park stands like a sightless
Lighthouse beside the lake.
It is very dark, there would be no moon
Even if the night were not thickly overcast.
The wind moans in the rustic carpentry,
But the rain returns silently to the water,
Without even a hiss or a whisper.
We have the shadows to ourselves,
The lovers, the psychopathic, the lonely,
Have gone indoors for the winter.
We have been here in other autumns,
Nights when the wind stirred this inland water
Like the sea, piled the waves over the breakwater,
And onto the highway, tore apart tall clouds,
And revealed the moon, rushing dead white
Over the city.

V

The absorbent, glimmering night
Receives a solitary nighthawk cry;
Marshalls its naked housefronts;
And waits.
The lights of a passing yacht
Jewel for a moment your windblown hair.
The shadows of the Lombardy poplars
Tilt like planks on water.
The sea breeze smells faintly of hospitals.
Far off,
On the desert coasts of the Antipodes,
Mountains slide silently into the sea.

VI

Paradise Pond

The minute fingers of the imperceptible air
Arrange a shadow tracery of leaf and hair
About your face.
Downstream a group of Hungarians from the mill,
Stiff with unaccustomed ease,
Catch insignificant fish.
A row of brown ducklings jerks itself across the water,
Moving like furry cartridges
Into some beneficent machine gun.
We shall arise presently, having said nothing,
And hand in vibrating hand walk back the way we came.

VII

I think these squalid houses are the ghosts
Of dinosaur and mammoth and all
The other giants now long rotted from the earth.
I think that on lonely nights when we,
Disparate, distraught, half a continent between us,
Walk the deserted streets,
They take their ancient forms again,
And shift and move ahead of us
For elbow room; and as we pass
They touch us here and there,
Softly, awestruck, curious;
And then with lurching step
Close in upon our heels.

VIII

"Whether or not, it is no question now,
Of time or place, or even how,
It is not time for questions now,

Nor yet the place."
The soft lights of your face
Arrange themselves in memories
Of smiles and frowns.
You are reading,
Propped up in the window seat;
And I stand hesitant at the rug's edge…
Whether or not… it is no question now.
I wonder what we have done
To merit such ironic lives.
Hesitant on the rug's edge,
I study the kaleidoscope
Before my toes, where some long
Dead Persian has woven
A cynical, Levantine prayer.

IX

After an hour the mild
Confusion of snow
Amongst the lamplights
Has softened and subdued
The nervous lines of bare
Branches etched against
The chill twilight.
Now behind me, upon the pallid
Expanse of empty boulevard,
The snow reclaims from the darkened
Staring shop windows,
One by one, a single
Line of footprints.

X

Out of the westborne snow shall come a memory
Floated upon it by my hands,
By my lips that remember your kisses.

It shall caress your hands, your lips,
Your breasts, your thighs, with kisses,
As real as flesh, as real as memory of flesh,
I shall come to you with the spring,
Spring's flesh in the world,
Translucent narcissus, dogwood like a vision,
And phallic crocus,
Spring's flesh in my hands.

XI

Someone has cast an unwary match
Into the litter of the tamarack woodlot.
A herd of silent swine watch the long flames
Blend into the sunset.
By midnight the fire is cold,
But long streamers of grey smoke
Still drift between the blackened trees,
And mingle with the mist and fireflies
Of the marsh.
I shall not sleep well tonight.
Tomorrow three days will have passed
Since I have heard your voice.

XII

After a hundred years have slept above us
Autumn will still be painting the Berkshires;
Gold and purple storms will still
Climb over the Catskills.
They will have to look a long time
For my name in the musty corners of libraries;
Utter forgetfulness will mock
Your uncertain ambitions.
But there will be other lovers,
Walking along the hill crests,
Climbing, to sit entranced

On pinnacles in the sunset,
In the moonrise.
The Catskills,
The Berkshires,
Have good memories.

XIII

This shall be sufficient,
A few black buildings against the dark dawn,
The bands of blue lightless streets,
The air splotched with the gold,
Electric, coming day.

XIV

You alone,
A white robe over your naked body,
Passing and repassing
Through the dreams of twenty years.

PHRONESIS

for Charles Henri Ford and Parker Tyler

I

And now old mammal, gall
He asked a question
He near and far asking
He said I must start at a place I remember and try and recall.
Fill that tube with blood and hold it to the light you will speedily
    see what was intended.
And what was discovered.

Of course certain rays won't penetrate.
Running a knife along the white edge of this cloister avoiding the
crevices avoiding the results.
Void and void.
The proper and peculiar area begins here the definitions are
a little frayed, it has been years but the partitions are
capable of interlocking, the catharsis, *narke*, the flash on
clash, narcosis, white white white the swift enveloping shutter.
Pull everything to the retina wall. Follow the blue, it is very
thin, speed, follow the blue, it is very thin, speed, follow the
blue and the abrupt.
The motions are adjusted.
Retroactive and ambivalent.
After they had been fed and fattened they did with them as was
the custom in that city. The blue and abrupt rocks. Sweet
haltered lovely cast and quaver.
A plaster hand holding a speckled egg lay on a small sod overhead
the four aluminum dirigibles and the sunlight the shadow
about which there was no question.
A handful of battered vertebrae.
Chew, chew, broad flat dun squares.
It is a far away rattle and readjustment. The waves lap lap the shore
stiffens on the hill the horses can be distinguished moving in
the moonlight.
Bright exhalation in the evening.
If a man can.
Nobody can.
The shoulders shift, swift pain.
If you can tell where it leaves off. You can if you follow the
chart closely. Cold water goes over granite. Snow falls. Pines
revolve. And dull cuts the instep. The symbols are peculiar
to this branch of the subject you will find them on the
back. Now. See this is where the expiration occurred. This
exhalation. Draying to be a light. You must be careful of
what you eat.
Edges. Edges.
Lay it against your cheek and see how cool it is, how much returns.

Lorn dawn clear wrists of wind. Drawn over all that has
intervened. Over the exploding lumber and the impenetrable
spots. Think about sincerity. Do you suppose he was
responsible for all that as they intimated.
Knowing much, dividing much from much.
Keep total arm and deep and ask.
They should look they haven't been exhausted by predecessors.
Muster. Drastic. The stars are easier. Lots of things are easier.
Watch for it as it comes round.
It just rattled through. It just hinged and clinked. Limped.
Slipped and tinkled.
It's over now and we didn't find it.
No we didn't find it.

II

Consular divides and the buttes glow.
The sagging noon
We will color the pages grey olive beige and blue turning them
slowly. We will break the backs of letters. There the snake
whirrs.
The scoria omits nothing.
O fugitive ostrich-porcupine.
Peel tendon from tendon.
Are you intent, standing for everything. I am the only
representative, the throb appeal, breaking.
Gasp and don't gasp, with your fists rub eyeballs and throat.
The mattresses lean against one another and the glass the doors
are stacked.
It is very dusty up here the light comes in through the little holes,
the slaughtered rectitudes lie around on the floor. The ink is
brown.
A pool cue chalked makes a sound.
A discreet enervating squeak.
The old bones scale and chip.
A horse with one blue eye.
That is the color of the sky and the little lake. Black horse pursuing

fracture. If you stop at the white hill top you will be among
them. A chest and wedges war.
An olive tree grows there. Whenever they want to pick an olive
they have to cut down the tree. It must be very inconvenient.
So you would think but they don't seem to mind it.
Sometimes they go by awfully fast. You've got to jump in between.
I mean the aftermaths.
A white column and a white crescent. A lion gate, the shifting
stone. The cabin smelled of iodoform, the walls were covered
with newspapers, rats ran behind them and made a terrific
noise. The horses bumped against the porch all night. You
used to sit in the purple shadow of a cluster of pines at the
edge of the clearing, reading and sewing. They had orange
trunks, forty feet to the first branches.
It is dawn in the markets, the polished fruits and vegetables, pink
masts at the end of the streets.

III

Sometimes.
A sort of erasure.
That quality. That white. Mater Immaculata.
Lady. Stars.
Sometimes from behind glass that slips a little the face of a wax
dummy cuts like a knife
Slicing a concentrated fecund curve
Think of Parmenides and a little glass box
A seamless glass box and a blue light
A silver plane a silver star the curve of an aluminum tube like a
curve of fruit.
Intense pain makes mice sweat.
Occasionally when they operated on a man they left a snowball
inside of him so now the snowballs have colored cords which
hang down outside the incision. You can never use a snowball
more than once so you might as well leave it in the patient
but it is against the law.
For if the eye were an animal vision would be its soul, *i.e.* vision

is the notional essence of the eye. The eye however is the matter of vision and if vision is wanting the eye is no longer an eye save in the meaning of a homonym, as a stone eye or a glass eye.

Soon the green will break into flame. Then it will be green no longer. It will be grey.

And the blue, will it always be blue.

Here one must apply a different standard. These forms are not measured by time, for time is the clocking of motion, the comparison of one motion with another, but by the aeon, *aevum*, which is the form of their relation, extraperipetal, to the celestial sphere. The internal relations of the celestial sphere are, viewed as a whole, simultaneous. From unique points within its manifold motion arises from the reference of any one point or finite system of points to the sum of their relations.

3 LOCAL MEN VANQUISH MONSTER IN FIGHT

San Mateo, May 26. – A desperate but victorious 2-hour battle with a giant neurone in which knives flashed and boat gaffs and trout hooks were used as spears, was the thrilling experience today of Charles Small, Earl Ross, and Edward Holtz of this city.

The huge cephalopod, said to be the largest ever captured on the northern California coast is now on exhibition in a local sport shop. It was hooked by Small, manager of the Peninsular Parcel Delivery Co., while he and his two companions were fishing for rock cod 12 miles out at sea off Princeton.

It took the combined strength of the three men to bring the monster to the surface. Instantly, said Small, the air was filled with flying tentacles. They swished around like whips. One was cut off by Ross as it wrapped itself sinuously around Small's leg. Another tentacle was severed as it twined into the propeller. At one time the fishermen feared the fighting spider of the sea would capsize the boat.

The creature measured 12 feet in diameter. Deep sea experts say that 14 feet is the maximum size for Pacific coast neurones, altho few of this dimension have been found. The suckers on the

tentacles close to the body measured one and one half inches
in diameter.

It is uneven dust and dark.
Spit and dusty eye
At Mott Haven the subway has two levels. The lower has a round roof and is very grey and full of waste paper and the subway wind and the subway smell. And a large black arrow. Negroes get off and on there and go up and down.
A cold toe and a coffee steam.
A blurred window and a green lunch room.
A slopped marble counter and a slow sword.
Why is it like alkali water.
And an omen.
When the icicle breaks it will not be because I tried to look through it.
Second verse.
If you cry they will love you if you try they will be a little frightened.
If you sit too late by the cold water nobody will be a loser.
If you *sculpe! limme! cisle!* the world will leap and bound about. They will love you. They will be tender and very neat.
When the cub reporter's buddy discovered atomic energy they left immediately for interstellar space. It was not until they landed on Mars that Dr. Fu Manchu emerged from the ice box.
Third verse. The hammer and sickle or Cut the Golden Bough.
Fourth verse. The assets deploy.
Consult the endeavor.
Prepare to.
Do not honor.
When the icicle breaks it will not be because I tried to look through it.
A darkness and no one to wonder.

Now drop like pencils the tubular bodies of the hosts of heaven.
Fra Angelico. Vacuum bottles of eternities these are the candles at your bier where you lie stiff and icy Sam Johnson there you lie

thin and sunken all the idealists crying
Ineluctable modality!
Ineluctable modality!
The darkness behind the darkness.
We will introduce Mr. Longfellow to the coal pocket in the galaxy
and the chamberlain of the court of the Duke of Brescia
of 1349. Draw up a chair boys it's warmer over here. The
neoplatonists like servants of the Fisher King bear past a
flame enveloped object. Does anybody know what it is?
Nobody knows.
Here come the unreal children one by one children of the definite
stars
So sweet their faces nonagonal paragonal and shining. They stand
in a row and sing.
Good morning dear teacher
Good morning to you
They join hands and dance and as they dance ring around the
rosie the rosie appears, a monstrous pellucid pie. Slowly the
lid lifts disclosing a moil of small animals live glass Christmas
tree decorations, a few resemble Hawaiian fish. Some fly some
hop some scamper some gasp for air. Then one by one they
die and as they die they burst and as they burst it smells and
when that happens all the children cry.
The hero enters. He is tall thin with platinum cheeks and
muscles of steel. He inspects Sam Johnson, signs him
with a rapid triple blessing. Johnson grows like a movie
flower, in slight jerks, fat and rubicund. Just before
he comes to life Longfellow (smiling) the Chamberlain
(asleep) the angels, archangels, principalities, powers, virtues,
dominations, thrones, cherubim, seraphim, (looking chilled)
the children (who have turned to plaster of paris, very
white) all disappear in a noisy smoke. The neoplatonists rush
through pursued by the Magna Mater.

IV

Rain falls on her glyptic eyelids
Beauty of vectors dies young and fair
A cleft altimeter hangs in the air
Caution. Between the smooth columns a drowse of colored paper falls.
A logarithmic spiral. I refer to the aforesaid aluminum.
A crimson ⊥ presses into the asphalt.
Intense pain makes mice sweat.
The mind, confined in this way to the definition, is seen to be epiphenomenal
Beneath the gold fillings of his teeth are secreted infernal machines but his voice is mild.
Mild hands the mild wash of mild seas on mild coasts mile on mile.
An orange T it is that emerges from the intersections and a blue ⊣ that creeps aimlessly about at the end of the streets.
And the neurones crawl over the paper. The paper crackles and it is wrinkled.
The young girls spin until they become invisible.
The subatomies of her despair cohere.
Day breaks, the breaking plates.
The three pale lights.
Smoke suspends in water.
The ostensive calm where the glaciers have always been.
It is dawn on the strained faces of the maidens who have been up all night
The sea is tendoned with electric herrings the prey of vast gulls.
The mountains are the color of the crows that flee from them screaming.
The flesh is thin on her cheeks like paper. Those who arrive will be confounded in her pale eyes. The grey swords will pass nothing will be asked of her they go to the unendurable torso and the gnawing mice.
The unbelievable cancer rises against the stars.
It is dawn in the valleys of the moon.
Your teeth. The breaking bones of your wrist and knee.

THE PLACE

for Yvor Winters

Unique planets break
the passing light
the serrate west the rose
graph oscillate and climbing
spark Antares needle and omen
germinate the apical blue
final crystal and absorbent
the thought
extends
secrets bloom
the bell wethers entangled in the waxen brush
the herd climbs out of dust
water speaks
cautious glockenspiel enshroud
nighthawk and bat
the grey herd bubbles
over the edge of the bench
meanders in the jackpine shadows
the Basquo's face spurts light
lambs stumble to calling ewes
the Basquo chews
speaks of Santander
of Yakima in winter
all night sheep speak intermittently
close at dawn
Utter bounty
after voluntary limit
cautiously anticipating
the single cosine
unambitious ballistics
minute focus
asymptotic object
before the fracture of the unsuspected calyx

or star
or haline signature
or the piñon that bloomed in the eclipse
unrequested
or crocus beneath oak leaf
Fabrics diadems spangles
the noetic flesh
the ivory Minoan diver
this curve
this tensile promise
fusile apostle
lucent somatic crystal
beneath purple hemlock
the law of freedom
cloth of gold
lily and lotus
Hermetic invisible
eyes pause between invisible
pillars suspended above the white
table

> And as they went on their journey they came toward evening to the river Tigris, and they lodged there. And when the young man went down to wash himself, a fish leaped from the water and would have devoured him. Then the angel Raphael said unto him, Take the fish. And the young man laid hold of the fish and cast it upon the land.

the lamp
or eye
Even the trough
even the closing scissors
where the northern boar
bled in the broken wall
the helmets turned slowly green
amongst the flat stones
The further room
the root of light
the staff

given in the Asian night
carried across Europe
planted in Glastonbury
the unguent
broken on the hair
Bread figs cheese olives grapes wine
the swords rest
mustered for war on the field of law
glories of kingdom
or lord of herds
and these
objects
the plume of mimosa
brushing the roof

CONFUSION

for Nancy Shores

I pass your home in a slow vermilion dawn,
The blinds are drawn, and the windows are open.
The soft breeze from the lake
Is like your breath upon my cheek.
All day long I walk in the intermittent rainfall.
I pick a vermilion tulip in the deserted park,
Bright raindrops cling to its petals.
At five o'clock it is a lonely color in the city.
I pass your home in a rainy evening,
I can see you faintly, moving between lighted walls.
Late at night I sit before a white sheet of paper,
Until a fallen vermilion petal quivers before me.

FUNDAMENTAL DISAGREEMENT WITH TWO CONTEMPORARIES

for Tristan Tzara and André Breton

1

"From any event intervals radiate in
all directions to other events, and the
real and imaginary intervals are separated
by a cone which is called the
null-cone."

gonaV

;

ing evIT

dras pRoG

2m3nL½

pros

*proS

instoting

tismaD

PROXY

gela

domi

immoderate

PROSPECT

savours curve doing instant conceptual bipartite

engine

West inclination 32

PERSPECTIVE

engine

ENGINE

MACHINE

CONCEPTUAL PERSPECTIVE ENGINE

x y z

motor-organ-organ-motor-. . . . . .ds!
number here
$\sqrt{2}$ to the left to the right
distribute
origin of vector
description of vectors
the personal pronoun
vvvvvvvvvvvv
vvvvvvvvvv
vvvvvvvv
v
i
modulatepersistendurereverserevolvereciprocate-oscillateperpetuate
ARRIVE
or pressure of significance
there exists an *a*
there exists an *i*
there exists at least one other entity *b*
valid
efficient
potent
which vests the prospect with originative continuity
the dominative pervasive accommodation of aspect
as the insertion localized as integer formaliter
thus acquiring trajectory
thus assimilating contingency
or the contingent as hiatus in the populous
meaning fused with recipient
amplitude coexists with discretion
importance endures with intervals
concentric and unique
not pendant
as an exterior
without contour
without projective meaning
shift digit

for this the fundamental number
of momentum
of retrograde traction
or of ingress
incarnate
tenuous
fluent
for this ophidian throat
twilight under the eucalyptus
stones sabers clouds kings nights leaves wishes arbors sparks
    shells wings mouths stars oranges fabrics ewes queens skins
    vehicles accents seeds cinders chutneys mixtures fevers apes
    eggs corpses mosses boxes shades irons glaciers
go up as if to be in or on
contemplate acumen distinguished as a formation
or the inane as mother of density
where the embassy of acquisition scrutinizes the monitor
or the spoon out of the sessile rainbow slides to the left of the
    mountains we are so prone to leave out of our calculations

2

"The sea cucumber when in danger of being eaten, eviscerates
    itself, shooting out its soft internal organs as a sop to the
    enemy while the body wall escapes and is able to regenerate
    a new set of viscera."

a

Profoundly and in state as casualty
the confusion lowered in
the reversible cross, the lowered
white cross thrust, glass baubled
integer in foam embroidery,
visual pollen seething between
the lashes, each focussed tendon

sown with eye bloom, each crowded
lily laminated with voracious
mouths. Ominous
the distinct difference. Lethal
the cleft intention. The flesh
motor in fog. The carnivorous
fungus of unpictured scene.
The gifts: a little cloud
a soiled handkerchief crumpled in a ball
the rose in alcohol
the brussels sprout in a sabot.
Electric and furry, that thing
hides in some worn
anonymous viscera, and now
summer being ended, the clocks
bulge, the liquescent
bulbs drop from the boughs, and splash
pale in the starlight on the stone.
That is your ambush, your gift, for your heels
will slide in the dark, your frosted onion
crash, its myriad capsules explode
ordure over the environs.

b

Now the hammock sword ensnares the febrile tree
palms ungloving haste across the sky
bloom veils off the wooly cormorant and race
of eye against returning
spears. So slice recurring
value, the spinner slicing
the red sphere concurs in taps
grounds soon and offers
which scattered crow or a blue sphere.
Revealing neither the arteries
of a fist nor peeling the iliac fascia.
A green bar

indifferent to imposition
reluctant as cruciform
cold as laminated, discovers
the horse wedge hammered
in crepuscular wind, or toss-pebbles
at night, late.
It was delivered in chunks and piled all over
at the end there was a termite left alone at the top.
Should the honey comb
tossed from the rail of the liner
sink slowly
down
beyond the reach of the sun's rays
lower than life
which is impossible.

c

Glitter ghost
flame death as rose blossom
the poinsettia smashed in night.
Once late between the graves
the dogs sitting in a circle
waiting in the grey sand
o narthex, narthex
the crescents broken everywhere.
The chinaman in the dawn hurried
north between the mountains.
The second day, before light, the dome
flamed, the boy
spoke of the sea
and something ancient in a white casket.
Then appeared
like a seal through a paper hoop
the scarlet egg of the lunation
roaring through the sky
uprooting the brass trees

passing noiselessly
over the deserted cities
over the ghosts in nickel shrouds
over the moss green and purple headlands
over the grey sea.
The children approach the hyena diffidently
they approach the guardian of embers
the sky filled with red hands
the wind heavy with dry salt
o narthex
broken on the walls

d

As from the citron kelp untangling in the purple bay
only brain caryatids return
hands jewelled with seeds
only the red dog circles the rocks
so from the ivory cautiously the spatulate question
intrudes, mutters itself, branches in the room of souls.
So the oak leaves, whittled in copper
parade death and astonishment
so, carefully as an animal in a dream, blue
with an icy pelvis
unaware of secrets, the chronometer
bursts, first crimson, in the triangle
of Leo, then orange
in the belt of Orion.
The grey larvae of the oak leaves
spill voluminously out of the proscenium.
Mackerel hang in the waterspout.
And eyelids are shorn like foreskins
in this religion
and the wand is weighted with eyeballs
and the ice cream skull weeps
that never should have stayed
that will never leave.

e

How shall the stars on the cheeks
of this mandrill find a number.
They have seen stars as intervals.
They have broken the vermilion legs of the jungle.
They wait
the owl
the moth
the tower in flames
the ibis with multiple moist paps.
None other waits.
The cross gouged in the hummock
waits like a trap.
Over the white trees the stars
iris out in the sky
metallic breaths cross the air
and distinct against the dry grass
the black bears
the red baboons
wait, and the little girl
so pale, so fragile waited
naked, whispering to herself.
In the ravines the pilgrims foundered in the mire
their jaws were broken, they died
and lay unburied.

THE SUFFICIENT

for Louis Zukofsky

ancre ridgedge et poissoble gongpoint
(or) KAniv ubiskysplice ubi danAe ubi diamondane
thru oat quiv   at place
at daybreak   shellbreak
as an act so many nerves so many kilowatt hours
and this locus mallet
sempiternal bomb
history is not independence
after the dialectic
the international
concatenation is not immanence
unable to escape stung to somatic
death by the innumerable
hypodermics
: so death :
"the dog
swims close to earth"
and the yucca bloom from his shoulders
the perennial
aseity donated
each anniversary or immediate
transfinite the dark
nebula given
to the anvil improved
instrument not
doubt or the voracious
well where through a telescope
the soles of chinamen can dimly
be discerned
as
per se and paradigm
nor take place
but posit nor ask needles

of april for a stone this stone (those
calculi) or aurora this
web and thread or silver
crest million grunions
or vegetable strand governor
important not doubt
the cauliflower
doubts and grows
doubting
no firecracker
but insisting source and symbiosis
the myth that is true
a se
stoned in the synagogues
patronized by the occult
but the word
this and this as quality
fountain and fountchart
only its metric transcends
as value this gratuity
verb home
all verbs transitive
in the dative presence
and itself mirrored
invariant as grace, as the answer
plenum

INTO THE SHANDY WESTERNESS

for William Carlos Williams

Do you understand the managing.
Mornings like scissors
Leaves of dying.
Let event particle e. Point track m-n.
Cooling grey slender ascenders.
Congruence. Yes? that's what you thought it would be?
A flag waves, a kite climbs. Clouds climb, advancing impalpable edges.
The whole mottled sky turns slowly on its zenith, the same clouds go round and round the horizon.

As A is.
A triangular chessboard squared in two tones of grey, P to K3, KN X B.
It's very cold under the table. A cold window.
When he was little he used to go out to the barn and put his cheek against a cow and cry and cry. When he swam in the pasture creek the little fish tickled his legs.
Something is going to cut.
Something is going to break.
I don't see it I can't hear it but it's swinging.
One goes swiftly back. One goes forward. Two move to the left. A voice.
The steel column bores and bores into the ground. Presently the air is filled with ammonia fumes.
We will sing hymn number 366, "Art thou weary, art thou languid," 366
MY number, MY bleeding number. So I ups and tells em Why I was weary Why I was languid.

As B is.
Orange green yellow blue red violet.

Is there anybody there said the stranger. Is there any reason why after all these difficulties we should be subjected in this particular humiliating manner.

Orange. Row after row of shining minute faces. Green. A slight lurch and then the floor begins to climb smoothly steadily up up everything clatters against the altar. The celebrant is embarrassed. White discs fly from the cylindrical heads of the spectators and disappear out of the windows. Presently only their palpitating necks are left, hollow, dark purple inside.

It's pleasant to think of the cottages along the mountainside. The alfalfa ripening in the afternoon. The thin smoke of evening. The chill nights.

Assorted solutions, neat packages of peace were distributed by officious archangels. There was much unemployment, long breadlines everywhere in the dusty cities, quiet, no traffic, much patience. We came on, collecting visas, wasting our substance in bribes, asking, Who is king in this kingdom, who is your ruler, by what do you measure?

Whenever I think of England I see Wyndham Lewis standing in a high freezing wind on the plain where Modred and Arthur fought, dressed only in his BVD's painfully extracting thorns from his chapped buttocks. It grows dark rapidly.

When I think of France I see Marcel Duchamp on Michigan Boulevard in a raccoon coat and a number of young americans praying before a roller-coaster from which middle-aged frenchmen strapped to bicycles leap into tubs of cocacola.

Now the blue flowers return the gravel mornings.
Now the immaculate mistresses
And those we loved from afar.

It's yellow in the sunlight and blue around the corner and it's all been so simple. The grey furry plants and the white hands. The considerations, the ablatives. The conversation about death. The lace parasol.

He was naturally very neat.
He was particular about neckties and very proud of his razors. They gleamed on maroon plush. His watch lost sixty seconds every four weeks neither more nor less. He sat on the screen porch smelling faintly of citronella and spoke slowly and distinctly of love. Then he died. And she hadn't made up her mind. So she walked under the lace parasol avoiding the decayed catalpa blossoms that littered the sidewalk.

It grows dark. A shitepoke flies up from the canal. That's a shitepoke he says to the boy. For supper hasenpfeffer. The rabbits are getting at the tomato sets, bad. Tourists are camping down at the woodlot at the corner. You can see their fire from the back door. When they came for water Nero snapped at the man. Now he looks over at their fire and barks every few minutes. On both sides of the walk about every ten feet all the way to the gate bushel baskets are turned upside down over the peonies. As it gets darker they disappear.

MEMORANDUM

for Horace Gregory

If distraught shall be the word or not,
Or understanding, or misunderstanding,
Terror, no not, or any glazed thing,
Impervious or treacherous, as final
And distraught before the last, the bright
Consummate flower. And he the sensual
And the dark rebel, bound now outward,
Gone out haunted by the quincunx of heaven,
By Fomalhaut and pulsing Algol,
By Orion and the dim thick nebula,
Observed by the indifferent eye
Of the cassowary, the understanding
Crimson nostrils of sharks in tepid
Bright oceans, and distraught, stoned by fetishes,
Or dead, and the grave marked with an oar,
Vibrating in the wind till the next spring tide,
The pale sea collapsing sleepily,
Booming on the shingle in the sun filled fog
Distraught by the inorganic eye
Of the jerking squid, the irrefutable stare.
Or restless nights unwashed and thirsty,
Sleeping among the stones and alkali dust,
The dwarf owls barking from their burrows.
Or distraught, terror within and the sword without,
A hundred miles of wind driven sand,
The fuel exhausted, the cold freezing the eyes.
Statistics. Kisses. Assassins. Bombs.
Pricing and weighing. Parting and being born.
Distraught or not, the iron at the throat.

The functioning total then,
Metabolic or catabolic,
Posits the germinal unit –
Position, created encapsulate –
The marvelous onion exploding
In successive exfoliations
Of purpose, falling away
In the primary discourse,
The resolution of vector tension –
He loves me, he loves me not.
Where the Bighorn scrambles over the snow
And disappears and the glaciers
Are a little smaller each year,
Where during an eclipse of the moon
A great white owl flew over the icefields
Calling like a bell.
Transparent granules
Radiate over the brain, leaving a path
Of glimmer behind like slugs in the evening.
The evening disappears in the sky
Over the basalt beach. They have lost something
Amongst the ferns and she stands
Holding a lantern while he searches
On hands and knees.
There is a slight wind
Which always arises from the opposite
Shore when the water has become white
In the evening.

The geminal unit –
If you can find the street you will find
No difficulty in finding the shop
Where they sell little boxes of ashes.

Each leaf is an encyclopedia
Slowly reading itself, keeping
Inviolate the secret of its
Discrimination, falling slowly
Through the counterglow of which it is a part.

Beyond Neptune the beckoner
Is known to pass, as birds seen falling
Skyward in the water's mirror
Transmute that curved opening in space
To song. Weighted, neural transversals
Gather against the bone, thus, explode and fuse
Thus, and leave their spoor like dinosaurs
In that quick lime.

So rises in the
Responsibility of achievement
The idea of birds, the theorem
Of the wing, the transit of the sphere –
Rising against the net of dark the bright
Planes, the shadows jangling in a crackle of light.
On the last ellipse the loadstone passes;
The iron falls in the night; the cloven
Merges; the focus whirls in the gulf;
The curve of grace spreads, remembering
Over the contour of the vase
The tangent creeping *ultra Herculis Columnas.*

THE CRISIS

for Dorothy Van Ghent

I

earth upon earth
between the confines of the day
and night earth took
of earth the careful clay of earth
compound with wrong and all woe
saying war
death destruction in these hands I bear
and form from the war
of earth and earth fear
on the irremediable ways
earth hypocrite to trusted earth
the faithless sky
the sly sea offer only
the old lie
a naked corpse tossed by nameless waves
earth in the earthen urn thrown
now the howling dogs advance in glimm'ring
light now earth in fogs falls stumbling
at last to earth and we falling
in dazed sleep drunken
surfeited with earth
wandering in the waste
dominion of birth
know of earth
little nor how nor why

II

What the Stars Say and A Prayer to the Stars

They wish, that they may also perceive things. Therefore, they say that the star shall take their heart, with which they do not a little hunger, the star shall give them the star's heart, the star's heart, with which the star sits in plenty. For the star is not small, the star seems as if it had food. Therefore, they say, that the star shall give them of the star's heart, that they may not hunger.

The stars are wont to call, "Tsau, Tsau." Therefore, the Bushmen are wont to say that the stars curse them the springbok's eyes, the stars say, "Tsau, Tsau." I am one who was listening to them. I questioned my grandfather, what things it could be who spoke thus. My grandfather said to me that the stars were the ones who spoke thus. The stars were the ones who said "Tsau" while they cursed the people the springbok's eyes. Therefore, when I grew up, I was listening to them. The stars said, "Tsau, Tsau." Summer is the time when they sound. Because I used to sleep with my grandfather, I was the one who sat with my grandfather, when he sat in the coolness outside. Therefore, I questioned him about the things which spoke thus. He said the stars were the ones who spoke thus, they cursed the people the springbok's eyes. My grandfather used to speak to Canopus, when Canopus had newly come out he said, "You shall give me your heart, with which you sit in plenty, you shall take my heart, with which I am desperately hungry. That I might also be full like you. For, I hunger. For, you seemed to be satisfied, hence you are not small. For, I am hungry. You shall give me your stomach, with which you are satisfied. You shall take my stomach, that you may also hunger. Give me also your arm, you shall take my arm, with which I do not kill. For, I miss my aim. You shall give me your arm. For, my arm, which is here, I miss my aim with it." He desired that the arrow might hit the springbok for him, hence he wished the star to give him the star's arm, while the star took his arm, with which he missed his aim. He shut his mouth, he moved away, he sat down, while he felt that he wished to sit and sharpen an arrow.

from Bleek–Bushman Texts

III

the sky turns violet
o you friend
the earth turns violet
o you friend
only the wind blows
o you friend
only the small birds flown
o you friend
from behind the disc of the sun
the rays of the sun pull groaning
pull groaning why o why
delay so long o lord of lords
for the lamb fallen in the herd shall I look
shall I look for the small lamb lost from the herd
shall I look o you friend
for the young ram stumbled in the herd
o you friend
for the ewe lost from the herd
o you friend
shall he take the bow
he of the sure eye the strong one
shall he take the axe
he of the sure arm the strong one
o you friend

shall he take the noose
he of the sure wrist the strong one
o you friend
this is the shining day of his advent
the clear-eyed the bright haired one
o you friend.

from Seligman – The Veddah

IV

Constable of the singular hearts that appear
Beaded with smoke on the confines, the meanders
Of a night of small discrete flares
And dragonish twilight, she met you carrying
The pastries of inferno heaped in a tray
Upon your head. "Be seated in a wilderness"
She said, "and tell me your story."
You smiled, produced the covert omen,
The mangled segilla she had feared.
Her fingers splayed in the moss and through the trees
Behind her filed the white lewd hypocrites
One by one, emaciate and nude.
A freight train growled on a far
Edge, moaned at a crossing where fireflies
And cat tails were. She advanced a silken leg,
A hand beringed and aqueous, against
Your thigh. She said, "Your cheeks are polished tin.
Your eyes, the restless larvae of your brain
Feed in my bones. See how the meteors, falling
Are reflected in your forehead, stream
In the sky and course above your eyebrows.
That force is yours to use, compulsion
Is your inheritance." She leaned near,
Breathed in your nostrils. We saw you then
Press a stiff hand to your rigid eyes, open
Your lips and close them silently again,

Arise, pulse like a spring against a weight
And go to where the chalk-eyed man of small
Machines waited your bargaining.
She followed, caressing your hands, weeping
A little, begged you wait, saying,
"Beware the forest horror stops
You where the paths cross. The guillotine
Animal crouches on the low branches,
Clockwork terrors tick in the bushes, and the moon's
Light falls slice by slice without pause
Without mercy. Dare you go there
Alone?" We heard your answer "I have gone
Where only the sea moved. I have moved
Painfully over the ancient mud.
Where the silent kingdoms
Of the luminous fishes swept like swift
Constellations a mile above. Only the sea
In large blocks moving in the years,
And the bones of drowned men
Picked clean in passage circling down."
She said, "I know and I am satisfied
We trust each other. Let us go."
The chalk-eyed pedlar rose as you approached
Hunched his back and wet his lips. You showed
Your little silver. He nodded
Sympathized and looked askance, at last
Sighed and fished in his pack, produced
A gyroscope, a coffee grinder, a saw,
A carburetor, an easy death, a patent trap,
Six obvious absolutes. Six candidates
Storming your Pantheon in a little row.
You watched him wrap them in an old newspaper
Counted your change, returned his bow,
And paced the wind along the forest aisles,
She gliding lambent by your side.
Presently the blind persistent moles

Crept sleek from the earth, black
In the moonlight, and devoured
The pastries lying on the ground.

v

The great year climbs the blackened sky,
The whirling equinoxes close their term,
The moon turns to the earth her unknown face.
Loneliness –
The flesh and the bones ragged with wounds.
Where have the chanting litanies wound away?
What flaring visions burn out day?
Let the luminous vaults of the sequoia
Resound with song of this last splendid bird.
Announce the climacteric convocation,
The passages and the conflagrations
And here mark out in air a sphere for wings
And drive away tamed spayed fates and furies.
Prohibit the ritual meek physician
Thumb shuttering eyelid forefinger to lip
And every overstuffed iota, every
Amoebic despot deprive of passport.
Let only the regal dream, the magniloquent
Geometric abstract emperor come near,
Let the ending only song fracture the long
Throat made supple with a lifetime's silence.
Let the maimed with age the clay eyed mourner
Go away weeping each in his own midnight,
For now the conjunct dual flame speeds toward
The whirling corolla of the eclipse.
Giver and receiver at last are one.
Vision roars in the loud forge of dream
And over the translucent surface
Of the molecule sweep the glimmering
Shadows of planets moving

Within its hot entrails.
Enumeration decayed in that benignity,
No integer between Polaris and the Southern Cross,
All victory placeless in that ubiquity,
Sown with mirrors fire drenched
Beyond possession beyond meaning,
This duality had devoured
The bowels of a promethean logic
And now at the end after the many
Failures and catastrophes, from the rock
Rang out the shuddering voice of the victim,
Wrung from the glutted trunk, ripping the air.
Finally monad and triad,
All your secret tireless principles,
Shrink to a last ember, and the jawbone
Pulverizes, the teeth seed furrowed soil.
Seventy years thought froze the fontanelles,
Sancta Sophia has crashed at last
Only a few gold wires thread the dust
Of all those singular embroideries,
The wheel swings on itself and wavers to a stop.
Neither history nor genesis forever now,
Though such a truth as may
Shall spread its words on walls
And such a beauty may coquette
From gauze thigh and red lip,
From now henceforward
All midnights wait,
The head in the hands,
The urn upon the knee.

ŌKEANOS AND THE GOLDEN SICKLE

for R.E.F. Larsson

Where is the toothed estuary the toothed
Wave, the ancient expense of fog-pale
Green water, that she should move
So sure in brittle languor
Over serrate sand? That she
Should never sing? Let us forget
The white drawn lips, the watery
Weak flesh. Ah lady, draw the long
Throated violins, the occult single bell
Nearer that we may pluck
Old music in an unknown wind.
Why should she tread the opulent
Promenade, the long avenue
Of narrow trees with so tired
Grace, with such immorally
Instinctive ease?
Give over ivory keys
And ominous untroubled
Drums and let the music be
Sharp, and friable, and somehow
Softer than the old elementalisms.

WHEN YOU ASKED FOR IT

for Frances Prudhomme

Dear Friend,

...... the day the seal came up the beach and mother fed him fish from the porch of the cottage all the children were away on a hike. However, when we went to the mountains the snow was just melting off the highest valleys and when it left it left carpets of yellow snow lilies with fragile watery stems. They say the deer eat them but we didnt see any, only tracks. They were timid for the trappers had just left the month before and in this locality these gentlemen are not adverse to killing a deer now and then for meat in the long winter. And there were whistling coneys that whistled almost a tune, we saw lots of them, and porcupines, and once an old bear sat up across the canyon and looked at us for quite a time, he sat so still nobody saw him until John whispered, "Theres a bear across the canyon looking at us, sh-h." The girls had to scream but that didnt faze him, he kept right on looking, and after a while he got tired and went away. We used to bathe in the creeks which flowed right off the snow, and was it cold. The fishing was poor and we didnt see many birds but the fir trees stood up all around with a beautiful taper and ever so slightly purplish......

In the evening by the flowers
In the evening by the green bronze
Trickle of watered wines the blossoms purple lips
And the wind and the wool of the surf blown diminishing in over
grey sand
Star in the east
Star in the west
Wish that star was in my breast
Entomological emperor
Master of the insect catalog
The long narrow white pages and the legs many jointed pasted
down with little bands of transparent paper

Gone
Some of these days
Gone
Some of these days
Gone
Some of these days
Gone
Some of these days
Gone

Gone
Knowing
That is knowledge
That is hard a hard mystery
Even Father Orkings doesnt know
Beyond the windward horizon lie beds of weak flowers
They are crushed in places and in places the rain has beaten them
into the sand
They are white and it is evening
We have instant death
Some of these days I am going to throw myself up for grabs
Alum
Alum pencilled on the cheeks
And the right angles that go in opposite directions the grey light
the yellow barred windows
(wanted and wanted)
The air filled with flying hands
A stack of china about to fall
Eyes in the ice
Teeth
And the lines recede
There is nothing but receding lines and a cross in electric lights
There is a flayed airplane

The axe was deeply imbedded when I tried to lift it out of the
encyclopedia a shudder of pain crept out on my diaphragm
and then then they crawled out of its white flaky flesh
hundreds of them and then I wanted to pull wool I wanted to
pull wool along spines
I know quiet
Weir
I know old fences
Some of these days
Gone eyes
Air
When you asked for it did you get it
Were they many

Were they hard
Put the T square there
The triangle there and the compass
Sift the evening
And the filmy filmy smoke
Pink and grey
Question the subaltern
Question the beautiful delicate lady
You know what she means to you
Silver and saffron all slick and tinkle
She leans on the arm of the master physicist
He wears a leather jacket and his face is silver
He draws question marks rapidly on the backs of envelopes

(are you there)
Are you waiting for us patiently as you said you would
And did you get it
Do you know do you believe do you transpire do you
Come to color
Relieving capture and devolving arc
Intransitive

This is not for us this is for the people down the street with the same name they have a little boy they dress him in very clean wash suits and he sings all day
Intransitive
Come to color
Between the edge of cube and cube the twilight thickens day deserts the eastward windows the cypress groves along the westward sea
Come to color and devolving arc
Claws are rapid clutch is rapid big figures walk past

(the T square)
How white it is and how beautiful the lines look
On every roof is a flagpole thin tapering tipped with a black ball the fire escapes go swiftly up and down and the escaping

firemen go swiftly up and down them
When you asked
They were many
There were a lot of bronze horses and marble goddesses and we saw we must walk very swiftly across this square and turn up the alley to the light in the doorway
Inside each shop a light burns above a cheap iron safe

(are you there)
Hold my hand and keep out of the rushes
Nothing will hurt you everybody loves you and I want you to be very happy
She cried and said Ive got to go I really ought to go
The master physicist
You mustnt do that he said we dont advise it it interferes with the work of the committees and interrupts the sessions of the congress
Goodbye o lady goodbye
When you asked for it
It is a little novel
We arranged a collusion
We arranged a beatified nisus
Leaping and washing the very dark place
O the lithe wavering wisp
Leaping and washing
There is always a procession of strange geezers just a little to the left and to the rear solemnly and very slowly going down many steps sometimes they are around a corner or obscured by the thick trees
Where ever you go
Have you stayed so long by the sea watching the sun and the sand-pipers running along the edge of the water the sea weed rolling under the surface
Because he was an odd child
Try not to caper and call when the institutions are busy because nothing is more disagreeable than that half questionable activity in times of great strenuous searchings

Mary was her name
She was very neat very studious and inclined to affect chastisements
Question this endeavor
Mary are you enquiring
Herbert are you piercing the planks the cords the cubicles one after another
Name the series you have uncovered
The river was beautiful there at the sea mouth full of colorless intense light in the twilight the fog poured in from the sea between two of the lower hills small rodents appeared and disappeared abruptly
Give me your hand
Herbert
Mary
Slowly obstructing the narrow valley the rectilinear ogre slowly
Devouring
She had not tried to make this an edge of the type demanded but she had hoped a lot of you
Clarion and clarion o so
Mary you know what it has been like
I do Herbert
Its a long evening the light lasts a long time
Everything is so quiet
I want you to uphold it though
True and the balances swinging
Do you know me at all
Close
There is too big a jump and too sure a requisition
Do long a sound bowling
Hands smoothing and smoothing
Right and right
Do

Am I a good woman
Who are you that you should wonder all the grass a wave it
The wire curls and curls slow
Greased green the thin kind line
Right cause to make much
I dont like the woods there are things under the roots
I tried and tried
Make fast there make fast
Mary we know what comes in at the deposition we really
    sympathize with you a lot
12345678
Nobody will help enough though the pressure is too great
I know I know

Doing this for us you blossom
Deter deter granting deter
Deter granting
Here I am
I have waited and wondered and thats all you have to say to me
Glass put the hand back
A long black middle creak
Dont gape
Hope and knowledge
Its your own fault though youre a fool and you know it
I certainly was
Take
Now there is one here see it off to the left and then you go that way
    along and cold cotton bale wet wood hope and hope hope
    and knowledge
Breathing little books and your gloves and your hands
But I dont wear gloves
Not even in winter
Not even in winter
Sometimes little vertigo sometimes little knowledge
Come near

Noise and night
I saw my sister in a white nightgown walking amongst purple tree trunks in a heavy fog very slow and with a gentle smile just like she was laid away
My brother died when he was ten years old he had dark red hair he died from a fall
Thats a big stone
Yes thats a big stone we are going to build a fire over it and then throw water on it sometimes the pieces fly a long way one killed a cow last spring a long sliver of granite
Right between the eyes

Deep moist walk
Tamaracks crack in the wind but not here it is quiet here with noises like night in the city
The hill slip
It wont do a bit of good it wont help
Hope and knowledge

Its been so difficult you cant possibly imagine how terrible it has
been trying and trying and never getting anywhere and never
knowing never being able to see it
Ive lacked attention for long construction
Its lonely and constant
Its dark now the trees look like teepees
Grey
Right between the eyes
Deep moist walk
O hold fast to me hold fast to me

We tried very hard to make it what we thought it had ought to be
Resilient sympathy and the hands
Walking together reading aloud in the evening
The green utterly beautiful twilight
The pistons rock and plunge it is very white there is an unshaded electric globe and one man in grey striped overalls far down on a gallery watches the slow movement of red and green lights across a board once in a great while he throws a switch

and the fresh copper bars gleam for an instant
The heart beating and beating one feels it now the diaphragm
slipping over undulant waves as one walks the abrupt shudder
of peristalsis
He knows her lips all her little nerves her web of capillaries her
capsules of mysterious fluids

Twilight
A number of people on a wide street
A palm turned upward at a table the marble cold against the back
of the hand
Trout swimming in the window
The gold fillings in teeth
I get to thinking of him
When I see him I notice his socks need mending

My eyes ache and I have a confused headache
See them coming inexorably the narrow hooves of their horses
their voices hoarse with dust their robes spectacular in the
sunlight their swords whirling above their heads
When a man has grown close to a woman and we were so close
You had better ask the captain
But his splendor terrifies me he is all alone on the bridge and the
wind presses against him
Perhaps Ive hurt him terribly if I could only go away I could forget
about it but I see him all the time and when I dont see him
I worry about him
I feel as though something were striking my face with the edge
of a hand vertically down the center of my face and across
my eyes
A door was opened in the ceiling and something was poured into
this room
Where is the cat
In the corner
There is an arrow here pointing up those long stairs there is sweat
on the walls
The old woman is a long way down the tunnel it is difficult to
see her because of the dust and the imperfect illumination

but she seems to be picking up things and she is in a great hurry
I believe you can get out to the end of it if you try of course its very frail

If I only had a little money
His pride
He is working across the river I know he doesnt like his job there was so much he wanted to do perhaps he can never recover a lot of the things I am taking with me there is a lot I can never recover

Blue veins beneath the chalky skin the bones showing through yellow the hair on the hands frizzled as though it had been singed
The leaves of the eucalyptus the leaves of the madrone spin in the wind ferry boats crawl over the water and disappear behind the islands as the fog comes in a siren moans then another
Why dont you try a little harder why do you forget the things that were so important you used to be so careful

I need money so badly I could go away as it is Im caught out here it costs so much to live in New York when I dont see him I wonder how he is getting along what he is doing now
Maybe he is in his room reading maybe he is walking along one of those empty streets where the railroads cross one another walking and thinking
He needs me so much

There is a faint odor of burning oil the hissing and crackling of a long spark several lids slap shut
Stretch out your arm and strain your fingers wide apart
The graph looks like a row of canine teeth the gold leaf rises and falls charging and discharging
Dont worry about it dont think I mean everything I say it will be all right

A PROLEGOMENON TO A THEODICY (1925–1927)

For
Mildred
Andrée

A PROLEGOMENON TO A THEODICY

I

a

This the mortared stone
Heated
The green lying over
The tinsel white that ascends
The rocker
Aboard aboard
It rustles rustles
Should he acquiesce to forever flow
No one shall ever enervate this structure
Where the worm walks
The fatigued worm
The countless green multiple umbrellas
And the red vestments
The toy balloons
Slowly it shifts all the lions grey
Shall you. Lion.
When you were young they called you Lilith
When you were young
It goes around it lies off
This is a squash
Thunder
More thunder
Still more
The little steel keys
Lock and revolve
And lock but
It is black scarred
Of what it was
When it stops transparent on the screen
Fish
Black

b

Has it been
No or has it
.alpha .gamma
The parallelogram of forces
The wishing cry the wishing
Is there a hole there where you walk or is there
Nothing
Is there an eyeball was it a demand or was it
A gift
In which nothing was given
Little planes of pain inserted in the brain
Needles in the tongue
"when you asked for it did you get it
were they many were they hard"
Remember that I told you there is nothing to
Be afraid of
I said there is nothing
I said it is a ghost it is a dream a
Joke an ontological neurosis
I told over and over
I said there is nothing
It is not an abyss
It is not even
A pit
Hope and hope muscle and muscle
O the pressure it presses o to get away to get
Away where it doesn't press where it isn't
Always pressing and pressing
Can't you understand
Can't you just forget and just believe believe
What. Believe
Nothing
Just believe
Living
Be
Be living   it is not even a pity nor the other thing

You think it is
If it was as you think someone would have
Told you o yes by now someone would
Don't you think someone would

c

The bell any bell and ring
The gold curves that wind up over the gold
The far shimmer
The exfoliate pentacles
The barging nosing lurging
Heave heavy
The dark
The cope of flesh the amethyst morse of pain
The unobtained ostensorium
They erected a sign
They said this is a sign
This is our own heraldry
In this way do we divide color from color
And it spreads it spreads over the sky the leaves
Of the canna
Wine brown o unanswered typhoon
Take a coarse comb and comb your vermicular throat
The red flowers that bleach in the sun
The roar crossed by the fine wires
In the haze the golden cumuli approach invisibility
The undersides of the forearms turn up
The lines on the palms shift like a graph of eels
It goes down down without alteration
With a chipper
Chirr
Down

d

I think secretly
Could it have for all the world have been just that

How have the blanketed eyes
Sensation drains through the body
The plague of grasshoppers blown out to sea, drowned, washed
ashore heaps of them ten feet high rotting on miles of coast,
stench in the air far inland
And one razor branch of bamboo in the sunlight in the twitter
As speaks the *cor anglais* the banal stab
And piston swims the air
The lucid crystal breaks always and recedes quantum
By quantum retreating
Engine of revelation
The beauty which was not otherwise than we could believe
As speaks the celesta
As speaks the ineffable triangle
The note which could never be interrupted and would never stop
O merle. O. O.   O. O. O.   O.
The gnomom falls erratic on the tangled thicket
The odor of raspberries crushed in the hot sun
Apparition
A mouthful of sticks and dactyls
It should be observed that this principle leads unavoidably to
endless regress
We ferry the Skagit pulling ourselves along a cable
The mountains are purple and grey the valley is green the river
is white
Milk of glaciers
In Horseshoe Basin the snow bled as the horses crossed it
A snarl of leaves
The curve of flesh
Evening and a light
I walk in the sunset
I walk in the sunrise
In the meantime I have been up all night
I have seen at a speed of three hundred kilometers a second the
great nebula of Andromeda rushing upon me
The acoluthic sensation is still with me
The procession of cynocephali
Hysteresis   the shattered stone

e

I told you how it was
I keep telling you over and over how it
Is
It is so easy to tell it over and over it is
So hard to get you to believe me
I take scenes I take places I say now isn't
This true
And this yes and this yes yes
Yes I don't know what else to say but
I want something else
I want and want always wear and wear
Always
Always
But you can't have it don't you realize there
Isn't any more there isn't any more at all not
At all
Greedy orphans of life
The bones are not broken the infinitely fine
Brainpan is still full to the pulsing
And there you stand "sad thin a trifle withdrawn"
And you stay that way
It isn't the way to stay
You ask presents
Surprise packages
What have you brought
Have you brought anything
Will you ever bring anything
Go into the sterile mountains into the region
Of minute stone
The puma that circles the pyramidal peaks
The eyes that dry revolve
Can you ask and after returning
Is it the same sewing and humming a little
Tune a little tumrtumrtumtumtum
O wise in moan
O infinitely wise and bent

And bowed and in the heart bowed down
Just born to die
Nobody will ever know anything about it
And I have nothing more at all to say.

II

We were interested in ways of being
We saw lives
We saw animals
We saw agile rodents
Scala rodent
The harmonic pencil
Scala rodent
Emits its fundamental
The stricken plethora
A bottle of water against a very blue sky
A toppling shutter
The final peninsulas of space
Germinate in the secret ovoid perimeter
e.g.: scholia
The white hill
Elastic fatigue
The white lax hill and immediately the iced antelope
The line warps
The meridian of least resistance ascends the sky
The brain ferments
The curdled brain
The repercussion
The bullweaver
Obsessed by an ideograph
A mechanical bracelet
A small diesel engine
First one and then the other
Air congeals in water
The mural rift

A kind of going
The little block falls
The little wooden block
That long snarl of coast in the Mediterranean
The heart inclines
The four triangles
The fifth
The fingers jerk
The green cheek
The fourth
The image in the portal
The resin curls
The soggy mitten
The third
The cleaved cough
The second
The closing ribs
The first
The double envoi
The grackle breaks
Sweat
The diverse arrows
The anagogic eye

III

This is the winter of the hardest year
And did you dream
The white the large
The slow movement
The type of dream
The terror
The stumble stone
The winter the snow that was there
The neck and the hand
The head

The snow that was in the air
The long sun
The exodus of thought
The enervated violin
The oiled temples
The singing song and the sung
The lengthy home
The trundling endless stairs
The young stone
Homing and the song
The air that was there
Flayed jaws piled on the steps
The twirling rain
And laying they repeat the horizon
Ineffably to know how it goes swollen and then not swollen
Cold and then too warm
So many minor electrocutions
So many slaps of nausea
The keen eyelids
The abrupt diastole
That leaves you wondering
Why it was ever despite their assurances unlocked
Stars like lice along the scalp
The brainpan bitten burning
And dull on one foot
And dull on one foot
O cry aloud
O teeth unbound
Don't you know that the stone walk alone
Do you know the shredded brow
Are you aware
Do you take this forever concentric bland freezing to touch
Let the scarlet rustle
Let the globes come down
Let the oblate spheroids fall infinitely away
Forever away always falling but you can always see them
The creak

The squeak that makes you slightly open your mouth
Patiently to be strangled
It is gone away somewhere
It is Winter
Reason
Winter
Ache

IV

Black
Blue-black
Blue
The silver minuscules
In early dawn the plume of smoke
The throat of night
The plethora of wine
The fractured hour of light
The opaque lens
The climbing wheel
The beam of glow
The revealed tree
The wine crater
The soft depth
The suspended eye
The clouded pane
The droning wing
The white plateau
The hour of fractured light
The twisted peak
The cold index
The turquoise turning in the lunar sky
The climbing toe
The coastwise shout
The cracking mirror
The blue angle

The soothed nape
The minute flame
The silver ball
The concave mirror
The quivering palm
The conic of the wing
The trough of light
The rattling stones
The climbing humerus
The canyon bark
The unfolding leaves
The rigid lamp
The lengthy stair
The moving cubicle
The shifting floor
The bending femur
The rigid eye
The revealing lamp
The crackling anastomosis
The initial angle
The involved tendon
The yellow light
The acoluthic filaments
The general conic of the wing
The revealing eye
The crazed pane
The revelation of the lamp
The golden uncials
The revelation of the mirror

v

It is now a decline
A decline and an understanding
A shining water
A voiced multitude

A broken alphabet
The avian corpse
The little birds

The reeling breath
The colored leaves
The hills

The white stone
The dark arch
The lowest rhythm
Opaqueness

The tapers
Call
The pieces
The nostrils

Stoning
Striping nerves
The knuckles
The clicked eyes
The point of jaw
The mill stone
Coruscate
She returns
The tiring touch
Solace sometime
The living palm

The passing year
Ye that by night stand in the
house of the Lord

Lift up your hands in
the sanctuary
And praise the Lord
The Lord that made
Heaven and earth
Blessing out of Sion
Give thee
Sicut erat
No cancelled brow
In principio
Peace says
Et nunc
Velvet
Peppermint
Spinning silver
Et semper
The beauty
Et in saecula
Cras amet

Saeculorum	Amavit
Qui nunquam	Vale
Veil	Saeculorum

VI

a

Asking is
Dream of deign
A coming so a come sowing
Day of drain
Leap of light
Strain strain the pinguid night long and told on sacrosanct
And told on drought
Song bell
Now sweep
Now ask
Dive glass, aside and lean
To the process the point comes the marching point the rocking icons all the flare of dark the recross and cross of waters underground
Hung white on that black
Agios
The crackling black *o theos*
Qui labia Isaiae Prophetae calculo mundasti ignito

b

The germ of gold
Old
The story said, the moving waters
The illimitable thought that grows enlarges beyond the possibility of horizons
Forever going over the grey
Clasp soft and deign

Apollo moved
The air of flutes
Atalanta and the germ of gold
Persephone the germ of parchment red the granular carbon
    chromosomes
Between the eye and spiral thought the ceiling of the eye
The photosphere of buds
Of ice
Of leaves of gold
Is this the question
Is this the chute threat mountain
The crumbling femur
    Though the tree die and wither, whence
        The apricots were got.

c

Bubbles bitten by the chalky teeth
Lantern of the incessant sands
Grace encapsulate of grace unfolds
As
The chorded arc of eyes
Day of drain
Dire glass
The nerves in the cheek extinguished one by one psalm by psalm
The tenebrae of breath
Agios
The theory handed down from the Pythagoreans appears to have
    the same import. For some of this school maintain that the
    sunmotes in the air are the soul…
            Agios
                    … others that
The soul is the principle which sets these in motion
Ischyros
Nostalgia of the tongue
Grey water
The shuttling barge

Air of gold
The floating egg
White

But as to the knowledge of the Word and of the things beheld in the Word, he is never in this way in potentiality. He is always actually beholding the Word and the things seen in the Word. For the bliss of Angels consists in such vision and beatitude, and does not consist in habit but in act, as the Philosopher says.

d

Square
Agios ischyros
The stricken flint
The tongs of name
Athanatos
The trefoil flame
Nostalgia of the throat
Lumen Christi
The oldest oak
Bracken
Deo gratias
Sursum corda
Extraordinary cube sugar multiple retroactive fragments
Habemus ad Dominum
The every presence whirl
The spinning eye
The deepest air
The shadow laid across the noonday air
Eleison imas
The single wing
And the feather forever floating a thin spiral down forever in the air of noon

VII

a

The casual reverberation is not restitution
The doing must claim
A claimed doing
As there are passages in ambivalence
As the passages to Canopus
As the transit of residing
As the bifurcation that will never equalize
Shall we commit mitosis as mayhem, in the dark
And as you spoke they spoke
The gongs of name
Confusing a difficulty
(A difficult memorandum: a difficulty)
Eroding the essential plethora
The epact of the minute brain
Bargaining answers
Bargaining music
Stave sanctity
The upright eyes
The pole of light
Stave eyes
Audible folding that cannot be watched sheds dichotomies
Stars burst
Jaws squirm beneath the ingrained claw
Eyes break the capsules of the strange arithmetics in claps of light
Stave eyes
And then to square the black square and the placental necessity
    in a stone acre
In a paralyzed night

b

Evasion is not contradiction
Aside is not against

This is that method
This one is aside
This one is against
Two
Oppose two
There is that trend
It is not enough to go posting in causes
It is not accurate to ask
It is not the case
Is the cause
Accepting collapsible perimeters to enquire
To encourage
To evolve differences
The partition of Athanasius
The partition of Sabellius
Now is the time and we go aside and they go away
The geminal eyes separate
The armature warps
Nothing to be avoided was disowned because nothing expected was expected
In all cases the concomitant values will always separate in such a way that the postulates gone to their creating will remain forever separated
Is the cause
Is the answer
To survey avenues of approximations may be held sufficient in more primitive organizations
The compass of two constants
Nothing under the only necessity will suffice
Not growing
Not doing

c

Doing is doing (doing as doing)
Nothing unwound
Evasion is consistent in equals

Evasion is pleasant on occasion
Green is green
That is, when there are polarities there is a pole, at least there is a polarizing activity
If there is not a necessity it does not mean that such a necessity is an impossible necessity. It means there are equals. It means there is measure in occasion
It is at least that
Green is green
When the activity is circular it means a center
When there are vortices it means at least an eye, it may mean a hand, it may mean germination
As a spiral
It is not always possible to suppose configuration
It is not even always possible to suppose intensification
It is not possible to suppose signification
Something
The cause is the case
Not in this place
The simultaneous cause is not however the perfect simultaneous cause
Not perfect in this place
The fusion of Athanasius
The fusion of Sabellius
Now is the time for reversal of position in height
The crumbs of iron crawl
The beam bends
Perhaps if you were given one rubber neurone and then went far away it could be said: this is the case, likewise: this is the cause, as in the economy of a microcosmos there exist polar and antipolar determinants.

VIII

The grammar of cause
The cause of grammar

The being of grammar
The place of being
The magnificent being of division
The gradient of change
The invisible triangle of difference
Of division
The parsed challenge
If the extended injunction remains it will be almost possible to observe the dispersion of the closing and unclosing follicles
A constellation of difference
The constellations of stimuli
The binder bent
As death by night by sleep
The humor of not being
The periodic variation which descends like a curtain of cold fire from the aurora borealis
Commutative and optative eclipsed by an invisible companion
Spun on an harmonic ladder
Even the most primitive elements of consciousness will be seen to emerge as concepts
The cold tangle of bowels slides on itself
"Hunting badgers by owllight"
The curtain of glow bends on itself
The unnumbered thuribles will clink and the suave etiologic fog go up from the exterior world
Those worlds that bloom against the blessing retina, etiolate across unnumbered distances and disgulphing years
Hunting owls by flint light as with noiseless vibratory insistence the vast hieroglyphic machine traces the great and little lines of conscience
And "Faith sits triumphant on a car of gold
Of Tubal's making, where blew sapphires shine"
Of Tubal's, that is, the discipline of severed choice from satellite to sepulcher
As: "the choice of death rather than dishonorable wealth reveals character, the choice of a nectarine rather than a turnip does not."

IX

a

The bell
Too softly and too slowly tolled
And the first wave was snow
The second ice
The third fire
The fourth blood
The fifth adders
The sixth smother
The seventh foul stink
And unnumbered beasts swam in the sea
Some feather footed
Some devoid of any feet
And all with fiery eyes
And phosphorescent breath
The enduring bell
The wash of wave
The wiry cranes that stagger in the air
The hooded eyes struggling in the confused littoral
The smoky cloak
Those who walk
Those who are constrained
Those who watch the hole of wavering dark
There is no order in expectation
The feet fall
Even the enemy of cold labor
Of the mighty tongue
The gull matted on the sand
Worms spilling out of the beak
The cervical agony
Unplumbed and unforgotten caves
A cry sent up in expectation
A mouth filling the sky
Shaping the words of the victor

The bell
A voice
Blessed are the dead who die
The generations of generations

b

They were in an unstable condition
Floating about in a putrid fog
Throughout the tangled forest
Between the charred trunks
Over the yellow marshes
Some squirmed after the manner of lizards
Some were upright with their arms held up
Some lay with their knees partly drawn up
Some lay on their sides
Some lay stretched at full length
Some lay on their backs
Some were stooping
Some held their heads bent down
Some drew up their legs
Some embraced
Some kicked out with arms and legs
Some were kneeling
Some stood and inhaled deep breaths
Some crawled
Some walked
Some felt about in the dark
Some arose
Some gazed, sitting still

c

Imperceptible light
Scintilla animae
In slumber behold the compass swinging
Behold the man swung in the way
The early meditation

The morning light in the throat
And the shield hung from the lintel
Swayed in the wind
Slowly the immense creaking screw
Turns
Nor the canker
Turns
Nor the entangled bone
Turns
Nor the salt of the sea
Turns
Nor the broken glass
Turns
Only a sudden confusion
Turning
And the secret appearance of the twilight lion
Turning
The hands clutching the knees
The bloody ankles
Which might devour
Which might trample
Which shall dissolve in the hands
And the instruments
And the broken gate
And a small light
The bent woman who admits the visitor with questions
The throat dry and dust in the hair
He sees him alive
The tired men converse watching the wrestlers under the arc-light
You stand in the house at night

X

a

In those days
In a pool of noise

Down the unending staircase goes the mother who shall not die
till she finds her daughter
The winding labor
The well of lost destinations
He that is comely when old and decrepit surely was very beautiful when he was young. And he considered that they who had fallen asleep with godliness had great grace laid up for them, for their works follow them. Beneath the heavy trees in an ivory chair dozed the master of those who know.
Now it would be useless for a thing to be moved unless it were able to reach the end of that movement, hence that which has a natural aptitude for being moved towards a certain end must needs be able to reach that end.
A traveller who has lost his way should not ask, Where am I? What he really wants to know is, where are the other places? He has his own body, but he has lost them.
An Aristotle was but the rubbish of an Adam and Athens but the rudiments of Paradise.

b

The torch
At that time
The bell
At that hour
Throughout the obscure machine
The slow unlocking and locking shifts
The blue gleams stir
The stellar vectors converge on the microscopic paradigm
Behold the man Gabriel, whom I had seen in the vision at the beginning, flying swiftly touched me at the time of evening sacrifice.
A movement athwart the gradients of thought
The larvae of the brain
A song in the peace of sleep
The larval brain
The rhythmic bell

The vested day
At that hour
The angel Gabriel seized the evil spirit and tied it up in the desert
of upper Egypt

c

He descends five hundred steps
They hear his breathing secretly
The murmur of the midnight air
The unendurable fragrance
O woe unto him
The breath of God
The embowelled wanderers
The spark
Light by night to travellers
Remembering happiness
Separating night from night
Hearest thou what curious things all the caves of night answer
The bright leaves reflect the severe light
Is the labor lost
The ululating she-goat
The cloud of sparks
The manifold bars of gold
The broom of light
The sweeping glow
The burnished ladders of the intellect
The silver spiral of the will
Tense in the telic light

d

Light
Light
The silver in the firmament
The stirring horde
The rocking wave

The name breaks in the sky
Why stand we
Why go we nought
They broken seek the cleaving balance
The young men gone
Lux lucis
The revolving company
The water flowing from the right side
Et fons luminis
The ciborium of the abyss
The bread of light
The chalice of the byss
The wine of flaming light
The wheeling multitude
The rocking cry
The reverberant scalar song lifts up
The metric finger aeon by aeon
And the cloud of memory descends
The regnant fruitful vine
The exploding rock
The exploding mountain cry
Tris agios
The sapphire snow
Hryca hryca nazaza

IN WHAT HOUR (1940)

The next chapter is concerned with the puzzling fact
that there is an actual course of events which is in itself
a limited fact, in that metaphysically speaking,
it might have been otherwise.
– A.N. Whitehead

FROM THE PARIS COMMUNE TO THE KRONSTADT REBELLION

Remember now there were others before this;
Now when the unwanted hours rise up,
And the sun rises red in unknown quarters,
And the constellations change places,
And cloudless thunder erases the furrows,
And moonlight stains and the stars grow hot.
Though the air is foetid, conscripted fathers,
With the black bloat of your dead faces;
Though men wander idling out of factories
Where turbine and hand are both freezing;
And the air clears at last above the chimneys;
Though mattresses curtain the windows;
And every hour hears the snarl of explosion;
Yet one shall rise up alone saying:
"I am one out of many, I have heard
Voices high in the air crying out commands;
Seen men's bodies burst into torches;
Seen faun and maiden die in the night air raids;
Heard the watchwords exchanged in the alleys;
Felt hate speed the blood stream and fear curl the nerves.
I know too the last heavy maggot;
And know the trapped vertigo of impotence.
I have traveled prone and unwilling
In the dense processions through the shaken streets.
Shall we hang thus by taut navel strings
To this corrupt placenta till we're flyblown;
Till our skulls are cracked by crow and kite
And our members become the business of ants,
Our teeth the collection of magpies?"
They shall rise up heroes, there will be many,
None will prevail against them at last.
They go saying each: "I am one of many";
Their hands empty save for history.
They die at bridges, bridge gates, and drawbridges.

Remember now there were others before;
The sepulchers are full at ford and bridgehead.
There will be children with flowers there,
And lambs and golden-eyed lions there,
And people remembering in the future.

AT LAKE DESOLATION

The sun is about to come up and the regiments lie
Scattered in the furrows, their large eyes
Wet in the pale light and their throats cut.
At noon the plow shearing the purple loam,
And the hands of the plowmen, the blood
Black on the knuckles. He has asked.
He has seen the naked virgins and matrons
Impaled and disemboweled. He has asked.
He has seen water wafering
Over stones. He has asked. He has seen
The roan gelding break through the alkali crust,
Sink rampant in the fetid mud. He has asked.
Moving towards hot crepuscular horizons,
He has asked. He has seen the nude children
Run screaming. He has asked. Their eyes
Festering their nostrils scalded. He has asked.
The fermented pulp oozes through the rotting fruit skin,
The unborn phoenix screams within the breakfast eggs.
The horrible abundances, the little blind answers
Like maggots, the dukes on the towering moor
Benighted in their cardboard armor; and he,
Locked in the vertebrae of the Sierra, saw
The sharp alley of night, the trail
Glimmering and feet pausing and going
On beside him; and beyond the tangled
Thicket and the thorns saw
Hakeldama, the potter's field,
                    Full of dead strangers.

GENTLEMEN, I ADDRESS YOU PUBLICLY

No marvel though the leprous infant dye
When the sterne dam envenometh the dug
– EDWARD III

They said no one would ever care
They said it would never make any difference
And after the years of waiting
I didn't it hadn't mattered originally
It didn't matter then
But why do they stand so
Why do they never go
What are they waiting for
What monstrous new planet
Glowing in a cloud of omen
Must appear poised on their red-hot alps
And now bolting from sleep
And unbelieving hearing
In the night echoing and reechoing
The glaciers walking or the midnight
Recurrent smashing of a train wreck
But nobody knows now
They said there were many
Before the wars
Now nobody cares
This knife is guaranteed to float on water
It's made for you take it it's yours
As you lie under the rocking stars on the organic
Vertiginous lift of the ocean
It will float out chill and sly
Creeping under the sternum in an inexplicable
Shiver nothing much will happen
The eyes half-open the hair floating
The starlight glittering on the moist teeth
They will remain the same
Only the heart and lungs will stop

But the breast will go on rising
Falling with the undulant ocean
Each night thereafter the corpuscular
Animation of the sea will shine more thickly
Until at last
Aureate and upright
Walking waist deep on the breaking combers
Some one screaming sees it from a boat

HIKING ON THE COAST RANGE

On the Anniversary of the Killing of
Sperry and Conderakias in the
San Francisco General Strike
Their Blood Spilled on the Pavement
Of the Embarcadero

The skirl of the kingfisher was never
More clear than now, nor the scream of the jay,
As the deer shifts her covert at a footfall;
Nor the butterfly tulip ever brighter
in the white spent wheat; nor the pain
Of a wasp stab ever an omen more sure;
The blood alternately dark and brilliant
On the blue and white bandana pattern.
This is the source of evaluation,
This minimal prince rupert's drop of blood;
The patellae suspended within it,
Leucocytes swimming freely between them,
The strands of fibrin, the mysterious
Chemistry of the serum; is alone
The measure of time, the measure of space,
The measure of achievement.
                                        There is no
Other source than this.

A LETTER TO WYSTAN HUGH AUDEN

Frightening a Child

It's not wise to go walking in the ruin.
Lest they should fall the cracked walls are held with chain,
All the lintels are covered with willow shoots
And the stones have shifted in the winter rain.
Leave the gate unclimbed and with untampered seal,
There are much better places to take the air.
The broken mosaics are best left unseen,
The robin's eggs in the shattered clock unclaimed.

Others have climbed to the tower's top to wish,
And kiss the face carved there unobliterate,
And fallen or been robbed or drowned the same day.
The rocks that line the moat are sharper than steel
And keep the bones that plunged to calling voices.
Men have died there helpless in the gathering ice.
The arches are all awry that once held taut.

You've a future before you that's still unseen,
Let glories of exploration go unclaimed.
You can break some far more profitable seal
Than keeps out vagrants and keeps in wind and rain.
There's only trouble waiting in the ruin,
You're better off playing in the sun and air,
Or making wild salads out of bracken shoots,
Or weaving violets in an endless chain.

Advising an Adult

No wish to leave unseen
No day to pass unclaimed
The unobliterate seal
The steel rain

Voices in the old ruin
Flayed hands seen in the air
Ice black on the green shoots
The taut chain

REQUIEM FOR THE SPANISH DEAD

The great geometrical winter constellations
Lift up over the Sierra Nevada,
I walk under the stars, my feet on the known round earth.
My eyes following the lights of an airplane,
Red and green, growling deep into the Hyades.
The note of the engine rises, shrill, faint,
Finally inaudible, and the lights go out
In the southeast haze beneath the feet of Orion.

As the sound departs I am chilled and grow sick
With the thought that has come over me. I see Spain
Under the black windy sky, the snow stirring faintly,
Glittering and moving over the pallid upland,
And men waiting, clutched with cold and huddled together,
As an unknown plane goes over them. It flies southeast
Into the haze above the lines of the enemy,
Sparks appear near the horizon under it.
After they have gone out the earth quivers
And the sound comes faintly. The men relax for a moment
And grow tense again as their own thoughts return to them.

I see the unwritten books, the unrecorded experiments,
The unpainted pictures, the interrupted lives,
Lowered into the graves with the red flags over them.
I see the quick gray brains broken and clotted with blood,
Lowered each in its own darkness, useless in the earth.
Alone on a hilltop in San Francisco suddenly
I am caught in a nightmare, the dead flesh
Mounting over half the world presses against me.

Then quietly at first and then rich and full-bodied,
I hear the voice of a young woman singing.
The emigrants on the corner are holding
A wake for their oldest child, a driverless truck
Broke away on the steep hill and killed him,
Voice after voice adds itself to the singing.
Orion moves westward across the meridian,
Rigel, Bellatrix, Betelgeuse, marching in order,
The great nebula glimmering in his loins.

ON WHAT PLANET

Uniformly over the whole countryside
The warm air flows imperceptibly seaward;
The autumn haze drifts in deep bands
Over the pale water;
White egrets stand in the blue marshes;
Tamalpais, Diablo, St. Helena
Float in the air.
Climbing on the cliffs of Hunter's Hill
We look out over fifty miles of sinuous
Interpenetration of mountains and sea.

Leading up a twisted chimney,
Just as my eyes rise to the level
Of a small cave, two white owls
Fly out, silent, close to my face.
They hover, confused in the sunlight,
And disappear into the recesses of the cliff.

All day I have been watching a new climber,
A young girl with ash blonde hair
And gentle confident eyes.
She climbs slowly, precisely,
With unwasted grace.

While I am coiling the ropes,
Watching the spectacular sunset,
She turns to me and says, quietly,
"It must be very beautiful, the sunset,
On Saturn, with the rings and all the moons."

THE MOTTO ON THE SUNDIAL

It is September and the wry corn rattles
Dry in the fields. It is dawn, the spider webs
Are white in the tracks of the cattle, the holes
Where they have torn up the grass roots, they are
Dry, sticky, no dew is on them. The morning
Comes, it is hot with the first dawn and windless.
The floury dust in the cowpath curls over no
Higher than my boot top and then settles
Into my crumbling footprints. The torn crows settle
Again into the dead elm, saying little.
McGregor, Iowa. I stand on the bluff
Looking out over the river, the water
Oozing past and the smell coming up from it,
Up from the scabby flat where the pigs stumble.
In Wisconsin smoke blooms over the forest,
Plumed at first and then flattening slowly.
I have seen the fog over the lotus beds,
White, curded and thick to the bluff's edge, the sun
Yellow over Wisconsin and the sky blue,
The air wet and jewelweed in the ravine,
Wet and the colored sandstone like wet sugar.
It is later than you think, fires have gone over
Our forests, the grasshopper screamed in our corn,
Fires have gone over the brains of our young girls,
Hunger over young men and fear everywhere.
The smell of gas has ascended from the streets,
Bloomed from the cartridges, spread from wall to wall,

Bloomed on the highways and seeped into the corn.
It is later than you think, there is a voice
Preparing to speak, there are whisperings now
And murmuring and noises made with the teeth.
This voice will grow louder and learn a language.
They shall sit trembling while its will is made known,
In gongs struck, bonfires, and shadows on sundials.
Once it has spoken it shall never be silenced.

CLIMBING MILESTONE MOUNTAIN, AUGUST 22, 1937

For a month now, wandering over the Sierras,
A poem had been gathering in my mind,
Details of significance and rhythm,
The way poems do, but still lacking a focus.
Last night I remembered the date and it all
Began to grow together and take on purpose.
    We sat up late while Deneb moved over the zenith
And I told Marie all about Boston, how it looked
That last terrible week, how hundreds stood weeping
Impotent in the streets that last midnight.
I told her how those hours changed the lives of thousands,
How America was forever a different place
Afterwards for many.
                    In the morning
We swam in the cold transparent lake, the blue
Damsel flies on all the reeds like millions
Of narrow metallic flowers, and I thought
Of you behind the grille in Dedham, Vanzetti,
Saying, "Who would ever have thought we would make
    this history?"
Crossing the brilliant mile-square meadow
Illuminated with asters and cyclamen,
The pollen of the lodgepole pines drifting
With the shifting wind over it and the blue

And sulphur butterflies drifting with the wind,
I saw you in the sour prison light, saying,
"Goodbye comrade."
                                        In the basin under the crest
Where the pines end and the Sierra primrose begins,
A party of lawyers was shooting at a whiskey bottle.
The bottle stayed on its rock, nobody could hit it.
Looking back over the peaks and canyons from the last lake,
The pattern of human beings seemed simpler
Than the diagonals of water and stone.
Climbing the chute, up the melting snow and broken rock,
I remembered what you said about Sacco,
How it slipped your mind and you demanded it be read into the
    record.
Traversing below the ragged arête,
One cheek pressed against the rock
The wind slapping the other,
I saw you both marching in an army
You with the red and black flag, Sacco with the rattlesnake banner.
I kicked steps up the last snow bank and came
To the indescribably blue and fragrant
Polemonium and the dead sky and the sterile
Crystalline granite and final monolith of the summit.
These are the things that will last a long time, Vanzetti,
I am glad that once on your day I have stood among them.
Some day mountains will be named after you and Sacco.
They will be here and your name with them,
"When these days are but a dim remembering of the time
When man was wolf to man."
I think men will be remembering you a long time
Standing on the mountains
Many men, a long time, comrade.

THE NEW YEAR

for Helen

I walk on the cold mountain above the city
Through the black eucalyptus plantation.
Only a few of the million lights
Penetrate the leaves and the dripping fog.
I remember the wintry stars
In the bare branches of the maples,
In the branches of the chestnuts that are gone.

A VERY EARLY MORNING EXERCISE

Chang Yuen is on the threshold of a remarkable career.
He is a minor official in Nanking;
However he is intimate with the highest circles in the capital.
Great things are predicted for him;
But he has literary tastes.
He works listlessly and stays up all night;
He wishes times were quieter;
He wishes he could become a monk;
He longs for what he calls social cohesion;
He wishes he lived in a more positive culture.
Anonymously he has published a learned paper,
"On the Precision of Shinto as an Agnostic Cultural Determinant."
At times he believes the world is on the verge
Of a Great Spiritual Rebirth.
He is very fond of Rimbaud, Bertrand Russell, and Tu Fu.
He wishes he could live in Paris.

He crosses the bridge by the Heavenly Inspiration Textile Works.
The long building quivers all over with the rattle of machinery.
In the windows the greenish lights
Wink as the people pass before them.

Porters plunge in and out of vast faint doorways.
Against the fence faces gleam in a heap of rags.
Chang Yuen pauses on the bridge muttering,
"The concubines of the Above One
Dance in transparent gossamer
In the evening at the Purple Phoenix Pavilion."
He thinks of the girls he could have bought for ten dollars
In Shantung during the famine.
He says aloud softly,
"Il faisait chaud, dans la vallée
Bien que le soleil se fût couché depuis longtemps,"
He thinks of the son of his very important friend Won;
He is fourteen years old and goes out at night in Shanghai,
With rouged cheeks in the streets of the International Settlement.
He decides to take his opium more seriously.
Pear blossoms fall in the fog,
The tide stirs in the river,
The first dawn glows at the end of the streets.

ANOTHER EARLY MORNING EXERCISE

One hundred feet overhead the fog from the Pacific
Moves swiftly over the hills and houses of San Francisco.
After the bright March day the interior valleys
Suck great quantities of cool air in from the ocean.
Above the torn fog one high, laminated, transparent cloud
Travels slowly northward across the lower half of the half-moon.
The moon falls westward in a parabola from Castor and Pollux.
I walk along the street at three in the morning.
It is spring in the last year of youth.
The tide is out and the air is full of the smell of the ocean.
The newly arrived mocking birds are awake
In the courtyard behind the houses.
I pass a frosted refrigerated window
Where five disemboweled white hares

Hang by their furred hind paws from a five-spoked rack.
The unlit florists' windows are full of obscure almond blossoms.
I have been sitting in Sam Wo's drinking cold aromatic liquor.
"What did Borodin do in Canton in 1927" –
The argument lasted five hours.
My friend Soo sympathizes with the Left Opposition;
He told me I had murdered forty thousand bodies on Yellow
    Flower Hill.
"Those bodies are on your shoulders," he said.
He ordered stewed tripe and wept eating it,
Clicking his chopsticks like castanets.
Whatever Borodin did it was probably wrong;
History would be so much simpler if you could just write it
Without ever having to let it happen.
The armies of the Kuo Min Tang have taken the birthplace
    of Tu Fu;
The Red Army has retreated in perfect order.
I wonder if the wooden image erected by his family
Still stands in the shrine at Ch'eng Tu;
I wonder if any one still burns paper
Before that face of hungry intelligence and sympathy.
He had a hard life he hated war and despotism and famine;
The first chance he got he quarreled with the Emperor.
Venomous papers dry their ink on the newsstands;
A chill comes over me; I walk along shivering;
Thinking of a world full of miserable lives,
And all the men who have been tortured
Because they believed it was possible to be happy.
Pickets keep watch by the bridge over the mouth of the Sacramento,
Huddled over the small fires,
Talking little,
Rifles in their hands.

AUTUMN IN CALIFORNIA

Autumn in California is a mild
And anonymous season, hills and valleys
Are colorless then, only the sooty green
Eucalyptus, the conifers and oaks sink deep
Into the haze; the fields are plowed, bare, waiting;
The steep pastures are tracked deep by the cattle;
There are no flowers, the herbage is brittle.
All night along the coast and the mountain crests
Birds go by, murmurous, high in the warm air.
Only in the mountain meadows the aspens
Glitter like goldfish moving up swift water;
Only in the desert villages the leaves
Of the cottonwoods descend in smoky air.
        Once more I wander in the warm evening
Calling the heart to order and the stiff brain
To passion. I should be thinking of dreaming, loving, dying,
Beauty wasting through time like draining blood,
And me alone in all the world with pictures
Of pretty women and the constellations.
But I hear the clocks in Barcelona strike at dawn
And the whistles blowing for noon in Nanking.
I hear the drone, the snapping high in the air
Of planes fighting, the deep reverberant
Grunts of bombardment, the hasty clamor
Of anti-aircraft.
                        In Nanking at the first bomb,
A moon-faced, willowy young girl runs into the street,
Leaves her rice bowl spilled and her children crying,
And stands stiff, cursing quietly, her face raised to the sky.
Suddenly she bursts like a bag of water,
And then as the blossom of smoke and dust diffuses,
The walls topple slowly over her.
                                        I hear the voices
Young, fatigued and excited, of two comrades
In a closed room in Madrid. They have been up

All night, talking of trout in the Pyrenees,
Spinoza, old nights full of riot and sherry,
Women they might have had or almost had,
Picasso, Velasquez, relativity.
The candlelight reddens, blue bars appear
In the cracks of the shutters, the bombardment
Begins again as though it had never stopped,
The morning wind is cold and dusty,
Their furloughs are over. They are shock troopers,
They may not meet again. The dead light holds
In impersonal focus the patched uniforms,
The dog-eared copy of Lenin's *Imperialism*,
The heavy cartridge belt, holster and black revolver butt.
    The moon rises late over Mt. Diablo,
Huge, gibbous, warm; the wind goes out,
Brown fog spreads over the bay from the marshes,
And overhead the cry of birds is suddenly
Loud, wiry, and tremulous.

NEW OBJECTIVES, NEW CADRES

Before the inevitable act
The necessity of decision,
The pauper broken in the ditch,
The politician embarrassed in the council,
Before the secret connivance,
Before the plausible public appearance,
What are the consequences of this adultery?
Ends are not consequences,
Enthusiasm is not integrity,
Hope is not knowledge.
Implements can turn into products,
Concessions into purposes.
By what order must the will walk impugned,
Through spangles of landscape,

Through umbers of sea bottom,
By the casein gleam of any moon
Of postulates and wishes?
Our objectives are not our confidantes,
We cannot retire to the past or the future
Like Franz Josef to his hasenpfeffer mistress.
We found that out.
Who so chooses may look at history
As a plumed courtier gracefully
Bowing himself backwards out of a window.
The treads of the tanks bang on the cobblestones,
The famous Jewish comedian is castrated in an alley,
The coalition cabinet is apprehended at the border,
The minister for foreign affairs commits suicide.
Grown for fear and fattened into groaning
The clawed eyelid or the crushed flower stalk,
Or the undeviating lockstep
The inert incurious onanist,
The rubicund practical prankster,
We wake never in this dispensation
For them or their inchoate brethren,
We watch imaginary just men
Nude as rose petals, discussing a purer logic
In bright functionalist future gymnasia
High in the snows of Mt. Lenin
Beside a collectivist ocean.
But see around the corner in bare lamplight,
In a desquamate basement bedroom,
He who sits in his socks reading shockers,
Skinning cigarette butts and rerolling them in toilet paper,
His red eyes never leaving the blotted print and the pulp paper.
He rose too late to distribute the leaflets.
In the midst of the mussed bedding have mercy
Upon him, this is history.
Or see the arch dialectic satyriast;
Miners' wives and social workers
Rapt in a bated circle about him;

Drawing pointless incisive diagrams
On a blackboard, barking
Ominously with a winey timbre,
Clarifying constant and variable capital,
His subconscious painfully threading its way
Through future slippery assignations.
We do not need his confessions.
His future is more fecund than Molly Bloom –
The problem is to control history,
We already understand it.

AUGUST 22, 1939

> *...when you want to distract your mother from the discouraging soulness, I will tell you what I used to do. To take her for a long walk in the quiet country, gathering wildflowers here and there, resting under the shade of trees, between the harmony of the vivid stream and the tranquillity of the mother-nature, and I am sure she will enjoy this very much, as you surely will be happy for it. But remember always, Dante, in the play of happiness, don't use all for yourself only, but down yourself just one step, at your side and help the weak ones that cry for help, help the prosecuted and the victim; because they are your friends; they are the comrades that fight and fall as your father and Bartolo fought and fell yesterday, for the conquest of the joy of freedom for all and the poor workers. In this struggle of life you will find more love and you will be loved.*
>
> – Nicola Sacco to his son Dante, August 18, 1927

> *Angst und Gestalt und Gebet*
>
> – Rilke

What is it all for, this poetry,
This bundle of accomplishment
Put together with so much pain?

Twenty years at hard labor,
Lessons learned from Li Po and Dante,
Indian chants and gestalt psychology;
What words can it spell,
This alphabet of one sensibility?
The pure pattern of the stars in orderly progression,
The thin air of fourteen-thousand-foot summits,
Their Pisgah views into what secrets of the personality,
The fire of poppies in eroded fields,
The sleep of lynxes in the noonday forest,
The curious anastomosis of the webs of thought,
Life streaming ungovernably away,
And the deep hope of man.
The centuries have changed little in this art,
The subjects are still the same.
"For Christ's sake take off your clothes and get into bed,
We are not going to live forever."
"Petals fall from the rose,"
We fall from life,
Values fall from history like men from shellfire,
Only a minimum survives,
Only an unknown achievement.
They can put it all on the headstones,
In all the battlefields,
"Poor guy, he never knew what it was all about."
Spectacled men will come with shovels in a thousand years,
Give lectures in universities on cultural advances, cultural lags.
A little more garlic in the soup,
A half-hour more in bed in the morning,
Some of them got it, some of them didn't;
The things they dropped in their hurry
Are behind the glass cases of dusky museums.
This year we made four major ascents,
Camped for two weeks at timberline,
Watched Mars swim close to the earth,
Watched the black aurora of war
Spread over the sky of a decayed civilization.

These are the last terrible years of authority.
The disease has reached its crisis,
Ten thousand years of power,
The struggle of two laws,
The rule of iron and spilled blood,
The abiding solidarity of living blood and brain.
They are trapped, beleaguered, murderous,
If they line their cellars with cork
It is not to still the pistol shots,
It is to insulate the last words of the condemned.
"Liberty is the mother
Not the daughter of order."
"Not the government of men
But the administration of things."
"From each according to his ability,
Unto each according to his needs."
We could still hear them,
Cutting steps in the blue ice of hanging glaciers,
Teetering along shattered arêtes.
The cold and cruel apathy of mountains
Has been subdued with a few strands of rope
And some flimsy ice axes,
There are only a few peaks left.
Twenty-five years have gone since my first sweetheart.
Back from the mountains there is a letter waiting for me.
"I read your poem in the New Republic.
Do you remember the undertaker's on the corner,
How we peeped in the basement window at a sheeted figure
And ran away screaming? Do you remember?
There is a filling station on the corner,
A parking lot where your house used to be,
Only ours and two other houses are left.
We stick it out in the noise and carbon monoxide."
It was a poem of homesickness and exile,
Twenty-five years wandering around
In a world of noise and poison.
She stuck it out, I never went back,

But there are domestic as well as imported
Explosions and poison gases.
Dante was homesick, the Chinese made an art of it,
So was Ovid and many others,
Pound and Eliot amongst them,
Kropotkin dying of hunger,
Berkman by his own hand,
Fanny Baron biting her executioners,
Makhno in the odor of calumny,
Trotsky, too, I suppose, passionately, after his fashion.
Do you remember?
What is it all for, this poetry,
This bundle of accomplishment
Put together with so much pain?
Do you remember the corpse in the basement?
What are we doing at the turn of our years,
Writers and readers of the liberal weeklies?

NORTH PALISADE, THE END OF SEPTEMBER, 1939

The sun drops daily down the sky,
The long cold crawls near,
The aspen spills its gold in the air,
Lavish beyond the mind.
This is the last peak, the last climb.
New snow freckles the granite.
The imperious seasons have granted
Courage of a different kind.
Once more only in the smother
Of storm will the wary rope
Vanquish uncertain routes,
This year or another.
Once more only will the peak rise
Lucent above the dropping storm,
Skilled hand and steadfast foot accord

Victory of the brain and eye.
Practice is done, the barren lake
That mirrors this night's fire
Will hold unwinking unknown stars
In its unblemished gaze.

"Now winter nights enlarge
The number of our hours,"
They march to test their power,
We to betray their march.
Their rabbit words and weasel minds
Play at a losing game.
Ours is the unity of aim,
Theirs the diversity of pride.
Their victories on either side
Drive more deep the iron.
Ours is the victory to claim,
Ours is the peace to find.

TOWARD AN ORGANIC PHILOSOPHY

Spring, Coast Range

The glow of my campfire is dark red and flameless,
The circle of white ash widens around it.
I get up and walk off in the moonlight and each time
I look back the red is deeper and the light smaller.
Scorpio rises late with Mars caught in his claw;
The moon has come before them, the light
Like a choir of children in the young laurel trees.
It is April; the shad, the hot headed fish,
Climbs the rivers; there is trillium in the damp canyons;
The foetid adder's tongue lolls by the waterfall.
There was a farm at this campsite once, it is almost gone now.
There were sheep here after the farm, and fire

Long ago burned the redwoods out of the gulch,
The Douglas fir off the ridge; today the soil
Is stony and incoherent, the small stones lie flat
And plate the surface like scales.
Twenty years ago the spreading gully
Toppled the big oak over onto the house.
Now there is nothing left but the foundations
Hidden in poison oak, and above on the ridge,
Six lonely, ominous fenceposts;
The redwood beams of the barn make a footbridge
Over the deep waterless creek bed;
The hills are covered with wild oats
Dry and white by midsummer.
I walk in the random survivals of the orchard.
In a patch of moonlight a mole
Shakes his tunnel like an angry vein;
Orion walks waist deep in the fog coming in from the ocean;
Leo crouches under the zenith.
There are tiny hard fruits already on the plum trees.
The purity of the apple blossoms is incredible.
As the wind dies down their fragrance
Clusters around them like thick smoke.
All the day they roared with bees, in the moonlight
They are silent and immaculate.

Spring, Sierra Nevada

Once more golden Scorpio glows over the col
Above Deadman Canyon, orderly and brilliant,
Like an inspiration in the brain of Archimedes.
I have seen its light over the warm sea,
Over the coconut beaches, phosphorescent and pulsing;
And the living light in the water
Shivering away from the swimming hand,
Creeping against the lips, filling the floating hair.
Here where the glaciers have been and the snow stays late,

The stone is clean as light, the light steady as stone.
The relationship of stone, ice and stars is systematic and enduring:
Novelty emerges after centuries, a rock spalls from the cliffs,
The glacier contracts and turns grayer,
The stream cuts new sinuosities in the meadow,
The sun moves through space and the earth with it,
The stars change places.
                                        The snow has lasted longer this year,
Than anyone can remember. The lowest meadow is a lake,
The next two are snowfields, the pass is covered with snow,
Only the steepest rocks are bare. Between the pass
And the last meadow the snowfield gapes for a hundred feet,
In a narrow blue chasm through which a waterfall drops,
Spangled with sunset at the top, black and muscular
Where it disappears again in the snow.
The world is filled with hidden running water
That pounds in the ears like ether;
The granite needles rise from the snow, pale as steel;
Above the copper mine the cliff is blood red,
The white snow breaks at the edge of it;
The sky comes close to my eyes like the blue eyes
Of someone kissed in sleep.
                                        I descend to camp,
To the young, sticky, wrinkled aspen leaves,
To the first violets and wild cyclamen,
And cook supper in the blue twilight.
All night deer pass over the snow on sharp hooves,
In the darkness their cold muzzles find the new grass
At the edge of the snow.

Fall, Sierra Nevada

This morning the hermit thrush was absent at breakfast,
His place was taken by a family of chickadees;
At noon a flock of humming birds passed south,
Whirling in the wind up over the saddle between

Ritter and Banner, following the migration lane
Of the Sierra crest southward to Guatemala.
All day cloud shadows have moved over the face of the mountain,
The shadow of a golden eagle weaving between them
Over the face of the glacier.
At sunset the half-moon rides on the bent back of the Scorpion,
The Great Bear kneels on the mountain.
Ten degrees below the moon
Venus sets in the haze arising from the Great Valley.
Jupiter, in opposition to the sun, rises in the alpenglow
Between the burnt peaks. The ventriloquial belling
Of an owl mingles with the bells of the waterfall.
Now there is distant thunder on the east wind.
The east face of the mountain above me
Is lit with far off lightnings and the sky
Above the pass blazes momentarily like an aurora.
It is storming in the White Mountains,
On the arid fourteen-thousand-foot peaks;
Rain is falling on the narrow gray ranges
And dark sedge meadows and white salt flats of Nevada.
Just before moonset a small dense cumulus cloud,
Gleaming like a grape cluster of metal,
Moves over the Sierra crest and grows down the westward slope.
Frost, the color and quality of the cloud,
Lies over all the marsh below my campsite.
The wiry clumps of dwarfed whitebark pines
Are smoky and indistinct in the moonlight,
Only their shadows are really visible.
The lake is immobile and holds the stars
And the peaks deep in itself without a quiver.
In the shallows the geometrical tendrils of ice
Spread their wonderful mathematics in silence.
All night the eyes of deer shine for an instant
As they cross the radius of my firelight.
In the morning the trail will look like a sheep driveway,
All the tracks will point down to the lower canyon.
"Thus," says Tyndall, "the concerns of this little place

Are changed and fashioned by the obliquity of the earth's axis,
The chain of dependence which runs through creation,
And links the roll of a planet alike with the interests
Of marmots and men."

A LETTER TO YVOR WINTERS

Again tonight I read "Before Disaster,"
The tense memento of a will
That's striven thirty years to master
One chaos with one spirit's skill.

As usual, disaster has returned.
Its public and its private round
Are narrow enough – we will have learned
Them quite by heart before we're underground.

Tonight Orion walks above my head
While I pace out my human mile;
At noon the same immeasurable tread
Will move toward Atlas from the Nile.

He too returns upon his ordered path,
While change seeps through his interstellar veins –
The Bull before him in immobile wrath,
The sword and cloud of light against his reins.

These thin imagos that abide decay,
The minds of Winters, Rexroth, and their like,
To fight these senile beasts what else have they
Than "clouds of unknowing,"
Swords that shall not strike?

AN EQUATION FOR MARIE

This dream prorogued
Is not a cause
Is uncaused
And has no seeming

This cause dreams
Of no forlorn notion
Walks
In no dreaming

These eyes seek
Sources in speaking
Lips terminating
In not speaking

This hair suspends
In its atmosphere
Fire particles and sparks
Of wishing truly

This body traverses
Hyperbolas of seeing
Recurs on a conchoid
Another bending above it

If this is waking
In a mode of dreaming
In a mode of causing
Without preceding

For it is being
And no seeming

SONGS FOR MARIE'S LUTEBOOK

1

The blue-eyed grass is opening now,
    Careless of frost,
Out with the first spring wind to blow,
    Careless of cost.

If we could act with such sublime
    Careless confidence,
We might not find with passing time,
    Careless indifference.

2

The sea is quiet, the wind gives over,
    The still heat descends,
Deer drowse in the chamisal cover,
    Where the land ends.

Close to each other on the last crest
    We lie stretched prone,
Watching the sun carry slowly west
    The immense noon.

The day with imperceptible motion
    Declines its light,
Until on Atlantic shores of ocean,
    Steps the night.

Suddenly we know daylight slipping
    Between the trees
And feel bright dawn awake the sleeping
    Antipodes.

3

From the plum the petals blow,
    Powdering your bright hair.
You mourn that they go –
    They sift through windy air.

All your grief won't bring them back,
    Another year they've gone.
Now the myriad leafbuds crack,
    The purple fruit comes on.

4

What years are these that warm your breast,
Their clear flames in your eyes and hair,
That you in their jeweled hours are dressed
So fair and debonaire?

Do you forget that this apparel
You shall not always own?
Time counts the coin you so imperil,
At last calls home his loan.

Shall we youth's wage in wrangling waste
And turn his trade amiss,
And when it is too late for haste,
Remember this?

(Tune: "Greensleeves")

GIC TO HAR

It is late at night, cold and damp
The air is filled with tobacco smoke.
My brain is worried and tired.
I pick up the encyclopedia,
The volume GIC to HAR,
It seems I have read everything in it,
So many other nights like this.
I sit staring empty-headed at the article Grosbeak,
Listening to the long rattle and pound
Of freight cars and switch engines in the distance.
Suddenly I remember
Coming home from swimming
In Ten Mile Creek,
Over the long moraine in the early summer evening,
My hair wet, smelling of waterweeds and mud.
I remember a sycamore in front of a ruined farmhouse,
And instantly and clearly the revelation
Of a song of incredible purity and joy,
My first rose-breasted grosbeak,
Facing the low sun, his body
Suffused with light.
I was motionless and cold in the hot evening
Until he flew away, and I went on knowing
In my twelfth year one of the great things
Of my life had happened.
Thirty factories empty their refuse in the creek.
The farm has given way to an impoverished suburb
On the parched lawns are starlings, alien and aggressive.
And I am on the other side of the continent
Ten years in an unfriendly city.

FALLING LEAVES AND EARLY SNOW

In the years to come they will say,
"They fell like the leaves
In the autumn of nineteen thirty-nine."
November has come to the forest,
To the meadows where we picked the cyclamen.
The year fades with the white frost
On the brown sedge in the hazy meadows,
Where the deer tracks were black in the morning.
Ice forms in the shadows;
Disheveled maples hang over the water;
Deep gold sunlight glistens on the shrunken stream.
Somnolent trout move through pillars of brown and gold.
The yellow maple leaves eddy above them,
The glittering leaves of the cottonwood,
The olive, velvety alder leaves,
The scarlet dogwood leaves,
Most poignant of all.

In the afternoon thin blades of cloud
Move over the mountains;
The storm clouds follow them;
Fine rain falls without wind.
The forest is filled with wet resonant silence.
When the rain pauses the clouds
Cling to the cliffs and the waterfalls.
In the evening the wind changes;
Snow falls in the sunset.
We stand in the snowy twilight
And watch the moon rise in a breach of cloud.
Between the black pines lie narrow bands of moonlight,
Glimmering with floating snow.
An owl cries in the sifting darkness.
The moon has a sheen like a glacier.

THE APPLE GARTHS OF AVALON

for the author of the REALMS OF BEING,
both as greeting and as farewell

Here the face turns
East, wisdom an unwilling
Forced acquisition, turning,
Turns west; the far retinas enfold
Oriented corridors of an ontology
Of mountain fog and cloud and snow-
Fed pool of unspecked depth. The turning
Face flushes from the welding point
Bubble of a sun in stone
Sea. He,
Chaperon of a neural frazzle, frayed
In a confusion of multiple demands,
Finds, bright in native reflex,
Awareness tired with waiting; saying,
"Wisdom has been wished
On us. We who wrought an accurate
Exhaustive positivism, having
Constructed a submarine apparatus
Of unique causation, arise
To an unexpected traumatic
Pacific shallow."

These things,
Like fruit dropped in crystal
Water off coral beaches, stand
Alone, remote and warm. The luscious
Fruit of this seized surety attracts
And holds him, Sebastian, electric
In its daedal realm. The dropped
Brittle bubbles rise, minute and myriad,
Off fecund contours; and green,
Blue, and blue-green, and fainter

Purple strata quiver,
Flash, and penetrate the eye. Thought,
Transmuted in this polyphony,
Peers the sea reaches; the edge
Of cognition wavers; the inviolate,
Skeptical architecture shatters
About him. Sebastian
Parts lips cauterized
By hypnosis in a world drawn
Suddenly closer to the sun.
Reintegrated, strives for swift
Articulation that shall be
Consonant to this scholia of a chaos made
Perfect and rhythmic and entire.

The epochal purity arriving
Out of condensation and rarefaction,
The ingenerable
In its generation proffering
In a realm, the conquest of caustic
Focus, the ascetic mode
Of apprehension, saying,
"Out of this, once known as death, we pluck
This thistle, life, elicited
After painful labor in the discreet.
We who murdered to dissect, penitent,
Come sentient at this time, in its way
An end, to tactile convictions in edges, blooms
And wavers, the lissome, infinite contingency."

A world of risibles, a world of teems
Of plums, of carrots, and the clotted creams
Of pieced acreages of pale frail greens –
The carbon crystal loam that busts
With cabbage laughter and spinach dreams,
Explodes its fronded fireworks
Out of the belly's wine,

And all the cervine maidens wince away.
The brown road winds down between
The yellow hills and the red trees; the hound
Runs rabbits in the stubble fields and cracks
A million barks against the frosty sun;
And Otto turns the squashes one by one,
His pipe emitting rare fat thistledowns,
Ascending in the autumn clarity.
Ladies your pointed eyes and toes
Curl as last night's leaves uncurl.
The coiffeur curls up and dyes the sculptor he…
…Ah, plummets of abundance fall light years
Through glassy air to burst upon the earth.

(The difference between a coiffeur and a sculptor is that the coiffeur curls up and dyes, while the sculptor makes faces and busts.)

THE HEART UNBROKEN AND THE COURAGE FREE

It is late autumn, the end of Indian summer.
It was dry and warm all day, tonight it is cold.
In the light of the quarter moon the hoarfrost
Glows dimly on the dry long grass. A breeze starts
And stops and starts and makes waves on the hillside.
At the edge of the wild raspberry bushes
Four sooty spots bob about against the white frost.
They are rabbits with cold noses and cold toes.
Castor and Pollux blur in the first edge of fog.
Your breath is visible like fine autumn down,
Your eyes are polished with moonlight,
I look at them, they are the color of snow.

ORGANON

1

Intact as concave
For cause as varnished
Marginal dreamed and finally
Insistent the thick
Leaf or morning dim
And expanding in the
Piece and cave the
Breaking shell in
The fist of the adhesion of the living
Hand the wall paused and
Preserved so spoken the question
Perduring therefore in
Living thought may risk
Assault of what selection
Surprises the total
Of temptations and disasters
Slow
Credentials of catastrophe
The flamboyant
Awaiting in the
Occurring over no
Theft of sign no
Inch of air
Elude
For
He who expected the endurance avoided the concomitants
Others seeking
Elsewhere
Thick leaf and slope
Of loess
And harsh
Leather and eyeball

Of dyed sandstone
Squat foetid men in the dim
Room and the living
Bone strode in air the living
On the ground the book
Cut with knives
With morning
And interrogation
The preserved confused
Reality
Intact
Tactile

2

Lost in white of an implacable
Unity, disguised and separate,
The emergent is not thus present
To question or even thus present
For fact. For fact, tangled in solvents
Of disintegrate and partial shock,
Is pain and pain alone, is never
Quick cause nor parent nor child thereof.
Who is this who surprises coffins
In the sky early in the morning,
Whose eyes were welded in the desert?
Not a dream but a knife, neither peace,
But many small live bombs like maggots,
Squirming in the shadow of cactus,
Replace the micrometers, the hands
Of distinctions; and the living spleen,
Moving spongewise across the ceiling
Of the liver, now painstakingly
Erases the auguries bitten by process,
Obliterates the spoor
Of razors and of sleep; now ether
Rains from the stone, hastily ignites;

And the bombs speak like small birds chirping –
And the little iota, the thing
That caused so much worry to so few,
Spinning like burning paper in wind,
Passes beyond the range of vision.

3

The minutes of the tongue are gone in,
And the volumes are closed behind them,
The small prisms and large ellipsoids,
The peppers withering in the heat.
Being accumulates negatives
Thus, electrolyzed, indifferent,
Hoarding deprivation as passage
Through entity of luminous flux
Of zeros exploding asymptotes
Hands Lips Fingers Mallets Tapers Orbs
The insect agile in utter sky,
Omnivorous, constructed, intact,
And the petals crawling, and the heat,
And the falling copper and the felt stone.

4

As fact wastes out of experience
Leaving no promise of conservation
Or perpetuity of those ultimates
Deposited in the experient,
And deaths and negatives waste being;
The erosion of being to what is,
Elimination in logic, and passage
Of history, effective equally –
And only values prime and promised
Surviving, and only dubiously –
Being as vital becomes a postulant

Of hope, a struggle of *sein* and *sosein*,
Whose only assurance is moral.

Distinction implies difference: awaited
Predicate and cleft particular
As a demonstrable otherness, as fact
And factual presuppose in act,
An act, comparison, configuration –
Always constitutive, primitive
And elicited first for presentation
As assertable pattern, precise,
Intransitive, adjective, impersonal;
Or difference implies distinction
As being imperative separateness
Of epistemic material,
Imperative enumerability
For proposition and decision.

It is a wise one in the early morning
Met in two halves and a wise
Standing as a thing act being
Gracious or divisible the
Opposition standing the
Channels cross and return this being
This instant thing and small as
Verb affect going a minute
Verb green to a hooded term
Shape part one and go back
Go back a gentle being
Being and gone to a meant term
Doing this is the stop
But wait but wait a box
Wait a bar going and a place
For the white meters crossing
The plug makes the glass hand
Square or once squared and the crossed

Metric going being
Falling

If difference is a being thing
And a pointing raises moving
Or stops break and dry
So instant make or growing
So meaning asking
And shall have been in cause
Risen is a mark or two no a
Question as is thing and
Removal desire not divide
Volume not the preceding
And weight not value
For pain and parts
Risen saying going
Moves doubted or off
Small one careful
Whereupon a way
Lift
Know
Pass

If in the imagined case it can
Be or is less than it is or there
Are two rights to the number
The chance speaking wages position
And the effort is going effort
In the way the travel out
Knows shape and the in mover
Forms then possible as thought
Opens as petals and close
Darkens large as dim long
Gathers or force a granted
To wing motion this is a less
Instant and the dividing
A mode happen in tight

And a place place
To speak it was there
A single old

DATIVE HARUSPICES

Film and filament, no
Donor, gift without
Reciprocity, transparent
Tactile act, an imaginary
Web of structure sweeps
The periphery of being, glass
Entities point, the fundamental
Entails arise, ominous
Real, augurs move in sleep
Voices break the vast
Indifferent sarcophagus, this
Source and word, secret, never
Fractured by volition
Seventy years
Hidden, the hangman
In the navel, or
An eye in the oblivion
Of an instantaneous
Being of a differential
Flexible beyond assent
Sentient webs morseled with fact
Parcel now in the sky, compact
Parabolas branch in a capsule
Punctured with instants, ominous of items
Stars Palps Needles
Where the central summation extrudes
Inhibited muscular tensors, what
Recall of pentacles, bulbs
Uttered in scissors loan, are being

Is sown on the rent
Tumuli, what ing in the ever
Lasting (there are no horizons
In mountains, but
Dispersed minutes itemize the skyline, stones
Are accepted by canyons with uniform
Acceleration and snow
Disturbed by wind hovers in sun
Light in the passes) directrices
Of becoming, courteous
In the differentials
With what fact
For an endless time being
Watching luminous songs utter
The round earth visible
As the moon moves
Men move from a distance
Men sleep overhead
A word a fire
Occurs endures for
Generations a slow body
Swings in space warm
Water pulled by the moon
Fog descends on the nostrils
Having died in its
Heart what pulse will
Ripen planes lift in dark
And move mice sleep
A sloth moves head down
The child sleeps
Guarded by an arrow
In what hour

VALUE IN MOUNTAINS

1

There are those to whom value is a weapon,
Collectors of negatives and ascertables,
And those to whom value is horror,
Themselves collected by evaluation;
Who, recurrently dispossessed in each judgment,
Seizing or seized by presented fact,
Explode in a fury of discreet instants.
    Being is social in its immediacy,
Private in final implications;
Life is built of contact and dies secretly;
So existants live in history and die out
In fulfillment of individuals.
    Thus value is a food and not a weapon
Nor a challenge, process, not result, of judgment,
The morituri te salutamus
Of unique atomic realizations,
Enduring only in their eschatologies.

2

The shields of the peltasts of
The imagination quiver in the
Imagination the flourish
Of fire curves on the border
The eyelids gold and blue
The place of penumbras
Iris and pupil
Frosted or a star
Falling past Deneb
Past Aldebaran
Falling all night
Heavy as the songs

Arhythmic atonal
That drift with smoke
Across water
Or the cry rising
From between the buttes
The myrmidons
Of the imagination emerge
From stones
And sleep

3

Peace above this arch urged and bent, rising out
The frieze that not till high cold air in that time
Grown earthward vatic, incomprehensible
In trees inverted and copper galls of bloom,
Spoke death as speaking wrought; rhymed the butterflies;
Pared away rinds of thinking finer than thought;
Constructed tissues of a death of moments;
The translucent frieze of petals, of blue leaves,
Opposed blocked men with red granite molar hands;
Opposed the somnolescent will in its fact;
Bespoke the exfoliation of decay;
Compressed the angles at which the rods had leaned;
Stirred in the mind; settled the beams of passage;
Spoke death as fact, as fiat of becoming.
    The three shamans in their castle cubicles
Restored the prisms; replaced the discs and cubes;
Wrenched the taut lines welded in the cone of rays.
    Death spoke in atoms, speaking fine blown parsings
Of collected passage, syntax of the crumb.

4

He strikes the two rocks
He casts the four seeds
He marks in the dust
He draws three triangles
He burns the five feathers
He barks like the coyote
He paints his face white
He runs away

Has the arrow stood erect
The cones falling in cold water
All night the bell
And the delicate feet
A thousand leaves spinning
In the cube of ten thousand leaves
Or the cube that descends like a mist
The speaking voice will issue
From between immaculate red
And white alternates

The immediate fact
Is not perdurable
And speaking is being memory
The prisms falling in snow
Or web of air
And silver target
And the unique
Note
Of the stricken

EASY LESSONS IN GEOPHAGY

for Hart Crane and Harry Crosby

pulldo pulldo shows quoth the caliver
– EASTWARD HOE

1

The Leonids having fallen
The tinkles having fallen
The silver having fallen silently
Having the fog
Having the colorless margin
Having the gold bees
The act having been forgotten
The right hand having turned sinister
Can the indifferent arms be raised
Moving in the tree tops
Sounding the long horn
Seeing the red animals
Floating among the transparent medusae
Canopus hears the moon hears
The night the members
Of the body move in the sea
In the saline transparent sea
Auguries of struggle urge the somatic
Community fluent webs run
Through the viscera the head
Appears in air the nostrils
The eyes open the lips open the whites
Of the eyes shine over
The groundswell the great conch speaks
The knowledge of war spreads over the water
The brittle bones watching
The spider

In a bar of light
In the sound of water

2

"In time all haggard hawks will stoop to lure"
The needle digests the eagle
The tile eyeballs
The painted marbles
The falsetto tornado interrupts itself
With shaved foxhounds
With unworthy insights
With hand-painted paraboloids
With cotton metronomes
With little beetles
The needle digests the eagle
They have programs in going
Away went conquests
Away went nodes and interruptions
Away went unmistakable punctuations
The kite screams and falls screaming
And falls blood streaming from its eyes
And falls its beak shattered
And falls in a tangent to the horizon
And falls whirling
And falls in mixed helices
And falls screaming
And falls into the spinning freezer
The resilient thumb presses the patent mattress
Three glimmers replace the hair
The scalp moves in recurrent conchoids
The undulation digests the albatross
Little cubes
The base whistle continues
Endures like the green hippocephali
Endures like the Gulf of Spoiled Botanies

Endures like the mincer
Endures like the worms of longitude
Ostriches digest needles
The dead are fed to the vultures
And the broken rhythmic vertigo recurs continually

3

"Born into it
Proved by external effects
Proved by internal effects
Thus literally living in a blaze of reality"
Is it fear to meet as he might meet fear
Meeting himself in the burnt forest
Is it fear avoiding the personal
Pronoun avoiding the eponymoi of myself
Amongst the innumerable black infusoria
I come so to the comet traps
I come so to the gegenschein
I come so to the more obscure aurora
I come so to the vital organs
Arranged on a shelf above the body
Guarded by the effigies of their patrons
When they spoke of a man they said you see
That was a different time in another
Place they spoke of another they said instead
Of succulents do you prefer kelp
Or cactus instead
Of the calipers the splintered ice

4

I passed the black fountain
I passed the swathed man
I passed the meteorite
I passed the tireless mice
I passed the long shark of the dawn

I passed the multitude of gelid eardrums
There are no teeth in most orchids
The bas-relief tilts in the wall
Flowers explode beneath the feet of the horses
And the earthquake announces its genesis by whistling in the
thermometers, and
Announces its approach by obscuring the pulsations of the flowers
The earthquake speaks gently and distinctly in a foreign language.

Born into it
Proved by external effects
Proved by internal effects
Light is reddened by age, it loses energy as it gets older, traveling
through space.

A LESSON IN GEOGRAPHY

of Paradys ne can not I speken
propurly ffor I was not there
– Mandeville

The stars of the Great Bear drift apart
The Horse and the Rider together northeastward
Alpha and Omega asunder
The others diversely
There are rocks
On the earth more durable
Than the configurations of heaven
Species now motile and sanguine
Shall see the stars in new clusters
The beaches changed
The mountains shifted
Gigantic
Immobile
Floodlit

The faces appear and disappear
Chewing the right gum
Smoking the right cigarette
Buying the best refrigerator
The polished carnivorous teeth
Exhibited in approval
The lights
Of the houses
Draw together
In the evening dewfall on the banks
Of the Wabash
Sparkle discreetly
High on the road to Provo
Above the Salt Lake Valley
And
The mountain shaped like a sphinx
And
The mountain shaped like a finger
Pointing
On the first of April at eight o'clock
Precisely at Algol
There are rocks on the earth
And one who sleepless
Throbbed with the ten
Nightingales in the plum trees
Sleepless as Boötes stood over him
Gnawing the pillow
Sitting on the bed's edge smoking
Sitting by the window looking
One who rose in the false
Dawn and stoned
The nightingales in the garden
The heart pawned for wisdom
The heart
Bartered for knowledge and folly
The will troubled
The mind secretly aghast

The eyes and lips full of sorrow
The apices of vision wavering
As the flower spray at the tip of the windstalk
The becalmed sail
The heavy wordless weight
And now
The anguishing and pitiless file
Cutting away life
Capsule by capsule biting
Into the heart
The coal of fire
Sealing the lips
There are rocks on earth

And

In the Japanese quarter
A phonograph playing
"Moonlight on ruined castles"
Kōjō n'suki

And
The movement of the wind fish
Keeping time to the music
Sirius setting behind it
(The Dog has scented the sun)
Gold immense fish
Squirm in the trade wind
"Young Middle Western woman
In rut
Desires correspondent"
The first bright flower
Cynoglossum
The blue hound's tongue
Breaks on the hill
"The tide has gone down
Over the reef

I walk about the world
There is great
Wind and then rain"
"My life is bought and paid for
So much pleasure
For so much pain"
The folded fossiliferous
Sedimentary rocks end here
The granite batholith
Obtrudes abruptly
West of the fault line
Betelgeuse reddens
Drawing its substance about it
It is possible that a process is beginning
Similar to that which lifted
The great Sierra fault block
Through an older metamorphic range

(The Dog barks on the sun's spoor)

Now

The thought of death
Binds fast the flood of light
Ten years ago the snow falling
All a long winter night
I had lain waking in my bed alone
Turning my heavy thoughts
And no way might
Sleep
Remembering divers things long gone
Now
In the long day in the hour of small shadow
I walk on the continent's last western hill
And lie prone among the iris in the grass
My eyes fixed on the durable stone
That speaks and hears as though it were myself

NORTHAMPTON, 1922–SAN FRANCISCO, 1939

All night rain falls through fog.
I lie awake, restless on a twisted pillow.
Fog horns cry over the desolate water.
How long ago was it,
That night with the pear blossoms
Quivering in the pulsating moonlight?
I am startled from sleep
By the acrid fleshy odor of pear blossoms.

Somewhere in the world, I suppose,
You are still living, a middle-aged matron,
With children on the verge of youth.

ICE SHALL COVER NINEVEH

But have you heard that, once upon a time, the city of Nineveh stood where now one sees the snow fields of the Gurgler Glacier? I do not know myself whether it is true or not. They say that a pilgrim came there and asked for bread. The people were miserly and gave him only a sour crust. He rebuked them, and after his departure, ice came and covered their city. I have heard that he was one of the Three Wise Men....

Austrian guns were mounted on the south peak of the Ortler, and all the way down to the Payer hut we shall find the remains of cables up which supplies were carried during the last weeks of conflict....

Tomorrow when you cross the Stelvio, you will see the galleries and rock-cut trenches where many men lived and died. They were mountain men like those cutting hay in the fields by which we passed. There was no hatred in their hearts. Word came from the cities that they must go out and kill.

"Ice Shall Cover Nineveh" – J. Monroe Thorington
SIERRA CLUB BULLETIN, 1933

1

Distant on the meridian verges
And the soft equinoxes calling
Altair burns over the glacial
Pyramid it is evening
And the nighthawks pass over me
The great heron lifts from the water
And goes away the evening deepens
The stars come out and the owls under them
Dew falls between the mountains
And the Milky Way
Treeless and desolate
The lake lies under the last mountain
The moon rises and falling
Fringes of storm clouds blow over it
The wind barks in the cleft of the mountain
Sheep bells move in the valleys under me
The owls spiral close to the ground
The rain thickens and they go away
Lightning unwinds over the summit
I turn in sleep and speak aloud

2

Under the surgical and unnoticed
Sun now the gray rare
Condor goes over his swimming
Shadow over the matted alpine
Hemlock and gold trout waltz and
Flash in the volatile water
The mind splinters in attenuate air
The trail curls
Movement whistles into pain
The ache of bone the ache
Of immemorial blood
The sun goes under

The prostrate wood
The stars come over
The standing stone
Sacrifices and populations dissolve
We shall go away and not know when
Awakened at night and far away
In dense valleys bright life needles every clod
Neither fortified in dolmen nor reclined
In tumulus shall white throat and quick hand hide
Nor eye escape the rasp of powdering time

3

We would hear the sheep bells at night
And sometimes by day with the wind changing
But we spent two days hunting and calling
Because the tableland was full of wrinkles
With all sizes of lakes in them and covered
With stones the size and color of sheep
And then coming back from the pass
She saw in the dark his pipe glowing
And there he was standing against a big rock
A shadow on the pale stone watching the moon rise
Nothing would cook in water at that height
We lived for a week on fried fish bacon and flapjacks
Cooked over the cow dung of the herd
That had been through there two years back

4

The donations of this pattern
Intractable fact or hopeful
Platonism await the issue
Of type or archetype
Of being and existence
Desire anxious and faint
With expectation

Where the shrill
Gasp of spume the cord of water
Hangs from the arid granite
In the lacunae
Of space the interstices
Of the brain
Black wing and rose head
The yellow climbing bird
In the blue haze
Singing over the chasm
Or conversely who shall question
The donor who shall accept
With courtesy and illumination
The chill ground light
The clouds still orange and purple the sky
Unfathomed green
And dark cumbrous and busy
The bears in the huckleberries
Dampness rising from the meadow
The broken moon arriving
Ubiquitously through cloven rock
Or who shall sieve history
The adamant occasion
In bright obstinacy
From this obdurate avalanche

5

No ritual nor prayer shall let
Ungrind this molar precision of
Catastrophe nor shall bespeak
The stars of this vacant absolute
Tragedies swarm polarized between
Cerebrum and cerebellum infest
The wainscotting infest the medulla
Infest the endocrines
Light entering your eyes becomes

Brilliant with worms
All through the twilight air
Creeps a fog of nematodes
And no unguent
No moonlight wafer setting
In your final sky shall still
The roar of falling iron and stone
Falling with lightning and indifference
Beyond knowledge
And beyond interruption

6

Discover the apostleship of diffidence
As gently as bubbles circle out from
The foot of this waterfall and the sun
Declines as carefully find out the torc
And tension of this straight evangel as:
"Again they walk with me who once beside
Me walked the careful feet beside me waked
The meadow lark from the starlit white wheat"
(The song countered against a sun of three thousand suns
The inch-long blur of wings the humming bird
Hung in the fecund air) speak to the fractured
Moments of the aspen the military
Precise marsh iris intercolumniate
With fir and hemlock in smoke of twisted juniper
Memory ascends the mind
Goes up
Assents
The moon early after sundown
The emerald
Long mountain meadow
At the far end
Thirty
Red cattle
Below the peaks

7

A white body prone beneath meteors
And no moon in the moist night
Let a note ring in the immobile forest
The warped gong shuddering as the swung beam struck
Across the peaks clouds rise against the snow
The small eyes
Birds' feet
Flies' wings
And all voice still
Only the catheaded bird wavers through the sequoias
Only the bear snuffs shuffling and the marten
Stretches slit-eyed on a branch and sleeps
And the bronze body prone all day beneath
The hunting hawks all day soaring
Spirals in the narrow canyon sky
Falling suddenly to the moved grass
The two red-tailed hawks in the evening go off across the
    mountain
Let the gong speak in the impenetrable granite

8

The sudden eyes of gravid mice
The sunset on the blades of stone
The wide glow of a star falling across
Scorpio in the final altitudes
The crisp utterance of Spica in the evening
The light white in the pools water falling
Luminous through the bat quick air
Glory flashes once and is gone and we go
Stumbling but this is a slow omnivorous
Glory and endures as the mind shrivels
And the electric cancer of the eclipse
Crawls into the sky over the snow

9

Fear no more the eye of the sun
Nor the covert lemming's glance
You the invisible medusa
Have seen at twilight
And the waters wash on shell beaches
Pale blue in the long pale days
And the doe and the new fawn cross the bars
Of sunlight under the marsh lodgepole pines
Fear no more Polaris' sword
Nor the noiseless water vole
Nor any brilliant invertebrate
Nor molten nematode
Only the inorganic residues
Of your aspiration remain
Combed over by constellations
Vivisected by blades of wind
Fear no more the chill of the moon
No brisk rodent fear
Nor thirty years' dreams of falling
For frozen on the fixed final summit
Your mineral eyes reflect the gleaming
Perpetual fall of a cube of singular stone
Coursing its own parabola
Beyond imagination
Unto ages of ages

10

You return breathless having startled
Phoenixes in the arroyos and seen
On porphyry altars the pelican
Rend itself tirelessly and the creature
With uncounted eyes
And who now creaking in rust soft armor

Will bring this taper to the outer room
O the lost phalanxes the engulfed Gemini
Where the guillotine animal flies over the drowned lands
And the bleached heads turn incuriously
And no hand lifts
This Prometheus breeds his own eaglets
At first daybreak a voice opens crevices in the air
Fear no more
The horns of those gray hunters wind along
Ridges more inaccessible than dreams
Speak not let no word break
The stillness of this anguish
The omniscience of this vertigo
These lucent needles are fluent
In the gold of every memory
The past curls like wire

11

And now surprised by lunar mountain avatars
The avid eyes of gravid mice entice
Each icy nostrum of the zodiac
Sidelong on quivering feet the giants tread
The white Excaliburs the zero saws
The igneous granite pencils silvering
The plunge of light the coneys barking
The white lips speak and Danae
Danae writhing in the fluent metal
The camels the llamas the dogsleds the burros
Are loaded and go off in the white distance
And green over them the nova grows above the pass

12

Shall ask no more then forget the asker
Shall fail at laughter and in the dark
Go mumbling the parched gums fumbling the baggy heart
Bark with the mice in the rubbish bayed at by rats
The glaciers are senile and covered with dust but the mountain cracks
The orange-red granite breaks and the long black slivers fall
Fine ice in the air and the stone blades falling and the opening vault
The high milk-blue lake tipping over its edge in a mile-long wavering waterfall
And for these weapons in what forge and from what steel
And for this wheat what winnowing floor what flail

THE PHOENIX AND THE TORTOISE (1944)

For Marie

I would not have you less than mutable,
Leaf wickered sunlight on your lips,
And on your lips the plangent, unstable
Laughter of your copious heart.

WHEN WE WITH SAPPHO

"...about the cool water
the wind sounds through sprays
of apple, and from the quivering leaves
slumber pours down..."

We lie here in the bee filled, ruinous
Orchard of a decayed New England farm,
Summer in our hair, and the smell
Of summer in our twined bodies,
Summer in our mouths, and summer
In the luminous fragmentary words
Of this dead Greek woman.
Stop reading. Lean back. Give me your mouth.
Your grace is as beautiful as sleep.
You move against me like a wave
That moves in sleep.
Your body spreads across my brain
Like a bird filled summer;
Not like a body, not like a separate thing,
But like a nimbus that hovers
Over every other thing in all the world.
Lean back. You are beautiful,
As beautiful as the folding
Of your hands in sleep.

We have grown old in the afternoon.
Here in our orchard we are as old
As she is now, wherever dissipate
In that distant sea her gleaming dust
Flashes in the wave crest
Or stains the murex shell.
All about us the old farm subsides
Into the honey bearing chaos of high summer.
In those far islands the temples
Have fallen away, and the marble

Is the color of wild honey.
There is nothing left of the gardens
That were once about them, of the fat
Turf marked with cloven hooves.
Only the sea grass struggles
Over the crumbled stone,
Over the splintered steps,
Only the blue and yellow
Of the sea, and the cliffs
Red in the distance across the bay.
Lean back.
Her memory has passed to our lips now.
Our kisses fall through summer's chaos
In our own breasts and thighs.

Gold colossal domes of cumulus cloud
Lift over the undulant, sibilant forest.
The air presses against the earth.
Thunder breaks over the mountains.
Far off, over the Adirondacks,
Lightning quivers, almost invisible
In the bright sky, violet against
The grey, deep shadows of the bellied clouds.
The sweet virile hair of thunder storms
Brushes over the swelling horizon.
Take off your shoes and stockings.
I will kiss your sweet legs and feet
As they lie half buried in the tangle
Of rank scented midsummer flowers.
Take off your clothes. I will press
Your summer honeyed flesh into the hot
Soil, into the crushed, acrid herbage
Of midsummer. Let your body sink
Like honey through the hot
Granular fingers of summer.

Rest. Wait. We have enough for a while.
Kiss me with your mouth

Wet and ragged, your mouth that tastes
Of my own flesh. Read to me again
The twisting music of that language
That is of all others, itself a work of art.
Read again those isolate, poignant words
Saved by ancient grammarians
To illustrate the conjugations
And declensions of the more ancient dead.
Lean back in the curve of my body,
Press your bruised shoulders against
The damp hair of my body.
Kiss me again. Think, sweet linguist,
In this world the ablative is impossible.
No other one will help us here.
We must help ourselves to each other.
The wind walks slowly away from the storm;
Veers on the wooded crests; sounds
In the valleys. Here we are isolate,
One with the other; and beyond
This orchard lies isolation,
The isolation of all the world.
Never let anything intrude
On the isolation of this day,
These words, isolate on dead tongues,
This orchard, hidden from fact and history,
These shadows, blended in the summer light,
Together isolate beyond the world's reciprocity.

Do not talk any more. Do not speak.
Do not break silence until
We are weary of each other.
Let our fingers run like steel
Carving the contours of our bodies' gold.
Do not speak. My face sinks
In the clotted summer of your hair.
The sound of the bees stops.
Stillness falls like a cloud.
Be still. Let your body fall away

Into the awe filled silence
Of the fulfilled summer –
Back, back, infinitely away –
Our lips weak, faint with stillness.

See. The sun has fallen away.
Now there are amber
Long lights on the shattered
Boles of the ancient apple trees.
Our bodies move to each other
As bodies move in sleep;
At once filled and exhausted,
As the summer moves to autumn,
As we, with Sappho, move towards death.
My eyelids sink toward sleep in the hot
Autumn of your uncoiled hair.
Your body moves in my arms
On the verge of sleep;
And it is as though I held
In my arms the bird filled
Evening sky of summer.

RUNAWAY

There are sparkles of rain on the bright
Hair over your forehead;
Your eyes are wet and your lips
Wet and cold, your cheek rigid with cold.
Why have you stayed
Away so long, why have you only
Come to me late at night
After walking for hours in wind and rain?
Take off your dress and stockings;
Sit in the deep chair before the fire.
I will warm your feet in my hands;

I will warm your breasts and thighs with kisses.
I wish I could build a fire
In you that would never go out.
I wish I could be sure that deep in you
Was a magnet to draw you always home.

LUTE MUSIC

The earth will be going on a long time
Before it finally freezes;
Men will be on it; they will take names,
Give their deeds reasons.
We will be here only
As chemical constituents –
A small franchise indeed.
Right now we have lives,
Corpuscles, ambitions, caresses,
Like everybody had once –
All the bright neige d'antan people,
"Blithe Helen, white Iope, and the rest,"
All the uneasy remembered dead.

Here at the year's end, at the feast
Of birth, let us bring to each other
The gifts brought once west through deserts –
The precious metal of our mingled hair,
The frankincense of enraptured arms and legs,
The myrrh of desperate invincible kisses –
Let us celebrate the daily
Recurrent nativity of love,
The endless epiphany of our fluent selves,
While the earth rolls away under us
Into unknown snows and summers,
Into untraveled spaces of the stars.

FLOATING

Our canoe idles in the idling current
Of the tree and vine and rush enclosed
Backwater of a torpid midwestern stream;
Revolves slowly and lodges in the glutted
Waterlilies. We are tired of paddling.
All afternoon we have climbed the weak current,
Up dim meanders, through woods and pastures,
Past muddy fords where the strong smell of cattle
Lay thick across the water; singing the songs
Of perfect, habitual motion; ski songs,
Nightherding songs, songs of the capstan walk,
The levee, and the roll of the voyageurs.
Tired of motion, of the rhythms of motion,
Tired of the sweet play of our interwoven strength,
We lie in each other's arms and let the palps
Of waterlily leaf and petal hold back
All motion in the heat thickened, drowsing air.
Sing to me softly, Westron Wynde, Ah the Syghes,
Mon coeur se recommend à vous, Phoebi Claro;
Sing the wandering erotic melodies
Of men and women gone seven hundred years,
Softly, your mouth close to my cheek.
Let our thighs lie entangled on the cushions,
Let your breasts in their thin cover
Hang pendant against my naked arms and throat;
Let your odorous hair fall across our eyes;
Kiss me with those subtle, melodic lips.
As I undress you, your pupils are black, wet,
Immense, and your skin ivory and humid.
Move softly, move hardly at all, part your thighs,
Take me slowly while our gnawing lips
Fumble against the humming blood in our throats.
Move softly, do not move at all, but hold me,
Deep, still, deep within you, while time slides away,
As this river slides beyond this lily bed,

And the thieving moments fuse and disappear
In our mortal, timeless flesh.

ANOTHER SPRING

The seasons revolve and the years change
With no assistance or supervision.
The moon, without taking thought,
Moves in its cycle, full, crescent, and full.

The white moon enters the heart of the river;
The air is drugged with azalea blossoms;
Deep in the night a pine cone falls;
Our campfire dies out in the empty mountains.

The sharp stars flicker in the tremulous branches;
The lake is black, bottomless in the crystalline night;
High in the sky the Northern Crown
Is cut in half by the dim summit of a snow peak.

O heart, heart, so singularly
Intransigent and corruptible,
Here we lie entranced by the starlit water,
And moments that should each last forever

Slide unconsciously by us like water.

NIGHT BELOW ZERO

3 AM, the night is absolutely still;
Snow squeals beneath my skis, plumes on the turns.
I stop at the canyon's edge, stand looking out
Over the Great Valley, over the millions –

In bed, drunk, loving, tending mills, furnaces,
Alone, wakeful, as the world rolls in chaos.
The quarter moon rises in the black heavens –
Over the sharp constellations of the cities
The cold lies, crystalline and silent,
Locked between the mountains.

THE ADVANTAGES OF LEARNING

I am a man with no ambitions
And few friends, wholly incapable
Of making a living, growing no
Younger, fugitive from some just doom.
Lonely, ill-clothed, what does it matter?
At midnight I make myself a jug
Of hot white wine and cardamon seeds.
In a torn grey robe and old beret,
I sit in the cold writing poems,
Drawing nudes on the crooked margins,
Copulating with sixteen year old
Nymphomaniacs of my imagination.

HABEAS CORPUS

You have the body, blood and bone,
And hair and nail and tooth and eye.
You have the body – the skin taut
In the moonlight, the sea gnawing
At the empty mountains, the hair
Of the body tensile, erect…
The full barley ears whip and flail
In the rain gorged wind and the flame
Of lightning breaks in the air

For a moment and vanishes;
And I tell you the memory
Of flesh is as real as live flesh
Or falling stone or burning fire...
You have the body and the sun
Brocaded brown and pink naked
Wedded body, its eternal
Blood biding the worm and his time.

PLINY – IX, XXXVI – LAMPRIDIUS – XXIX

When I remember that letter of Pliny's –
The daily round of a gentleman
Of letters in the days of Trajan –
Masseuses of assorted colors
Before breakfast, all of them learned
In the Greek poets, philosophic
Discourses in the bath, flute players
For lunch, along with mathematics,
Roast peacocks for dinner, and after,
Mixed maenads, or else astronomy,
Depending on the mood and weather –
I am overcome with amazement.
Here I sit, poor, proud, and domestic,
Manipulating my typewriter;
And beyond my library window,
Inordinately luxuriant,
Suffused with esoteric giggles,
The remote daughters of my neighbors
Return from high school.

HARMODIUS AND ARISTOGEITON

Last night, reading the Anthology,
I could find no epitaph for you.
I suppose it was naive to look.
Alexander and Justinian,
The brocaded Paleologoi,
French drunkards and sleepy Turks,
Have ruled over Athens since your day.
So, late by these many years, take this:

Your act is vocal still. Men grow deaf.

INVERSELY, AS THE SQUARE OF THEIR DISTANCES APART

It is impossible to see anything
In this dark; but I know this is me, Rexroth,
Plunging through the night on a chilling planet.
It is warm and busy in this vegetable
Darkness where invisible deer feed quietly.
The sky is warm and heavy, even the trees
Over my head cannot be distinguished,
But I know they are knobcone pines, that their cones
Endure unopened on the branches, at last
To grow imbedded in the wood, waiting for fire
To open them and reseed the burned forest.
And I am waiting, alone, in the mountains,
In the forest, in the darkness, and the world
Falls swiftly on its measured ellipse.

~

It is warm tonight and very still.
The stars are hazy and the river –
Vague and monstrous under the fireflies –
Is hardly audible, resonant
And profound at the edge of hearing.
I can just see your eyes and wet lips.
Invisible, solemn, and fragrant,
Your flesh opens to me in secret.
We shall know no further enigma.
After all the years there is nothing
Stranger than this. We who know ourselves
As one doubled thing, and move our limbs
As deft implements of one fused lust,
Are mysteries in each other's arms.

~

At the wood's edge in the moonlight
We dropped our clothes and stood naked,
Swaying, shadow mottled, enclosed
In each other and together
Closed in the night. We did not hear
The whip-poor-will, nor the aspen's
Whisper; the owl flew silently
Or cried out loud, we did not know.
We could not hear beyond the heart.
We could not see the moving dark
And light, the stars that stood or moved,
The stars that fell. Did they all fall
We had not known. We were falling
Like meteors, dark through black cold
Toward each other, and then compact,
Blazing through air into the earth.

~

I lie alone in an alien
Bed in a strange house and morning
More cruel than any midnight
Pours its brightness through the window –
Cherry branches with the flowers
Fading, and behind them the gold
Stately baubles of the maple,
And behind them the pure immense
April sky and a white frayed cloud,
And in and behind everything,
The inescapable vacant
Distance of loneliness.

VITAMINS AND ROUGHAGE

Strong ankled, sun burned, almost naked,
The daughters of California
Educate reluctant humanists;
Drive into their skulls with tennis balls
The unhappy realization
That nature is still stronger than man.
The special Hellenic privilege
Of the special intellect seeps out
At last in this irrigated soil.
Sweat of athletes and juice of lovers
Are stronger than Socrates' hemlock;
And the games of scrupulous Euclid
Vanish in the gymnopaedia.

BETWEEN TWO WARS

Remember that breakfast one November –
Cold black grapes smelling faintly

Of the cork they were packed in,
Hard rolls with hot, white flesh,
And thick, honey sweetened chocolate?
And the parties at night; the gin and the tangos?
The torn hair nets, the lost cuff links?
Where have they all gone to,
The beautiful girls, the abandoned hours?
They said we were lost, mad and immoral,
And interfered with the plans of the management.
And today, millions and millions, shut alive
In the coffins of circumstance,
Beat on the buried lids,
Huddle in the cellars of ruins, and quarrel
Over their own fragmented flesh.

GAS OR NOVOCAIN

Here I sit, reading the Stoic
Latin of Tacitus.
Tiberius sinks in senile
Gloom as Aeneas sank
In the smoky throat of Hades;
And the prose glitters like
A tray of dental instruments.
The toss head president,
Deep in his private catacomb,
Is preparing to pull
The trigger. His secretaries
Make speeches. In ten years
The art of communication
Will be more limited.
The wheel, the lever, the incline,
May survive, and perhaps,
The alphabet. At the moment
The intellectual

Advance guard is agitated
Over the relation
Between the Accumulation
Of Capital and the
Systematic Derangement of
The Senses, and the Right
To Homosexuality.

IT ROLLS ON

Irresolute, pausing on a doubtful journey;
Once more, after so long, the unique autumnal
Wonder of the upper Hudson about me;
I walk in the long forgotten
Familiar garden. The house was never
Reoccupied, the windows are broken,
The walks and the arbors ruinous,
The flower beds are thickets,
The hedges are shattered,
The quince and hawthorns broken and dying.
One by one the memories of twenty years
Vanish and there is no trace of them.
I have been restless in many places
Since I rested in this place.
The dry thickets are full of migrating
Grey-green warblers. Since last fall
They have visited Guatemala and Labrador
And now they are bound south again.
Their remote ancestors were doing the same thing
When I was here before. Each generation
Has stopped for an autumn evening
Here, in this place, each year.

DELIA REXROTH

died June 1916

Under your illkempt yellow roses,
Delia, today you are younger
Than your son. Two and a half decades –
The family monument sagged askew,
And he overtook your half-a-life.
On the other side of the country,
Near the willows by the slow river,
Deep in the earth, the white ribs retain
The curve of your fervent, careful breast;
The fine skull, the ardor of your brain.
And in the fingers the memory
Of Chopin études, and in the feet
Slow waltzes and champagne twosteps sleep.
And the white full moon of midsummer,
That you watched awake all that last night,
Watches history fill the deserts
And oceans with corpses once again;
And looks in the east window at me,
As I move past you to middle age
And knowledge past your agony and waste.

ANOTHER ONE

Septimius, the forms you know so well,
The olla of callas, the multiform
Guitar, the svelte girl torso and slick thigh,
Surprise you and become you unaware.
You get drunk like one of your spotless nudes;
I hear that you resemble a still life
Between sheets; and your conversation ticks
From certitude to tock;
But not with me.

ANDRÉE REXROTH

died October 1940

Now once more gray mottled buckeye branches
Explode their emerald stars,
And alders smoulder in a rosy smoke
Of innumerable buds.
I know that spring again is splendid
As ever, the hidden thrush
As sweetly tongued, the sun as vital –
But these are the forest trails we walked together,
These paths, ten years together.
We thought the years would last forever,
They are all gone now, the days
We thought would not come for us are here.
Bright trout poised in the current –
The raccoon's track at the water's edge –
A bittern booming in the distance –
Your ashes scattered on this mountain –
Moving seaward on this stream.

PRECESSION OF THE EQUINOXES

Time was, I walked in the February rain
My head full of its own rhythms like a shell,
And came home at night to write of love and death,
High philosophy, and brotherhood of man.

After intimate acquaintance with these things,
I contemplate the changes of the weather,
Flowers, birds, rabbits, mice, and other small deer
Fulfilling the year's periodicity.

And the reassurances of my own pulse.

AGAIN AT WALDHEIM

Light upon Waldheim
– Voltairine de Cleyre on the Haymarket martyrs

How heavy the heart is now, and every heart
Save only the word drunk, power drunk
Hard capsule of the doomed. How distraught
Those things of pride, the wills nourished in the fat
Years, fed in the kindly twilight of the books
In gold and brown, the voices that had little
To live for, crying for something to die for.
The philosophers of history,
Of dim wit and foolish memory,
The giggling concubines of catastrophe –
Who forget so much – Boethius' calm death,
More's sweet speech, Rosa's broken body –
Or you, tough, stubby recalcitrant
Of Fate.

Now in Waldheim where the rain
has fallen careless and unthinking
For all an evil century's youth,
Where now the banks of dark roses lie,
What memory lasts, Emma, of you,
Or of the intrepid comrades of your grave,
Of Piotr, of "mutual aid,"
Against the iron clad flame throwing
Course of time?
Your stakes were on the turn
Of a card whose face you knew you would not see.

You knew that nothing could ever be
More desperate than truth; and when every voice
Was cowed, you spoke against the coalitions
For the duration of the emergency –
In the permanent emergency

You spoke for the irrefutable
Coalition of the blood of men.

STRENGTH THROUGH JOY

Coming back over the col between
Isosceles Mountain and North Palisade,
I stop at the summit and look back
At the storm gathering over the white peaks
Of the Whitney group and the colored
Kaweahs. September, nineteen thirty-nine.
This is the last trip in the mountains
This autumn, possibly the last trip ever.
The storm clouds rise up the mountainside,
Lightning batters the pinnacles above me,
The clouds beneath the pass are purple
And I see rising through them from the valleys
And cities a cold, murderous flood,
Spreading over the world, lapping at the last
Inviolate heights; mud streaked yellow
With gas, slimy and blotched with crimson,
Filled with broken bits of steel and flesh,
Moving slowly with the blind motion
Of lice, spreading inexorably
As bacteria spread in tissues,
Swirling with the precise rapacity of starved rats.
I loiter here like a condemned man
Lingers over his last breakfast, his last smoke;
Thinking of those heroes of the war
Of human skill, foresight, endurance, and will;
The disinterested bravery,
The ideal combat of peace: Bauer
Crawling all night around his icecave
On snowbound Kanchenjunga, Tilman
And Shipton skylarking on Nanda Devi,

Smythe seeing visions on Everest,
The mad children of the Eigerwand –
What holidays will they keep this year?
Gun emplacements blasted in the rock;
No place for graves, the dead covered with quicklime
Or left in the snow till the spring thaw;
Machine gun duels between white robed ski troops,
The last screaming schusses marked with blood.
Was it for this we spent the years perfecting
The craft of courage? Better the corpse
Of the foolhardy, frozen on the Eiger
Accessible only to the storm,
Standing sentry for the avalanche.

STILL ON WATER

Solitude closes down around us
As we lie passive and exhausted
Solitude clamps us softly in its warm hand.
A turtle slips into the water
With a faint noise like a breaking bubble;
There is no other sound, only the dim
Momentous conversation of windless
Poplar and sycamore leaves and rarely,
A single, questioning frog voice.
I turn my eyes from your entranced face
And watch the oncoming sunset
Powder the immense, unblemished zenith
With almost imperceptible sparkles of gold.
Your eyes open, your head turns.
Your lips nibble at my shoulder.
I feel a languid shudder run over your body.
Suddenly you laugh, like a pure
Exulting flute, spring to your feet
And plunge into the water.

A white bird breaks from the rushes
And flies away, and the boat rocks
Drunkenly in the billows
Of your nude jubilation.

UN BEL DI VEDREMO

"Hello NBC, this is London speaking…"
I move the dial, I have heard it all,
Day after day – the terrible waiting,
The air raids, the military communiqués,
The between the lines whispering
Of quarreling politicians,
The mute courage of the people.
The dial moves over aggressive
Advertisements, comedians, bands hot and sweet,
To a record concert – La Scala – *Madame Butterfly*.
I pause, listening idly, and suddenly
I feel as though I had begun to fall
Slowly, buoyantly, through infinite, indefinite space.
Milano, fretting in my seat,
In my lace collar and velvet suit,
My beautiful mother weeping
Happily beside me. My God,
How long ago it was, further far
Than Rome or Egypt, that other
World before the other war.
Stealing downstairs to spy on the champagne suppers;
Watching the blue flame of the chafing dish
On Sunday nights: driving over middle Europe
Behind a café au lait team,
The evenings misty, smelling of cattle
And the fat Danubian earth.
It will never be again
The open work stockings,

The lace evening gowns,
The pink roses on the slippers;
Debs eating roast chicken and drinking whiskey,
On the front porch with grandpa;
The neighbors gaping behind their curtains;
The Japanese prints and the works of Huneker.
Never again will a small boy
Curled in the hammock in the murmurous summer air
Gnaw his knuckles, reading *The Jungle*;
Never again will he gasp as Franz Josef
And the princesses sweep through
The lines of wolf caped hussars.
It is a terrible thing to sit here
In the uneasy light above this strange city
And listen to the poignant sentimentality
Of an age more dead than the Cro-Magnon.
It is a terrible thing to see a world die twice,
"The first time as tragedy,
The second as evil farce."

ADONIS IN WINTER

Persephone awaits him in the dim boudoir,
Waits him, for the hour is at hand.
She has arranged the things he likes
Near to his expected hand:
Herrick's poems, tobacco, the juice
Of pomegranates in a twisted glass.
She piles her drugged blonde hair
Above her candid forehead,
Touches up lips and eyelashes,
Selects her most naked robe.
On the stroke of the equinox he comes,
And smiles, and stretches his arms, and strokes
Her cheeks and childish shoulders, and kisses

The violet lids closed on the grey eyes.
Free of aggressive Aphrodite,
Free of the patronizing gods,
The cruel climate of Olympus,
They feed caramels to Cerberus
And warn him not to tell
The cuckold Pluto of their adulteries,
Their mortal lechery in dispassionate Hell.

ADONIS IN SUMMER

The Lotophagi with their silly hands
Haunt me in sleep, plucking at my sleeve;
Their gibbering laughter and blank eyes
Hide on the edge of the mind's vision
In dusty subways and crowded streets.
Late in August, asleep, Adonis
Appeared to me, frenzied and bleeding
And showed me, clutched in his hand, the plow
That broke the dream of Persephone.
The next day, regarding the scorched grass
In the wilting park, I became aware
That beneath me, beneath the gravel
And the hurrying ants, and the loam
And the subsoil, lay the glacial drift,
The Miocene jungles, the reptiles
Of the Jurassic, the cuttlefish
Of the Devonian, Cambrian
Worms, and the mysteries of the gneiss;
Their histories folded, docketed
In darkness; and deeper still the hot
Black core of iron, and once again
The inscrutable archaic rocks,
And the long geologic ladder,
And the living soil and the strange trees,

And the tangled bodies of lovers
Under the strange stars.
                    And beside me,
A mad old man, plucking at my sleeve.

WEDNESDAY OF HOLY WEEK, 1940

Out of the east window a storm
Blooms spasmodically across the moonrise;
In the west, in the haze, the planets
Pulsate like standing meteors.
We listen in the darkness to the service of Tenebrae,
Music older than the Resurrection,
The voice of the ruinous, disorderly Levant:
"Why doth the city sit solitary
That was full of people?"
The voices of the Benedictines are massive, impersonal;
They neither fear this agony nor are ashamed of it.
Think... six hours ago in Europe,
Thousands were singing these words,
Putting out the candles psalm by psalm...
Albi like a fort in the cold dark,
Aachen, the voices fluttering in the ancient vaulting,
The light of the last candle
In Munich on the gnarled carving.
"Jerusalem, Jerusalem,
Return ye unto the Lord thy God."
Thousands kneeling in the dark,
Saying, "Have mercy upon me O God."
We listen appreciatively, smoking, talking quietly,
The voices are coming from three thousand miles.
On the white garden wall the shadows
Of the date palm thresh wildly;
The full moon of the spring is up,
And a gale with it.

INCARNATION

Climbing alone all day long
In the blazing waste of spring snow,
I came down with the sunset's edge
To the highest meadow, green
In the cold mist of waterfalls,
To a cobweb of water
Woven with innumerable
Bright flowers of wild iris;
And saw far down our fire's smoke
Rising between the canyon walls,
A human thing in the empty mountains.
And as I stood on the stones
In the midst of whirling water,
The whirling iris perfume
Caught me in a vision of you
More real than reality:
Fire in the deep curves of your hair:
Your hips whirled in a tango,
Out and back in dim scented light;
Your cheeks snow-flushed, the zithers
Ringing, all the crowded ski lodge
Dancing and singing; your arms
White in the brown autumn water,
Swimming through the fallen leaves,
Making a fluctuant cobweb
Of light on the sycamores;
Your thigh's exact curve, the fine gauze
Slipping through my hands, and you
Tense on the verge of abandon;
Your breasts' very touch and smell;
The sweet secret odor of sex.
Forever the thought of you,
And the splendor of the iris,
The crinkled iris petal,
The gold hairs powdered with pollen,

And the obscure cantata
Of the tangled water, and the
Burning impassive snow peaks,
Are knotted together here.
This moment of fact and vision
Seizes immortality,
Becomes the person of this place.
The responsibility
Of love realized and beauty
Seen burns in a burning angel
Real beyond flower or stone.

WE COME BACK

Now, on this day of the first hundred flowers
Fate pauses for us in imagination,
As it shall not ever in reality –
As these swifts that link endless parabolas
Change guard unseen in their secret crevices.
Other anniversaries that we have walked
Along this hillcrest through the black fir forest,
Past the abandoned farm, have been just the same –
Even the fog necklaces on the fencewires
Seem to have gained or lost hardly a jewel;
The annual and diurnal patterns hold.
Even the attrition of the cypress grove
Is slow and orderly, each year one more tree
Breaks ranks and lies down, decrepit in the wind.
Each year, on summer's first luminous morning,
The swallows come back, whispering and weaving
Figure eights around the sharp curves of the swifts,
Plaiting together the summer air all day,
That the bats and owls unravel in the nights.
And we come back, the signs of time upon us,
In the pause of fate, the threading of the year.

MARTIAL – XII, LII

This is your own lover, Kenneth, Marie,
Who someday will be part of the earth
Beneath your feet; who crowned you once with roses
Of song; whose voice was no less famous
Raised against the guilt of his generation.
Sweetly in Hell he'll tell your story
To the enraptured ears of Helen,
Our joys and jealousies, our quarrels and journeys,
That unlike hers, ended in kisses.
Her spouse will smile at impetuous Paris
When he hears the tale of our sweet lust.
Laura and Petrarca, Waller and his Rose,
Grim Dante and glowing Beatrice,
Catullus and Lesbia, and all the rest,
Transparent hand in hand, will listen,
A tremor on their shadowy flesh once more.
And when at last I welcome you there
Your name will stand for memory of living
On the tongues of all whom death has joined.
You shall know this when you see my grave snowless
Winter long, and my cold sleepfellows
Shifting themselves underground to warm
Dead bones at my still glowing ashes.

THEORY OF NUMBERS

Think, as we lie in this sweet bed,
With the lamplight dim on books
And pictures of three thousand years,
And the light caught in the wine
Like Mars or Aldebaran:
Vaulted over the winter mountains,

The night sky is like the pure
Space of the imagination –
Defined by infinite star points,
Interrupted by meteors,
And the fleshy fires of planets
That move like infusoria.
The moon is as sheer as glass;
Its globe dissolves in illusion;
Out from it flow mysterious
Lines and surfaces, folding
And unfolding without limit.
The *Carmina Burana* –
Differential geometry –
"Dum Dianae vitrea
While Diana's crystal lamp"
Proof of the questionable
Existence of integrals –
And this bloody sacrament,
This linking of corpuscles
Like atoms of oxygen,
This Matrimony called Holy,
This is the lens of intention,
Focusing liability
From world to person, from passion
To action; and conversely,
The source of potential in fact.
The individual – the world –
On the bookshelves there is only
Paper soiled by history.
The space of night is infinite,
The blackness and emptiness
Crossed only by thin bright fences
Of logic.
                    Lying under
The night sky's inexhaustible
Equation, and fallen from it,

Uncountable hexagons
Of snow blanket the streamlined
Volcanic stones, and the columns
Of hexagonal basalt,
And the hexagons of wax
And honey where the bees sleep.

ANDRÉE REXROTH

Purple and green, blue and white,
The Oregon river mouths
Slide into thick smoky darkness
As the turning cup of day
Slips from the whirling hemisphere.
And all that white long beach gleams
In white twilight as the lights
Come on in the lonely hamlets;
And voices of men emerge;
And dogs barking, as the wind stills.
Those August evenings are
Sixteen years old tonight and I
Am sixteen years older too –
Lonely, caught in the midst of life,
In the chaos of the world;
And all the years that we were young
Are gone, and every atom
Of your learned and disordered
Flesh is utterly consumed.

HORNY DILEMMA

I have long desired to shine
As the modern Juvenal.
However, when I survey
The vast jungle infested
With bushmasters and tsetse
Flies imperviously stretched
From A… B… to C….
D…. E…, from M….
N…., to Y…. Z….,
I resign myself perforce
To Martial's brief excursions.

INCENSE

Her boudoir is ornamented with
The works of the Bloomsbury mystics –
Limited editions in warped vellum;
There is also a mauve draped prie-dieu
And a New Mexican crucifix.
Sinister and intimidating
As this environment might appear,
Her ecstasies can be distinguished
From those of Lais the agnostic
Only by their singular frequency.

A NEOCLASSICIST

I know your moral sources, prig.
Last night you plunged awake screaming.
You dreamed you'd grown extremely old,
Lay dying, and to your deathbed,

All the girls you'd ever slept with
Came, as old as you, to watch you die.
Comatose, your blotched residues
Shrivelled and froze between stiff sheets;
And the faces, dim as under
Dirty water, incurious,
Silent, of a room full of old,
Old women, waited, patiently.

PAST AND FUTURE TURN ABOUT

Autumn has returned and we return
To the same beach in the last hours.
The Phoenix and the Tortoise is finished.
The gratuitous discipline of finality
Falls on our lives and shapes our ends.
Ourselves as objectives, our objects,
Pass from our hands to the hands of time.
Reconsidering and revising
My life and the meaning of my poem,
I gather once more within me
The old material, sea and stone.

The green spring that comes in November
With the first rains has restored the hills.
Seals are playing in the kelp beds.
As the surf sweeps in they can be seen
Weaving over one another in
The standing water. In the granite
Cliffs are swarms of dark fish shaped patches
Of rock oriented to the flow lines
Of the hot magma. Nobody knows
Exactly what caused their formation,
Deep in the blind earth under the blind
Jurassic world, under the dead

Franciscan series, what disorder,
What process. On the wet sand lie
Hundreds of jellyfish with pale
Lavender organs at their hearts.
The sun will dry them and leave only
A brittle film. There are more hundreds
Pulsing through the water, struggling
Against the drive of the rising tide.
Down the beach beyond a tangle
Of barbed wire an armed sentry stands,
Gazing seaward under his helmet.

Carapace or transfiguration –
History will doubtless permit us
Neither. Eventually the will
Exhausts itself and turns, seeking grace,
To the love that suffers ignorance
And time's irresponsibility,
The Cross cannot be climbed upon.
It cannot be seized like a weapon
Against the injustice of the world.
"No one has ever seized injustice
In his bare hands and bent it back.
No one has ever tried to smash evil,
Without smashing himself and sinking
Into greater evil or despair."
The Satanic cunning represents
Itself as very strong, but just
A trifle weaker than its victim.
This is the meaning of temptation.
The Devil does not fool with fools.

It is easy to read or write
In a book, "Self realization
Is responsible self sacrifice."
"The will to power, the will to live,
Are fulfilled by transfiguration."

"The person is the final value;
Value is responsibility."
As the world sinks in a marsh of blood,
You won't raise yourself by your bootstraps,
However pious and profound.
Christ was not born of Socrates,
But to a disorderly people,
In an evil time, in the flesh
Of innocence and humility.

"The self determining will." What self?
What determination? History
Plays its pieces – "The Japanese
Adventure was shaped on the countless
G'oto tables of a hundred years."
Black slowly immobilizes white.
Evil reveals its hidden aces.
As the Philosopher observes,
"Fear is the sentiment of men
Beaten and overcome in mind,
Confronted by an imminent evil
Which they take to be too much for them
To resist and more than they can bear."
And again, appropriately, in the *Rhetoric*,
"We are never afraid of evil
When we are in the thick of it
And all chance of escape has vanished.
Fear always looks to flight, and catches
With the fancy's eye some glimpse
Of an opening for the avoidance
Of evil."

"O my Father, all things
Are possible unto Thee, if it be
Possible let this cup pass from me.
Nevertheless, not my will, but Thine."

The self determining will accepts
The responsibility of all
Contingency. What will? What self?
The Cross descends into the world
Like a sword, but the hilt thereof
Is in the heavens. Every man
Is his own Adam, left to itself,
The self unselfs itself, the will
Demands autonomy and achieves
It by a system of strategic
Retreats – the inane autonomy
Of the morally neuter event.
Conversion, penitence, and grace –
Autonomy is a by product
Of identification.

What was our sacrifice worth?
Practically nothing, the waste
Of time overwhelms heroes,
Pyramids and catastrophes.
Who knows the tropical foci
Of the Jurassic ice floes?
Who has seen the frozen black mass
That rushes upon us biding
Its light years? Who remembers
The squad that died stopping the tanks
At the bridgehead? The company
Was bombed out an hour later.
Simonides is soon forgotten.
The pressure of the unfound
Future is the pressure of the lost
Past, the brain stiffens with hope,
And swims in hallucination
Beating its spinal column
Like a flagellate in a mild
Solution of alcohol,
And pressed against it, mantis

To mantis, the cobwebbed body –
The caput abdominale.
As for that thin entelechy,
The person, let him wear the head
Of the wolf, in Sherwood Forest.

We return? Each to each, one
To another, each to the other?
Sweet lovely hallucination –
The sea falls through you, through the gulf
Of wish – last spring – what was value?
The hole itself cuts in its self
And watches as it fills with blood?
The waves of the sea fall through
Our each others indomitable
As peristalsis.

        Autumn comes
And the death of flowers, but
The flowered colored waves of
The sea will last forever
Like the pattern on the dress
Of a beautiful woman.

Nineteen forty-two and we
Are selves, stained, fixed, and mounted
On the calendar – and the leaves
Fall easily in the gardens
Of a million ruins.

        And deep
In the mountains the wind has stopped
The current of a stream with only
A windrow of the terribly
Red dogwood leaves.

THE PHOENIX AND THE TORTOISE (1940–1944)

For Marie

I

Webs of misery spread in the brain,
In the dry Spring in the soft heat.
Dirty cotton bolls of cloud hang
At the sky's edge; vague yellow stratus
Glimmer behind them. It is storming
Somewhere far out in the ocean.
All night vast rollers exploded
Offshore; now the sea has subsided
To a massive, uneasy torpor.
Fragments of its inexhaustible
Life litter the shingle, sea hares,
Broken starfish, a dead octopus,
And everywhere, swarming like ants,
Innumerable hermit crabs,
Hungry and efficient as maggots.

This is not the first time this shingle
Has been here. These cobbles are washed
From ancient conglomerate beds,
Beaches of the Franciscan series,
The immense layer cake of grey strata
That hangs without top or bottom
In the geological past
Of the California Coast Ranges.
There are no fossils in them. Their
Dates are disputed – thousands of feet,
Thousands and thousands of years, of bays,
Tidemarshes, estuaries, beaches,

Where time flowed eventless as silt.
Further along the beach the stones
Change; the cliffs are yellow with black
Bands of lignite; and scattered amongst
The sand dollars in the storm's refuse
Are fossil sand dollars the sea
Has washed from stone, as it has washed
These, newly dead, from life.

And I,
Walking by the viscid, menacing
Water, turn with my heavy heart
In my baffled brain, Plutarch's page –
The falling light of the Spartan
Heroes in the late Hellenic dusk –
Agis, Cleomenes – this poem
Of the phoenix and the tortoise –
Of what survives and what perishes,
And how, of the fall of history
And waste of fact – on the crumbling
Edge of a ruined polity
That washes away in an ocean
Whose shores are all washing into death.

A group of terrified children
Has just discovered the body
Of a Japanese sailor bumping
In a snarl of kelp in a tidepool.
While the crowd collects, I stand, mute
As he, watching his smashed ribs breathe
Of the life of the ocean, his white
Torn bowels braid themselves with the kelp;
And, out of his drained grey flesh, he
Watches me with open hard eyes
Like small indestructible animals –
Me – who stand here on the edge of death,
Seeking the continuity,

The germ plasm, of history,
The epic's lyric absolute.

What happened, and what is remembered –
Or – history is the description
Of those forms of man's activity
Where value survives at the lowest
Level necessary to insure
Temporal continuity.
Or "as the Philosopher says,"
The historian differs from
The poet in this: the historian
Presents what did happen, the poet,
What might happen. For this reason
Poetry is more philosophic
Than history, and less trivial.
Poetry presents generalities,
History merely particulars.
So action is generalized
Into what an essential person
Must do by virtue of his essence –
Acting in an imaginary
Order of being, where existence
And essence, as in the Deity
Of Aquinas, fuse in pure act.
What happens in the mere occasion
To human beings is recorded
As an occurrence in the gulf
Between essence and existence –
An event of marginal content.

In the artificially bright
Evening of the clocks of war,
In the last Passover of the just,
We too prepare symbolic supper.
The low fog coils across the sun,
And falls back, and the powerful

Gold Aton blades of the desert sun
Shine again on the desert land
And over the fogbound ocean.
One side of the canyon is frigid
With shadow, and the other busy
In the dense heat. I build the fire
At the stream's edge. The flames are pale
In the sunlight, thick and fleshy
In the reflections on the water.
While I wait for the water to boil
I stand, abstract, one breathing man,
On the suture of desert, sea,
And running water brief as Spring.
Sagebrush and seaweed, sand and granite.
Mice and plankton, sterile and swarming,
Steam and spume, inhale and exhale –
Out of this the ancient Chinese
Built up their whole cosmology –
Rest that dissipates into motion,
And motion that freezes into rest.
And you ride up, hungry, shouting
For supper, on a red stallion,
Breasts quivering in their silk blouse.
Yin and Yang… possibly history
Is only an irritability,
A perversion of the blood's chemistry,
The after effects of a six thousand
Years dead solar cyclone.

In the twilight…
Here, on the soft unblemished skin,
Where ear and jaw and throat are joined,
Where a flush begins to spread
Under the glittering down;
Here, where the gracious eyebrow
Tapers over the orbit and onto the edge
Of the blue shadowed temple;
Here, on the lips curled back

To begin a smile, showing the teeth
And the tongue tip... kisses in the evening,
After supper on the anniversary
Of the white gift of sacramental flesh.

Of what body. Through what years. In what light.

Value and fact are polar aspects
Of organic process. As plus
Is to minus a value: "virtue"
And minus is privative "fact";
So minus is to virtue, "sin."
That is, quality is the aspect
Assumed in perspective of polar
Antitheses of achievement.
How comfortable, and how verbal.

The free laughter and the ivory feet
Treading the grapes – the tousled hair –
The dark juice rising between the thighs
Of the laughing, falling girl, spreading
Through the dark pubic hair, over
The laughing belly.

                    The law by which
We live is the law by which we die.
Again, "as the Philosopher says,"
The ground of individuation
Is the ground of communication.
As pure potentials, the mistresses
Of Alexander and the bedmates
Of the perdurable fellahin
Return finally from history
To the common ground of all discourse.

Found in the smashed tent on Everest –
"Dear Noel,
            We'll probably start

early tomorrow (8th) in order
to have clear weather. It wont be
too early to start looking out
for us either crossing the neckband
under the pyramid or going
up to the skyline at 8 p.m.
yours ever,
Geo. Mallory"

When process is defined as the field
Suspended between positive
And negative, the Absolute One
And the Absolute Many, the poles
Of being short circuit in reason.
The definition dissolves itself.
Anode and cathode deliquesce
By virtue of inherent structure.
Unavoidably the procedures
Of logic flatter the Deity.

Not want and fear, but the rigid
Vectors of the fallible mind
Confuse all pantheons and haunt
Geometries – and if not fear
And danger, then danger and desire.
Always the struggle to break out
Of the argument that proves itself,
Past procedure as perimeter,
Past the molecular landslide,
Past the centrifugal perspectives
Of precipitous gain and loss,
Past the attrition of estate…
On the frontiers, all boundaries fuse,
Peaks, passes and glaciers, kisses,
Lips and epistemologies.
And the wardens of ontology,
The lethal sophists and policemen,

Patrol the surveyed boundaries.
In the bistros and academies
Rhetoricians seek the absolute
Hallucination. In the bureaux
Of policy it is put in practice.
History is the chronicle
Of the more spectacular failures
To discover vital conflict.

Not want and fear, but danger and desire…
Contemporary mysticism
Accounts for all motivation
By the bitch's tit and the dropped pup.
(The vectors don't explain themselves.)
Well might the aging précieux cry out,
"Zénon! Cruel Zénon d'Elée!"
Or turgid Webster lucidly say,
"Like diamonds we are cut with our own dust."

Danger and desire, or jealousy
And fear of pain, the constant pressure
For the lesser, immediate, good…
The three tragedians saw lives
As strung on doom, like the lion's teeth
On his still tensile sinews;
Persons as trophies, the savage
Jewelry of continuity
From "pure function to pure potential,"
And Karma, the terrifying
Accumulation of bare fact.
And in dynamic antithesis,
The person as priest and victim –
The fulfillment of uniqueness
In perfect identification,
In ideal representation,
As the usurping attorney,
The real and effective surrogate.

Iphigenia at Aulis –
The ritual person emerges
As term of responsibility.
Doom or responsibility –
Fashionable superstition builds
The world from "intervals at which
Accidents are likely to happen."
Catastrophic contingency
In physics or theology,
God as pure fiat, the person
As pure caprice, ends in the worship
Of history as demonic will,
The pandemic destroying Europe.

The lucid Socratic drama
Defines tragedy by example;
Aristotle's recipe book
Neglects to explain why tragedy
Is tragic, the hero, heroic.
Even the Angelic Doctor,
When he came to deal with angels,
That is, personality as such,
Produced the perfect anti-person.
Scotus – Luther – Kierkegaard – Barth –
The dark Gothic demonolatry,
Or the spotless imitation man,
One of David's noble lay figures –
The Oath of the Horatii –
The flesh made of highly polished lead.

The problem of personality
Is the problem of the value
Of the world as a totality,
The problem of immortality
As a basic category –
That passed away, so will this.
The moraine creeps on the meadow;
The temples dissolve in the jungle;

The patterns abide and reassert
Themselves; the texture wears through the nap.

All the terminals coalesce
In the region that defines reason.
In this wilderness as men say
Are the trees of the Sun and the Moon
That spake to King Alexander
And told him of his death.

And they took
The head of Bran, and came to Harlech
And the three birds of Rhiannon
Came and sang to them for seven years;
And it seemed as though the birds were far
Distant over the sea, and yet
They were clear, and distinct, and close.
And they went to Gwales in Penvro
To a kingly and spacious hall
That overlooked the sea. And the third
Door that looked towards Cornwall was closed.
And they placed the head in high honor,
And dined and drank and were happy,
And remembered none of their sorrow.
And after fourscore years, on a day,
Heilyn ap Gwynn opened the door
To see if Bran had spoken the truth.
And they looked out over Cornwall
And Aber Henvelen, and as they looked,
They saw all the evils they had suffered,
And all the companions they had lost,
And all the old misery, and the death
Of their good lord, all as though once again,
It was happening there, in that same spot.
And they could not stay, but went to London,
And buried the head in the White Mount.

The perfect circle. The perfect term.

Endurance, novelty, and simple
Occurrence – and here I am, a node
In a context of disasters,
Still struggling with the old question,
Often and elaborately begged.
The atoms of Lucretius still,
Falling, inexplicably swerve.
And the generation that purposed
To control history vanishes
In its own apotheosis
Of calamity, unable
To explain why anything
Should happen at all.

One more Spring, and after the bees go,
The soft moths stagger in the firelight;
And silent, vertiginous, sliding,
The great owls hunt low in the air;
And the dwarf owls speak at their burrows.
We walk under setting Orion,
Once more in the dim boom of the sea,
Between bearded, dying apple trees,
In the shadows of the Easter moon;
And silent, vertiginous, the stars
Slide over us past the equinox.
The flowers whirl away in the wind like snow.
The thing that falls away is myself.
The moonlight of the Resurrection,
The moon of Amida on the sea,
Glitters on the wings of the bombers,
Illuminates the darkened cities.
The motion of Egyptian chisels
Dissolves slowly in the desert noon.

It is past midnight and the faint,
Myriad crying of the seabirds
Enters my sleep. The wind rises.

I hear the unbelievably
Distant voices of the multitudes
Of men mewing in the thoroughfares
Of dreams. The waves crowd on the beach.
A log falls in the fire. The wind
Funnels the sparks out in the moonlight
Like a glowing tree dragged through dark.
I see in sudden total vision
The substance of entranc'd Boehme's awe:
The illimitable hour glass
Of the universe eternally
Turning, and the gold sands falling
From God, and the silver sands rising
From God, the double splendors of joy
That fuse and divide again
In the narrow passage of the Cross.

The source of individuation –
The source of communication –
Peace, the conservation of value –

Came Jesus and stood in the midst, and
Saith unto them, "Peace be unto you."
And when he had so said, he shewed
Unto them his hands and his side.

The fire is dense again in the dark.
I turn my face into shadow
And fall again towards sleep,

Amida,
Kwannon, turn from peace. As moonlight
Flows on the tides, innumerable
Dark worlds flow into splendor.

How many nights have we awakened –
The killdeer crying in the seawind.

II

I am cold in my folded blanket,
Huddled on the ground in the moonlight.

The crickets cry in congealing frost;
Field mice run over my body;
The frost thickens and the night goes by.

North of us lies the vindictive
Foolish city asleep under its guns;
Its rodent ambitions washing out
In sewage and unwholesome dreams.
Behind the backs of drowsy sentries
The moonlight shines through frosted glass –
On the floors of innumerable
Corridors the mystic symbols
Of the bureaucrats are reversed –
Mirrorwise, as Leonardo
Kept the fever charts of one person.
Two Ptahs, two Muhammad's coffins,
We float in the illimitable
Surgery of moonlight, isolate
From each other and the turning earth;
Motionless; frost on our faces;
Eyes by turns alive, dark in the dark.

The State is the organization
Of the evil instincts of mankind.
History is the penalty
We pay for original sin.
In the conflict of appetite
And desire, the person finally
Loses; either the technology
Of the choice of a lesser evil
Overwhelms him; or a universe

Where the stars in their courses move
To ends that justify their means
Dissolves him in its elements.
He cannot win, not on this table.
The World, the Flesh, and the Devil –
The Tempter offered Christ mastery
Of the three master institutions,
Godparents of all destruction –
"Miracle, Mystery, and Authority" –
The systematization of
Appetitive choice to obtain
Desire by accumulation.

History continuously
Bleeds to death through a million secret
Wounds of trivial hunger and fear.
Its stockholders' private disasters
Are amortized in catastrophe.

War is the health of the State? Indeed!
War is the State. All personal
Anti-institutional values
Must be burnt out of each generation.
If a massive continuum
Of personality endured
Into grandchildren, history
Would stop.

"As the Philosopher says,"
Man is a social animal;
That is, top dog of a slave state.
All those lucid, noble minds admired
Sparta, and well they might. Surely
It is highly questionable
If Plato's thesis can be denied.
The Just Man is the Citizen.

Wars exist to take care of persons.
The species affords no aberrants.

Barmaid of Syria, her hair bound
In a Greek turban, her flanks
Learnedly swaying, shivering
In the shiver of castanets,
Drunk, strutting lasciviously
In the smoke filled tavern…

What nexus gathers and dissolves here
In the fortuitous unity
Of revolving night and myself?
They say that history, defining
Responsibility in terms
Of the objective continuum,
Limits, and at the same time creates,
Its participants. They further say
That rational existence is
Essentially harmonic selection.
Discarding "is," the five terms
Are equated, the argument closed.
Cogito and Ergo and Sum play
Leapfrog – fact – process – process – fact –
Between my sleeping body and
The galaxy what Homeric
Heroes struggle for my arms?

Fact and value, process and value,
"Process, not result of judgment,"
Or, result, not process of judgment,
Or, judgment, not result of process,
Or, judgment of result, not process,
The possible combinations
Can be found by arithmetic
Or learned in the School of Experience.
The whalebone sieves the whale food

From the plankton, the plankton
Finally dissolves the whale,
Liberating the whalebone.
Liberty is the mother
Not the daughter of order.

Value evolves in decision;
History passes, pedetentim;
The results of decision dissolve.
The assumption of history
Is that the primary vehicle
Of social memory is the State.

The nighthawks cry in the saffron
Twilight over the smoky streets
Of Chicago. It is Summer.
Victimae paschali, the wise
Jubilant melody of the
Easter Sequence breaks in the Mass.
The song of the monks is like laughter.
It is Spring, intense and sunlit.
The fieldpieces bang on the warped streets
Of Boston. Riots sweep over the world.
Midsummer – the harvest over.
The American polity
Discards its chrysalis of myth.
Ribbentrop and Stalin exchange smirks,
The fruit falls from the tree. Summer ends.

Was it Carnot who said, "The end
Justifies the means"? Or was it Marx?
Or Adams? "As teleology
Subsides to a minimum, achievement
Rises to a maximum." "The sum
Of conflagration is tepidity."
The infinitely cool, Virgin
Of Dynamo; the term: entropy

Or fecundity; the bleak Yankee
Purposiveness always gnawing:
"You have nothing to lose but your chains."
They are willing to pay any price.
They can be bought for any price.

As the Philosopher says,
That only is natural which contains
The principle of its own change within
Itself; what comes by chance is accident.
Being is statistical likelihood;
Actuaries conjure the actual.
In the words of the Stagirite,
"Nature comes apart at the joints."
Or, a theory of history,
"Physiologists and physicians
Have a fuller knowledge of the human
Body than the most anxious mother."

"The inhabitants of the world
At each successive period
In its history have beaten
Their predecessors in the race
For life, and are, in so far, higher
In the scale." So Darwin himself.
Natura non facit saltum.
The Franciscan series under me
Revolves with the planet, a mile thick
Mummy of blank catastrophe.

Gilbert White in his garden, Darwin
Poking around on the *Beagle*,
Franklin vanishing in the Arctic,
"There is no such thing as negative
Historical evidence."

The vast onion of the actual:
The universe, the galaxy,

The solar system, and the earth,
And life, and human life, and men's
Relationships, and men, and each man…

History seeping from capsule
To capsule, from periphery
To center, and outward again…
The sparkling quanta of events,
The pulsing wave motion of value…

Marx. Kropotkin. Adams. Acton.
Spengler, Toynbee. Tarn building empires
From a few coins found in a cellar…
History… the price we pay for man's
First disobedience… John of Patmos,
The philosopher of history.

His body huddled on the whirling
Earth, dipping the surface of sleep
As damsel flies sting the water's skin
With life. What is half remembered
In the hypnogogy of time;
Ineradicable bits of tune;
Nicias in rout from Syracuse;
Scarlet Wolsey splendid on the Field
Of the Cloth of Gold; More on trial;
Abélard crying for that girl;
"More than my brother, Jonathan,
Of one soul with me,
What sin, what pollution,
Has torn our bowels asunder."
The burnt out watch fires of Modena;
Or Phoebi claro – love, dawn, and fear
Of treacherous death; the enervated
Musical, dim edge of sleep;
Archdeacon Stuck on McKinley
Singing, "Te Deum laudamus…"
In the clenching cold and the thin air;

Lawrence dying of his body,
Blue gentians burning in the dark mind;
The conflict of events and change.

In their hour the constellations
Of Autumn mount guard over me –
Aquarius and Capricorn,
Watchers of my birth and of the turn
Of the apocalyptic future;
Noah and Pan in deadly conflict,
Watched by Fomalhaut's cold, single eye.
These are the stars that marched over
Boethius in meditation,
Waiting the pleasure of the Goth;
And once Chinese philosophers
Saw all the visible planets
In conjunction in Capricorn,
Two thousand, four hundred, forty-nine
Years before Christ.

The thinne fame
Yit lasting, of hir ydel names,
Is marked with a fewe lettres...

Loken up-on the brode shewinge
Contrees of hevene, and up-on
The streit site of this erthe...

Liggeth thanne stille, all outrely
Unknowable; ne fame maketh yow
Not know.

III

Softly and singly an owl
Cries in my sleep. I awake and turn
My head, but there is only the moon

Sinking in the early dawn.
Owls do not cry over the ocean.
The night patrol planes return
Opaque against the transparent moon.
"The owl of Minerva," says Hegel,
"Takes her flight in the evening."
It is terrible to lie
Beside my wife's canvas chrysalis,
Watching the imperceptible
Preparation of morning,
And think that this probably is not
The historical evening we thought;
Waking in the twilight like bemused
Drunkards; but the malignant
Dawn of the literate insect,
Dispassionate, efficient, formic.

Irrelevant appetite dissolves
The neurones of a deranged nation –
Nucleus of alcohol, fibers
"Meandering in pellucid gold."
Remorse and guilt stiffen the tissues
With hypnotic dread of penitence.
Stone lodges against the heart
A blank total of catastrophe –
The bloody heart, suspicious
And ruined, but still the irritant
In the vitals of this iron mollusc,
Still the cause of its daily
Frightened secretions of mud.

The ant has perfect statistical
Intelligence, "a thoroughly
Humean approach to the problem
Of causality." History starts
With the dislocation of units,
The creation of persons,

A phenomenon of diffusion
In the high tension gap between
Technology and environment.
On the edges of riparian
Egypt and Mesopotamia
The dense family societal body
Acquired leucocytes within
And parasites without. "History
Is the instability
Of the family constellation."
Its goal is the achievement
Of the completely atomic
Individuality and the pure
Commodity relationship –
The windowless monad sustained
By Providence. History
Ceases in a change of phase –
The polarization of its parts
In a supernatural kindred.

Shogun or Mikado – the Sun King
Eighteen centuries before Christ
Or after – amateur lockmakers
With pussy mistresses – the pure form
Of the cutting edge of power –
Man reduced to an entelechy –
"I lay down my pen in horror,
Not at the thought of Ivan's
Atrocities, but at the thought
That high minded, noble men
For years found it expedient
To bow to his will, to act
As instruments of his monstrous crimes."
"Politics is the art of choosing
The lesser evil." "The State, that's me."
Splendid as a rococo
Sunburst, with its powdered face buried

In the immortal buttocks
Of little Murphy, St. Thomas More
Or venereal Anne Boleyn –
Posterity in gratuity
Has provided both with beautiful
Apocryphal testaments.

The flow of interoffice
Memoranda charts the excretions
Of societal process,
The cast snakeskin, the fleeting
Quantum, Economic Man.
Novelty comes to be considered
The unpredictable, process
The clean columbarium
Of consumed statistical
Probabilities. Pascal
Merges with Hume; the stresses
Of the architecture are computed
By roulette; "the foundations
Are ingeniously supported
By the superstructure"; the agent
For insurance evicts that agent
Once thought more noble than the patient,
And his ontology along with him.
In the words of the Philosopher
King, Faustina's husband, "If I don't,
Somebody else will. Think of the good
I can do with my authority."
John Maynard Keynes visits the White House.

"Salvation equals autonomy."
All major religions have said so,
Whatever their founders thought.
Six thousand years of struggle
For autonomy, and what's to pay?
The terrified Phi Beta Kappas

Cower behind the columns
They afforded the masses,
Whispering, "E pluribus unum."
Or the Sufi, shrouded in white wool,
Meditating in dead Ctesiphon,
Spinning the erotic metaphors
Of self abandonment – wine, rubies
And perfumed buttocks – for the jackals
And cactus – the slow self destruction
Of the human, consumed away
By the inaccessible sun
Of absolute unity.

Hippias and Socrates
Contending for the title
Of Most Autonomous Greek.
Hippias who duplicated
The cube; who came to Olympia
With all that he had about
His body the work of his own hand –
A ring and seal, a strigil
And vanity case, high shoes and cloak,
And underwear, and a belt,
A perfect imitation
Of the finest Persian leather work;
Who came to Olympia
Carrying tragedies, dithyrambs,
Epics, learned treatises,
And all of his own composition,
Rhetorically sublime,
Grammatically immaculate,
Besides a system of mnemonics;
Who stood in public in all
The Greek cities and had an answer
For all questions; who came to Sparta
With a theory of the Beautiful
All his own, and many ingenious

Contrivances in mathematics,
And found a people interested
Only in archaeology
And history – their own history
And the ruins they had made elsewhere.
And Socrates, playing practical
Jokes on the imperium.
As the Philosopher says,
"All men desire to know." A highly
Undetermined appetite.

Atomization versus
Autonomy – the odds are with
The side with the most matériel.
The most resistant elements break
Under sixty centuries
Of attrition; only a species
Of hysteresis preserves
A sort of residue, overplus
Of past renunciation.
The saint becomes a madman,
The sage a crank, the beggar
A pauper, the courtesan
A whore or enthusiast.
Time's crystals lodge against the bitter
Heart at last, even the perfected
Heart of flesh.

Eva and Ave,
The swords of history – jealousy,
The fear of autonomous action,
The sharer of the gaudy apple
Of Atalanta and Paris,
Persephone's parchment red
Globule and its carbon chromosomes,
The germ of gold and the counter-heart;
And conversely, the hara-kiri

Sword of history, the goal
Of pure undetermined fiat,
Duns Scotus' Immaculate Virgin,
The sentimental climax
Of aged Goethe's vision,
"The form of the cutting edge –"
And as contradictory, Murphy
Cuddling that sword in tickles,
And lovely bemused Lesbia
Kneeling in every Roman alley.

And somewhere the irreducible
Fused unity and duality,
The fluent, liquid source of number.
The busy Myrmidons, those sly men,
Retreat to the last river,
The continuity of the germ plasm,
The animal tribute to a brief
Eternity. The Philosopher:
"Matter is the tendency
To immediate ends. An exact
And adequate material force
Must always deflect another force.
As the new form evolves, the prior
Recedes reciprocally into
Pure potentiality."

The institution is a device
For providing molecular
Process with delusive credentials.
"Value is the reflection
Of satisfied appetite,
The formal aspect of the tension
Generated by resolution
Of fact." Overspecialization,
Proliferation, gigantism.

Would it have been better to have slept
And dreamed, than to have watched night
Pass and this slow moon sink? My wife sleeps
And her dreams measure the hours
As accurately as my
Meditations in cold solitude.
I have lain awake while the moon crossed,
Dragging at the tangled ways
Of the sea and the tangled, blood filled
Veins of sleepers. I am not alone,
Caught in the turning of the seasons.
As the long beams of the setting moon
Move against the breaking day,
The suspended light pulsates
Like floating snow. Involuntary,
I may live on, sustained in the web
Of accident, never forgetting
This midnight moon that already blurs
In memory.
                    As certain
As color passes from the petal,
Irrevocable as flesh,
The gazing eye falls through the world.
As the light breaks over the water
One by one, pedetentim,
The stakes of the nets appear
Stretching far out into the shallows,
And beyond them the dark animal
Shadow of a camouflaged cruiser.

IV

Dark within dark I cling to sleep,
The heart's capsule closed in the fist
Of circumstance; prison within
Prison, inseparably dark,
I struggle to hold oblivion

As Jacob struggled in a dream,
And woke touched and with another name.
And on the thin brainpan of sleep
The mill of Gaza grinds;
The heart condenses; and beyond
The world's lip the sun to me is dark
And silent as the moon that falls
Through the last degrees of night into
The unknown antipodes. I lie
At random, carelessly diffused,
Stone and amoeba on the verge
Of partition; and beyond the reach
Of my drowsy integrity,
The race of glory and the race
Of shame, just or unjust, alike
Miserable, both come to evil end.

Eventually history
Distills off all accumulated
Values but one. Babies are more
Durable than monuments, the rose
Outlives Ausonius, Ronsard,
And Waller, and Horace's pear tree
His immortal column. Once more
Process is precipitated
In the tirelessly receptive womb.
In the decay of the sufficient
Reasonableness of sacraments
Marriage holds by its bona fides.

Beneath what shield and from what flame.

The darkness gathers about Lawrence
Dying by the dead Mediterranean –
Catullus is psychoanalyzed
Between wars in lickerish London.
Another aging précieux

Drinks cognac, dreams of rutting children
In the Mississippi Valley,
Watches the Will destroy the logic
Of Christopher Wren and Richelieu.
Schweitzer plays Bach in the jungle.
It is all over – just and unjust.
The seed leaks through the gravel.

The light grows stronger and my lids
That were black turn red; the blood turns
To the coming sun. I sit up
And look out over the bright quiet
Sea and the blue and yellow cliffs
And the pure white tatters of fog
Dissolving on the black fir ridges.
The world is immovable
And immaculate. The argument
Has come to an end; it is morning,
And in the isolating morning
The problem hangs suspended, lucid
In a crystal cabinet of air
And angels where only bird song wakes.

"Value is the elastic ether
Of quality that fills up the gaps
In the continuum of discreet
Quality – the prime togetherness."
The assumption of order,
The principle of parsimony,
Remain mysteries; fact and logic
Meet only in catastrophe.
So long ago they discovered that
Each new irrational is the start
Of a new series of numbers;
Called God the source of systematic
Irrationalization of given
Order – the organism that

Geometricizes. And that vain
Boy, systematically deranging
Himself amongst the smoky cannoneers
Of the Commune, finding a bronze
Apotheosis as the perfect
Provincial French merchant who made good.
The statistical likelihood
Of being blown to pieces.

"Value is the reflection
Of satisfied appetite."
The State organizes ecstasy.
The dinosaur wallows in the chilling
Marsh. The bombs fall on the packed dance halls.
The sperm seeks the egg in the gravel.
"Novelty is, by definition,
Value-positive."

"Value
Is a phase change in the relations
Of events." Does that mean anything?

Morning. It is Good Friday Morning;
Communion has passed to Agony
And Agony is gone and only
Responsibility remains; doom
Watches with its inorganic eyes,
The bright, blind regiments, hidden
By the sun-flushed sky, the remote
Indestructible animals.
Value, causality, being,
Are reducible to the purest
Act, the self-determining person,
He who discriminates structure
In contingency, he who assumes
All the responsibility
Of ordered, focused, potential –

Sustained by all the universe,
Focusing the universe in act –
The person, the absolute price,
The only blood defiance of doom.

Whymper, coming down the Matterhorn,
After the mountain had collected
Its terrible, casual fee,
The blackmail of an imbecile beauty:
"About 6 PM we arrived
Upon the ridge descending towards
Zermatt, and all peril was over.
We frequently looked, but in vain,
For traces of our unfortunate
Companions; we bent over the ridge
And cried to them, but no sound returned.
Convinced at last that they were neither
Within sight nor hearing we ceased;
And, too cast down for speech, silently
Gathered up our things and the little
Effects of those who were lost
And prepared to continue
The descent. When, lo! a mighty arch
And beneath it a huge cross of light
Appeared, rising above the Lyskamm
High into the sky. Pale, colorless,
And noiseless, but perfectly sharp
And defined, except where it was lost
In the clouds, this unearthly
Apparition seemed like a vision
From another world; and appalled,
We watched with amazement the gradual
Development of two vast crosses
One on either side… Our movements
Had no effect on it, the spectral
Forms remained motionless. It was
A fearful and wonderful sight;

Unique in my experience,
And impressive beyond description,
Coming at such a moment."

Nude, my feet in the cold shallows,
The motion of the water surface
Barely perceptible, and the sand
Of the bottom in fine sharp ridges
Under my toes, I wade out, waist deep
And swim seaward down the narrow inlet.
In the distance, beyond the sand bar,
The combers are breaking, and nearer,
Like a wave crest escaped and frozen,
One white egret guards the harbor mouth.
The immense stellar phenomenon
Of dawn focuses in the egret
And flows out, and focuses in me
And flows infinitely away
To touch the last galactic dust.

This is the prime reality –
Bird and man, the individual
Discriminate, the self evalued
Actual, the operation
Of infinite, ordered potential.
Birds, sand grains, and souls bleed into being;
The past reclaims its own, "I should have,
I could have – It might have been different –"
Sunsets on Saturn, desert roses,
Corruptions of the will, quality –
The determinable future, fall
Into quantity, into the
Irreparable past, history's
Cruel irresponsibility.

This is the minimum negative
Condition, the "Condition humaine,"
The tragic loss of value into
Barren novelty, the condition
Of salvation, out of this alone
The person emerges as complete
Responsible act – this lost
And that conserved – the appalling
Decision of the verb "to be."
Men drop dead in the ancient rubbish
Of the Acropolis, scholars fall
Into self-dug graves, Jews are smashed
Like heroic vermin in the Polish winter.
This is my fault, the horrible term
Of weakness, evasion, indulgence,
The total of my petty fault –
No other man's.

And out of this
Shall I reclaim beauty, peace of soul,
The perfect gift of self-sacrifice,
Myself as act, as immortal person?

I walk back along the sandspit,
The horizon cuts the moon in half,
And far out at sea a path of light,
Violent and brilliant, reflected
From high stratus clouds and then again
On the moving sea, the invisible
Sunrise spreads its light before the moon.

My wife has been swimming in the breakers,
She comes up the beach to meet me, nude,
Sparkling with water, singing high and clear
Against the surf. The sun crosses
The hills and fills her hair, as it lights

The moon and glorifies the sea
And deep in the empty mountains melts
The snow of Winter and the glaciers
Of ten thousand thousand years.

THE SIGNATURE OF ALL THINGS (1949)

For Marie

I cook young hearts
With overheated learning.
Eros is the starter of wisdom.
He lights the torches
Of the relay race of youth.
– Cephalos

BETWEEN MYSELF AND DEATH

to Jimmy Blanton's music:
SOPHISTICATED LADY, BODY AND SOUL

A fervor parches you sometimes,
And you hunch over it, silent,
Cruel, and timid; and sometimes
You are frightened with wantonness,
And give me your desperation.
Mostly we lurk in our coverts,
Protecting our spleens, pretending
That our bandages are our wounds.
But sometimes the wheel of change stops;
Illusion vanishes in peace;
And suddenly pride lights your flesh –
Lucid as diamond, wise as pearl –
And your face, remote, absolute,
Perfect and final like a beast's.
It is wonderful to watch you,
A living woman in a room
Full of frantic, sterile people,
And think of your arching buttocks
Under your velvet evening dress,
And the beautiful fire spreading
From your sex, burning flesh and bone,
The unbelievably complex
Tissues of your brain all alive
Under your coiling, splendid hair.

~

I like to think of you naked.
I put your naked body
Between myself alone and death.
If I go into my brain
And set fire to your sweet nipples,

To the tendons beneath your knees,
I can see far before me.
It is empty there where I look,
But at least it is lighted.

I know how your shoulders glisten,
How your face sinks into trance,
And your eyes like a sleepwalker's,
And your lips of a woman
Cruel to herself.
                                        I like to
Think of you clothed, your body
Shut to the world and self contained,
Its wonderful arrogance
That makes all women envy you.
I can remember every dress,
Each more proud than a naked nun.
When I go to sleep my eyes
Close in a mesh of memory.
Its cloud of intimate odor
Dreams instead of myself.

MONADS

As the sun comes in the window,
And shines through the aquarium,
The water turns green in the light.
The swirling dinoflagellates
Make rockets in their own thick clouds,
Like the rockets that plunge along
The Yosemite waterfalls.
Lucretius, Leibniz – I wonder –
Are there windows in the flagellates?
I muse over an inward picture
Of the meteoric dust

Floating in the black sea deeps
And eddying in the sunlight
In the stratosphere.

THE SIGNATURE OF ALL THINGS

My head and shoulders, and my book
In the cool shade, and my body
Stretched bathing in the sun, I lie
Reading beside the waterfall –
Boehme's *Signature of All Things.*
Through the deep July day the leaves
Of the laurel, all the colors
Of gold, spin down through the moving
Deep laurel shade all day. They float
On the mirrored sky and forest
For a while, and then, still slowly
Spinning, sink through the crystal deep
Of the pool to its leaf gold floor.
The saint saw the world as streaming
In the electrolysis of love.
I put him by and gaze through shade
Folded into shade of slender
Laurel trunks and leaves filled with sun.
The wren broods in her moss domed nest.
A newt struggles with a white moth
Drowning in the pool. The hawks scream,
Playing together on the ceiling
Of heaven. The long hours go by.
I think of those who have loved me,
Of all the mountains I have climbed,
Of all the seas I have swum in.
The evil of the world sinks.
My own sin and trouble fall away
Like Christian's bundle, and I watch

My forty summers fall like falling
Leaves and falling water held
Eternally in summer air.

~

Deer are stamping in the glades,
Under the full July moon.
There is a smell of dry grass
In the air, and more faintly,
The scent of a far off skunk.
As I stand at the wood's edge,
Watching the darkness, listening
To the stillness, a small owl
Comes to the branch above me,
On wings more still than my breath.
When I turn my light to him,
His eyes glow like drops of iron,
And he perks his head at me,
Like a curious kitten.
The meadow is bright as snow.
My dog prowls the grass, a dark
Blur in the blur of brightness.
I walk to the oak grove where
The Indian village was once.
There, in blotched and cobwebbed light
And dark, dim in the blue haze,
Are twenty Holstein heifers,
Black and white, all lying down,
Quietly together, under
The huge trees rooted in the graves.

~

When I dragged the rotten log
From the bottom of the pool,
It seemed heavy as stone.

I let it lie in the sun
For a month; and then chopped it
Into sections, and split them
For kindling, and spread them out
To dry some more. Late that night,
After reading for hours,
While moths rattled at the lamp –
The saints and the philosophers
On the destiny of man –
I went out on my cabin porch,
And looked up through the black forest
At the swaying islands of stars.
Suddenly I saw at my feet,
Spread on the floor of night, ingots
Of quivering phosphorescence,
And all about were scattered chips
Of pale cold light that was alive.

FOR A MASSEUSE AND PROSTITUTE

Nobody knows what love is anymore.
Nobody knows what happened to God.
After midnight, the lesbians and fairies
Sweep through the streets of the old tenderloin,
Like spirochetes in a softening brain.
The hustlers have all been run out of town.
I look back on the times spent
Talking with you about the idiocies
Of a collapsing world and the brutalities
Of my race and yours,
While the sick, the perverted, the malformed
Came and went, and you cooked them,
And rolled them, and beat them,
And sent them away with a little taste
Of electric life from the ends of your fingers.

Who could ever forget your amiable body,
Or your unruffled good sense,
Or your smiling sex?
I suppose your touch kept many men
As sane as they could be kept.
Every hour there is less of that touch in the world.

LYELL'S HYPOTHESIS AGAIN

An Attempt to Explain the Former
Changes of the Earth's Surface by
Causes Now in Operation
subtitle of Lyell: *Principles of Geology*

The mountain road ends here,
Broken away in the chasm where
The bridge washed out years ago.
The first scarlet larkspur glitters
In the first patch of April
Morning sunlight. The engorged creek
Roars and rustles like a military
Ball. Here by the waterfall,
Insuperable life, flushed
With the equinox, sentient
And sentimental, falls away
To the sea and death. The tissue
Of sympathy and agony
That binds the flesh in its Nessus' shirt;
The clotted cobweb of unself
And self; sheds itself and flecks
The sun's bed with darts of blossom
Like flagellant blood above
The water bursting in the vibrant
Air. This ego, bound by personal
Tragedy and the vast

Impersonal vindictiveness
Of the ruined and ruining world,
Pauses in this immortality,
As passionate, as apathetic,
As the lava flow that burned here once;
And stopped here; and said, "This far
And no further." And spoke thereafter
In the simple diction of stone.

~

Naked in the warm April air,
We lie under the redwoods,
In the sunny lee of a cliff.
As you kneel above me I see
Tiny red marks on your flanks
Like bites, where the redwood cones
Have pressed into your flesh.
You can find just the same marks
In the lignite in the cliff
Over our heads. *Sequoia*
Langsdorfii before the ice,
And *sempervirens* afterwards,
There is little difference,
Except for all those years.

Here in the sweet, moribund
Fetor of spring flowers, washed,
Flotsam and jetsam together,
Cool and naked together,
Under this tree for a moment,
We have escaped the bitterness
Of love, and love lost, and love
Betrayed. And what might have been,
And what might be, fall equally
Away with what is, and leave
Only these ideograms

Printed on the immortal
Hydrocarbons of flesh and stone.

SHARP IN MY HEART

Come, O my love, and lay you down.
Come, O my love, and lay you down.
The summer is gone,
And the leaves turn brown.

The summer is gone, and the leaves fall down.
The summer is gone, and the leaves fall down.
I loved you well,
And you did me wrong.

I loved you well, and you broke my heart.
I loved you well, and you broke my heart.
Love me once more,
And forever part.

Love me once more, though I know you lie.
Love me once more, though I know you lie.
Leave me a memory
For the day I die.

Leave me a memory that I can't forget.
Leave me a memory that I can't forget.
I can see those hours
Go past us yet.

I can see those hours, as the summer drew near.
I can see those hours, as the summer drew near.
Sharp in my heart,
Like diamonds clear.

Sharp in my heart, the leaves turn green.
Sharp in my heart, the leaves turn green.
Your innocent face
I wish I never had seen.

(Tune: in Matteson and Henry, *Beech Mountain Folk-Songs and Ballads*, Schirmer, N.Y., 1936)

BLUES

The tops of the higher peaks
Of the Sierra Nevada
Of California are
Drenched in the perfume of
A flower which grows only there –
The blue *Polemonium*
Confertum eximium,
Soft, profound blue, like the eyes
Of impregnable innocence;
The perfume is heavy and
Clings thickly to the granite
Peaks, even in violent wind;
The leaves are clustered,
Fine, dull green, sticky, and musky.
I imagine that the scent
Of the body of Artemis
That put Endymion to sleep
Was like this and her eyes had the
Same inscrutable color.
Lawrence was lit into death
By the blue gentians of Kore.
Vanzetti had in his cell
A bowl of tall blue flowers
From a New England garden.
I hope that when I need it

My mind can always call back
This flower to its hidden senses.

YUGAO

Tonight is clearer and colder.
The new half moon slides through clouds.
The air is full of the poignant
Odor of frost drying earth.
Late night, the stillness grows more still.
At last, nothing moves, no sound,
Even the shunting freight trains
In the distance stop.
                                        I go out
Into the ominous dark,
Into the garden crowded with
Invisible, impalpable
Movement. The air is breathless
Under the trees. High overhead,
The wind plunges with the moon
Through breaking and driving clouds.
I seem to stand in the midst
Of an incomprehensible
Tragedy; as though a world
Doubled against this were tearing
Through the thin shell of night;
As though something earth bound with its
Own glamorous violence
Struggled beside me in the dark.
On such nights as this the young
Warriors of old time take form
In the Noh plays; and, it may be,
Some distraught, imagined girl,
Amalfi's duchess, Electra,
Struggles like an ice bound swan,

Out of the imagination,
Toward a body, beside me,
Beyond the corner of the eye;
Or, may be, some old jealousy
Or hate I have forgotten
Still seeks flesh to walk in life.
If so, I cannot see her.
I can call, plain to the mind's eye,
Your bright sleeping head, nested
In its pillow, and your face, sure
And peaceful as your moving
Breath. You, wandering in your dream,
Watched over by your love for me.

JANUARY NIGHT

late, after walking for hours on the beach,
a storm rises, with wind, rain, and lightning

In front of me on my desk
Is typewriter and paper,
And my beautiful jagged
Crystal, larger than a skull,
And beyond, the black window,
Framing the wet and swarming
Pointillism of the city
In the night, in the valley
And spread on the distant hills
Under the rain, and beyond,
Thin rivulets of lightning
Trickling down the sky,
And all the intervening
Air wet with the fecundity
Of time and the promises
Of the earth and its routine

Annual and diurnal
Yearly and daily changeless
Motion; and once more my hours
Turn in the trough of winter
And climb towards the sun.

DELIA REXROTH

California rolls into
Sleepy summer, and the air
Is full of the bitter sweet
Smoke of the grass fires burning
On the San Francisco hills.
Flesh burns so, and the pyramids
Likewise, and the burning stars.
Tired tonight, in a city
Of parvenus, in the inhuman
West, in the most blood drenched year,
I took down a book of poems
That you used to like, that you
Used to sing to music I
Never found anywhere again –
Michael Field's book, *Long Ago*.
Indeed it's long ago now –
Your bronze hair and svelte body.
I guess you were a fierce lover,
A wild wife, an animal
Mother. And now life has cost
Me more years, though much less pain,
Than you had to pay for it.
And I have bought back, for and from
Myself, these poems and paintings,
Carved from the protesting bone,
The precious consequences
Of your torn and distraught life.

HOJOKI

Spring

Venus in the pale green sky
Where the Pleiades glimmer
Under a bar of dark cloud,
The moon travels through the L
Formed by Jupiter and Saturn
In conjunction below Gemini –
The year marches through the stars
Orion again walks into the sea.
The horned owl sits on the tree
By my hut and watches me
As I gather a handful
Of sticks and boil my rice.
He stays there through the growing dusk,
I can hardly see him when
He flies off in the starlight.

Spring

Fine warm rain falls through the maple
And laurel leaves, and fills the narrow
Gorge with a pulse like life.
The waterfall is muffled,
And my ten foot square hut lies
In the abysm of a sea
Of sibilant quiet.

Autumn

I lay aside the Diurnal
At the light drenched poetry
Of St. Ambrose that converted
St. Augustine to a world
More luminous and more lucid

Than one where light warred with dark.
I ponder what it is I find
Here by my hut in the speech
Of falling water's swift conjunction.
What have men ever found?
I think of Buddha's infinite
Laugh in the Lankavatara,
Lighting up all the universes.
The steep sides of the gorge enclose
Me like the thighs of a girl's
Body of bliss, and illusion,
And law. The end of dry autumn –
The narrow water whispers
Like the rustle of sheer, stiff silk.

Summer

A thing unknown for years,
Rain falls heavily in June,
On the ripe cherries, and on
The half cut hay.
Above the glittering
Grey water of the inlet,
In the driving, light filled mist,
A blue heron
Catches mice in the green
And copper and citron swathes.
I walk on the rainy hills.
It is enough.

Winter

Very late, a thin wash
Of cirrus cloud covers half
The sky and obscures
A three quarter moon.
Since midnight it has turned warmer.

There will be rain before morning.
There is no wind.
Everything holds still
In the vaporous light.
I walk along the stream.
Its voices are rich and subdued.
The alders overhead blend their bare twigs
And catkins with the moonlit clouds
Into one indistinct, netted haze.
The hills, covered with wet young grass,
Are intangible as billows of fog.
The decaying leaves on the path
Break the light into a hazy shimmer.
The thin bladed laurel leaves
Look like Su Tung-p'o's bamboos.
Two deer bounce away from me
Through the woods, in and out
Of the shadows like puffs of smoke.
The moon grows very dim.
The air does not move at all.
The stream deepens its voices.
I turn to go back to my hut,
And come on the cloudy moon
And the light filled sky
Reflected through the bare branches
In a boundless, velvety pool.
I stand and gaze and remember
That if this were my home country,
In a few hours, slow, still, wet, huge,
Flakes of snow would be falling
Through the windless dawn.

Spring

I sit under the old oak,
And gaze at the white orchard,
In bloom under the full moon.

The oak purrs like a lion,
And seems to quiver and breathe.
I am startled until I
Realize that the beehive
In the hollow trunk will be
Busy all night long tonight.

ANDRÉE REXROTH

Mt. Tamalpais

The years have gone. It is spring
Again. Mars and Saturn will
Soon come on, low in the West,
In the dusk. Now the evening
Sunlight makes hazy girders
Over Steep Ravine above
The waterfalls. The winter
Birds from Oregon, robins
And varied thrushes, feast on
Ripe toyon and madrone
Berries. The robins sing as
The dense light falls.
                                        Your ashes
Were scattered in this place. Here
I wrote you a farewell poem,
And long ago another,
A poem of peace and love,
Of the lassitude of a long
Spring evening in youth. Now
It is almost ten years since
You came here to stay. Once more,
The pussy willows that come
After the New Year in this

Outlandish land are blooming.
There are deer and raccoon tracks
In the same places. A few
New sand bars and cobble beds
Have been left where erosion
Has gnawed deep into the hills.
The rounds of life are narrow.
War and peace have passed like ghosts.
The human race sinks towards
Oblivion. A bittern
Calls from the same rushes where
You heard one on our first year
In the West; and where I heard
One again in the year
Of your death.

Kings River Canyon

My sorrow is so wide
I cannot see across it;
And so deep I shall never
Reach the bottom of it.
The moon sinks through deep haze,
As though the Kings River Canyon
Were filled with fine, warm, damp gauze.
Saturn gleams through the thick light
Like a gold, wet eye; nearby,
Antares glows faintly,
Without sparkle. Far overhead,
Stone shines darkly in the moonlight –
Lookout Point, where we lay
In another full moon, and first
Peered down into this canyon.
Here we camped, by still autumnal
Pools, all one warm October.
I baked you a bannock birthday cake.

Here you did your best paintings –
Innocent, wondering landscapes.
Very few of them are left
Anywhere. You destroyed them
In the terrible trouble
Of your long sickness. Eighteen years
Have passed since that autumn.
There was no trail here then.
Only a few people knew
How to enter this canyon.
We were all alone, twenty
Miles from anybody;
A young husband and wife,
Closed in and wrapped about
In the quiet autumn,
In the sound of quiet water,
In the turning and falling leaves,
In the wavering of innumerable
Bats from the caves, dipping
Over the odorous pools
Where the great trout drowsed in the evenings.

Eighteen years have been ground
To pieces in the wheels of life.
You are dead. With a thousand
Convicts they have blown a highway
Through Horseshoe Bend. Youth is gone,
That only came once. My hair
Is turning grey and my body
Heavier. I too move on to death.
I think of Henry King's stilted
But desolated *Exequy*,
Of Yuan Chen's great poem,
Unbearably pitiful;
Alone by the Spring river
More alone than I had ever
Imagined I would ever be,

I think of Frieda Lawrence,
Sitting alone in New Mexico,
In the long drought, listening
For the hiss of the milky Isar,
Over the cobbles, in a lost Spring.

A LETTER TO WILLIAM CARLOS WILLIAMS

Dear Bill,

When I search the past for you,
Sometimes I think you are like
St. Francis, whose flesh went out
Like a happy cloud from him,
And merged with every lover –
Donkeys, flowers, lepers, suns –
But I think you are more like
Brother Juniper, who suffered
All indignities and glories
Laughing like a gentle fool.
You're in the *Fioretti*
Somewhere, for you're a fool, Bill,
Like the Fool in Yeats, the term
Of all wisdom and beauty.
It's you, stands over against
Helen in all her wisdom,
Solomon in all his glory.

Remember years ago, when
I told you you were the first
Great Franciscan poet since
The Middle Ages? I disturbed
The even tenor of dinner.
Your wife thought I was crazy.
It's true, though. And you're "pure," too,

A real classic, though not loud
About it – a whole lot like
The girls of the Anthology.
Not like strident Sappho, who
For all her grandeur, must have
Had endometriosis,
But like Anyte, who says
Just enough, softly, for all
The thousands of years to remember.

It's a wonderful quiet
You have, a way of keeping
Still about the world, and its
Dirty rivers, and garbage cans,
Red wheelbarrows glazed with rain,
Cold plums stolen from the icebox,
And Queen Anne's lace, and day's eyes,
And leaf buds bursting over
Muddy roads, and splotched bellies
With babies in them, and Cortes
And Malinche on the bloody
Causeway, the death of the flower world.

Nowadays, when the press reels
With chatterboxes, you keep still,
Each year a sheaf of stillness,
Poems that have nothing to say,
Like the stillness of George Fox,
Sitting still under the cloud
Of all the world's temptation,
By the fire, in the kitchen,
In the Vale of Beavor. And
The archetype, the silence
Of Christ, when he paused a long
Time and then said, "Thou sayest it."

Now in a recent poem you say,
"I who am about to die."
Maybe this is just a tag
From the classics, but it sends
A shudder over me. Where
Do you get that stuff, Williams?
Look at here. The day will come
When a young woman will walk
By the lucid Williams River,
Where it flows through an idyllic
News from Nowhere sort of landscape,
And she will say to her children,
"Isn't it beautiful? It
Is named after a man who
Walked here once when it was called
The Passaic, and was filthy
With the poisonous excrements
Of sick men and factories.
He was a great man. He knew
It was beautiful then, although
Nobody else did, back there
In the Dark Ages. And the
Beautiful river he saw
Still flows in his veins, as it
Does in ours, and flows in our eyes,
And flows in time, and makes us
Part of it, and part of him.
That, children, is what is called
A sacramental relationship.
And that is what a poet
Is, children, one who creates
Sacramental relationships
That last always."
    With love and admiration,
    Kenneth Rexroth.

MAXIMIAN, ELEGY V

for Mildred

The sky is perfectly clear.
Motionless in the moonlight,
The redwood forest descends
Three thousand feet to the sea,
To the unmoving, silent,
Thick, white fog bank that stretches
Westward to the horizon.
No sound rises from the sea;
And the forest is soundless.
Here in the open windows,
Watching the night together,
I cannot understand what
You murmur, singing sweetly,
Softly, to yourself, in French.
O lady, you are learned,
In your hands as they touch me,
In lips that sing obscurely,
In secret, your private songs.
Your face looks white and frozen
In the moonlight, and your eyes
Glitter, rigid and immense.
The illusion of moonlight
Makes you look terror stricken.
And behind you the firelight
Draws black and red frightening
Toppling patterns on the walls.
An airplane crosses, low down,
And fills the landscape with noise
Like an hallucination.
Alive or dead, the stiff heart,
As the hours slide through moonlight,
Squeezes blood and memory.
The fog climbs up the mountain,

And leaves only one star in
The fog bound wood, like an eye
In a tomb. Without warning
Your voice breaks, and your face
Streams with tears, and you stagger
Against me. I do not speak,
But hold you still in my arms.
Finally you say, "I am not
Weeping for our own troubles,
But for the general chaos
Of the world." I feel you hurling
Away, abandoned on
A parachute of ruin.
A violent shuddering
Overcomes me, as though all
The women like you who had
Ever lived, had stepped across my grave.

BLOOD AND SAND

If there ever was a spoiled darling,
It was you, García Lorca.
The sensation of three continents,
That was you, García Lorca.
You were asked to dinner everywhere.
You were divine, Federico.
What went on in you, Federico,
Orestes doubling for Dwight Fiske?
Everyone threw his love at your head,
Those ailing loves, Federico,
With the channering worm in their garlands.
Hot Spain showed you her bare belly.
You saw the black solar plexus
Hollow with maggots. No love there.
No love. You made a concert program

Out of synonyms for agony,
The frightful parching agony
Of the lovers of Lot's wife.
You bore your own caesarian
Children daily, and all black stones.
They kept you pregnant, Federico,
With the chemicals of their unlust,
With their ugly devouring sperm,
With their pustulant, corrosive blood.
You watched the monster, Federico,
That Yeats saw stirring in the desert.
You never took your eyes off it.
It watched you, García Lorca.
Then one day it walked. It never
Noticed you again, Federico.

THE GIANT WEAPON

Yvor Winters' new book comes on the anniversary of the day that I met my wife. We read it while troop trains move in the valley below us.

Today *The Giant Weapon* came,
Fresh from the press, and fresh
From fifteen years' growth and decay –
The annual sweet flesh
Of plums in the stunning summer,
Tightening each powdered line;
The sterile heat of autumn;
Lashing rain, and sharp wine,
And talk above disordered books
In winter evenings;
And the long wet forgetful walks
Under the swallows' wings,
Trillium past the orchard's edge;

Dogs drifting to old age;
Youth sifting over the children;
Time yellowing the page.
The Giant Weapon? The pattern?
The mind? The obdurate
Flesh? Or is it perhaps Janet
And you consecrate
In duality Plato said
Was the creative source
Of the many? Weapon or tool –
The wielded sovran force
Waste nor ruin shall overcome.
Flesh dead in lethal rain,
And the vain mind dissolved in hate,
Kisses at the dark train,
And children born of dead fathers,
And pressed flowers and blood
Stained snapshots – the creative will
Stirs the seed from the mud.
And the lost world we hunted, each
In proud flesh or tough mind,
Found, in doubled vision no cost
Of time or death shall blind.

FOR THE CHINESE ACTRESS, GARDENIA CHANG

When Tu Fu was a small boy
He saw Kung Sung as she danced
With two swords, and years later
He remembered, and she lived
In his memory, always
Refining his perception,
As meditation on her
Sure grace had once taught Chang Hsu
The secret of powerful

And subtle calligraphy.
Now, days later, you are still
Clear and intact in my mind,
Your arch, small, transcendent face,
Your voice, so pure, light, and dry,
All your body's movement like
Thought in some more noble brain,
All your presence vivid as
The swords that whirled about you.
I know I shall remember
You for many, many years.
Your vision in my memory
Will teach and guide my vision,
Like the contemplation of
The deep heart of a jewel.

AUSONIUS, EPISTLE VII

A letter from a flier,
"We came back up the Moselle
In the twilight, and I thought
Of your friend Ausonius..."
Bright midnight, the Easter moon
Shepherds a sky of fleeces.
Reading, drinking Château Ausone,
I puzzle out those fluent pictures,
The footprints of Tu Fu grown old,
Hungry, lost on the Great West Road,
Dead, hostage of streams and rivers.
On the radio a piece
For the morticians, the Fauré
Requiem, sentimental,
Its themes remotely Japanese,
When they are not Gregorian;
And after it, a newscast,

The same story, fugitive,
Durable, as a torch of grass.
Paulinus and Bodhidharma,
The intact soul vanishes
In wildfire. Jungle or glacier,
The filth of the world strangles
One hundred million young men.
One hundred million men in arms!
More than lived in all Athens,
From beginning to end. Tonight,
The Feast of the Resurrection,
Easter, in a year of war,
The radio concert's choice
Is appropriate enough,
A sentimental Frenchman's
Ideas of death and rebirth,
The language of Roman ruin,
Of the fall of Jerusalem,
Tunes about cherry blossoms.
"Here alone in the night's heart,
In the midst of ten thousand sorrows,
I bribe the spring with wine."

ADVENT

for Brother Antoninus

Rorate coeli, desuper, et nubes pluant
justum. Aperiatur terra, et germinet
Salvatorem.

The year draws down. In the meadows
And high pastures, the green grass veins
The grey. Already the stubble
Fields are green. Orion stands

Another year over California,
Simple and lucent, guarding the full moon.
Dew descends from heaven
Good pours from the clouds.
The earth wavers on its whirling track.
We milk by lantern light. The shadows
Of the cattle are illimitable.
The lantern light knots in gouts of gold.
As the sun retreats, and the moon
Turns its face away and back again,
Following the spinning earth
Like our following lanterns
Through the dark, back to the white breath
Of the cattle, back to the smell
Of hay and dung and milk,
Back to the placental
Dark in the abandoned ruins,
God goes again to birth.

LUCRETIUS, III, 1053–1076

Baudelaire knew what it was like,
The typewriter keys red hot,
All the paint brushes a yard long,
The paint mixed with chewing gum.
I write letters and don't send them;
Dream away my poverty;
Make dozens of incredibly
Bad sketches; reread the great
Masterpieces; review my
Greek and Chinese, and discover
My vocabulary is gone;
Take my pulse; start out on walks,
And return home; my mind deep
And clear like the Deipnosophists.

Jean-Jacques, Amiel, Bashkirtsev,
It is possible to produce
A very influential
Ontology out of such
Material, of guaranteed
Ecumenical provenance.
Porch and Garden up to date,
Kierkegaard and Sacher-Masoch,
"One feels like a man about
To be executed." Niebuhr
Discovers that everyone
Is his own Wanda Guillotine.
Liberal Protestantism
Goeth at last to its long home,
Only a few hours behind
The Capitalist System.
Die Ausrottung der Besten.
Just think, all the patronesses
Of the surrealistes feel
Like this all the time. In fact
Practically every female,
With an income, in our set does.
"In the cold autumn moonlight
The cicada dies by its shell."
Even in jail, Mirabeau
Found work for idle hands to do.
The Rule of St. Benedict
Is very explicit about
The sickness that destroyeth
In the noonday.

One advantage
Of being learned, is that
There is no fix you can get in
Where you won't find company.
Even if your advisors
Cannot be called very helpful.

NO!

I have closed my ears, I refuse
To listen to my mouth weeping.
I have closed my mouth, I refuse
The taste of my weeping eyes.
I have closed my eyes on the past
As you want it remembered for
The rest of life, called "forever."
I was not there. I was away.
At the Poles, in the Amazon.
I am not going to have been
Where you say I was. You fancy
You can force me to have lived
The past you want. You are wrong.

A CHRISTMAS NOTE FOR GERALDINE UDELL

Do the prairie flowers, the huge autumn
Moons, return in season?
Debs, Berkman, Larkin, Haywood, they are dead now.
All the girls are middle aged.
So much has escaped me, so much lies covert
In memory, and muffled
Like thunder muttering through sleep, that woke me,
To watch the city wink
Out in the violet light under the twisting rain.
Lightning storms are rare here,
In this statistically perfect climate.
The eucalyptus shed
Branches, doors banged, glass broke, the sea smashed its walls.
I, in my narrow bed,
Thought of other times, the hope filled post war years,
Exultant, dishevelled
Festivals, exultant eyes, dishevelled lips,

Eyes dulled now, and lips thinned,
Festivals that have betrayed their occasions.
I think of you in *Gas*,
The heroine on the eve of explosion;
Or angry, white, and still,
Arguing with me about Sasha's tragic book.
Here in the empty night,
I light the lamp and hunt for pad and pencil.
A million sleepers turn,
While bombs fall in their dreams. The storm goes away,
Muttering in the hills.
The veering wind brings the cold, organic smell
Of the flowing ocean.

STONE AND FLOWER

for Kathleen Raine

Here in America,
By the other ocean –
Your book, two years delayed –
In the spring evening.

I look from my window
Over a steep city,
From a hilltop higher
Than most of your England.

West of the dark mountains,
Over the white ocean,
That female planet burns,
Twisting in the green sky.

I think of you at work –
Against the apathy

Of war, all the squalor
Of ruin, your sure word:

Stone and flower moving
Each into the other
Their unmeasured cycles –
The perfume in the rock,

The fossilized pollen,
Phosphate in the petal,
The rose between the breasts,
The eyes' bag of diamonds.

My dear Kathleen, others
Have evoked a poet's
Responsibility,
And never raised a ghost

Out of the permanent
Wreckage of a world where
Wars are secret or not,
But never, never, stop.

Your poems give meaning to
The public tragedy
To which they lend themselves
On their own terms, as when

One sharp, six pointed star
Of snow falls from the black
Sky to the black water
And turns it all to ice.

GAMBLING

Thoughts of you spatter my thought.
Black drops fall from the sword edge
Of thunder. White cards scatter
Black and red equivocal
Hearts and spades. Death passes me
Daily and splashes her fierce
Chemicals in my hair. Clock
Ticks change voice and speak your name.
What a dish life is, with its
Sour grapes and broken glass.
I can remember your breasts,
That smell of marzipan.

ME

The bleeding hearts in the garden
Bloom early, but never fruit.
Every year they have spread further,
Underground, by creeping rootstocks.
Zeno's arrow in my heart,
I float in the plunging year.

THE LIGHT ON THE PEWTER DISH

Driving across the huge bridge
Above San Francisco Bay,
The United States Navy
Anchored, rank by deadly rank,
In the water under me,
And over me the sky filled
With hundreds of bombing planes,

My mind wandering idly,
I was suddenly aware
That Jacob Boehme flourished
During the Thirty Years' War.

ME AGAIN

They say I do not realize
The values of my own time.
What preposterous nonsense!
Ten years of wars, mountains of dead,
One hundred million armed men
And billions of paper dollars
Spent to disembowel mankind.
If they go on forever,
They will have realized less
Value than I can in one hour
Sitting at my typewriter.

ON A BEAUTIFUL BAR BUTTERFLY IN THE BLACK CAT

Vinea submittit capr(e)as non semper edulis.
She-goats bred in vineyards are not always edible.

VALUE NEUTER

Traders, parsons, and stoolpigeons,
Always confuse value and price.
The long epistemological
Debauch of modern philosophy –
The police-professors mull over
Pilate's question. Judas consults
The best income tax attorneys.

DISCRIMINATION

I don't mind the human race.
I've got pretty used to them
In these past twenty-five years.
I don't mind if they sit next
To me on streetcars, or eat
In the same restaurants, if
It's not at the same table.
However, I don't approve
Of a woman I respect
Dancing with one of them. I've
Tried asking them to my home
Without success. I shouldn't
Care to see my own sister
Marry one. Even if she
Loved him, think of the children.
Their art is interesting,
But certainly barbarous.
I'm sure, if given a chance,
They'd kill us all in our beds.
And you must admit, they smell.

FACT

In the encyclopedia
Are facts on which you can't improve.
As: "The clitoris is present
In all mammals. Sometimes, as in
The female hyena, it is
Very large."

DE FERA DORMITA

Annos tres vesperi, passer venit, sub tecto
Vestibuli somno. Quid fecit bello Europa?
Annos tres, hieme aestateque, idem passer,
Capite velato, dormiens in tenebra glauca.

William Carlos Williams

BONAPARTISME

Napoleon on St. Helena
Read Homer. I am depressed
And read over my own manuscripts.
Pencilled on a list of books
And groceries I find two lines:
"High in the east a morrow soft and sweet.
This hour, this is our last hour glass."
I no longer remember
If they are mine or another's.

FURTHER ADVANTAGES OF LEARNING

One day in the Library,
Puzzled and distracted,
Leafing through a dull book,
I came on a picture
Of the vase containing
Buddha's relics. A chill
Passed over me. I was
Haunted by the touch of
A calm I cannot know,
The opening into that
Busy place of a better world.

UNDER SORACTE

Another day, deep in the stacks,
Where no one had come for years.
Walled in by the forbidding tomes
Of Migne's *Patrologia*,
I stood, reading the heart tearing
Plaints of Abelard. All at once
I realized that for some time
I had been smelling a sweet, light
Perfume, very faint, and very chic;
And then I heard the shiver
Of thin bracelets, and a murmur
That went on and paused and went on again;
And discovered that beyond me
In the next aisle a boy and girl
Made love in the most remote
Corner of knowledge.

THE DRAGON AND THE UNICORN (1952)

"What is love?" said Pilate, and washed his hands.

ROSA MUNDI

Bright petals of evening
Shatter, fall, drift over Florence,
And flush your cheeks a redder
Rose and gleam like fiery flakes
In your eyes. All over Florence
The swallows whirl between the
Tall roofs, under the bridge arches,
Spiral in the zenith like larks,
Sweep low in crying clouds above
The brown river and the white
River bed. Your moist, quivering
Lips are like the wet scarlet wings
Of a reborn butterfly who
Trembles on the rose petal as
Life floods his strange body.
Turn to me. Part your lips. My dear,
Some day we will be dead.

I feel like Pascal often felt.

About the mid houre of the nicht

FIRE

The air is dizzy with swallows.

Sunset comes on the golden
Towers, on the Signoría.
In the Badía, the light goes
From the face of Filippino's
Weary lady, exhausted with
The devotion of her worshipper.
Across the face of the Duomo
The Campanile's blue shadow
Marks the mathematics of beauty.

In San Miniato the gold
Mosaics still glitter through
The smoky gloom. At the end
Of the Way of the Cross, the dense
Cypress wood, full of lovers,
Shivering with impatience.
As the dark thickens, two by two
They take each other. Nightfall, all
The wood is filled with soft moaning,
As though it were filled with doves.

LEDA HIDDEN

Christmas Eve, unseasonably cold,
I walk in Golden Gate Park.
The winter twilight thickens.
The park grows dusky before
The usual hour. The sky
Sinks close to the shadowy
Trees, and sky and trees mingle
In receding planes of vagueness.
The wet pebbles on the path
Wear little frills of ice like
Minute, transparent fungus.
Suddenly the air is full
Of snowflakes – cold, white, downy
Feathers that do not seem to
Come from the sky but crystallize
Out of the air. The snow is
Unendurably beautiful,
Falling in the breathless lake,
Floating in the yellow rushes.
I cannot feel the motion
Of the air, but it makes a sound
In the rushes, and the snow

Falling through their weaving blades
Makes another sound. I stand still,
Breathing as gently as I can,
And listen to those two sounds,
And watch the web of frail wavering
Motion until it is almost night.
I walk back along the lake path
Pure white with the new snow. Far out
Into the dusk the unmoving
Water is drinking the snow.
Out of the thicket of winter
Cattails, almost at my feet,
Thundering and stamping his wings,
A huge white swan plunges away.
He breaks out of the tangle,
And floats suspended on gloom.
Only his invisible
Black feet move in the cold water.
He floats away into the dark,
Until he is a white blur
Like a face lost in the night,
And then he is gone. All the world
Is quiet and motionless
Except for the fall and whisper
Of snow. There is nothing but night,
And the snow and the odor
Of the frosty water.

GOLDEN SECTION

Paestum of the twice blooming
Roses, the sea god's honey
Colored stone still strong against
The folly of the long decline
Of man. The snail climbs the Doric

Line, and the empty snail shell
Lies by the wild cyclamen.
The sandstone of the Roman
Road is marked with sun wrinkles
Of prehistoric beaches,
But no time at all has touched
The deep constant melodies
Of space as the columns swing
To the moving eye. The sea
Breathes like a drowsy woman.
The sun moves like a drowsy hand.
Poseidon's pillars have endured
All tempers of the sea and sun.
This is the order of the spheres,
The curve of the unwinding fern,
And the purple shell in the sea;
These are the spaces of the notes
Of every kind of music.
The world is made of number
And moved in order by love.
Mankind has risen to this point
And can only fall away,
As we can only turn homeward
Up Italy, through France, to life
Always pivoted on this place.

Finally the few tourists go,
The German photographers, the
Bevy of seminarians,
And we are left alone. We eat
In the pronaos towards the sea.
Greek food, small white loaves, smoked cheese,
Pickled squid, black figs, and honey
And olive oil, the common food
Of Naples, still, for those who eat.
An ancient dog, Odysseus' dog,
Spawned before there were breeds of dogs,

Appears, begs, eats, and disappears –
The exoteric proxy of
The god. And we too grow drowsy with
White wine, tarry from the wineskin.
The blue and gold shafts interweave
Across our nodding eyes. The sea
Prepares to take the sun. We go
Into the naos, open to the
Sky and make love, where the sea god
And the sea goddess, wet with sperm,
Coupled in the incense filled dark,
As the singing rose and was still.

Mist comes with the sunset. (The Yanks
Killed the mosquitoes.) Long lines of
Umber buffalo, their backs a
Rippling congruence, as in the
Paintings of Krishna, file across
The brilliant green sea meadows,
Under banners of white mist.
The fires of the bivouacs of
Spartacus twinkle in the hills.
One train comes with the first stars.
Venus over the wine dark sea.

All the way back the train fills
And fills up, and fills again,
With girls from the fish canneries,
And girls from the lace factories,
And girls from the fields, who have been
Working twelve hours for nothing,
Or at the best a few pennies.
They laugh and sing, all the way
Back to Naples, like broad bottomed,
Deep bosomed angels, wet with sweat.

Under the second moon the
Salmon come, up Tomales
Bay, up Papermill Creek, up
The narrow gorge to their spawning
Beds in Devil's Gulch. Although
I expect them, I walk by the
Stream and hear them splashing and
Discover them each year with
A start. When they are frightened
They charge the shallows, their immense
Red and blue bodies thrashing
Out of the water over
The cobbles; undisturbed, they
Lie in the pools. The struggling
Males poise and dart and recoil.
The females lie quiet, pulsing
With birth. Soon all of them will
Be dead, their handsome bodies
Ragged and putrid, half the flesh
Battered away by their great
Lust. I sit for a long time
In the chilly sunlight by
The pool below my cabin
And think of my own life – so much
Wasted, so much lost, all the
Pain, all the deaths and dead ends,
So very little gained after
It all. Late in the night I
Come down for a drink. I hear
Them rushing at one another
In the dark. The surface of
The pool rocks. The half moon throbs
On the broken water. I
Touch the water. It is black,
Frosty. Frail blades of ice form

On the edges. In the cold
Night the stream flows away, out
Of the mountain, towards the bay,
Bound on its long recurrent
Cycle from the sky to the sea.

MIRROR

The afternoon ends with red
Patches of light on the leaves
On the northeast canyon wall.
My tame owl sits serenely
On his dead branch. A foolish
Jay squalls and plunges at him.
He is ignored. The owl yawns
And stretches his wings. The jay
Flies away screaming with fright.
My king snake lies in inert
Curves over books and papers.
Even his tongue is still, but
His yellow eyes are judicial.
The mice move delicately
In the walls. Beyond the hills
The moon is up, and the sky
Turns to crystal before it.
The canyon blurs in half light.
An invisible palace
Of glass, full of transparent
People, settles around me.
Over the dim waterfall
The intense promise of light
Grows above the canyon's cleft.
A nude girl enters my hut,
With white feet, and swaying hips,
And fragrant sex.

ONLY YEARS

I come back to the cottage in
Santa Monica Canyon where
Andrée and I were poor and
Happy together. Sometimes we
Were hungry and stole vegetables
From the neighbors' gardens.
Sometimes we went out and gathered
Cigarette butts by flashlight.
But we went swimming every day,
All year round. We had a dog
Called Proclus, a vast yellow
Mongrel, and a white cat named
Cyprian. We had our first
Joint art show, and they began
To publish my poems in Paris.
We worked under the low umbrella
Of the acacia in the dooryard.
Now I get out of the car
And stand before the house in the dusk.
The acacia blossoms powder the walk
With little pills of gold wool.
The odor is drowsy and thick
In the early evening.
The tree has grown twice as high
As the roof. Inside, an old man
And woman sit in the lamplight.
I go back and drive away
To Malibu Beach and sit
With a grey-haired childhood friend and
Watch the full moon rise over the
Long rollers wrinkling the dark bay.

EMPTY MIRROR

As long as we are lost
In the world of purpose
We are not free. I sit
In my ten foot square hut.
The birds sing. The bees hum.
The leaves sway. The water
Murmurs over the rocks.
The canyon shuts me in.
If I moved, Bashō's frog
Would splash in the pool.
All summer long the gold
Laurel leaves fell through space.
Today I was aware
Of a maple leaf floating
On the pool. In the night
I stare into the fire.
Once I saw fire cities,
Towns, palaces, wars,
Heroic adventures,
In the campfires of youth.
Now I see only fire.
My breath moves quietly.
The stars move overhead.
In the clear darkness
Only a small red glow
Is left in the ashes.
On the table lies a cast
Snake skin and an uncut stone.

DOUBLED MIRRORS

It is the dark of the moon.
Late at night, the end of summer,
The autumn constellations
Glow in the arid heaven.
The air smells of cattle, hay,
And dust. In the old orchard
The pears are ripe. The trees
Have sprouted from old rootstocks
And the fruit is inedible.
As I pass them I hear something
Rustling and grunting and turn
My light into the branches.
Two raccoons with acrid pear
Juice and saliva drooling
From their mouths stare back at me,
Their eyes deep sponges of light.
They know me and do not run
Away. Coming up the road
Through the black oak shadows, I
See ahead of me, glinting
Everywhere from the dusty
Gravel, tiny points of cold
Blue light, like the sparkle of
Iron snow. I suspect what it is,
And kneel to see. Under each
Pebble and oak leaf is a
Spider, her eyes shining at
Me with my reflected light
Across immeasurable distance.

THE DRAGON AND THE UNICORN (1944–1950)

For Marthe

εἰμὶ δ᾽ ἐγὼ τὰ μὲν ἄλλα φαῦλος
καὶ ἄχρηστος, τοῦτο δέ μοί πως ἐκ
θεοῦ δέδοται, ταχὺ οἵῳ τ᾽ εἶναι γνῶναι
ἐρῶντά τε καὶ ἐρώμενον. Σώκρατες.
– Socrates, in the Lysis

I

"And what is love?" said Pilate,
And washed his hands.

All night long
The white snow falls on the white
Peaks through the quiet darkness.
The overland express train
Drives through the night, through the snow.
In the morning the land slopes
To the Atlantic, the sky
Is thicker, Spring stirs, smelling
Like old wet wood, new life speaks
In pale green fringes of marsh
Marigolds on the edges
Of the mountain snow drifts. Spring
Is only a faint green haze
On the high plains, only haze
And the fences that disappear
Over the horizon, and the
Rails, and the telegraph
Poles and the pale singing wires
Going on and on forever.

All things are made new by fire.
The plow in the furrow, Burns
Or Buddha, the first call to
Vocation, the severed worms,
The shattered mouse nest, the seed
Dripping from the bloody sword.
The sleepers chuckle under
The wheels, mocking the heartbeat.
We think of time as serial
And atomic, the expression
By mechanical means of a
Philosophical notion,
Regular divisibility
With a least common divisor
Of motion by motion, so
Many ticks to a century.
Such a thing does not exist.
Actually, the concept
Of time arose from the weaving
Together of the great organic
Cycles of the universe,
Sunrise and sunset, the moon
Waxing and waning, the changing
Stars and seasons, the climbing
And declining sun in heaven,
The round of sowing and harvest,
And the life and death of man.

The doom of versifying –
Orpheus was torn to pieces
By the vindictiveness of
Women or struck down by the
Jealousy of heaven.

The doom of the testicles –
Chiron's masculinity
Was so intense that all his

Children were adopted and
Later destroyed by the gods.

The deed done, Orestes draws
His steel penis like a snake
From its hole. The sun and moon
In Capricorn, Electra,
The little she-goat, bleats and squirms,
Her brother between her thighs,
From whose wounds pour forth both blood
And water, the wine of whose
Maidenhead turns to water
Of baptism, the fiery
Mixture of being and not being.
The artist is his own mother.

Chicago, the train plunges through
A vast dome of electric gloom.
Cold wind, deepening dark, miles
Of railroad lights, 22nd
And Wentworth. The old Chinese
Restaurants now tourist joints.
Gooey Sam where we once roared
And taught the waiters to say
Fellow Worker, is now plush.
As the dark deepens I walk
Out Wentworth, grit under my feet.
The smell of frying potatoes
Seeps through the dirty windows.
The old red light district is
Mostly torn down, vacant lots
Line the railroad tracks. I know
What Marvell meant by desarts
Of vast eternitie. Man
Gets daily sicker and his
Ugliness knots his bowels.
On the site of several

Splendid historical brothels
Stands the production plant of
Time-Luce Incorporated.
Die Ausrottung der Besten.

Do not cut a hole in the
Side of a boat to mark the
Place where your sword dropped and sank.

In experience each present
Time includes its past and as the
Future appears it is included
In it. Only when we come to
Compare the time of one group of
Facts with another do we have
To imagine a common factor,
The instant. As one time is
Measured against the other, both
Are considered to lie in a
Neutral medium of serial
Instants, or against a linear
Background of dots in series.
With hardly any exceptions
The great philosophers have held
That this kind of time is unreal.

Women of easy virtue,
Nanda and Syata, came
To Buddha before the first
Enlightenment. Ambipali,
A whore richer than princes,
Before the last Nirvana.
Jesus was born in Rachel's tomb,
John's Salome his midwife.

A freshman theme, "It is the
Contention of this paper

That the contemporary world
Is fundamentally corrupt."

The logical positivist,
The savage with an alarm clock,
"It seems to me that human
Spiritual evolution
Progresses from a maximum
To a minimum of
Imagination. It seems
That the pattern of history
Leads man from fantasy to
Reason, from a mythical
To a logical condition.
Perhaps progress consists in
Getting rid of that over
Whelming power of fantasy
Which seems to dominate children
And primitive peoples."

The greatest dragon painter
Who ever lived was Ssu Ma
Tsien. Awesome, terrifying,
His dragons left spectators
Weak and giddy for hours.
When they were shown to the Son
Of Heaven, he had to take
To his bed and thunderstorms
Drenched the Five Regions. The real
Dragons were very flattered.
The Dragon Court decided
That in fact they weren't quite so
Frightening; and as a mark
Of favor the Dragon King
Appeared before Ssu Ma Tsien
As a model for future
Dragons. The painter became

Unconscious with terror and
Never again was able to
Paint dragons because of his
Continuous shuddering.

"The progress of science is
A transition to new and
Better information. Often
The old must be discarded
As false and inadequate.
Philosophy progresses by
Deepening and enriching the
Understanding of principles
Already known. Philosophy
Which discards the past is suspect.
Art, however, does not progress."

Clear after a three day storm,
Phosphorescence in the sea
Off Ireland, the air tropical,
The pole stars high in the sky.
The sun enters the second
Moon of Spring. The hawk turns to
A dove. Hoar frost becomes dew.
The next day, Easter, nineteen
Forty-nine, from Fastenet
All along the coast the bells
Ringing in the birth of the
Irish Republic. Easter
Night, the odor of land off
Holyhead, the special smell
Of Wales, of herbs and turf smoke.

"The human soul is infinitely
Richer than it is aware of.
Its being is so broad and deep
That it can never wholly

Develop and comprehend
Itself in the consciousness.
Man is a mystery to
Himself, a riddle which will
Never be solved in consciousness,
For, should he ever attain to
The internal intuition
Of his whole being he would
Be swallowed up and consumed
In himself." So Leibniz says.

The great black pseudo classical
Victorian public buildings
Of Liverpool, bombed-out shells,
Everybody too busy
To fix them up. So Rome died,
They were always going to
Get at the ruins next year.
Coal smoke and Spring move down the
Brick-lined gas-lit streets on the
Chill wind from the Mersey.
The Youth Hostel recommends
"A Jew bloke, decent chap, yu knaow,
Runs a plice called Troicycle Ouse."
Friendly as a six months pup,
Enthusiast for the adult
Tricycle, bronzed from tricycling
Over England. It is Pesach,
An austerity Passover,
With matzoth and fish and chips.

Christ blessed the cup with the Kadusha
Sabbath prayer over the wine.
Malkuth, the embodied Glory –
The Mother of God was a
Temple prostitute deflowered
By a chance passerby, or

The Virgin of the Ages –
Essentially the same thing.

I visit the neogothic
Cathedral, almost as handsome
As Sacré-Coeur, the window
Of Gordon bringing opium
And Christ to the Chinese is still
In storage since the war. Down
The hill to Chinatown, sleepy
In Spring sunlight, I eat lunch with
Two Lancashire and two Welsh whores –
Ham and greens, pork tripe and pea pods,
The best meal I'll get in England.
To me, fresh from the States, the girls
Look awfully poor. I will learn
More cosmopolitan standards.
They are full of songs, dirty jokes,
And wisecracks, say "Yu knaow" every
Third word, act remarkably
Like French girls and utterly
Unlike the bitter London drabs.
Lancashire, if you forget
It is supposed to be English,
Is a musical language
Something like Irish and Welsh.
One of the Lancashire girls
Is a long-legged blonde with
Very knowing eyes, named Clarice.
I spend the night with her and
In the morning she makes breakfast
With two eggs apiece, takes me
Back to bed again for a long
Farewell embrace, then takes me
To the station and helps me
To get my baggage sorted,
Some in a rucksack, the rest

Off to London. I change clothes
In the baggage room, she tips
The baggage clerk, and we do it
One last time amongst the dark
Piles of trunks and suitcases.
She weeps as she sees me off
On the bus to Chester and
Refuses to take any money.
It hasn't taken me long
To find the only place where
I will find friends in Europe.

As the Philosopher says,
"Love is the desire to be
United to the beloved,
To be transported out of
Oneself into the beloved.
So love prefers the least contact
To the greatest distant joy."

Just as the time of mathematics
Is a convention of measure,
So past, present, and future
Are qualifications of
Knowledge. They have no being
Outside the experience
Of possible and consequent.
They are the way discursive
Knowledge comes to us, and their
Essential relation is
One of inclusion. The past
Is less experience than the
Present and it than the future.

The tremendous exaltation
Of North Wales glowing with Spring –
Birds and wild flowers everywhere,

Too many to name, the rock walls
And high hedges and sunken fields
Covered with violets and bluebells,
Daffodils at the woods' edges,
Black Welsh cattle and chubby sheep.
Topping the hills above Conway
The Snowdon mountains rise through the
Clouds, unmistakable Tryfan
Dramatic as the great peaks of
Caucasus and Himalaya,
Faint purple aslant the sun with
Blue snow patches, Conway castle
Mellow lavender stone in the
Early evening. Llanrwst,
Capel-Curig, Betws-y-Coed,
Idwal Cottage, Llanberis,
Beddgelert, all the beautiful
Names and the dark blue-eyed people
With their musical voices.
I walk at night through the thick forest
Spotted with light by the half moon.
Owls cry all about me, and off
In a nearby meadow, in a cloud
Of moonlight, the grate of a
Corncrake. Suddenly the wood gives
Way to an orchard, nightingales
In the midst of blooming pear trees.

Yang Kuei-fei was hanged on a
Pear tree, and a black bird flew
Away with her bloodstained veil.
Augustine hung his childhood
In a pear tree. In our day
Psychoanalysts decided
It was somebody's penis
And not a pear tree at all.

Climbing Tryfan and the Glyders
With a young telephone lineman,
The rock greasy in driving mist.
The mountains show themselves
A few seconds at a time
But from Tryfan for a quarter
Hour, the sea and islands,
All the purple peaks of Wales
Mottled with soft white clouds,
To the east a brilliant rainbow.

Light is the aptitude of
A point to generate a
Sphere of graded intensity
Indefinitely large.
As the Philosopher says,
"The noblest way to possess
A thing is to possess it
In an immaterial
Manner, that is, possessing
Its form without its matter.
This is the definition
Of knowledge." The dragon
And the unicorn, earth and air.

Pont Aberglaslyn in whirling
Mist like a Chinese painting.
Down to the sea at Port Madoc,
I swim in the cold water.
Pwllheli and Aberdaron
In stiff wind, the busses filled
With plump farm women with baskets.
No one speaks English, everyone
Has that odor of herbs and turf,
The strange gnome-like smell of Wales.
At Aberdaron no boat to
Bardsey, too stiff a wind, so

I loaf four days in a place
Where man is still good, tight grey
Houses, the hedges filled with
Flowers and the sky with birds,
Even the sheep look clean and
Intelligent. The girls have
Plump bright cheeks, deep eyes, and round
Bottoms. In the evening talking
On the old bridge below the
Watermill they sound like thrushes.

If we think of time as really
An aspect of experience
It is easy to realize
That its serial character
Is that of inclusion series,
Like Chinese boxes or the tubes
Of a telescope, and the time
Of the mathematician is
Simply the surface along which
The elements of experience
Fit into each other. Each
Person's experience grows
From an insignificant
Indivisible atom to
An infinite universe.
Each simpler experiential
Level telescopes into
The more complex as we look back
And analyze experience
And see it as consequential.
We call this time and the simpler
We attribute to the past and
Imagine a still more complex
In the future. Actually,
Of course, no one has ever

Seen either the past or the
Future, we live in the present.

No sign of the wind letting up,
So I leave Brenda Chamberlain
To her island of ten thousand birds
And go on to Dolgelley and climb
Cader Idris in the evening
And sleep on top in a mist
Like cotton wool so dense I can't
See my primus stove when I stand
In the dark. My flashlight shines
Against mist like a plaster wall.
After midnight the sky clears
And the soft Summer stars move
Over me from England to the sea.

The heart's mirror hangs in the void.
Vision blossoms in the night
Like stars opening in the brain.
Jehovah created the world
In six days. The Bible does not
Mention the nights. He holds the
Creation of the night in
Concealment for His own ends.
There is no reality
Except that of experience
And experience is the
Conversation of persons.

The next day, up the river
Through the hills, through Llangadfan
And the high moors of the Border.
I stop in a fisherman's inn
Just this side Welshpool. Cold mutton
And black beer for supper. The guests

Are English, decent people, but
Too much like drawings in *Punch*.
I go into the pub, full of
Peasants singing and drinking beer.
No one speaks English except
To me, but they are all very
Friendly and buy me drinks and
Ask wistfully if I think
America plans to go to war.
Not having been in the habit
Of using "we" when I mean the
State Department, it takes time
To explain that America
Is several different persons,
Some of them like Welsh peasants.
They are curious about John
L. Lewis, who is to Wales what
Giannini is to Italy.
The room reeks very pleasantly
Of the Welsh smell. I shall never
Know what it is, you can't ask,
"I say, what makes you smell so odd?"
Later, when I tried to get some
Information on the subject
From Dylan Thomas, he was quite
Put out. But my hiking guides,
Shropshire and the Border, North Wales,
Still smell in California.
In the morning, loud with birds,
Wales drops behind me. Never
Will I find better people
Or a more beautiful country.

All things, all entities of
Whatsoever nature are
Only perspectives on persons.
Each moment of the universe

Is a moment of choice, chosen
Out of the infinite system
Of possibility which forms
The content of experience,
The continuously shifting
And flowing organism
Of relationships, its form
Determined by the character
Of the willing agent, its
Contents the evaluative
Strands and strains, the perspectives
Connecting with all other persons.
Each moment of the universe
And all the universes
Are reflected in each other
And in all their parts and
Thence again in themselves.
It is simpler to see this
As a concourse of persons, all
Reflecting and self-reflecting
And the reflections and the
Reflective medium reflecting.

Sunday, Shrewsbury and crowds
Boating on the Severn. Back and
Forth and up and down Shropshire
Through the entranced landscape.
Always before I had thought
Housman a conventional
Sort of Theocritan, Versailles
Peasant kind of poet, but it
Is all just as he says. Broom,
Hawthorn, cherry, the wind on
Wenlock Edge, the Clun villages
Drowsing away the centuries,
Clee Beacon above Ludlow and
The bell in the pure tower

Of St. Lawrence scattering
The quarters over the town.
No redcoats marching to drums,
No hangings at the moment –
He neglected to mention
The haunting color of the glass
In St. Lawrence, like the blue eyes
Of Welsh queens. Hiking along
The road by Onwy, a young
Veterinarian gives me a ride.
He is leaving for London
And America next week
And taking a last drive over
Shropshire, so I see it all again,
From Shrewsbury to Leominster,
From Much Wenlock to Montgomery.
He is a remarkably
Civilized young man with few
Of the appetites of commerce,
But he says of Wenlock Edge,
"Chap wrote a poem about it,
Couldn't make head or tail of it."
Oh well, it's all there and
He could see it, anyway.
After supper we walk in
The park of Ludford above
The town and the castle hazy
With evening fires, with Clee
Beacon in the distance on the
Long swell of hill above the
Tower of St. Lawrence, all paling
And then gone in the darkness.
We bid farewell and promise
To look each other up. Poor
Bastard, he doesn't know what is
Going to happen to him, he's
To teach at Pullman, Washington.

Every item of this cosmos
Of possibilities is the
Mode by which I apprehend
A person. Each person chooses
His own time and space as he
Continuously adjusts
Himself to other persons
With whom he is in closest
Contact. They of course may appear
Not only as persons. For the
Moment an onrushing train
Seems more important than a
Distant wife or dead mother.
South to Hereford, swinging a
Stick of Housman's cherry cut
On Wenlock Edge, a great red
Lion of a Cathedral, and
Across to the Wye, the placid
River winding through meadows,
Orchards, and forests, the apples
All in bloom over red and white
Hereford cattle, the people
Friendly and open, bright and clear –
Westerners. A wind comes up
In the afternoon and the boats
Of fishermen revolve on the
River. St. Briavel's high on the
Hills above the river, the road
Climbing through apple orchards full
Of nightingales, past stone-troughed,
Terraced fish ponds, like the aging
Cassiodorus built himself,
"Pleasant is the glittering
Of the sun today on these
Banks because it flickers so,"
Tired of the court of the Goth
And the empty-headed Senate,

In the last ruin of the world
In Squillace, fourteen hundred
Years ago.

St. Briavel's Hostel,
A purple ruined castle,
The gate house and some of the front
Repaired and rebuilt, the rest
Tapering off gently into
Rubble. The inhabitants
Completely improbable.
Two youths, not together, who
Have both read my poetry.
A steel spectacled, balding
Australian social science
Teacher, "educator" he
Called himself, full of the most
Arrant nonsense about both
Baden-Powell and Wilhelm Reich –
The B-P Spirit and Free Love
For Infants, a combination
He explained dialectically
(As Hilary Belloc says,
It must be frightful to live
Where you have to travel ten
Days to meet somebody who
Doesn't dot his capital I's).
A precocity of ten
With a mother who looked like
Something by Gutzon Borglum,
Who knew literally everything.
She thought Petrie better than Breasted,
The body of Montezuma a fake,
Disapproved of Schliemann,
Thought Picasso was declining,
Stalin would have more trouble with
Tito than he had with Trotsky,

Simone de Beauvoir wrote atrociously,
Genet was an American fad,
The planet Pluto was smaller
Than estimated, Einstein
Did not compare with Clerk Maxwell,
Joe Lewis was unbeatable,
The greatest strain in racing
History was Man o' War's.
The curious thing about all
These opinions is their soundness.
By the fire, playing a game
Involving the guessing and
Plotting of quadratic curves,
The child says, "Mother dear, I find
This random talk excessively
Distracting." They're from Cambridge,
Castle-crawling this trip, did
Cathedrals last year, mountains next.

Morning, down through the river
Meadows and the Forest of Deane,
The last taste of King Arthur's world,
To Tintern Abbey, rooks wheeling
In the crystal sky through pure
Gothic planes and spaces as I
Eat lunch from red sandstone purple
With time. The vast muddy Severn,
Bristol vast and busy but still
About St. Mary Redcliffe
With the hushed voice of an age
Founded on contemplation.

States like men are born in blood,
Die first in the heart and head.

The history of choice which
The person traces through his

Chiliacosm, through all the
Possible universes of
All his possibilities, like
A worm track through cheese, is what
Has been called the empiric
Ego – the self of Buddhist and
Similar polemic. It has,
Obviously, no existence
Except as the perspective
On shifting perspectives.

Bath a stageset for Terence,
One of the world's unlikely
Cities, as freakish as Venice.
In the midst of the colonnades
And the swarming well-fed people,
Bath Abbey, immense and absurd,
Like the skeleton of a
Whale or a dirigible,
Built by Walpole Gothicizing,
The most eighteenth century
Product of the Middle Ages.

All the possibilities of
Any instant and of any
Series of instants are both
Unlimited, but they are
Only the possibilities
Organized and structured by those
Specific situations, the
Possibilities of just those
Consequences and no others.

The close of Wells Cathedral
Gold and green in the afternoon,
Inside, the combination
Of Protestant destruction

And British worship of the dead
Is beginning to pall on me.
Glastonbury at twilight,
The Tor over the hollow land,
The Graal procession and the court
Of the Fisher King behind the mist,
The black-robed queens and the dead
Arthur in a barge on the river.

But consequence is only
Possibility seen backwards,
So the manifold which garbs
The person and which he thinks
Of as himself and as all the
Content of his experience –
The universe – all he has done,
Knows, plans, or hopes, all his ideas
And sensations, however
Delusional or illusory –
Is his responsibility.
We each choose in all its details
The exact world we live in.
Do you complain of war, famine,
Pestilence, treason, and murder?
They exist because you choose them.
They are the consequences
Of the movements of your will.

Night in Somerset alone
Under the windy stars, an inn
Where the host kept me till midnight
Talking of Amuriky in
The soft speech of Somerset,
Like Quaker talk without their pride.
Exeter half in ruins,
The cathedral shored up and closed.
Cornwall like tepid barley water.

Over the hills and fields to
Derek Savage's thatched clay
Cottage in a narrow moist
Valley by a ruined mill.
Three days of hospitality
And passionate talk. How good
To meet someone in this world
With his own convictions and
Careless of gossip and fashion.
The only young English poet
Of working class extraction –
Barker is Irish, Thomas, Welsh –
But certainly by far the most
Distinguished both in appearance
And opinions. Connie
Savage an educated Kate Blake.

"One morning as I was sitting
By the fire, a great cloud came
Over me, and a temptation
Beset me; but I sat still.
And it was said, 'All things come
By nature,' and the elements
And the stars came over me,
So that I was in a manner
Quite clouded with it. But as
I sat still under it and
Let it alone, a living
Hope arose in me, and a true
Voice which said, 'There is a living
God who made all things.' Instantly
The cloud and the temptation
Vanished away, and life rose
Over it all; my heart was glad,
And I praised the living God."

"They betray the Truth," says Derek,
Sitting amongst his children.
No answer to Pilate's question.

High above Yarcombe the wind
Dies at sunset and I rest
In a hanging meadow. The land
Falls away for long blue miles
Down the trough of glacial valley.
In the deep resonant twilight
The stars open like wet flowers.
Young rabbits play on the hummocks
And vanish as a white owl comes
Cruising low over the ground.
He lights on a post and inspects
Me with curious owl-like quirks.
I go on in the starlight.
Lights of farms and villages
On the high ridges reflect
The constellations. Down
The hill in the soft thick night
The nightingales are singing, bird
After bird, for mile on mile.

George Fox was a bloody man,
A ranter who went naked.
Out of his violent heart
Peace poured through his skin like dream,
Like a moonlight around him.

Finnan haddie and tomatoes
For late supper in Yarcombe Inn.
Next day, a Thomas Hardy wind.
Crimson orchids in the hedgerows.
Salisbury Cathedral
A form at least as pure as
Chartres, like a stone waterfall

Descending or a fountain
Of stone ascending to heaven.
Inside, the hideous British
Necrophilia and the rancid
Stink of the Church of England.

I am walking westward along
The road across Salisbury
Plain in the great wind of the place,
Like a trade wind; and my mind is
Full of the climbing silver-grey
Cascade of the cathedral spire.
All around me larks are throwing
Themselves frantic into heaven.
The air is shivering with the
Singing of a thousand larks.
Closer to earth there are hoopoes
With their lunging flight and their strange
Desolate crying; and dashing
Away from my walking, great hares
And moorhens. All at once I come
Around a copse and see the road
Stretching away to the west, white
In the glare of late afternoon,
And beside it, purple, immense
With shadow, Stonehenge, lonelier
Than ten thousand years.

Alone, deep in contemplation
An hour, and then a little yellow
Man in chambray shorts and jumper
Pops up and asks, "Excuse, please,
Is possible could be natural
Phenomenon?" He turns out
To be a Karen, studying
To be a pilot at the airfield
Nearby, with all the jungle's

Note-taking greed for Western
Learning and science. Another
Logical positivist.
"All things come by nature." On the
Way back, lovers walking, arm in
Arm, out of Amesbury, towards
The sunset and the ancient stone.

All the past is not apparent
In most presents, certainly not
Those of high or complex order,
But neither is all the space of
The foreground apparent between
Parallel lines as they recede.
Of course, the past is all there, it
Is simply not all relevant.

Coming up the hill looking back
Over Winchester, the looping
River and the vast cathedral –
The fog with sun breaking through –
Two aged men in an ancient
Churchyard cleaning the gravestones
Under a calling cuckoo.

England is gone and London,
Sicker than New York, takes its place.

The spider monkeys revolve
Over their island with ghostly
Jollification. A rhesus
Masturbates, observing
Himself in a hand mirror.
Death and taxes, the affairs
Of gods and men, go their way.
And Hseuh-fung said that
Even these inconsequential

Creatures carry the Buddha
Mirror in their hearts. Kew Gardens,
Beyond Lebanon's cedars,
Sequoias from California,
Poor and spindly in the smoke
And lifeless London sunlight.

Tense tiger-eyed women who take
My lack of inhibitions for
An invitation to the games
Of scatological children.
The editor of ——, his
Power gone, being treated
Like a nigger by drunken
Cryptostalinist fairies.
The Chelsea set being refined,
Which means insulting each other
In sundry complicated ways.
The London Anarchist Group
Like a debating club at an
Exclusive Kansas private school.
Emma Goldman said, years ago,
"You're not British anarchists,
You're just British." A blonde barrage
Balloon, the power behind
——, a frantic
Imitation of Mary
McCarthy, Rita Hayworth,
And Simone de Beauvoir Sartre.
——'s hideous caddy
Bubbling like a poisoned pudding.
Intellectual parties,
Orgies of foolish snobbery,
Bad manners, and illiteracy.
The Irish are not considered
Human, the Scotch and Welsh subject
To worse chauvinism than

Can be found in the Deep South.
Everywhere, hate, covetousness,
And envy of money-grubbing
Americans. More talk of
Money than I have ever heard.
However, my pension is
A haven of old ladies,
Coal smoke, and cat piss, presided
Over by a retired colonel
Who eats breakfast in morning clothes.
"When I was military
Advisor to the Sultan of
Abadabad, we knew how
To handle fellows like Pollitt,
Gave them a whiff of grape, that
Quieted them, no more trouble."
I thought whiffs of grape were given
Only in Henty's boys' books.
The last total male in London.

Walking through Soho on Greek Street,
One of the soiled drabs who are the
Special fauna of the place comes
Up and says, as they all do,
With exquisite English tact,
"Come along." I say, "How much?"
She says, "Thirty shilling." I say,
"What've you got worth thirty shilling?"
She says, "Ow, if you wants them
Circus tricks they's French girls over
On Romilly Street'll oblige
You for a pound." I say, "Thank you."
As I cross Romilly Street
A girl comes towards me, tall, heavy
Black hair like a Mexican girl,
Exophthalmic, dark blue-grey eyes,
Full hips and the heavy breasts of

Provence, narrow waist, spectacular
Legs on skyscraper heels. She says,
"Allô?" I say, "Que fais?"
She says, "Vous parlez français?"
I say, "Un petit peu." She
Speaks hardly any English.
I explain that I have
A very special rendezvous
But I will come back at eight
And we can go to dinner.
She says, "Vous me trouverez ici
Tout le temps, si je ne travaille pas
Dans ma chambre. Restez ici."
We go to the Club Suisse and then
To the Gargoyle. We become fast
Friends and I introduce her to
All the right people as an
Existentialiste. She tells me that
She was the lover of a French
Communist who turned out to be
A finger man for the Nazi
Extermination squads, so she
Can never go back to Paris.
This seems to me a good record
To run for office on in
Present-day Paris, but she
Is definite and expressive
About what would happen to her.
She is a Nizarde, "Nini" for
Andrée, (I thought Nini was Jeanne),
Certainly the most impressive
Woman to enter a room with
I have ever known and one of
The very best lays. She tells me
She is a sadist "seulement
Pour le commerce." But as the nights
Go on she gets quite rough and I
Spend the days in a tingle.

"Les Anglais sont bêtes, saints,
Et pervers." "Et lourds et plausibles."
"Oui, oui, oui, très plausibles!"
The night before I leave London
I give her two boxes of nylons
Which I had brought for a Chelsea
Writress who turned out to be
Too refined for nylons. They are
Opera length and deep brownish black.
She is enraptured and takes
Off all her clothes and puts them on.
For a while she struts before me
Making French noises of approval,
And then suddenly turns and butts
My shoulder and weeps violently,
"Ah, le monde est méchant, mon
Petit, le monde est très méchant."

It is doubtful if the world
Presents itself in any
Important aspects under
The forms of serial time
And atomic space. It is
True that the intellect has
Come to be conditioned by them,
But important experience
Comes to us in freedom and
Is realized as value,
And the intellect alone
Can know nothing of freedom
And value because it is
Concerned with the necessary
And they are by definition
Unnecessitated. Love
Of course is the ultimate
Mode of free evaluation.
Perfect love casts out knowledge.

The *Daily Mail*, "We view with some
Amusement the naïveté
Of the Italians, who are
Permitting themselves to be
Chivvied by the Americans
Into a most unwise over-
Expanded hydroelectric
Development. The French are
To be commended for having
Resisted and continuing
To resist similar coaxing
From the new 'bosses' of Europe.
With true Gallic sagacity,
They cling to well-known facts,
And show no desire to substitute
Electricity derived from
Coal for the inferior
Product derived from water."

The dragon and the unicorn.

II

The Art of Worldly Wisdom
Comes to me by air across
The continent and over
The Atlantic. I get a beer
And cut open the package
On the Place de l'Opéra,
Hideous and jangling with
The Sahibs of the Plan Marshall
And their nasty virgin daughters.
Poems twenty-five years old –
All that old agony and
Wonder strikes me in the face
In the glare of downtown Paris,
The bankrupt faubourg of hatreds

And Bonapartes. I take the bus
To the Closerie des Lilas
And sit on the leafy terrace
Looking at the book in amazement.
Was it all true once? Just like
It says? I cannot find the past.
It is only anecdotes
For company and the parching
Of a few more hidden nerves
Each year.

I get up and go
To dinner to the room of my
Only friend on this continent,
A blonde Bretonne servant girl
Who earns forty francs an hour
(Three-fifty to the dollar).
Her little boy has TB
And impetigo and doesn't
Even own a ball except one
He ingeniously made of rags.
She has just lost her job, but
We have potage Parmentier,
Salade, haricots verts, cheval,
And pommes with fines herbes and black
Coffee fresh roasted and ground
For each cup, and cerises
Which she has managed to chill
By some occult process. I bring
Some Pelure d'oignon. We sit
In the great heat of the long
Drought of nineteen forty-nine
And eat cherries and discuss
The papers which must be signed
So the boy can go to a
Sanatorium in the Pyrenees,
The hirondelles like angels

Of St. Michael over the roofs.
Suddenly into the court
Of this slum, under the beams
Of heat and the crushing sun,
"La Vie en rose" always on
Somebody's radio, the past
Returns, the youth, the agony,
And the vertigo and the love
That always failed or broke or turned
Away. And with the past and its
Bound loyalty and love, comes,
I suppose, the art of worldly
Wisdom as guest to this feast
Of horse meat and fugitive
Loyalty and passing faith.

We put Christian to sleep and go
To the Gaîté Montparnasse,
La Lune dans le fleuve jaune. Irish
Plays are all the rage this season.
After it is over I ask
Léontine what she thinks of it.
"Comme ci – comme ça, one revolution
Is much like another."

Said Pilate, "What are facts? Don't
Talk to me about facts, I
Am fact." Who can escape from
The shadow of his own head?

Cornemuse, musette, and vielle,
Full of calvados and poiré,
We dance Gaelic flings older than Rome,
On the Rue Vercingétorix.

The first real Fourteenth since the war,
Yvonne and I lie on the quai

Watching the illuminations.
The years pass, the Summers go,
And our few days fall away
From us like the falling stars;
But that glory of rockets,
Showered on sky and river,
On our nightbound eyes and lips,
Will always last. That is what
"Always" means, and all it means.

So each creates his own world,
Polar and antipolar,
Medium, end, and result
Of the act of will, falling
Sparkling through the void, spools of
Good and evil turned on the
Seven-bladed lathe of heaven.

Raindrops spatter the Marne with
Quick discs, a rainbow appears
Over the handsome nineteenth
Century Château Ménier
(Now deserted by debased taste
For a functionalist villa).
The young wheat, just turning gold,
Grows close against the marble walls.
A broken stream trickles through
Wrecked bear pens and aviaries.
We make love in the deep bed
Of the little forest while
Birds cry in the rain over us.

Many women have said goodbye
To me and someday we will say
Goodbye also. At last the hands
Unbraid themselves and the head turns
Away taking the eyes and lips

Away finally forever.
The cords of the heart that were so
Tightly knotted are untied.

Gauguin's last picture – what word
In the final painting fever
In Tahiti? Brittany –
Sunless Winter evening,
Snow, grey sky, not a flush
Of color, blackish brown buildings,
No orange, no green, no red anymore.

Jacqui doesn't believe in
Wasting time. In the dancing
She keeps saying, "Quand faisons-nous
Une poudre? Votre ami, il trouve
Le jitterbug meilleur que l'amour."
At last he and Carmen get
A surfeit of Antillais jazz
And we go to a hotel.
Just before dawn Jacqui uses
The bidet and then leans out
On the balcony, with her
Lovely bottom reared against
The warm empty night above
The tracks of the Gare du Nord,
And says, "Les étoiles, les étoiles
Reculantes, elles s'éloignent
De nous. How you say étoiles
En anglais?" Did she read that
In a book? If so, what book?

The mechanical constructs of
Space-time are by definition
Not accessible to the will.
That is why they were invented.
Choice is only between persons.

The will is the instrument
Of interpersonal concourse.

Late night, walking from La Villette
All the way to Montparnasse –
As I come near the river,
Fog gathers around the lights,
And the whores swim in and out
Of the dark like drowned women.
Crossing the Isle St. Louis,
Where Restif carved his memoirs,
And time has forgotten itself,
Out of a high window floats
A girl's voice – Guillaume Machaut –
"Douce dâme" – with its heart-
Breaking cadence on the word
"Seulement," and that is all –
The black river and the fog
Glowing faintly in the light
Of a waning quarter moon.

When one act of will is compared
With another, when it is
Necessary to find a
Neutral component of all
Possibilities, the unit
By which to measure potencies,
Space-time is invented, but it
Is no more real in an absolute
Sense than the ruler is part of
The cloth which the tailor measures.

August… south through stubble fields
To the South and Italy.
The middle age of Summer.
Light and shadow both lie long
On the haystacks and poplars.

The world's most hideous
Suburban villas pass by us
In a series of discreet winces.
The narrow level fields of
The Isle de France, looking like
Indiana, the dusty forests.
Orléans and the Loire, at once
The tensions of the narrow
Gutted North relax.
Pompadour in her portraits
By Boucher and Fragonard,
The heads on the bodies of
Some sphinxes, France at her best,
The best years of her best king –
The thought of the thinking flesh.
Blois and François's folly, that
Damned staircase that looks as though
It was about to fall down.
Incredible that it has stood
So long. "The Thirteenth, greatest
Of centuries," it's possible.
St. Nicolas, buffeted
By the centuries, but still
Nobler than the vanity
Of even the best monarch.

Dinner in a peasant auberge,
Everybody inspects the
Vélos. "De Paris en Italie?
Incroyable! Formidable!"
Grilled pork chops, fried potatoes,
Tomatoes, beans in vinegar,
Fresh cheese, pears, wine, and coffee,
And the magnificent bread
Of Touraine. Just looking at it,
We weep for joy after the
Rancid papier-mâché turds

They sell in Paris. We shake
Hands with everybody and
Pedal on down the river,
Wobbling, heavy with food.

We camp on the Loire, the vélos
Parked under a rose bush, the
Sleeping bags under acacias,
And careen down the swift current,
Impossible to stand, much less
Swim against it. Two owls chatter
In the trees as the twilight
Comes, lavender and orange
Over the white reaches of
Water and the whiter sandbars,
And the first starlight dribbling
On the rushing river.

Although the possibilities
Of each instant are infinite
They are the possibilities
Of only that instant, that point
Of triangulation in which
The person places himself
In relation to others. You
Can move only from one point.
This necessitous character
Of consequence is what
Has given rise in the West
To the conception of sin,
In the East to that of Karma.

Chaumont, brilliant in the sun,
The working of a consistent
Principle, the best of the
Big châteaux. Amboise dull and
Hot in August midafternoon,

And then a cool hand, over
The chapel doorway the high
Relief of St. Eustache and
The cruciferous stag, almost
As touching as Pisanello's.

High above the Loire on the way
To the Cher and Chenonceaux –
The Pagode de Choiseul.

ETIENNE FRANÇOIS, DUC DE CHOISEUL,
PENETRE DES TEMOIGNAGES
D'AMITIE, DE BONTE, D'ATTENTION,
DONT IL FUT HONORE PENDANT
SON EXIL PAR UN GRAND NOMBRE
DE PERSONNES EMPRESSEES DE SE
RENDRE EN CES LIEUX, A FAIT
ELEVER CE MONUMENT, POUR
ETERNISER SA RECONNAISSANCE.
1760.

In the center
Of a geometrical
Forêt, his hunting park,
Waiting the patience of the best
Of kings, he and his friends in
Mandarin coats and powdered
Wigs, duchesses and the girls
Of the neighbors in transparent
Trousers, playing chinoiseries
Under the colored lanterns.
Ten petits-scouts and a chef-scout,
Scrambling up the staircases.
The chef-scout looks like Raimu,
Is this the B-P facies?
From the top, all of golden
Touraine in the August glitter.

He outwitted Catherine
And expelled the Jesuits;
Walpole says, "Gallantry without
Delicacy was his constant
Pursuit," a compliment from that
Source. Achilles loafing in Hell
With his harem, Philoxena,
Briseis, Iphigenia,
Helen, and Penthesilea.

It is true that being is
Responsibility, beyond
The speculations of Calvin,
St. Thomas, or Augustine,
Ontology is ethical.

Chenonceaux, the sun low and
Fishermen poling a boat
Under the arches, a boy
Wading up to his arms along-
Side in the weedy water.
Bléré, a foire and carrousel,
All the world drunker than peach
Orchard boars, dashing about
On bicycles. A fine dinner
With lots of the mild local wine,
At the next table a party
Of Anglaises with Rackham daughters,
Quite put about by the foire.
We camp by the Cher in the town,
Till two AM an orchestra
Plays beatless renditions of
Le Jazz. As the dawn comes under
The arches of the bridge, the first
Fishermen appear in the
Dewfall.
            Tours dusty, hot and bright.

Above the Loire, defacing
The landscape, a monstrously
Ugly moderne Franciscan church,
Windows like kaleidoscopes,
Rouault goosed up for the masses.
In Tours the streets are named for
The famous of France, of the world,
And of the locality, with
Biographical details
On each street sign, a brave custom.
The cathedral very English,
Shattered by Protestants.
We eat lunch under the chestnuts
In a bring-your-own café.

This terrifying picture
In which you are the cause of
The wars and disasters of
Your history is transcended
By the realization that
They are those possibilities
Which you have chosen to throw
Into sharpest perspective.

All day southward to Poitiers,
Through a world of rivers and
Castles, white shorn wheatfields and
Ripening grapes and suddenly
Tile roofs and cream-colored houses,
The mark of civilization,
Of Rome and the South. Poitiers
An outlyer of Ravenna,
Saint Jean a ruined provincial
San Vitale, Notre Dame
Romanesque with the last
Sense of the Arian mystery
Of the Goths in the narrow

Aisles around the apse. St. Hilaire,
The aisle arches interlaced
In quincunxes Sir Thomas missed.
Here the saintly pagan queen
Fought once more for Julian's
Lost cause and lost it again,
And Sweet William the Lewd, crowned
Poet, the first open flame
From the erotic gnostic fires.

Tant las fotei com auziretz
Cen ce quatre vint et ueit vetz,
Q'a pauc no .i rompei mos corretz
E mos arnes
E no .us puesc dir lo malaveg
Tan gran m'en pres.
Ges no .us sai dir lo malaveg
Tan gran m'en pres.
E.l pans fo blancs e.l vins fo bos
E.l pebr' espes.
                    White bread, good
Wine, and plenty of pepper.

Iam, dulces amico venito –
Dum caupona verterem –
If Hafiz is a mystic,
How many of the poems of
The Carmina Burana
Are at least as mystical?
Radegunde's tower, and the
Memory of Venantius
Fortunatus, that mild
And felicitous heart writing
Odes for gifts of plovers' eggs
And violets, compliments
On new dresses of lady saints,
And just once – exaltation –

Vexilla regis prodeunt
Fulget Crucis mysterium –
The royal banners forward go,
The Cross shines forth with mystic glow.
Radegunde's beauty still quivers
In the pages of Dill and Raby,
And Venantius' hymn still chills
The scalps of millions every
Second Sunday before Easter.

In the archetypal couple
Left is evil and right is good.
In their embrace left lies against
Right and right against left and
Good absorbs and transmutes evil.

Angoulême late at night with
Storm brewing, violent rain
On the steep streets after midnight.
Morning grey and vast over
Angoumois with a lace of lightning
Constantly above the valley
Of the Anguienne to the south.
The rain trickles out with a
High clear wind. The monument
To Carnot on the main Place,
Two female figures, one happy
And inspiring, one seated
And discouraged, (the Laws of
Thermodynamics?).
                                        The Rempart
De Beaulieu,
                        "PAUL VALERY
S'EST ARRETE ICI LE IX
DECEMBRE MDCCCCXXXI
'– O récompense après une pensée
Qu'un long regard sur le calme des dieux! –'"

And immediately beyond –

"EN MDCCCVI LE GENERAL
RESNIER, NE A ANGOULEME
MDCCXXIX–MDCCCXI
S'EST ELANCE DE L'ENDROIT,
TOUR LADENT, EFFECTUANT AINSI
LE PREMIER
VOL SANS MOTEUR AVEC UN
APPAREIL DE SON INVENTION
CONSTRUIT A ANGOULEME."

Through fields, vineyards, and forests,
The two rivers wind away
Below, the mellow civilized
Land stretches on and on southwards.
In the hanging gardens a white
And a colored peacock both
Titivating after rain,
A peahen and two peachicks
Busy catching worms. Down past
Terraced water, like St. Briavel's
And Cassiodorus' ponds,
Fat French goldfish jumping for
Post-rain insects, to the church
Of St. Ausone – canonized –
The old sentimentalist
And sensualist dreaming away
The centuries (the church is
New but the site ancient)
Amongst the chestnuts and peafowl
Waiting for Valéry and
Carnot and Le Général Resnier.
St. Pierre, neat, calm, and splendid,
On the façade St. George spitting
A sort of Gila monster,
Certainly one of the really

Great equestrian statues.
Vernet and Abadie dreaming
Of the glory of Langue d'Oc.
Over the hills into the
Dordogne watershed, all the farm
Houses built by Theodoric.
Périgueux – St. Front – Diana
Of Ephesus recumbent
On the fertile flesh of the Midi,
The white interior marked by
Abadie's lucid intellect.
The Arabic cavern of
St. Etienne, the ruins
Of another kind of vision.
The specialties of
Périgord, pâtés truffés,
Monbazillac, and brochet steamed
In wine, copies of the reindeer
On the walls of the restaurant.
In the slums under St. Front
An akimbo hotel full
Of elderly, very drunken
And very affectionate whores
Who try hard to entice us in.
High on the hills across the Isle
Where the Gallic chiefs lived once,
A deserted Theodoric
Farm, the well dry, red sunset
On the white breasts of St. Front.

The vélos plunge through heather
On the steep roads above the
Vézère. Les Eyzies, a good
Place for man to have started
In Europe, a pity he
Ever left. Today the natives
Are surely less civilized

Than the Cro-Magnons. An Auberge de la
Jeunesse Française camp in a cave,
All the jeunesse singing without
Stop, even during dinner,
The adolescent girls very
Unfrench with magnificent
Breasts. What is causing this change
In one generation in this
Country once without a mammal?
We leave for the river bank
And camp there in the evening.
It is easy to see the bison
Grazing in the meadows, smoke
Rising from the caves and huts.
Formidable bread, the best
We will ever find in France.

Deep in the bowels of mystery
Where young Cro-Magnons had their
Foreskins shorn, a wiry little
Peasant woman with a lantern
Says, "Regardez! Le dos! Les cornes!
Regardez! L'oeil! Le nez! La bouche!"
It is sad but true, the greatest
Cave artist was the Abbé Breuil.
On up to Lascaux, which if not
A fake points to lamentable
Taste amongst our protoplasts –
Sid Grauman's Cro-Magnon Theatre.

Every world is the reflection
Of the ones about it. Every
Event must take place in every
World in order. All existence
Is like an endless chain hanging
From infinite heaven and
Gradually drawn up. This world

Of yours seems like the last link,
But this is only an illusion
Of perspective. Within the
Atoms of your streaming blood
Millions of Troys burn every
Hour. This is the interest
You have taken in the concourse
Of persons of which you are a part.

Condat, we make camp back of a
Factory by the Vézère
And get dubious water
From a farm. The son is in
Training and runs round and round
The field till after dark. He
And his family are as poor,
As friendly, and as generous
As Neapolitans. We cook
Spaghetti with goat cheese on the
Primus and drink Monbazillac
Chilled from the twilit river.

Through Brive to Tulle, mean and dirty.
Through the mountains, lumbering
Villages, wood smoke in the air,
Old men and knitting women
And children watching the few
Cows and goats, the girls great flirts.
"Out at daybreak goes the farmgirl
With flock and spindle and fresh wool.
In her little herd are a lamb,
A donkey, a calf, and a heifer.
She frowns at the scholar sitting
On the turf, 'What are you doing,
Mister? Come and play with me.'"
You can always tell the

Prosperity of the country
And the value of labor
By who can afford to watch goats.

Argentât, camp in a pasture
On the upper Dordogne, the farm
Of a lean, wise old peasant with
A bustling tiny woman
He carefully lets us know
Is his mistress, not his wife.
Much talk of ordinary life
In the States, as distinguished from
The tourist businessmen they'd seen –
The price of beef, of bread, of clothes,
The financing of a farm,
The government farm programs,
Farm machinery, wages.
In the evening a foire
In Argentât, rather skimpy,
And in the night a thunderstorm
Cannonading the hillsides
And solid masses of rain. My
Himalayan tent leaks for the
First time in its life. Morning,
Broken clouds on the hills, swathes
Of mist on the river, and
Wading in mist to their shoulders,
Or with their heads lost in mist,
Fishermen like Chinese sages.
The French philosophy of
Fishing is at least as
Civilized as their attitude
Toward sex. They expect nothing but
Satisfaction from either.

Down the blue, winding river
Through forested hills to Beaulieu,
A fine portal on the church
And a hostel where the river
Teems with washerwomen,
Swallows, and fishermen.

The moral atom of this world,
The irreducible minimum,
Might be the aspect some person
Assumes to me as a speck
Of dust on the edge of the most
Remote imagined galaxy.
This of course is a relation
To myself projected and
Confounded with another.

A Harvest Fête on the local
Liberation Day, dancing
In the streets of Latronquière,
The procession led by a sword,
A flag on a spear, a loaf,
A sheaf king, and a full chalice,
A platter with cooked food – the Graal.
The sacraments of pagan Gaul
Will survive other liberations.

Through the highlands to Figeac,
A smelly town but still the France
Before three ruinous wars.
In the early morning old men
Busy whittling sabots, bakers'
Ovens like those in Pompeii,
Blacksmiths forging coulters, just
Like in Chaucer, cartwrights with
Spokeshaves at work on creamy
Sweet-smelling wood of new wagons.

The aubergiste is enchanted
To see me again, and produces
An excellent dinner and
In the morning, "un breakfast"
With scrambled eggs. Incroyable.

Rodez, back in civilization
After the Cantal, the cathedral
A red animal like Hereford,
And looted, too, like England.
Pound's wind blowing west through Langue d'Oc.

All day through the gorges and hills,
We get to Albi late at night,
A fine emergency repast
At our commercial hotel,
Bouillon, cassoulet with boiled beef,
Haricots verts with pommes, cold with
Oil and vinegar like Italy,
Wine as heavy as Burgundy,
Slabs of spongy white cheese, and great
Heaps of fruit, coffee, and anisette.
Then we walk slowly through the
Clear starlight to Sainte Cécile.

The stars over Sainte Cécile,
The five stars and the wide dark space,
Deneb and the cross of heaven,
The swan of Leda, black now,
His work done, and jewelled,
And climbing into his heart the
Vast uprushing, mountainous thought.
Beyond under the Pole Star,
The évêché silhouetted
Pale against the deep sky and
Stabbed with cross lights from the high
Windows of the ancient houses,

And from the highest, like a square
Cut topaz, a phonograph
Spilling "La Vie en rose,"
And inside the évêché
The rests of twisted Lautrec,
Lines like shrivelled mountain pines.

Ultimately the fulfillment
Of reality demands that
Each person in the universe
Realize every one of the
Others in the fullness of love.

Every day we eat ourselves
Drowsy in our little hotel
On the Vigan and sleep with
The rustle of the massive
Chestnut trees in our ears and
The warble of two small but
Softly musical fountains.
One of the chestnuts, blasted
In this year's historic drought,
Has just put forth new pale green stars
Of leaves and delicate tiers
Of unreal blossoms. The rest
Of the time we look at Cécile,
The finest integral work
Of art ever produced north
Of the Alps, a palisade
Of sequoias, the Karnak
Of Europe, the behemoth
Of orthodoxy that devoured
Langue d'Oc. And as the days go by,
The smoke of the Dominicans
Frying the population,
And the curses of the gunman

De Montfort, and the leaking
Pus of Papal hypocrisy
Form a film between the red
Brick cylinders, so noble
And aloof, and my eyes. I
Remember every day that
This fortress church is the symbol
Of the repression of all
That I love in France. The struggle
Of the vine, the olive, and the
Orange against coal, iron, and wool,
The lure of the narrow seas,
The soot of Flanders and the Rhine,
Against the clean blue classic sea.

Unless we can find somewhere
In the course of rebirth the
Realization of all
Persons through the transcendence
Of the self, what I have called
Extrapersonalization,
We must go on mopping the sea,
Quantitatively again
And again reorganizing
The universe of consequence
And possibility in terms
Of our appetites until we
Have entered into personal
Relations with every person
Who now appears as only
One of the electrons of
The present universe.

Rabasson, a filthy church
In a filthy village, the
Fourteenth-century frescoes

Like a healthy Puvis, sweet
As pictures in a child's bedroom,
De Monvel's Jeanne, but honest.

Crossing from the Tarn to the
Garonne, a black storm gathers
In the Pyrenees, breaks up
And lifts over the warm valley
And piles up against the Massif.
Only fringes of its skirts
Brush us as we race down miles
Of hills to Toulouse. Bright lightning
And quick thunder to the east,
And glimmers and murmurs over
The Pyrenees, and great white
Exploding drops in the late sun
So that you think for a moment,
"Here comes the hail." And at last
In twists of wind, hail does come and
Almost hammers us off our
Vélos just as we bump onto
The cobbles of Toulouse.

The true capital of France,
Toulouse like a happier,
Freer Spanish city, like
Mexico, or Los Angeles
Before the Baptists came.
Cassoulet with dark goosemeat
And Tolosian sausage, and
The faint flavor of saffron
And garlic, a formidable
Dessert and the wine of Toulouse,
Dry, bitter goat cheese from the
Pyrenees, and dense sweet coffee
Full of sparks like Italy.
All the leafy city – the

Allées and boulevards and parks
And squares full of bright hurrying
People, an atmosphere as
Bracing as nineteen twenty in
Chicago. How infinitely
Better off the modern world
Would be if Raimon had won
Instead of the Pope's gangster
And the king of the Isle de France.
Saint Sernin Gaudi's grandfather –
The split personality
Of the cathedral a symbol
Of the conquered city. An
Immense piscine where we
Swim until exhausted and
Bicycle home in the scarlet
Evening, the pale green moon
Over the red brick buildings.
In the museum some fine
Romanesque sculpture, some carved
Capitals, very Byzantine,
With biblical figures like
The Four Kings at San Marco.
An American male torch-
Singer in the main café.
Black-haired, black-eyed whores with heavy
Gold earrings, full-fleshed in thin
Translucent summer dresses.

France fell at Appomattox.
Louis-Napoleon had schemed
For a Mediterranean
Union, a commonwealth of Greece,
Spain, Turkey, Egypt, Italy.
In a generation the
British could have gone back to woad.
To flatter his wife and keep

Austria quiet on the
Adriatic, he bet on
Maximilian and the South.
Grant knew how to fight with railroads,
Juárez's bullets murdered
The last chance of a Latin
Roman Empire, Napoleon
Succumbed to the industrial
And banking North and bit Bismarck,
And that was the end of France.

At last we leave, bicycle
Through villages each with a
Red brick church with bells in a
Pierced gable, what we call "Mission,"
Out past Villefranche and camp
On the Canal du Midi under
The ancient plane trees; full moon;
Great Romanesque farmhouses
Each with an attached arched barn;
A bridge and lock; an old village
Across it; the silver canal
Curving away through black shadows
Of the dense trees; and at dawn
The quiet barges swishing past.

The person is transcended
By the reflection of himself
In the other in love, the
Unique is universalized
In the dual, any important
Crux of reality is
Only the emergence of
A person into a love
Perspective, experience
Has no other real content.

Heavy bicycling all morning,
Down hill in second gear against
A pounding southeast wind from the
Mediterranean, millions
Of cubic miles of transparency
With millions of tons of pressure
Rushing up from Africa.
At the watershed they change the
Trees on the canal to cypress
Because of the constant wind.

In Carcassonne a wistful young
Algerian silver miner
From the Pyrenees who finds
Us a place for lunch at three o'clock,
Incredible in France, and who
Begs us to stay with him that night
And tries to pay for our lunch.
Up to buggery or worse,
No doubt, but very touching.
The castle a tiresome visite.

Quillan, a fête in progress,
No one will feed or house us
In town, a fine restaurant
Under great trees, off on the
Highway, regal food and Blanquette
De Limoux, better than champagne,
Soft sheep cheese and sexual pears
And bunches of the new grapes,
Armagnac like Spanish brandy
And black Levantine coffee.
The Pyrenees and the moon and
The rushing river out the window.
Dancing in the jam-packed streets until
Almost dawn, and then out of town
On the vélos, we camp in

A pinewood, moonblades on the
Loud mountain water, the smell
Of the dry pines parching the nose.

The universe of persons
Is reflected in me as
The inexhaustible content
Of experience, as a
Mountain is reflected in
A mirror or as the moon
In water held in the hand.

Thunderstorms in the Pyrenees.
Very few of the peasants
Speak anything but perfect
Textbook French, all the dialects
Of France are fading away
Before the conquering State.

History assumes the State
As the extrapersonal
Vehicle of memory.
What is important is what is
Held in the sieve of polity.
The State is the great forgetter.

High in the mountains one of the
Few screen doors in France, bright brand-new
Copper, and near the sill a neat
Hole cut out for the cat.

Perpignan really like Latin
America, a pleasant, dusty,
Meaningless town. Two fatigued
Merlans for lunch, but saffron
In the rice, and southern wine.

Nightbound, we camp on the Etang
De Solces, mosquitoes in dense clouds
And flies that bite out pieces.
The primus fails, impossible
To reach the sea and swim, we
Fill the tent with DDT spray
And crawl in in spite of the thick heat,
Drink macabeu and go to sleep.
Next morning we encourage
The primus and cook last night's
Risotto for breakfast and drink
The rest of the macabeu.

My knowledge of the others is
Of all grades of indirection.
Love provides an object which may
Be known more and more directly.
In the sex act it may be
Known fully and directly
But only for so brief a time.

Narbonne, the first city of Gaul,
Ruined by the Pope, de Montfort,
And the French king, the cathedral
Only a grandiose choir,
All that was ever finished.
We have Narbonnese honey
At lunch, and find some real ice cream.

Béziers, here de Montfort butchered
Twenty thousand in one day.
The fortress church looms over the
Orb and the Plateau des Poètes.

Cette on its hill in the sea
Marshes, orange and cream-colored
Seventeenth-century houses

Doubled in the glassy canals.
Montpellier busy as
A city in America.

On into Nîmes, the best taste
Of Rome left in the world, fountains
And columns, boulevards and
Terraced water, all the city
Emanating from the old
Temple, as classical as Bath
But not compulsive about it.
Here at last is one place untouched
By the Normans or the English,
No sign of Gothic mentalism –
In fact, the best looking church
Is modern Romanesque. They say
The city was once Calvinist,
Now it seems hardly Christian.
Splendid food, a masterwork
Of a pâté truffé which the
Host carries about like a
Newborn baby, cèpes dipped in
Olive oil and grilled, guinea hen,
Dove, aubergines provençales,
Courgettes stuffed with spiced soft cheese,
Thick crinkly fresh noodles, rice
With saffron, wines like the small wines
Of Naples. The natives put ice in it!

A specialty of Nîmes –
The extraordinarily
Hard-boiled looking whores; like
The girls at Les Halles in Paris
Who circulate amongst the
Flying boxes and vegetables,
Hustling the camion drivers
In the dawn; the same dirty

Bare legs, short skirts, and bobby sox,
Teetering on novelty shoes
In the Jardin de la Fontaine at
Lunch time, their eyes hard in the sun.
Vice during siesta, the touch
Of the Mediterranean.
But where do they come from? Out of
Marseilles for a little rest?

A sudden cold wind at night and
Explosions of lightning and
Rivers of rain, all the lights
In town go out. We stand on
The balcony and watch the trees
And the fountain flash purple white,
And then plunge into black again.
The wind roars, the thunder bangs,
We make love by the open window.

Discursive knowledge, knowledge by
Indirection passes away
And love, knowledge by direction,
Directly of another, grows
In its place. There exists a point
At which the known passes through
A sort of occultation,
A zero between plus and
Minus in which knower and known
And their knowledge cease to exist.
Perfect love casts out knowledge.

The Pont du Gard as beautiful
As ever. Why can't a culture
Of businessmen and engineers
Make beautiful things? I walk
Across on top and then back
Under the small arches with

Idyllic frames of Provence
Slipping past me and suddenly
I notice the shells in the rock –
With my head full of the
Fossils of a million years,
Standing on this fossilized
Roman engineering, built of
Mudflats and fossil seas, springing
From cliffs with caves of fossil man –
Half-naked jeunesse with golden
Bodies scamper over golden
Stone, the air is full of swallows
Whirling above flowing water.

There are three ways of loving,
Modes of communication,
The realization via
The ground of possibility,
We touch each other through the
Material of love, the earth
Center which all share; or by means
Of ultimate inclusive
Action, the empyrean
Shared by all persons where the
Mythology and drama
Of the person is realized
In pure archetype; or face
To face in the act of love,
Which for most men is the way
In which the other modes are
Raised into consciousness and
Into a measure of control.

Provence hot, the hills grey with heat,
Miles of olive trees, silver green,
The color of Sung celadon,
The houses peach colored, over

Each doorway a grape vine, around
It the wall stained pale blue-green with
Copper sulphate spray. Avignon,
Beautiful across the river
But with a god damned visite;
(The legends and chauvinism
Of an ancien combattant,
Permitted, because he has given
A leg or arm to France to beg
In this tedious way. Splendid
Fellows, salty and wise, as who
Wouldn't have to be if this
Was all he got from a grateful
People, but hardly the screen
Through which to absorb The Past.)
And over all the lingering
Stink of the Papacy and
The present stink of English tourists.
The vélos roll down hill, mile
After mile beside rushing
Water after Aix. We go for
A swim in the cold piscine at
The Roman baths and on into
That city of small splendors.

Seldom has man made so perfect
A work of art of light and shade.
The Fromentins are fine in the
Cathedral, but they can't compare
With the green submarine light
Of the Cours Mirabeau broken
By pools of clarity at the
Small fountains at the crossings,
The dark gloom and black statue
Of King René at one end,
The white glare of the Fountain
Of Culture at the other.

Certainly the most civilized
Man ever to get mixed up
With a revolution has
An elegant monument.

The author of *Le Rideau levé*,
Approached as a colleague by
Sade in prison, repulsed him
Succinctly, "Mon Sieur, je ne suis
Pas ici pour avoir donné des
Confits empoisonnés aux femmes
De chambre." The existentialistes
Don't like him very much.

Granet painting in Rome, never
Forgot that light and shade. In
The museum his paintings with
Their stereoscopic values
Hang by his two portraits –
The famous Ingres, more handsome
Than Byron, and another
Of an old, old, dying man.
Lots of Cézanne watercolors
Full of peach blossoms and leaf flicker.

Milhaud, Cendrars, Tal-Coat, a place
Where men with balls can escape
The maggots of the Deux Magots.

Dinner at the Café Mistral,
Plover's eggs and tomatillos
In aspic, écrevisse, raw tuna
With chives, thick noodles with saffron,
Duckling with truffles and cèpes,
Fricassée of guinea hen,
A local wine, not still, not
Sparkling, but volatile like

The chiantis of Florence,
A dark blue cheese, and black, black
Coffee and Rémy Martin
And thick layers of cream –
And then like all the world we
Promenade on Mirabeau's
Fine street and eat glaces and
Drink more cognac and coffee.
At last the strange malady
Of France has vanished and the
Women once more are mammals.

At last the ability to
Know directly becomes a
Habit of the soul and the
Dominant mode in which
Possibility is presented
To the developing person.
As such it ceases to appear
As consequence and becomes
Conscious communion with a
Person. A duality
Is established which focuses
The reflection of the mountain
As an illuminating ray
On the mountain itself,
The moon dissolves in the water
Held in the palm of the hand.

Mile after mile of the fertile
Valleys and the arid mountains
Of Provence. All the world is
Out picking grapes – and great wheeled
Carts in long lines, hauling them
To the wineries. Young peasants
Pelt us with grapes as we ride past.

Fréjus, heavy-breasted and bruised
Whores, Senegalese and Indo-
Chinois soldiers brawl all night
In the streets, even the women
In the shops try to hustle me.

Saint-Raphaël, a California
Town, full of pastry shops and
English children and high-class tarts.
We camp on Cap Rouge and swim
In the warm sea, the Esterels
Over us, the Alps beyond Nice
Coming and going behind
High-piled storm clouds where at night
Sheet lightning wavers like an
Aurora.

                    Lunch in Cannes from
Heavy handfuls of bursting fruit.

Agape is built on philia;
Eros on agape; caritas,
The supernatural eros,
On eros; and caritas
Is again the foundation
Of a transformed philia.
Thus the process is a cyclic
Ascent of realms of value.

The vélos stagger in the wind
And we grind into Nice, the
Beverly Hills of the middle
Classes of Europe. A great
Sense of bustling fornication,
Raving beauties in the crowds
Offering themselves for free,
The small type advertisements

In the papers one long epic
Of classified eroticism –
"Tall, striking blonde, properly
Gloved and shod, desires exchange
Lessons in English for advanced
Lessons in French, will pay well."
Thank God, for once a city
Without any monuments!
Two days of promenading
And swimming in the sea and
Then the bus to Genova.

Love, like all the sacraments, is a
Miniature of being itself.
All things have an apparent
Meaning and an opposite
Hidden meaning brought forth by fire.
The phoenix and the tortoise,
The dragon and the unicorn,
Man, eagle, bull, and lion.

III

Zoroaster long ago
Said poetry presents us
With apparent pictures of
Unapparent realities.

The sleep which fell on Adam
Was the deep lassitude
Of divine contemplation.
Eve arose, a projection,
From his dreaming heart. Blake
Made a picture of it once.

Diana Marina, my
Favorite on the Italian

Riviera. Quiet, few
People, no foreigners.
We pass through the town and stop at
An albergo on the river.
The terrace overlooks the sea,
And we swim before dinner
In the sunset Mediterranean.
The owner is a fisherman.
He rows away, standing up,
And looking forward, Italian
Style, into pink and blue space.
We are too happy to be hungry.
We eat only pasta and wine,
Grignolino, the first blood
Of the South. As the padrona
Fills out my card, she says, "San
Francesco, eh? Giannin' è mort'
Oggi," in a sepulchral voice and
Passes me the Genova paper.
I must admit she moves me. It's a
Personal tragedy for her.
I walk in the early evening
On the empty spianato
And turn into town. In a
Very San Francisco–like
Café and billiard room I
Have that best of all heavy
Brandies, Vecchia Romagna.
After France, the toilet seems
As clean as a laboratory.
The streets are wide for Italy,
And the houses square and trim,
Like the seventeenth-century
Ones on the Piazza Navona.
The streets are flagged and all they need
Are the crossing blocks to look
Exactly like Pompeii.

Fireflies are dipping and
Wavering in thin clouds of
Sparkle two feet thick over
All the pavements. In the red
Light district, the beautiful
Deep breasted, long legged, regal
Necked Italian whores are
Wading with elegant carriage
Knee deep in glittering fireflies.

Poetry like the unclouded
Crystal and the uncut block,
And the details of the mirage of life,
Presents contemplation
With its instruments. Then isn't
Contemplation a kind of judgment?
It is all the judgment there is.
The others are paranoia.

As the Philosopher says,
The process of developing
Life complicates but enriches
The world. The process of thought
Simplifies but eviscerates
It. Contemplation is the
Preeminent process of
Developing life; yet it
Follows the form and movement
Of thought. Hence it both unifies
And enriches, and overcomes
The conflicting one and many.
Universalization
Of contemplation is wisdom.
Contemplation is the final
Form of responsibility,
The only truly effective
Mode, and source of all others.

There is no difference between
Love and contemplation as far
As the actual reality
Is concerned. What is taken in
In contemplation is poured out
In love. Love, as a description
Of the process, is the truer
Term because the person
Is more adequately defined.

Genova hot and roaring,
Considerably uglier than
Ashtabula or Gary.
Two coy lions guard the Duomo.
A comprehensive of Magnasco –
"Bad artists dislike painting
Dogs and horses, and prefer
Dragons, demons, and spirits."
A painter for the American
Fairies. A dock strike, Togliatti
Worrying the government,
Ragged workers and double
Breasted bureaucrats, nobody
Seems to know what it is about.
They do what they are told.
Spaghetti, boiled beef, cold
Fagiolini, black grapes, and
Purple inky wine in the
Ristorante Comunale.
We come in late, so all the
Waitresses and their lingering
Boy friends practice up their English.
Everybody very happy
To discover Americans
Who are not rich. My copy
Of *Umanità Nuova*
Creates a tremendous sensation.

Genovese art is dull, the most
Impressive things in town are
The old banking houses, one
Of the finest, with immense
Lanterns and elaborate
Ironwork, now the offices
Of Signor Giannini, the
Cavour of the Second World War,
Nonentity's new arrivéd guest.

The political innocence
Of the Italians is shown
In the fact that every city
Has a Via Cavour. The waste
Of history. Get what you can.
If you don't, somebody
Else will. "Entia non sunt
Multiplicanda praeter
Necessitatem," said Pilate.

The lover and the beloved
Rise above the levels of
Appetite, discursive knowledge,
Consequence, probability,
And enter into each other
Directly. Knowledge of each
Other becomes a mode of
Being, and through each other
The being of all the others
Is realized more and more
Directly. The lover first
Divorces himself from all
Desire to use the beloved.
This means divorcing himself
From all appetite for things.
If the lover desires only
Union with the beloved, and

Desires nothing else, he has
Nothing left to use the beloved
For except herself. The naked
Mutual being is enough
To satisfy all life's desires.
Love is mutual indwelling
Without grasping. It is knowledge
Of another as a state of
Being rather than a process.
Possession and being possessed
Are not a part of love. Indwelling
Is not possession. One does not
Possess oneself. The contract
Relationship of civilized
Love is lust, the balancing
Of possessive appetites.

The will to live or the will to
Power or the will to love.

The fire of the sexual act,
The wedding of light and darkness,
Boehme's scream and flame, the pregnant
Echo of the sound of eternity.

All the highway crowded with
Bicyclists and strolling couples.
Above Shelley's bay the olive
Hills fall away in terraces,
All under the trees, couples as
Beautiful as Praxiteles,
Fucking in the silvery shade,
In the hot perfumed air of
Pentecoste, celebrating
The descent of the dual flame.
We wait, in company with
Miles of cars and busses, high
On the ridge above Rapallo,

Beside a peasant rococo
Church we expect to suddenly
Start revolving and tinkling,
While the Communist Party
Uses the steep highway for a
Motorbike race. Rapallo –
Far worse than treason or dementia,
Pound endured this Atlantic City
Of Czechoslovak yachtsmen and
Swiss gamblers for twenty-five years!
Between the strips of grain are lines
Of poplars with vines growing
On a demountable trellis
Seven feet high. In other parts
Of Italy the vines grow
Directly on the mulberries.
Virgil says elm is the best,
But that was before they raised silk.

Viareggio, maybe the world's
Best beach resort. Nobody
There but Italians, quiet, clean,
Orderly, graceful, no rolly
Coasters, clip joints, or Shriners,
But lots of ice cream, coffee,
Brandy, good food, white sand, and
The warm and gentle purple sea.
During the war a regiment
Of boys from old Southern families
Was quartered in town.
Giosi says, as we walk in the
Moonlit pinewood, "Man, yo right down
In front. Man, ah relly dig yo.
Ah means, yo groovy, yo send me!"
She talks this way all the time
Under the impression she is
Speaking the English language.

It is the essence of love
To transcend consequence. Love
Is the total act of the
Person, all other activity
Is contributory to
The act of love, which is the
Special and definitive
Act of the person. That is
What a person is, a lover.

Having never read any of
These "Lost Art Treasures" books,
At Pisa we run across the lawns
To the Campo Santo, open
The door and rush inside. The shock
Is too much for me and I drop
Onto a bench made of a
Roman capital and gasp with pain.
An old gentleman, looking much
Like Victor Emmanuel, comes
Over and pats me on the head.
"Si, si, si, war is horrible.
You did not know the frescoes were
Gone? The Inglesi. Everywhere
In Italia they have
Destroyed the monumenti.
The Tedeschi and the Americani
Were careful, but the Inglesi
Are jealous of Italia.
Even today they are still
At war with us."

Cardinals
Saying vespers in the Duomo.
Isaiah's wizards who peeped
And muttered behind the altar.
But, says the judgment, "My hands shall
Find as a nest the riches

Of the people; and as one
Gathereth eggs that are left,
Shall I gather all the earth;
And none shall move the wing or
Open the mouth, or peep."

Here Pound
Stumbled to the pitiful
Conclusion of the longest
And most highly decorated
Hymn of hate in literature.

How easy it is to hate
A people who claim all the
Mundane advantages of a
Supernatural community
And carefully deny all the
Transcendental responsibilities.
Everybody tries it, as
Max Weber points out, but no one
So successfully as the Jews,
Who hurt only themselves.

"I can get it for you wholesale."
In fact, the Jewish middle class
Do it better than the Masons
Or the Knights of Columbus, quite
Automatically. The poor,
Far from B'nai B'rith, deep down
Underground from the Talmud,
Keep the ancient communion,
The pagan sensual bond,
Older than the Torah, old as
The new moon on the sacred pillar.
The atomized, secularized
Gentile wage slave can be excused
A little wistful envy.

Ancient Hebrew religion
Was essentially orgiastic,
In the sense that mystical
Fulfillment, the actual
Worship of the gods, consisted
In the physical act of
Begetting children before the
Lord. At the climax of sexual
Union, the goddess Shekinah,
Jehovah's embodied Glory,
Was made manifest over the
Marriage bed, coupled with her
Divine lover. It was from
Their union, really, that the seed
Of Israel descended to
The womb of the enraptured wife.
Post-exilic Judaism
Extracted from this mystic
Orgiastic cult only its
Ritual prohibitions
And injunctions, robbed of content.
The ancient religion survived
Occulted in the Kabbalah
And Chasidism, and in the
Stubbornly held folkways of
The Ghetto. For instance, the
Roofs of the little arbors
Built in the backyard to this day
By good Jews on the Feast of
The Great Mother, are purposely
Only a scant openwork,
So that she may descend and
Possess the husband and wife as they
Make love under the new moon.

In the shadow of the lingam
And yoni, the massebah,
On the feast of oil and wine,

From the arbors of Asiph,
From the embracing lovers,
Joy spread like a sweet incense
In the fire of communion.
Then the virgins of Israel,
Adorned with tabrets, went forth
In the dances of them that
Make merry. Then the winepress
Was trod with joy and gladness.
There was shouting at the vintage.
When the daughters of Shiloh
Came out to dance in dances,
The men came from the vineyards,
And every man took a bride.

She answered me so gaily,
She seemed to burn in love's first flame,
"Brother, our will is stilled by
The power of love which makes us
Wish only for what we have
And thirst for nothing else."

"Long as the feast of Paradise,
So long our love shall wrap us
In the rays of such a garment.

Brightness shall follow our ardor,
Ardor, our vision. All shall be
Gracious with its true value.

Here we do not repent, but smile
Not at sin which never comes to mind,
But at the value which orders

And provides. The love which moves
All being, penetrates the
Universe, and shines back, in

Some things more, in others, less."

When the Romans hunted him
Who had dared to speak against them,
Simon ben Johai took his son,
Eleazar, and they hid
Buried to their necks in a
Cave for fourteen years and a
Miracle fed them. And when
They came out the son's eyes burned
The mundane works of men with
Transcendental wrath, but the word
Of the father restored them.
And an ancient peasant came
And presented them with two sprays
Of myrtle. And Eleazar
Smelled them and found them perfumed
With the odors of Paradise.
And Simon ben Johai said,
"It is the perfume of the
Hidden bride in heaven, the
Sabbath, the cloud of glory."
And Eleazar remembered
The bride wreaths of Israel.
And his father said to him,
"This is the work which the Lord
Has made, let us rejoice and
Be glad in it." And they went
To Rome and healed the daughter
Of the Emperor of the
Devil which had entered her.

Antisemitism is
An exceptional folly
In the roster of lunacy.
Actually, the power

Of the rabbinate has been
So absolute that the Jew
Has wasted millennia
Tangled in a meaningless
Legalism and has not
Functioned as a social
Or economic competitor
Of the Gentile world at all.
The Elders of Zion doubtless
Conspired, but only to enslave
And make impotent their own race.
Once I had the sentimental
Hope that some of the old ways
Would come back in Palestine
In the secular kibutzim.
But today ex-radical
And liberal Jews call Buber
A crypto-Christian and traitor
To his blood, and go to parties
At the homes of rich and silly
Women, and hop around by
Candle light, making noises
Like Fanny Brice, while a
Grimjawed, double-breasted
Bureaucrat gathers in the take.
What price Utopia in dollars?
A kibutz for every taste.
Down the chute to destruction, the
Last bourgeois nationalism.

Who is the "English King" buried
At Lucca? An historical
Mystery like the Chartres
Fellow, come home to die after
A life spent in High Asia
In the service of the Great Khan.

After Chase and Sanborn's coffee
At Leland's Bar, the American
Fairies cruise the Lungarno,
Hunting tall, broadshouldered, hungry
Florentines. At the local court
Of the king and queen of the set
Who commute between Florence
And Tangiers, a party for
Their world's leading poet.
My mother used to say, "A snob
Is a person who mimics the
Manners of those above him."
All the hell of American
Italy. I look in the door
And flee back to Florence, and run
Into miles of Communists
Marching under the immense icons
Of Stalin, Molotov, Togliatti,
And

MAO TSE TUNG
POETA E GUERRIERO

I am convinced the Dogana
Allows no heterosexual
American under forty
Past the Italian border.
Under the arcades of the Uffizi
At night lie sleeping family
After family, cuddled
Around their babies. In the
Piazza, the orchestra
Plays "La Vie en rose." The waiter
Gives me my change – the first new coins
Stamped "Repubblica Italiana."
Boethius and Theodoric,
Dante and Machiavelli,
Rienzi, Emperors, and Popes,

Arnold of Brescia, Federigo,
Are as dead as Mazzini.
The long pain of history
In my heart is too much for me.
The blonde wife of the band leader
Sings, "Mene, mene, tekel, upharsin."

Why this sudden outburst of
Homosexuality?
The American mass culture
Has identified the normal
Sex relation with the stuffing
Of an omnivorous and
Insensate vagina with
Highly perishable and
Expensive objects of non
Utility. Useless value
Has replaced use value and has
Been linked with sex satisfaction.
Since every young American
Male knows that very soon the State
Is going to take him out and
Murder him very nastily,
He is inclined to withdraw from
The activities prescribed for him
In the advertising pages.
Since it is physically
Impossible to realize
The fullness of love except
Between a man and woman,
This is at best a sort of
Marking time before execution.
For similar reasons, children
In the highschools take heroin.
Why not? They gave Christ narcotics
On the cross. You cannot expect
To terrify children with

Atom bomb drills and quiet them
With Coca-Cola. During the
Last months of the Second War,
The Japanese had begun
An experimental, routine
Administration of shock
Therapy to all combat troops.
Only the decorticated
Will be able to survive the
Last horrors of the profit system.
French radical youth, like
The Wandervögel before them,
Have a better way of marking
Time until the monsters destroy
Each other: Keep uncompromised;
Stay poor; try to keep out from
Under the boot; love one another;
Reject all illusions; wait.
"Antisemitism" said
Marx, "is the socialism of
Fools." Homosexuality
Is the revolt of the timid.

Boswell: "Sir, what is the chief
Virtue?" Johnson: "Courage, Sir,
Without it, opportunity
To exercise the others
Will often be found wanting."

On his first visit to the States
Wells was asked what most impressed him.
He said, "The female schoolteachers.
In two generations they will
Destroy the country." It took one.

In the Uffizi I prefer
To spend most of my time with the

Even tempered Greeks and Romans.
Pictures in galleries always
Look to me like dressed meat in
Butcher shops. From Cimabue
And Simone Martini,
Arrows point across the river
To Bronzino, and via
Raphael, to Picasso.
Without Florence, there isn't
Really any modern painting,
But just the same, it looks cooked.
Straight through, from beginning to end,
It is all Mannerism.
In the churches you get tired
Of all the Taddis and Gaddis.
Why does no one ever point out
That the great Masaccios are
Compounded of the elements
Of Roman painting, and no
Others at all, and that each figure
Is derived from classic sculpture?
There is the same knowledge of
Good and evil, and in the face
Of it, the same serenity.

God is that person who
Satisfies all love, with whom
Indwelling encompasses
All reality. It is
Impossible to say if there
Exists only one god, the
Ultimate beloved of all
Persons. It would seem rather,
Since the relationship is
Reciprocal and progressive,
That there are as many gods
As lovers. Theoretically

One infinite god could
Satisfy all finite lovers –
But this concept comes from the
Insoluble residues of
The quantitative mathematics
Of infinitudes. It really
Has no place in the discussion
Of the love relationship,
Which knows neither finite nor
Infinite. The Shekinah
And Jehovah are only
An enlarged mirror image
Of the terrestrial embrace.
The sephiroth of the Kabbalah
Are the chakras of the Tantra.
The records of Hafidh, Rumi,
St. Theresa, even the crazed
Augustine, seem to be the
Records in each case of a
Unique duality. The
Object of love is a person
Like the lover, and the demands
On the definition of
A monotheistic god
Made by other philosophical
Considerations, largely
Of an arithmetical
Nature, make it unlikely
That such an entity could be
Also a person. There is here a
Collision of two exclusive
Modes of viewing reality.
Hence perhaps the peculiar
Subjective tension of the
Monotheistic mystic,
The reason why he always feels

His love as incomplete and
Destructive of his person.

Agathias Scholasticus:
Restless and discontent
I lie awake all night long.
And as I drowse in the dawn,
The swallows stir in the eaves,
And wake me weeping again.
I press my eyes close tight, but
Your face rises before me.
O birds, be quiet with
Your tittering accusations.
I did not cut that dead girl's tongue.
Go weep for her lover in the hills,
Cry by the hoopoe's nest in the rocks.
Let me sleep for a while, and dream
I lie once more in my girl's arms.

Under a lattice of leaves
Her white thighs in cloth of gold
That casts a glittering shade.
She turned to her left and stared at
The sun. My imagination
Was moved by her gesture, and as
I turned, I saw the sun
Sparkle all round, like iron
Pulled molten from the furnace.

Bright petals of evening
Shatter, fall, drift over Florence,
And flush your cheeks a redder
Rose and gleam like fiery flakes
In your eyes. All over Florence
The swallows whirl between the
Tall roofs, under the bridge arches,

Spiral in the zenith like larks,
Sweep low in crying clouds above
The brown river and the white
River bed. Your moist, quivering
Lips are like the wet scarlet wings
Of a reborn butterfly who
Trembles on the rose petal as
Life floods his strange body.

Turn to me. Part your lips. My dear,
Some day we will be dead.

I feel like Pascal often felt.

About the mid houre of the nicht

FIRE

The air is dizzy with swallows.

Sunset comes on the golden
Towers, on the Signoría.
In the Badía, the light goes
From the face of Filippino's
Weary lady, exhausted with
The devotion of her worshipper.
Across the face of the Duomo
The Campanile's blue shadow
Marks the mathematics of beauty.
In San Miniato the gold
Mosaics still glitter through
The smoky gloom. At the end
Of the Way of the Cross, the dense
Cypress wood, full of lovers,
Shivering with impatience.
As the dark thickens, two by two
They take each other. Nightfall, all

The wood is filled with soft moaning,
As though it were filled with doves.

In this way, lifted to this height,
These creatures trace the spoor of
The Eternal Value to the
End and pattern of all things.

The insoluble problems –
The order of nature, the
Ego and the other, the
Freedom of the will, evil,
Identity, time, mind and
Body, indeterminateness,
The economy of nature,
The unity of knowledge,
The principle of conservation,
Essence and existence, form
And content, act and power,
Rest and motion, the one and
The many, all these have no
Meaning in the fulfillment
Of love. All that is, needs, in
Its ultimate reality,
Some sort of definition;
But what we know of its
Apparent character would be
Better described as a
Community of lovers,
Rather than an Absolute
And its aspects, or a Creator
And his contingent creatures.

Maybe the Or' San Michele
Is an architectural
What is it, but every night
We walk around it a couple

Of times before we go home.
I can never forget those
Supple bodies and lithe faces –
In the summer twilight when
"The swallows and the bats change guard,"
In the perfumed smoke of Autumn,
And glazed with chilling rain.
I know of no intact building
Which gives you more of a sense
Of being a part of a
Civilized community.
And there around you on the streets
Are the same beautiful people
With the same potential in them.

As the Philosopher says,
He who contemplates a statue
Shares the thought of the artist;
The statue itself does not.
As the soul contemplates nature,
The spirit the light, and the mind
The stars, every eye sees into
The matrix from which it was born.

We walk by the Arno singing
Cowboy and hillbilly songs.
One night on the Via dei
Servii, I am singing "The
Wreck of the Ninety Seven"
At the top of my voice. When I
Get to the line, "His whistle broke
Into a scream," I go, "WHOO! WHOO!"
And scare a poor civilized
Florentine dog. He jumps straight up,
Rigid with terror, and then goes
Into paroxysms of shrill
Barking that may be lasting yet.

Lawrence, Lawrence, what a lot
Of hogwash you have fathered.
Etruscan art is just plain bad.
It is the commercial art
Of mercenary provincials,
On a par with Australian
Magazine covers. Where it is
Good at all, it was done by Greeks.
True, something of the secret
Prehomeric world lingers, but
Homer lingers in Canberra.
The Hellenistic Chimera
Which all the highbrows disdain
Is a better organized horror,
And the Apollo of Veii
A better hierophant of the
Great Mother of Crete and the Isles,
Than anything the natives did.
And by far the best Etruscan
Architect was Thomas Jefferson.

An enormous amount of
Misplaced ingenuity,
Especially since the rise of
Capitalist Protestantism,
With its "existential anguish,"
Has gone to the reducing
Of each basic context or
Description of experience
To a dilemma, and then
Resolving the dilemma
By calling it resolved, and
Calling the resolution
God. Actually our descriptions
Of experience run out
Into a very patent
Dilemma – experience itself,

Which is not exhaustible
By quantitative description,
And which is its own context.
Experience, to be known, must,
Obviously, be experienced.
The purely logical culs-
De-sac adduced as proofs of God
Are unworthy of the subject.
God is lover and beloved – a
Person – or he is nothing
Important. I see no way
Of proving his nonexistence,
But there is no way of proving
That the person experienced
By all the lovers of God
Is actually the same person,
And if the only absolute
Is a community of equals,
There is no room for him.
Experience is the
Manifestation of persons
One to another. It is
Possible for all experience
To be absorbed and evalued
By the manifestation of
One person, and all other
Persons and their manifestations
Seen only through the one lover.
But this is precisely the end
Of all persons – the opening
Of the Summum Bonum, the
Beatific Vision, and is
Found in the plenum of love,
The interlocking manifold
Of dualities, not in a monist
Absolute and its contingent beings.

San Lorenzo in Perugia –
A jewel box restored with
An exquisite sense of chic,
Which could not quite overcome
The strange, sterile, diseased murals
Of Aliense, that well-named painter –
Full of chairs for a concert,
The front rows marked CINEASTI.
A little door behind the
Altar. Fiat Lux! Assisi
Far away on its hill in the
Blazing air of Umbrian Summer.
At the Ristorante Comunale,
A fine Umbrian ham, mast fed,
Flesh like the game of Artemis.
When I tell an American
Where I eat, he acts as though
I had just come from Smolny Institute
And never speaks to me again.

This brings up the question, are
The other human beings,
The people around us who
Seem part of the unreal things
Of time and space, only more
Active, real? Are they all persons,
Potential objects of our love?
This question has no real meaning.
It is like, "Is compassion green?"
When viewed as part of the world
Of quantity, no. Just as the
Bursting of bombs, the falling
Of leaves or stars, are the voices
Of some person speaking to us,
Are perspectives on a person,
So the figures of clothed bipeds
Which surround us are similar

Perspectives. We assume from
Experience that if approached,
The person will in each case
Be present, usually more
Accessible than in the leaf
Or star. However, as part
Of the world of consequence
And possibility, "this crowd
Of men" is illusory.

Arezzo, a fine commercial
Hotel, our bedroom ceiling
Covered with Turks and tigers.
Splendid gnocchi and heady wine –
Montepulciano – strong for lunch.
After a day immersed in the
Lucid systems of Piero,
I realize that he had
The first true neoclassic mind,
Anti-expressive and hence
Expressive of every strange
Cold torture of the regular
Beating of the orderly heart.
Constantine's "we worship
Cold water and the moon, beaten
By the hawk's wings of vision."
Baudelaire might have painted it.

Siena, two American
Fairies sipping brandy before
The Cathedral, all the urchins
Crying, "Milioni! Milioni!"
Heady stuff for boys from Texas,
Especially just after lunch.
Sienese painting was so suave,
So civilisé, so sick,
So early doomed. The Southern

Sung were like this, but they managed
To keep it a good deal cleaner.
Rossetti knew his parents.

For the undeveloped heart,
The news or even the sight
Of the destruction of thousands
Of other human beings
May assume only the form
Of a distant cry, coming
Through the complexities of
Disaster, of one other
Person. An air raid may be
Only a distraction from
A letter to a sweetheart;
The famines and floods of China
Only transportation
Difficulties between hotels.
However, as the dual,
The beloved, is known and
Loved more and more fully, all
The universe of persons
Grows steadily more and more real.
Eventually loss or pain
To the least of these, the most
Remote known person of the
Other, is felt personally
Through the intense reality
Of the dual. There is no
Way of proving the existence
Of a person except by
Experience, but we assume
The appearance "human being"
Is always, at least potentially,
The immediate vesture
Of a person. None the less,
It must not be forgotten

That, as such, this appearance is
Only a sign of possible
Underlying reality
In a manifold of empty
Contingency. There is no
Self subsistence whatever
In the manifold as such.

A girl nun, praying cruciform,
Her face pressed against the
Portiuncula, suddenly
Utters a high, hawk-like scream
And faints. Over this blackened
Dolmen of love rises a
Monstrous vulgar church, worse than
Anything to be found in
America or Australia.

Assisi like a warm Lhasa.
To see the Giottos you buy light
By the minute from a slovenly
Franciscan. How little atheist
Sentimentalists know of this
Rotten, corrupt, dirty, venal,
Mercenary, and ignorant
Order, which has spent
Eight hundred years murdering
Its founder with at least
As conspicuous success as
The Christians have managed with Christ.

Intellectuals who admire
The architectonics of
Neo-Thomism, the liturgies
Of Solesmes, forget that they
Are not the expression of
A living church, but carefully

Constructed booby traps of
Archaism built by over-
Sophisticated Anglican
And Gallican agnostics.
From Newman and Duchesne
To Maurras and Daudet, the entire
Structure of fashionable
Neo-Catholicism has
Been declared heretical at
Each step of its evolution.
This is not Rome. The true face of
Rome is to be seen in Naples,
Franco's Spain, Santo Domingo.

In softheaded America,
Pseudo liberal folly
Has now reached such a pitch, it
Is considered unprogressive
To criticize the Papacy.

Trasimeno in thick mist.
Hannibal and the Romans
Struggle invisibly all
Around us. Midway of the lake
The mist vanishes and we
Look back into the turquoise
Morning. Villages, castles,
Fields, not a soul moving in
All the brilliance. It might be
Painted on gold leaf and gesso.

Soracte. I guess things were
Different in those days.
Now it is all arid squalor.
I would as soon have a farm
In the Salinas Valley.
Two vast hieratic oxen

Drowsily guard the approach
To a dismal shack, BAR HORATIO.
As we come down the highway
Through suburbs much like Cleveland,
The Tiber appears, and then a sign,
PONTE MILVIO. We enter
Rome in the tracks of the first
Triumph of barbarism
And religion, through crowding
Ghosts from Piero's fresco.

It was Rome on the fifteenth
Of October, as I sat
Musing amidst the ruins
Of the Capitol, while the
Barefoot friars were singing vespers
In the Temple of Jupiter –

Gibbon in Rome, Polybius
In Carthage, and Strabo in
Babylon, myself in New York.
The pomp and grandeur of evil
Soon passes, but always a new
Pustule opens somewhere on the earth.
Why should time come to an end?
The stars eat their own feces.
Hunger gives rise to series and
Series gives rise to consequence.

We live in the Pensione
San Giorgio, on the Piazza
Sant' Apostoli, an island
Of quiet in a city
As noisy as Newark, in the
Palace of Cardinal York,
The last legitimate Stuart
Claimant to the English throne.

The whole Piazza was once
A sort of little England.
Here Alfieri cuckolded
Bonnie Prince Charlie. Here the Old
Pretender set his jaw and died.
Here is the best beer in Rome,
And two of the best restaurants.
Although it is just around the
Corner, you can escape from the
World's largest wedding cake, which
Follows you all over town.

It didn't take the Renaissance
Long to find out that the Christian
Documents can be read in a
Kabbalistic sense, but the
Gospels, and especially Paul,
Can also be read as a new
Colonial policy for
Rabbinical Judaism.
An orgiastic religion
Is not easily centralized,
And almost impossible to
Bureaucratize. The declining
Roman Empire left thousands
Of bureaucrats unemployed.
Naturally they chose orthodox
Catholicism which was
Willing to compromise and
Absorb any ritual or doctrine
As long as it could be given
A new content – the power
Of the underemployed
Intellectuals of Rome.
Caiaphas assumed the triple
Crown – or the bloodthirsty Stoic
Philosopher Seneca –

It makes no difference –
A few generations later,
He would have been Pope.

San Clemente, a layer cake
Of the decay of mystery –
On top a Catholic church,
Below it, a Christian church,
Under the earth, a Mithraeum.

From the Middle Ages on,
With few exceptions the art of
Rome is WPA art.
It isn't as bad as the
Buckwheat cake Sumerian
Bas-reliefs of the history
Of education and science,
With which Roosevelt flooded These States,
But only because he had poorer
Material to begin with.
But it is obvious that
Every artist or architect
Who went to work for the Pope
Knew in advance he had sold out.
Only Raphael remained
Uncorrupted, but Raphael,
Like his archangelic namesake,
Was too pure to be a moral
Agent. Even the painting
Of the Counter Reformation –
The Pope's very own expression –
Is compromised. The Jesuit
Ceilings are not Tiepolo,
They are Tiepolo's mummy.
There are a few islands, the
Piazza Navona, where
Bernini for once stopped acting

Like a giddy matron, perhaps
The Lateran, which compares
Very favorably with the
Railroad station in Washington.
Of course there are the early
Mosaics, and the unchanged
Spaces of the basilicas,
And one little hidden church.
And there are always the great Greeks
And Romans. They must have been
Really a little like Plutarch
Describes them. We sit on the
Floor all afternoon in front of
The Ludovisi throne, and there's
The little flapper with her
New hair-do, and those haunted
Paintings in the Vatican,
Where Tanguy got, and spoiled, his stuff.
The critics tell you the Romans
Couldn't paint, and all that survives
Is provincial commercial art.
This may be very true, but
No other prosperous farmer
Known to history decorated
His walls like the Villa dei
Misterii. It doesn't
Matter, Fra Angelico
To Pontormo, some disorder
Of the conscience, some lesion
Of the sensibility,
Drove them to act up, to try
To exorcise with magic
The dilemmas of life in
This hard universe. Life cannot
Be outwitted. The Romans
Never act up. They miss no
Lie, no horror, and their judgments

Are as worldly and as
Devastating as the Roman Law.

In the Hebrew religion
There could be no mystical
Experience without marriage –
Kedeshim and Kedeshoth,
Every man and wife together.
Therefore each family became
A separate unit in the
Community of Israel.
The hierarchy of the Church
Forbade illumination
To all but celibates, and
Centralized authority
Under celibate bishops.
Sexual fulfillment became
Treason to the bureaucracy.
Heresy – all normal life
Seeking its normal end – went
Underground. When it reappeared
In the political vacuum
Of Provence for a brief moment
The bureaucracy liquidated
Its practitioners, "as a class,"
In history's bloodiest purge
Before the invention of progress.
However, in France, the Church
Was forced to tolerate a new
Morality. Whenever it could
It debased it to common
Promiscuity. Cardinals
And Kings were little better than
Whoremasters, but the Freemasons
Who led the French Revolution
Were both erotic mystics and
Political libertarians.

Rochester may have been perverse
When he translated the hymns
Of a jealous god into
Songs to his mistress. Mirabeau
Meant business with his Sophie.

Michelangelo was surely
A noisy man, and terribly
Conceited. After all, nothing
Ever happened to him that
Doesn't happen to all of us.
If you have tragedy to
Portray, you should be humble
About it, you are serving
The bread of communion.
"To many nakeds for a chapel,"
Said Evelyn. But I don't think it
Was the exposed privates of the
Mother of God made the Pope faint.
That's an arrogant, perverse, pride
Soaked wall, a good thing to look down
On the election of the Popes.
Maybe he intended it for
A portrait of the Papacy.
But the Moses was beautiful
Just before the church shut, looking
Like oiled ivory against
The wavering blackness in
The light of the vigil lamps.

The worship of art, the attempt
To substitute it for religion,
Is the blindest superstition
Of them all. Almost all works of
Art are failures. The successes
Occur hardly once in a
Lifetime even in periods

Of great cultural flowering;
And then they are likely to be
Unpretentious perfections,
Of modest scope, exquisite
As a delicate wine and
Often no more significant.
Better lump them all together –
"A good judge of wine, women,
And horseflesh" – than go posting
For the Absolute in the
Galleries of Fifty-seventh Street –
Or the Louvre – or the Uffizi.
The World's Masterpieces are
Too often by Vasari,
Benjamin West, Picasso,
Or Diego Rivera.

The Pope was once content to rule
The rulers, the masses were
Allowed their old worship under
A new nomenclature. Feudal
Methods of exploitation
Required a homogeneous
Society, a "natural"
Religion. New methods,
New cadres. Capitalism
Revived all the paranoid
Compulsions of rabbinical
Judaism, coupled with
A schizophrenic doctrine
Of the person as utterly
Alone, subsistent as a pure
Integer at the will of a
Uniquely self subsistent
Commander (hardly a lover),
Two things with wills. It required
The total atomization

Of society. The family
Hierarchy disappeared and the
Monogamous couple was
Substituted. Not a vehicle
Of mystic love, but an iron
Necessity for survival.

Says Evelyn, "Turning to the right
Out of the Porta del Popolo,
We came to Justinian's
Gardens, near the Muro Torto,
So prominently built as to
Threaten to fall any moment,
Yet standing so these thousand years.
Under this is the burying
Place of the common prostitutes,
Where they are put into the ground
Sans ceremony." In the
Rotonda Sant' Agostino,
A sign, WHORES WILL REFRAIN
FROM HUSTLING THE CUSTOMERS
DURING THEIR DEVOTIONS. From the
Albergo Inghilterra
To the Piazza di Spagna
Stretches a solid tide wall
Of crew-cut American fairies,
Elderly nymphomaniacs,
Double breasted, gabardined
Artisti. The latter have reduced
Hemingway to a formula.
"Let's go," Bill said. "Let's go," Pete said.
"OK, let's go," Joe said. It's like
Dante's terza rima, and the
Triad of the dialectic.
Honest. They write books about it.
Everybody on the prowl
For Cineasti and the Milioni

Of any sex. The Via
Vittorio Veneto
After dark is strictly graded.
On the terrace of the Doni
Sit the condottieri of
The Marshall Plan like Rameses.
The Cineasti and Milioni
Lounge over their highballs.
The artisti stand and bow.
The more expensive whores walk
The sidewalks. The poorer whores work
The side streets. The most expensive
Sit. At the entrance to the
Park are whores from Masereel
And Félicien Rops. Inside are
Italian boys who get paid.
Further inside are beringed
Cigar smoking Italians, who
All look like Mussolini's
Grandfather. They will pay you.
At the beginning of the street
Is the American Embassy.
Midway is an ESSO pump.
At the end is the devouring dark.

"La mauvaise conscience des
Bourgeois, ai-je dit, a paralysé
Tout le mouvement intellectuel
Et moral de la bourgeoisie.
Je me corrige, et je remplace
Ce mot 'paralysé' par
Cet autre: 'dénaturé.' "
So Bakunin says, and Marx,
"The bourgeoisie, wherever
It has got the upper hand,
Has put an end to all feudal,
Patriarchal, idyllic

Relations. It has pitilessly
Torn asunder the motley
Feudal ties that bound man to
His 'natural superiors,'
And has left no other nexus
Between man and man than naked
Self interest, than callous
Cash payment. It has drowned the
Most heavenly ecstasies
Of religious fervor, of
Chivalrous enthusiasm,
Of philistine sentimentalism,
In the icy water of
Egotistical calculation.
It has resolved personal worth
Into exchange value, and in
Place of the numberless
Indefeasible chartered freedoms,
Has set up that single
Unconscionable freedom,
Free trade. In a word, for
Exploitation veiled by
Religious and political
Illusions, it has substituted
Naked, shameless, direct, brutal
Exploitation."
For Dante,
Usury was the ultimate
Form of pederasty, in which
Buggery attempts to make
Its turds its heirs.

Sexual fulfillment was robbed
Of all meaning. The sex act became
A nervous stimulant and
Anodyne outside of the
Productive process, but still

Necessary to it as an
Insatiable, irrational
Drive, without which the struggle
For meaningless abstractions,
Commodities, would collapse.
This is the ultimate in
Human self alienation.
This is what the revolution
Is about. In a society
Ruled only by the cash nexus
The sexual relationship
Must be a continual struggle
Of each to obtain security
From the other, a kind of
Security, a mass of
Commodities, which has no
Meaning for love, and today in
America, no meaning at all.
The greater the mass of things,
The greater the insecurity.
The security of love lies
In the state of indwelling rest.
It is its own security.
This is what free love is, freedom
From the destructive power
Of a society coerced
Into the pursuit of insane
Objectives. Until men learn
To administer things, and are
No longer themselves organized
And exploited as things, there can
Be no love except by intense
Effort directed against
The whole pressure of the world.
In other words, love becomes,
As it was with the Gnostics,
The practice of a kind of cult.

Against it are arrayed all
The consequences of a
Vast systematic delusion,
Without intelligence or
Mercy or even real being,
But with the power to kill.

Centuries ago they tore down
Or remodelled all the best
Churches in Rome. But there is one
Which haunts the mind permanently,
Quattro Santi Coronati,
The only church in Rome where
Otto's sense of the holy
Lingers; a secret place where
Christianity still seems
A mystery religion.
It is perched on a rampart
Between the Esquiline and the
Palatine, and approached by two
Courtyards like a Norman castle.
The ancient frescoes in the
Sacristy chapel are a
Child's innocent idea of
The conversion of a king.
The church is restored and full of
Junk, but the awe is still there.
The Holy Place at Alamut,
The fortress churches of the
Crusaders, Krak, empty and
Sand blown in the empty desert,
Must have been something like this.
The Four Crowned Saints were artists who
Would not make idols for Caesar.

What is Capri to me, or me
To Capri? To Hell with the

Bourgeois scenery, said Gurly
To Big Bill Haywood. We live
Back of the Porta Capuana
Where the adolescent whores
Are too poor to buy stockings,
And rent their sleazy dresses
To each other around the clock,
And turn their tricks on the ground
Like the rug girls in New Orleans.
Twenty per cent of the male
Children of Naples are without
Domicile. An equal number
Have active tuberculosis.
Little girls have virtue, and so
The Church finds them domicile.
In the midst of boiling squalor,
The crazed faces of American
Cover girls on the magazines,
The special devils of this
Proliferating Hell, where
Only the innocent are damned.
In Sorrento the lace makers
Are called apprentices and work
For a bowl of polenta at lunch.
Babies are doped with bromides,
And rented around the clock, like
The whores' dresses, to beggar women.
You never see a beggar's baby
Awake, in a few months it is dead.
But the Church keeps the people
Fruitful, birth control is a
Prison offense. Everybody,
Except the tourists, gives to the
Beggars, the Church teaches Charity.
But they keep only a few
Lire a day, periodically
Boys on bicycles shake them down,

And collect the take for the
Lords of the lazzaroni,
Who pay off to the archbishop.
We go to call on the leading
Anarchist theoretician.
He patriotically denies
That conditions like this exist.
He sits in his expensively
Appointed office and questions
Us about how the theories
Of Wilhelm Reich, and the orgones,
Are doing in America.
I have been further round the shit
Pot looking for the handle
Than this bastard has been from home.
The Hell with him, the Museum
Is full of workers in rags,
Ebullient before the Greek
Statues. Three excited, stinking
Fishermen are having a
Violent argument in front
Of Barberi's portrait of
Luca Pacioli, with its face
Like a pure crystal and its
Crystal like a pure mind. I
Could be happy here. There is
All the world still left to win.

America is today a
Nation profoundly deranged,
Demented, and sick, because
Americans with very few
Exceptions believe, or when
They doubt are terrified to
Be discovered doubting, that
Love is measured entirely
In an interchange of

Commodities. The wife provides
Pop-up toast, synthetic coffee,
Frozen orange juice, two eggs of
Standard color, size, and flavor,
In the morning, at night the
Fantastic highly colored canned
Poisons which grace the cooking
And advertising pages
Of the women's magazines.
In exchange the husband provides
Her with the clothes and cosmetics
Of a movie courtesan,
A vast array of "labor"
Saving devices, all streamlined,
Presumably so they can be
Thrown, a car, never more than
Two years old, engineered with
Great skill to their social status,
A television set, a dream
House, designed by a fairy,
And built of glass and cardboard,
A bathroom full of cramped, pastel
Tinted plumbing. When they wish
To satisfy their passions,
They go to a movie. The
Sexual relation is
A momentary lapse from
The routine fulfillment of
This vision, which is portrayed
As love and marriage by thousands
Of decorticated and
Debauched intellectuals,
Who enjoy the income of princes.
Almost all advertising
In America today
Is aimed at the young married
Couple. Billions are consciously

And deliberately spent
To destroy love at its source.
Like the "fiends" who are picked up
In parks, an advertising
Man is a professional
Murderer of young lovers –
On an infinitely vaster scale.

You will find more peace and more
Communion, more love, in an hour
In the arms of a pickup in
Singapore or Reykjavík,
Than you will find in a lifetime
Married to a middle class
White American woman.

It feels like it's made of plastic.
It smells like it's perfumed with
Coal tar. It tastes like it's made
Of soybeans. It looks like an
Abandoned pee-wee golf course.
It is still and sterile
As a crater on the moon.

Sitting there, reading this in your
Psychoanalyst's waiting room,
Thirty-five years old, faintly
Perfumed, expensively dressed,
Sheer nylons strapped to freezing thighs,
Brain removed at Bennington
Or Sarah Lawrence, dutiful
Reader of the *Partisan*
Review's Book of the Month, target
Of my highbrow publisher, you
Think this is all just Art – contrast –
Naples – New York. It is not. Every time
You open your frigidaire

A dead Neapolitan baby
Drops out. Your world is not crazy.
But dead. It can only mimic
Life with the economics of
Murder. "War production and
Colonialization of
The former imperialist
Centers." This is the definition
Of Fascism. You are not just
Responsible. You are the dead
Neapolitan baby,
The other side of the coin.
I don't wonder you've never
Been the same since you left the
Tickets to *Don Giovanni*
In the orgone collector.

At the Pappagallo, cold squid,
Spaghetti with vongole,
Panini which here, after two
Thousand years, is still fine Greek bread,
Stuffed veal, grilled birds, cold spinach,
Washed down with Lachryma Christi,
And finished with tortoni and
Coffee like a skyrocket,
Laced with grappa aruta.
In Italy, as in America,
A symptom of a good restaurant
Is a wall covered with photos
Of opera singers. At the
Next table is a party of
Drummers from Lombardy. They
Agree with us about Naples.
"Italy is like America
With its Negroes. But here the
Negroes are white. These starving
People are the finest in

Italy. Once they escape from
The slavery of the Church and learn
The meaning of freedom, they will
Free Italy, just like they did
Before. Garibaldi's Thousand
Will some day be paid back with millions
Of a New Italy." It's
A word's been used a long time,
Italia Nuova.

In America today
Sex as such is regrettable,
But it can be channelized
Into socially useful forms.
From birth there exists a host
Of special policemen, the Black
Hundreds of Democracy,
Pediatricians, social
Workers, psychiatric social
Workers, psychiatrists, child
Guidance clinics, vocational
Guidance clinics, marriage guidance
Clinics, psychoanalysts,
Counselors, and psychologists.
Like most policemen they are
Largely homosexual
Sadists, and are thoroughly
Quantified, passionate pseudo
Marxists and Freudians. Their
Job is to see that sexual
Relations are kept as much like
A visit to a painless
American dentist as possible.

From the Greeks to the Normans
Communal life was especially
Strong, but from then on Naples

Has been without a polity.
Since the beginning of the
Middle Ages, it has been
A piece of real estate bandied
About between dynastic
Cadets and by-blows. Only
Under the pagan Frederick
Did it enjoy a brief moment
Of civilization. Which shows
What one civilized man can do.
The Renaissance started with
His sculptors, his coins are as fine
As the Arethusa of
Syracuse or the Bactrian Kings.
Aquinas grew up in his court
In the company of Arab
Mystics, troubadours, and Kabbalists.
Murat denied the Emperor
And dickered with Metternich
And ended like Black Christophe.
The Pope filled the vacuum.
Naples never had a Nineteenth
Century. If you advocated
Kindness to animals you'd
Be a revolutionary.
But in the local dungeon,
Held incommunicado,
Is Italy's first war resister.
Angevin, Spaniard, Bourbon,
What survives under priestcraft,
Starvation, terror, ignorance,
Is the soul of a Greek polis.

In America today
All basic experience is
Looked on as a morbid condition,
An actual serious sickness.

There are doctors specializing
In each of them – being born,
Childhood, puberty, fucking,
Parenthood, vocation, growing
Old, and dying. These crises
Of life are the matter of
The sacraments in more normal
Societies – baptism,
Confirmation, marriage,
Orders, communion, unction –
Moments when life necessarily
Transcends any quantitative
Experience altogether –
Windows into reality.
In America they are
Given into the aseptic
Hands of medical specialists,
From obstetricians to
Geriatrists. This is a
Picture of a nation gone
Stark raving mad, in the grip
Of mutually homicidal
Paranoia. So it is
Fitting that its sacrament
Should be the atomic bomb, the
Apotheosis of quantity.
The blazing mushroom cloud is
Just such a mystical vision
As one would expect of the
Managers of the du Pont
Industries and their enslaved
Physicists, of Mr. ——, who
Bears so fatal a resemblance
To the grinning monsters who
Are the heroes of the
Advertising pages.

Alchemy started as the
Craft of metals, ended in
Sex mysticism. Science
Started as a mystical
Doctrine of the pure atom,
Being as self subsistent,
Ended in catastrophe.

Against arithmetic man
There can be only vengeance.
A murder can be healed,
But vengeance is incurable.

We fill our rucksacks at a
Rôtisserie just like the ones
In Pompeii, with bread just like the
Pumice casts, and take the train
To the South. In our compartment
Is an aged widow who gives
Us a message for her sister
In San Francisco. She is
Travelling third class from Milan
To Palermo, erect on the
Board bench like a white hawk in
Black silk. Our wineskin from the
Pyrenees creates a sensation.
All the men cheer as we hold
It at arm's length and spurt the
Wine, usually, into our mouths.
Everybody takes a drink.
We figure they have decided
There are some good Americans.
Then we find out they think we're French.
We tell them we're Americans,
And then they do become friendly,
They were being cool before.

Paestum, the apex of the trip,
And the zenith of our years.

Helen's jewel, the Schethya,
The Taoist uncut block,
The stone of the alchemist,
The footstool of Elohim's throne,
Which they hurled into the Abyss,
On which stands the queen and sacred
Whore, Malkuth, the stone which served
Jacob for pillow and altar.

"And what is truth?" said Pilate,
"A,E,I,O,U – the spheres
Of the planets, the heavens'
Pentachord. A noir, E blanc,
I rouge, O bleu, U vert."
When in Japan, the goddess
Of the sun, attracted by
The obscene gestures of the flesh,
Came out from eclipse, she spoke
The first and oldest mystery,
"1, 2, 3, 4, 5, 6, 7,
8, 9, 10."

All things have a name.
Every mote in the sunlight has
A name, and the sunlight itself
Has a name, and the spirit who
Troubles the waters has a name.

As the Philosopher says,
"The Pythagoreans are
Of the opinion that the shapes
Of the Greek vase are reflections
Of the irrational numbers
Thought by the Pure Mind. On the

Other hand, the Epicureans
Hold them to be derived
From the curves of a girl's
Breasts and thighs and buttocks."

The doctrine of Signatures –
The law by which we must make
Use of things is written in
The law by which they were made.
It is graven upon each
As its unique character.
The forms of being are the
Rules of life.

The Smaragdine Tablet
Says, "That which is above is
Reflected in that which is below."

Paestum of the twice blooming
Roses, the sea god's honey
Colored stone still strong against
The folly of the long decline
Of man. The snail climbs the Doric
Line, and the empty snail shell
Lies by the wild cyclamen.
The sandstone of the Roman
Road is marked with sun wrinkles
Of prehistoric beaches,
But no time at all has touched
The deep constant melodies
Of space as the columns swing
To the moving eye. The sea
Breathes like a drowsy woman.
The sun moves like a drowsy hand.
Poseidon's pillars have endured
All tempers of the sea and sun.
This is the order of the spheres,

The curve of the unwinding fern,
And the purple shell in the sea;
These are the spaces of the notes
Of every kind of music.
The world is made of number
And moved in order by love.
Mankind has risen to this point
And can only fall away,
As we can only turn homeward
Up Italy, through France, to life
Always pivoted on this place.

Sweet Anyte of Tegea –
"The children have put purple
Reins on you, he-goat, and a
Bridle in your bearded mouth.
And they play at horse races
Round a temple where a god
Gazes on their childish joy."

Finally the few tourists go,
The German photographers, the
Bevy of seminarians,
And we are left alone. We eat
In the pronaos towards the sea.
Greek food, small white loaves, smoked cheese,
Pickled squid, black figs, and honey
And olive oil, the common food
Of Naples, still, for those who eat.
An ancient dog, Odysseus' dog,
Spawned before there were breeds of dogs,
Appears, begs, eats, and disappears –
The exoteric proxy of
The god. And we too grow drowsy with
White wine, tarry from the wineskin.
The blue and gold shafts interweave
Across our nodding eyes. The sea

Prepares to take the sun. We go
Into the naos, open to the
Sky and make love, where the sea god
And the sea goddess, wet with sperm,
Coupled in the incense filled dark,
As the singing rose and was still.

Mist comes with the sunset. (The Yanks
Killed the mosquitoes.) Long lines of
Umber buffalo, their backs a
Rippling congruence, as in the
Paintings of Krishna, file across
The brilliant green sea meadows,
Under banners of white mist.
The fires of the bivouacs of
Spartacus twinkle in the hills.
Our train comes with the first stars.
Venus over the wine dark sea.

All the way back the train fills
And fills up, and fills again,
With girls from the fish canneries,
And girls from the lace factories,
And girls from the fields, who have been
Working twelve hours for nothing,
Or at the best a few pennies.
They laugh and sing, all the way
Back to Naples, like broad bottomed,
Deep bosomed angels, wet with sweat.

Only in a secret place
May human love perfect itself.

In the mountains above Bologna
A ropewalk, two lean faced, copper
Skinned men, who tread like cats,
Spinning hemp. "Illyrians,"
Strabo called them Pelasgoi,

Who were here before Etruscan,
Greek, Celt, Roman, or Goth. A loud
Crowd of peasants swarming bees.
All the hundred armies passed
This way, but the peasants stayed.

The twilight asked the dark, "Why
Do you move away from me?" "I do
Not move myself. I am cast by
A body which I cannot
See, and which made me, and moves
Me, according to the laws of
Opacity and movement."

The shadows of the towers
Of Bologna move on the
Walls of the cramped, noisy square,
Red gnomons of history.
Ruskin called them Jove's spent thunder
Bolts. Carducci wrote his best poem
About them, a dialogue of
The long betrayal of Italy
By the Evil Twins, Church and Empire.

You go to Ferrara for
Lasagne verde. The art is
Rigid as the Palazzo
Diamante, there is just the
Moated Este castle and the
Food, but the food is worth it.

The sun enters the second
Moon of Autumn. The dove turns
To a hawk. Dew become hoarfrost.

Ravenna, October, night,
The Pleiades are rising
Over Dante's tomb with its

Always burning, blood-red lamp.
On the walls of the loggia,
Between the shadows of the
Columns and the curves of the
Arches, the Autumn wind sways the
Shadows of palm and laurel leaves.
Theodoric's tomb in the rain,
The monolith split by a bomb.
I ask about the ruined fort
Nearby. "Ah, signore, the Inglesi,
They hate and envy the Italia."
Doubtless true, but in this case,
No Inglese later than
Hawkwood. There is no question
The English rankled under
Their defeat by an army
Which couldn't handle the Greeks,
So they did as much damage as
Possible once the Pope and
Giannini presented them
With a defenseless ally.
The average Italian is
Convinced they are to blame for the
Condition of the Roman Forum.
The Communists control the town,
And it is a concentration
Point for the Pope and the USA.
The whole place broods under a
Fog of deadlocked hostility,
A dry hate as barbarous
As Mexico. Still, nobody
Hates Americans, they are
Children, good hearted, but misled,
By the Pope and the Inglesi.
Stalin's smartest move was to
Inveigle America
Into an alliance with

A power which is not only
Without divisions, but which
Can never, founded firmly as
It is on biological
Nonsense, do anything but fail.

We peek in the windows of
The Albergo Commercio.
The walls are covered with photos
Of opera singers. This is it.
Our room with its immense oaken
Letto matrimoniale
Is barren and noble. The food –
The food is beyond question
The best I have ever eaten
Cooked by an Occidental.
It is simple enough. The cook
Is an old woman. Usually
I loathe female cooking, but she
Makes magic over it. The cold
Green beans are just cold green beans,
The sliced eggplant has only
Been dipped in oil and garlic
And broiled, the steamed fish is just steamed,
The veal is the same national
Animal of Italy,
The guinea hen is baked, the birds
Are spitted and broiled. Nothing else.
It seems to be, as in the best
Chinese cooking, a matter
Of absolute accuracy
In timing and flavoring.
Impossible to believe,
She can turn out a better
Lasagne verde than can be
Found publicly in Ferrara.

It is unfortunately
The case, that the world in which
We live in is dominated
By two collectivities
Whose whole force is exerted
To depersonalize and
Quantify persons – the State
And the Capitalist System.
If a person is that which
By definition can never
Be added to anything else,
The State is precisely the
Mechanism by which persons
Are reduced to integers.
The State exists to add and
Subtract, divide and multiply
Population units. Its
Components have no more and
No less reality than the
Mathematics of the battlefield.
Similarly, Capitalism
Views all existence in the form
Of commodities. Nothing
Is valuable except to
The extent it will bring a
Profit on the market. Again,
The human being is reduced
To a special commodity,
Labor power, his potential
To make other commodities.
Labor power on the market,
Firepower on the battlefield,
It is all one, merely two
Aspects of the same monster.
The parliaments of the State
Are only highly ritualized
Capitalist market places.

The battlefield is only
The most advanced form of trade.

The equities of the State
Are only devices for
Postponing the decisions
Of violence to a more
Opportune moment. The ballot
Is a paper substitute
For the billy, the bullet,
And the bayonet.

McTaggart:
"Better worship a crocodile
Which being a sentient being
Has some value, than the State, which,
Being an instrument, has none.
As well worship a sewer pipe,
Which may have considerable
Instrumental value."

The times come round, once more all
Our hearts are breaking as the world
Drowns in a marsh of blood and fire.

How poor they were in the last hours.
What a little thing the tomb
Of Galla Placidia is.
An ordinary mechanic
In Los Angeles could contract
For a small monthly payment, and
Get as good a job when he died.
San Vitale's dimensions
Are not marked on the floor of
St. Peter's. The mosaicist
Of the Twenty-third Psalm was
Hardly Christian. You can see

Justinian's dissipated
Face any day at the Stork Club
Or on the Place Vendôme, and the
Exophthalmic, sex-crazed eyes of
Theodora glare through the smoke
Of every Harry's Bar
Around the world and wink across
The aisle in every airliner.
I hate to seem fashionable, but
I guess this is the art I like
Best in all of Italy.
Since the Greeks nobody knew
Better how to put together
The simplest forms and make the most
Complex harmonies – second hand
Columns, red bricks, and bits of
Colored stone and gilded glass.
Poor Richardson. They tried hard
To make Chicago look like this.

Every collectivity
Is opposed to community.
As Capitalism and the
State have become identical,
All existence assumes the
Character of a vast
Conspiracy to quantify
The individual and
Convince him that all other
Seeming persons are actually
Already successfully
And happily quantified,
And that all human relations
Are quantitative, commodity
Relationships. This means murder.
Every minute, in a million
Ways, the society in which

You live is trying to murder
You. War is the health of the State?
War against its own members.
And with the falling rate of
Profit, all commodities,
Including you, as a unit
Of labor power, become
War matériel, nothing more.

"A golden book, worthy of
The leisure of Plato or Tully."
I am older than Boethius,
Executed age forty-three.
"Whatever, therefore, comprehends
And possesses the whole fullness
And unlimited life at once,
Where nothing future is lacking
And none of the past flows away,
May be truly called eternal."
Here the last philosopher died,
In contemplation, "in the last
Gloomy hours of Theodoric."
And with the two, king and martyr,
Italy's last chance of life.
Nobody won but the Pope.
From this base Justinian's
Cuckold and eunuch accomplished
The decline and fall of the
Roman Empire in two fell swoops.
All in the name of the unity
Of the Divine Nature. I have
Always wondered about him. Did
It give Justinian a special
Thrill to screw a Monophysite?
Here Maximian wrote his
Elegies of impotence,
Of the tedium and horror

Of the end of the world.
I like to fancy that the
Bitter face of the Maximian
In the mosaic is his.
Here Dante died and Byron
Lusted and played cicisbeo.
Here the Risorgimento
And the Papacy stabbed at
Each other in secret. Now,
Every night in the Piazza
A loudspeaker blares, the voice, smooth
As a preacher's prick in a calf's arse,
Dripping with lachrymose evil,
Of a Passionist missioner.
On alternate weekends the Church
And the Communists march through the
Streets with their respective idols.

I see the water, I see
The fire, the air, and the earth,
And all their mixtures, come to
Decay and last but little.

Be still and let the years revolve.

There would seem to be some in whom
The potential personality
Of others is sacrificed
To the ever diminishing
Realization of the self,
Still considered in terms of
Possibility and consequence.
This is evil, the total
Distortion of the end of life.
All that we know of life is love,
All that we know of the world
Of happenings is that it is

Shot through and through with offers
Of love. What we realize
In the beloved is the
Growing reality of
All the others. The sacrifice
Of millions of human beings
Or one human being, for
The most sublime goals, is
A defeat of being itself.

It is obvious that the Jews
Or the Ukrainian peasants,
Or the Chinese middle class,
Cannot be exterminated
To advance even the most
Glorious future society,
Without destroying the inner
Reality, the persons, of
Their altruistic murderers.
But the universe of persons
Cannot in any way be
Manipulated as a
Condition of community,
Of love. The community
Is always there, beyond cause
And effect, or time and space,
And only contingencies
May be manipulated.
The politician works in
The materials of his
Own destruction – by definition.

I pay a visit to ——.
When she opens the door, she says,
"Don't blame me, they're just using
The place." All the American
Consuls in Italy, but one,

And their wives, are having a
Party. The men all look like
Gas station attendants, their wives,
Like their wives, except the one wife
Whose husband is away. She is
Très civilisée, oh, so
Continental, black haired,
Haggard, glare eyed, and brave, brave,
And oh, so witty. —— says,
"He was here this spring, driving
Mrs. Crosby to Paris."
The brave one says, "Bing? Oh! Bing! Bing!
You had an affair with Bing?
I have always wanted Bing,
Ravenously, ever since
I saw that gorgeous *Boys Town*."
This goes on without the least
Pause, all evening; except when
It gets extra loud, it is
Possible to ignore it.
Sometimes she is pretty funny.
They suspect the fact that I am
Some highbrow friend of ——'s and
All try to talk big. I find
That few of them speak Italian,
And that the principal source
Of diplomatic information
Seems to be their wives' servants.
As I listen, it occurs to
Me that most of Gertrude Stein is
This stuff, slightly dissociated,
And this is the class she spoke for.
They leave, but in a minute
Back they come. The brave one is
Raging. "Come with me. Come with me.
Protect me from them. They tried
To put me in a traghetto
That wasn't there, and besides

The man was drunk." We wearily
Go with them. Somehow I am
Left to pay the traghettatore,
To whom I whisper, "Viva
Il Pian' Marshall." "Si, si, dronk
Bambini." As I rejoin them
In the midst of freezing fog,
A consul says, "Do you play bridge?"
"Not any more than I can help."
"But you can?" "Yes." Instantly, I am
Dealt a card. The deal goes round
And the bidding starts. We are
Walking through a narrow lane
Almost invisible to
Each other in the blowing fog.
"Two hearts." "Three spades."
"Three hearts." My turn –
Fortunately we have reached
The door of the Danieli.
"Sorry," I say, "I must go on."
The brave one screams, "But you aren't
Coming in? You won't play bridge?"
"No." "But it's you, you, I want.
We'll play like madmen. We'll drink
Gallons and gallons of absinthe,
I'll trump your aces all night long,
Till the dawn comes up like thunder,
From the Lido 'cross the bay."
I go home. It isn't funny.
It will be hard to forget
That useless body and those
Nerve wracked, empty eyes.

The vulture is only female
And fertilized by the wind.
Viva videns vivo
Sepiliri viscera busto.

Neurosis develops first
In the vegetative system.
Man, when he fails as a man,
Dies first as a plant.
The divorce at Cana where
The wine turned into water.
Insanity is the crippling
Of the organ of reciprocity.

The snake bodied, tortoise beaked
Clutch footed Eumenides.

Tara, the Counter Buddha,
Is a supremely beautiful
Courtesan, born in a time
When history has filled its cup
With chaos and tragedy.
As the world is transfigured
By the Divine Couple at
Its apogee, so in the
Depth of its declension it is
Returned and redeemed by the
Coupling of the warrior and
The whore, the beggar and the queen.
The madman and beggar, and
The whore are sperm cell and egg
By which one society
Passes to another. Hence
The State in our time has turned
On them with a special savagery.

Jealousy is a kind of
Murder, murder is a kind of
Jealousy. The end of life
Is the full communion of
Lovers, the only absolute.
There is little doubt but what

There exist persons who view
The relation with others
And with the beloved as
Restrictive and acquisitive.
This is what evil is, the
Translation of the terms of
Illusion into the world
Of reality. What this
Means, of course, is that the real
Is thereby so much impoverished.
When this is the typical
Activity of the person,
We are safe in ascribing
Evil motives. The person
Is growing less and less
And life is being narrowed.
It is perhaps possible
That in the community
Of persons which is reality
The activity of the members
Goes both ways, as obviously
It does in man's history.

We sit above the rain-flooded
Piazza San Marco in a
Workers' club and talk to two
Young anarchist leaders. They ask
Me about California.
"Do I know Lily La Rue?"
"Oh yes, she gave a lot of
Money to the cotton strikers."
"La Verne De Vere?" "Oh yes, she sang
At an entertainment for Spain."
"Billy McAgy?" "Very well.
His father was a Wobbly,
Once he spoke for Tom Mooney
And filled the auditorium."

I notice their puzzled faces.
We are talking at cross purposes.
The Grapes of Wrath, is it true?
"One eighth true; in the book, one man
Is killed, actually there were eight."
"Then the American workers
Are fighters?" "Yes, they fought for
What they got. Now they have got it."
I ask them about the workers
In Venice. Like the middle class
Everywhere, they talk about the
Only workers they know – servants.
"In Venice, the workers are all
Gondoliers, or porters, or
Waiters, or hotel employees."
"Between Venice and Padova
Are miles and miles of the finest
Docks in Europe, all idle.
What about them?" On this subject
They have no information.

There are reasons for and against
Assuming that being is
In its nature progressive.
If being is essentially
Active, action would seem to
Imply a positive and
Negative, even beyond time.
Just as some persons move deeper
Into the plenum of the
Community of love, so
Others may be moving, or
All or some may move at times,
Towards the isolation of
The ego, not being, hate,
Ultimate atomization.

It is a great art in the
World, to know how to sell wind.
A meeting in a Renaissance
Palazzo to reunite the
Shattered Socialist Party.
Silone talks for an hour
All about Democracy.
Not a word about the problems
Of this country which is bleeding
To death. Not a word about
The Pope. It sounds like an
Enormously expanded
Luce editorial, but
Chambers was a better writer –
So much less emotional.
The Stalinists always measure
The success of their meetings
By the number of Negroes,
Youth, and women they bring out.
Here are five hundred gabardined
Employees and petty bourgeois,
No Sicilians or Trentinos,
One worker, a gondolier,
Who paces the floor and leaves early,
Five women, two aging copies
Of Beatrice Webb, and three housewives
With their husbands, who go to sleep.
As poor old Trotsky used to say,
"Power lies in the streets and
No one knows how to pick it up."

It is even possible
That the movement is circular,
That persons flow from pole to pole.
This was Boehme's belief and it
Has colored all German thought.
Even their most ambitious

Systems of morality,
Nietzsche's, for instance, seemed robbed of
Meaning by its application.
Its truth may at least be doubted.
The satisfactions of the
Community of lovers
Are inexhaustible and
The lure of love of person
For person so great that it
Seems likely that all persons
Are caught up eventually
In the full community of
Love or pass out of existence.
Of course this discussion is
Haunted by the terms of space
And time, possibility
And consequence. Actually
The community of lovers
Is always there. It grows, not
In time, like a vine on a rod,
But in compass and intensity,
State within state, like the wave
Motion of ripples from a stone,
If it moved both in and out
At once. The physical evils
Of pain and waste and loss are
Easily dismissed. Most thinkers
Have evaded the problem
By identifying them with
The problem of moral evil.
Pain, waste, and loss are inherent
In the world of contingency.
Death, sickness, suffering may
Fill us with an agony of
Compassion when we witness them
In others, and when they occur
To ourselves, move us but little.

It is love makes us suffer with
The poor doped babies of Naples,
They do not know they suffer.
As for ourselves in this world
Of acquiring and losing – we
Will die, probably painfully,
And lose all of it at once.
Moral evil, the denial,
Betrayal, or debauching
Of love is another matter.
The evil person, assuming
His existence, remains the
Mystery he has always been.
But one should never forget,
He appears only in the
Context of a collectivity,
And the person is real
Only in community.

We walk thousands of miles and look
At acres of Tintorettos.
We spend days in the Scuola
San Rocco. We do not miss a church.
At last in this floating city
We become disembodied.
The law of gravity dies out.
All solids interpenetrate.
All space is cobwebbed and netted.
The mind is entirely possessed
By the breathing vortex of
Creation itself. Fiat!
It is like nitrous oxide, but
Nitrous oxide with a meaning
That lasts after it is over.
"In St. Hildegarde of Bingen
The identification
Of idioretinal

Disturbances with the mystic
Light is unmistakable."
What happens when a culture
Peters out? How can these people
Live under a sky of the thought
Of "the mightiest mind that
Ever applied itself to painting"
And be so ordinary?
We find out. After a while
We are exhausted. Titian
Is so sane and solid, the flesh
And smoke and dark, and the orange flame
That rings like a somber bell
In his San Lorenzo seem more
Wise as well as more real. His
"Presentation" is less tricky
As well as a profounder judgment.
So we come back, one by one,
To the others, Bellini's
Mysterious, transcendent flesh,
Carpaccio's russet cube of dream,
Indecipherable Giorgione,
Veronese, Marlowe in paint,
And Tiepolo, so cultured,
And so dreadfully obscene.
When it dawns on me what St. Lucy
Is really up to, even I
Blush. We discover all sorts
Of things, for instance, that the
Guardi ceilings in the Ca'
Rezzonico are in pastel.
And every day I stop and look
At the four last rulers of Rome,
Clutching each other in fear.

And every day we eat well,
In this city of foul cuisine,

In the Casa Paganelli,
The cheapest hotel in town,
And we have real breakfasts with good
Caffè latte and fresh pastry
By the Tre Ponti and the Greek Church.
These are good places to know –
Venice is a tourist trap,
The first and greatest in the world.
Mostly we eat lunch on the street.
We suck jackknife clams still
Wiggling, walk along muzzling
Great dripping kakis, munch rotten
Medlars in churches and
Pickled polpi in palazzi.
All the Venetians have to do
Is put food on a stove to spoil it.
But the wines are wonderful,
Valpolicella, Bardolino,
And the small wines of Trentino.

All too often where we might,
By seeking, find a person,
We are content to hang a
Specter that haunts ourselves.
The triangle of consequence,
Result, action, and appetite,
Appetite, action, and result,
Spins like the coat of arms of the
Isle of Man, until it erupts
Into a kind of false being,
The ghost or demon of the deed.
The *Tale of Genji* is the
Story of generations
Of beauty destroyed by a
Devil which sprang from a moment
Of wrath and jealousy, and whose
Power grew for years until

It was dissolved by one pure act
Of gracious, casual compassion.

If we cannot be assured
That any human being
Or group of human beings
Is any more real than any
Of the other occasions of
The world, we cannot literally
Love our neighbor as ourselves,
Because love is reciprocal,
And in the majority
Of our encounters with our
Neighbors, they show no signs of
Wishing to transcend the thingness
They share with all impersonal
Experience, and enter
Into any personal, let
Alone a love relationship.
All we can do is to try
To love one another, and through
The beloved to love all
She loves, and to keep ourselves
Open to the love of others.

A day with the Giottos in
Padova, the best thing is the
Donkey. The Mantegnas were bombed.
Vicenza for Palladio,
And the Villa Valmarana,
And then on to Verona.
San Zeno and the arena,
And then lunch with Mardersteig.
No better printer anywhere,
One of those perfect craftsmen
In whom absolute devotion
And respect for a medium

Has produced a state of being
Which can only be called saintly,
A personality like a
Work of art, a true state of grace.
We both think of the portrait of
Luca Pacioli in Naples.
Autumn planting in Lombardy,
As the sower walks along
A puff of dark dust flies from
His hand and floats away with
Each cast. The grain is mixed with soil.

Sirmio, a dark blue grey sky
Above the grey blue lake, the sun
Breaking through the mountains at the
Far end, its light a pale, soft orange;
Dull red leaves on the hillsides,
Bright yellow poplars on the shores;
Everything else wet brown, dusky
Blue, and chalky white. Dürer
Painted his watercolors here,
And here Tiepolo found those
Terribly civilized color chords.
Catullus certainly picked
A lovely spot for himself.
I will never do as well.
But I have never been the lover
Of "the most depraved daughter
Of the Claudian line," either.

Milano, a big show of
Public Health work in Italy.
Very impressive, perfect
Techniques, as good as the States.
Behind these montages and
Movies are thousands of poorly
Paid, hard working idealists,

Many of them Americans.
The statistics of what they've done
Are very impressive, too,
Until you read the statistics
Of the real situation.
You can plug dikes with a finger,
But you can't plug a tidal wave.

Normally one would assume
That what appears as a group
Of human beings would be
An aspect of persons in
A community of love.
Unfortunately mankind
Appears collectively almost
Always as an instrumentality
Of the State, as malignant,
If not openly murderous.
I have never encountered
Even good will in any
Collectivity. I know of
No association of men
Which cannot be demonstrated
To have been, ultimately,
Organized for purposes
Of coercion and mutual
Destruction. By far the worst
Are the putative communal
And benevolent gangsters.
Lawrence pointed out long ago
That the most malignant form
Of hate is benevolence.
Social frightfulness has increased
In exact proportion to
Humanitarianism.
In the nation of the atom
Bomb, dentists inject narcotics

Before they clean your teeth. The
Society of Friends has the
Honor of having introduced
The concentration camp into
America, of course under
Very humane auspices.

Milanese food is world famous,
But when I want French food, I'll take
It straight without tomato sauce.
However, Milano has the
World's best snails, cared for better
Than most Italian babies and
Fed on vine leaves and polenta.

The Cathedral – why on earth
Did they want to try to build
A thing like that in Italy?
But Sant' Ambrogio, that is a
Different matter, its Milanese
Barn roof filled with flying golden
Geometry. And the Cena –
Leonardo has always
Annoyed me, he seems like a
Renaissance Marcel Duchamp,
And Freud was certainly right
About that sickening St. John.
But once in his life he was both
Transfigured and accomplished.
Fresh from the Scuola San Rocco,
And the Stanze of Raphael,
This tattered cloud of color,
Filled with the forms of gods and
Every tragedy of man,
Beggars all Italian painting.
We look at it all day long.
Just before the light goes, a group

Of schoolgirls comes in. They all stand
At the back and listen to their
Nun. Except one little blonde girl,
About twelve, with a face of
Untempered sensibility,
Who advances slowly, hands
Folded, lips parted, eyes rapt away.
We turn aside, as though we had
Pried on the vision of a saint.
I say to Marthe, "I would
Give anything in the world to
Have a daughter like that." Our
Daughter is already alive.
The next day we leave Italy.

To match the scarlet of the
Autumn leaves, the red sunlight
Glitters on the flowing stream.
Lago Maggiore, blue black
And grey with bands of silver.
Deep Autumn, the orange fruit
And olive grey bare branches
Of the kakis silhouetted
In dark air. And at the last
Italy only a dimness
And vastness of gold filled fog
Behind us in the narrow mountains.

There are more fallen leaves than I
Ever saw growing on the trees.

IV

Over Switzerland broods the
Anal ghost of Karl Barth's church
Of spiritual masochism,
Up to date religion for the

Inmates of a world in barbed wire,
And the miasma of Jung's
Health resort occultism,
For the bored wives of the screws.
Switzerland is the world's worst
Country – Kansas stood on end.

A real religion is not
Believed in, it is practiced.
Julian was not the reviver
Of paganism, but the
Unsuccessful founder of
A sect. So his competitors,
The Christians, except where they
Have been overcome by the
Ancient cults they tolerated,
Began as, and remain late
Hellenistic sectarians.
Neither Augustine nor Karl Barth
Are religious men. They are
Emotionally unstable
Philosophers. The savage fills
The gap between technology
And environment with
Projections of himself.
If he is successful he is
Unaware of the gap until
Confronted with a sewing machine.

The World Soul, the point where the
Sun's path crosses the ecliptic,
Moves through the constellations,
Slow as the waste of mountains
In the midst of falling water.
The Zodiac revolves like
A waterwheel of which the
Planets are the buckets and

Gathers light generated
By contemplation and pours
It into the lamps of the world,
The sun and moon. The world passes
Like a white pony which flashes
Past a gap in a hedge.

The year
6666
The rainbow will shine like a bride,
Adorned for the bed of her spouse.
A star will rise in the east and
Swallow seven stars in the north.
A star will appear at the Pole.
It will shine for seventy days.
It will have seventy stars.
Rome will fall into ruins.
The celestial ו will raise up
The terrestrial ה into the
Bliss of sexual union.

Love and do what you will.
Love slays what we have been,
That we may be what we were not.

Dans l'automne vaine
Les feuilles tombent
Des kakis, où les singes
S'agrippent dans leurs
Fourrures ahuries.

Paris at midnight, colder
Than a witch's tit. We cower
In our Italian clothes and hunt
A cab. A little jumping wisp
Of a man with bright Celtic eyes
Escorts us to the last cab
That won the battle of the Marne.

The porter, covered with luggage,
Is so drunk he can't see, and must
Be led like a dizzy camel.
"Votre voiture va plus?" "Oui, oui,
M'sieu, madame. Elle marche doucement
Avec les années de la sagesse."
Spurred, she explodes and shakes herself,
And starts off with only one lamp,
Peering weakly through the rain.
"Ah, la bonne auto! Elle a été
La bonne, et la camarade très
Fidèle!" entering Boulevard
St. Germain, a traffic cop
Whistles. She rears and quivers
And shuts her eye and dies.
The cop comes over, soaked with rain.
"Vous n'avez pas la lumière."
"Ah, mais oui, je n'ai qu'une, mais
Très efficace, toutes les fois
Qu'elle va, alors, elle éclaire!"
"J' comprends. C'est pour ça que j'vous ai arrêté.
Changez la lumière active
A la gauche. Faites sûr que ça
S'allume avant de repartir."
This is no enemy of the people.
He presses his lips and goes away.
The cabby changes the lamps.
Nothing happens. He tinkers with
The dashboard. Nothing happens.
He jumps out again and gently
Pats the light. It lights.
There is no lens and it lights up
His face, streaming with rain, suffused
With the great joy of relief
From a terrible fear. "M'sieu,
Madame, je vous disais n'est-ce pas,
Qu'elle était la bonne camarade?"
All the pathos and anguish

And heroism of the French
Working class hits us in the face
Like a bludgeon. "Nous ne sommes
Rien, soyons tout!" But when?
When? When? In the bitter rain
On the Boulevard St. Germain?

Edgar Quinet – not a whore out
In the storm. Our reservations
Have been forgotten. Two o'clock
Before we find a narrow bed,
And furiously make love,
To assure ourselves our blood
Still circulates. In the dark hall
Under a one watt lamp, a sign –

LE SILENCE
DE CHACUN
ASSURE
LE REPOS
DE TOUS

When they caught
Vaillant trying to blow the
Chambre to smithereens, the
Judge said, "But think of all the
Innocent people you would
Have killed." He replied, "There are
No innocent bourgeois."

We have
Fed you all for a thousand years
And you hail us still unfed.

Anyone in France with an
Income of over sixty dollars
A month is a rascal, and this

Includes existentialists,
Poets, artists, Communists,
All colors of labor fakers,
From anarchist to royalist.
They all piss through the same quill.
Ye are many, they are few.

There are only two classes,
Members of communities,
Members of collectivities,
And they have nothing in common.
Mankind will sink only deeper
Into mutual murder,
As long as collectivity
Robs them of their persons, starves
And dehumanizes them,
Deranges their desires, crazes
Them with insane appetites
Instead of the satisfactions
Of mutual love, provides them
With commodities which turn
To guns in their hands and bullets
In their bowels, and leaves them
Finally, perfect, abstract
Integers, anonymous white
X's in battlefield graveyards.

Between these two classes a
Struggle must go on until
Mankind is exterminated,
Or all abstract, coercive
Collectivities are destroyed,
And the satisfaction of
Human needs becomes a minor
Part of the fulfillment of
Personal desire, in a
Community of love.

La Nuit de la Libertaire
At the Mutualité.
An endless entertainment,
All the best raconteurs and
Singers of Paris donate
Their services, the bitter
Humor and passion of the
Dispossessed, gone from the States
With the old tramp carnivals
I followed once in Arkansas,
The voice of the Buttes Chaumont,
The true blague of Pig Alley.
At the end, mass chants by the
Auberge Jeunesse Laïque, "Spain
Will Rise Again," "Our Martyrs."
One by one, boys and girls step out
And sing a name. I am moved
As the foreign names ring out,
And then, unprepared, I hear,
"Parsons, Frank Little, Joe Hill,
Wesley Everest, Sacco,
Vanzetti." I weep like a baby.
Afterwards, when the dancing
Begins, we discover the cadres
In double breasted gabardines,
Sitting in a side room at a
Long table, solemnly sipping
Beer, like the Central Committee
In a Pudovkin movie.
They are horrified when we
Jitterbug with the young comrades.
No hope there. But along the
Beautiful rivers of France,
And in the mountains, next summer
Boys and girls will be making love,
And singing the songs of Joe Hill
In their own language. "Song on his

Lips he came, song on his lips he
Went. This be the burden of his
Refrain, soldier of discontent."
Hideux dans leur apothéose,
Les rois de la mine et du rail
Ont-ils jamais fait autre chose
Que dévaliser le travail?
Combien de nos chairs se repaissent!
Mais si les corbeaux, les vautours,
Un de ces matins, disparaissent,
Le soleil brillera toujours!

No collectivity against
Collectivities can function
To restore community.
You cannot creep from quantity
To quality. Today the world is full
Of the vendors of well policed
Utopias, preachers of
Progress by mass arithmetic.
They are all liars, knowingly
Using the language of being
To sweeten the poison of
Death. Never has the last circle
Of Dante's Hell been so crowded.
While there is a lower class,
I am in it. While there is
A criminal element,
I am of it. Where there is
A soul in jail, I am not free.

In the Italian museums
The paintings look like very
Expensive treasures, but still
Works of art; elsewhere in Europe
They look like loot; in England
Like badges of Empire and class

Distinction, collective Orders
Of Merit; in the United
States they look like tastefully
Chosen, beautifully shown
Merchandise. French painting
Never de-provincialized
Itself. Most of it is sterile
And concocted. Poussin – the
Darling of the aesthetes who think
Copland sounds like Bach.
Le Sueur, at once rigid and soft,
But in the Mass of St. Martin,
Uncanny as Easter Island.
The Nains, as academic
And Italianate as the Blue
And Pink Picassos which copy
Them. The Nineteenth Century
Largely the private conversation,
The symbols of a special
Antibourgeois way of life,
Of a secret revolutionary
Society. The Twentieth
A horrible collection
Of gadgets and infernal
Machines. Had Seurat lived things might
have been different. What have you?
The boudoir painters, certainly
As good as Tiepolo, but
With less scale and no arrogance;
Lorrain, a sentimental
Peasant, touched with the over-
Ripe infantilism you
Think of with Richard Jefferies;
David, a pompous bureaucrat,
Except for little Val d'Ognes,
But I doubt if he painted her;
Ingres, an inflated lapidary;

Courbet and Delacroix, the
Only French painters who ever
Seriously tried to be
Major artists, one corrupted
By Haldeman-Julius, the
Other full of fustian, but as
Gide replied, "Hugo. Hélas!"
Even the failure in Saint
Sulpice has a kind of
Renaissance arrogance and might
Well be hanging in Italy.
The "French Moderns" are aged men.
Actually contemporary
Painting is awful past belief –
With the exception of Tal-Coat,
Who is a man in his forties.
The growing point of painting
Today has moved to Seattle.

Americans who worship
Richardson despise Abadie.
Although it is the symbol
Of Neo-Catholicism
And the Black Terror after
The Commune, still, Sacré Coeur
Is equalled by few churches in
Paris, and no archaistic
Churches elsewhere. Trinity
May be in better taste, but
It was so patently built
For Boston consumption.
St. Vincent Ferrer looks like
Gothic by Kohler of Kohler.
Liverpool is the tomb of
An Empire's hypocrisy.
"Functionalist churches" are
For people who have forgotten

The very meaning of a sect,
Let alone a religion.
Sante Cécile in Albi was
Another "cry of triumph
Over the Wall of the Communards,"
Why shouldn't the ruling class
Be best when celebrating
Its most characteristic
Activity, mass murder?

There is a false impression
Abroad that American
Poetry has given up
The working class as a bad
Proposition and taken to
Form. This should be corrected.

Wine, women, and song,
Whiskey, pin-ups, and laxatives,
All the world raises hell about
Essenin and Mayakofsky.
Twenty-three poets of "anthology
Rank" have committed suicide
In the USA since 1900.
It is by far the commonest
Form of death amongst poets.
I am far better aware of
The evils of Stalinism
Than you are, you ex-Trotskyite
Warmonger. But it won't get you
Anywhere to tell me I should
Welcome the beast who devours me
Just because a bigger lion
Is eating somebody else on
The other side of the arena.

Love and lowliness and
Loyalty, these shall be

Lords in the land, truth to save.
For the world has lost his youth
And the times begin to wax old.

Léontine gives us a farewell.
"M. Kennet', un poète
Prolétarien, et sa femme,
Marthe, une jeune philosophe."
The tiny room is packed with guests;
A fat Italian sculptor who
Looks like a ragged, dying Wilde,
Epilepsy destroyed his hand,
Now he makes casts for the Louvre;
His silent, fat, Bretonne peasant wife;
A little wiry garagist,
Red faced, bright eyed, three times
Given up for dead with consumption,
Three years in concentration camps;
A Bretonne ex-seamstress who makes
Periodic trips to Belgium,
Where a girl can still find money;
Two neighbors, haggard young housewives,
Who eat and drink but hardly speak;
Léontine's first lover, an old
Shepherd from the Breton highlands,
With cheeks of purple morocco,
And eyes like a benevolent
Eagle. A wonderful dinner;
A pâté truffé; a brochet
Au beurre blanc; a bardatte,
The wild hare and woodcocks snared
By the shepherd; peas in cream;
Roast beef with a gravy of
Buckwheat flour, cream, and plums;
Choufleur farci; and a farsac'h,
The plum pudding of Brittany.
I bring the wine, Pelure d'oignon
(Just like in America,

The girls prefer rosé), and a
Bottle of Calvados. They admire
Marthe's dress. "From a couturière?"
"Certainly not, I made it myself."
The atmosphere perceptibly
Lightens. Everybody eats, drinks,
Tells stories, sings songs, recites
Poetry. Over the coffee
The garagist cuts loose. His
Repertory is formidable.
"La Poule qu'était batie trop étroite,"
"Toute la nuit sur la Tour Eiffel,"
"L'Hirondelle avec les hémorroïdes sèches"
(Hirondelles are bicycle cops),
And especially for the shepherd,
"Pompadour, ma belle angèle."
Léontine says, "He writes them all
Himself." I tell a story with
The punch line, "Ci-gît. Personne.
Son père utilise les
Produits Michelin." Great uproar.
The French all think their invention
Hilariously funny.
The shepherd is rather aloof
Until I tell him that once
I worked sheep, when I was a
Forest ranger in the Far West.
We get into a long discussion
Of shepherding. I draw pictures
Of pack saddles, herders' wagons,
Tie a diamond hitch around his
Fingers. He is in ecstasy.
"La même, la même chose. Formidable.
Très ingénieuse." He wants to leave
For Nevada on the instant.
"C'est très simple," I say,
"Ecrivez une lettre au

Senator McCarran, et
Il vous fera venir outre-mer
Par avion; alors, vous
Gagnerez trois cents dollars par mois
Dès que vous signerez." "Impossible!"
"Impossible, mais c'est vrai." "Incroyable!"
The eagle's face gets a little
Foolish with shock. Léontine says,
"C'est absurde. L'Amérique vous
Tuerait. En France tu es
Un pauvre des pauvres, mais tu
As la bonne vie. Aux Etats-Unis,
Tu serais seul, dans le désert
Avec des milliards de moutons,
Et les loups de la prairie,
Les très sauvages coyotes,
Les ours de la montagne,
Les grizzlys féroces, les rattle
Snakes, et les sournois Peaux-Rouges."
"Je n'ai pas peur. Dans les
Pyrénées une fois..." "Tu n'avais pas
Peur, mais tu es vieux. Quand
Etais-tu dans les Pyrénées?
Pendant la Grande Guerre. M'sieu
Kennet' dit que tu conduirais
Les grands troupeaux à travers des
Milliers d'hectares. C'est la
Vitesse américaine dans les
Déserts. Et quand tu terminerais
Le travail, puis, quoi? Pas de
Léontine. Pas de Montparnasse.
Rien que le cowtown, les cowboys,
Le jukebox, le pinball, le whiskey.
Vous ne savez pas jouer au poker."
The old wisdom comes back in his
Face and he smiles his sly smile.
"L'illusion d'un moment,

Ma chérie, ce n'est qu'un cauchemar.
Je n'irai pas à moins que
Tu n'y ailles aussi. Tu
Pourrais être une dancing-girl
Parmi les cowboys et les Peaux-Rouges."
The garagist raises his glass,
And says, "Ki Yi Yippee Yi Yi!"
He has come back from his own room,
Bringing a sheaf of drawings, and
A box of beautiful models.
As he shows them to me his face
Lights with exaltation, and his
Movements grow entranced and still
More quick. I am dumbfounded.
He has managed to discover
A fundamentally new
Application of a double
Torsion. I cannot tell through his
Excited language if he is
Aware of this or not.
He has perfect models of a
Stabilizer for the latest
Ford, a coupling for heavy trailers,
A gimmick for jet airplanes
I do not quite understand,
And last – "I hoped this at least
Could be sold in France" – a brake
For a bicycle, which is so
Revolutionary and
Efficient, I ask him if he
Can have it copied for me
In a model shop. "I do not
Use a model shop. I make them
Myself, in my spare time in the
Garage." "What do you do in the
Garage?" "I wash cars." No one speaks.
At last Léontine says, "There is

No place for a man like him
In France. No one will invest
Any money. They want big
Profits from the old machinery,
Making the old junk. The money
They put in gold in boxes
In the banks in Buenos Aires."
I look at him. He is in rags.
His cheeks are like splotches
Of red ink. In a year or so
He will be dead. If he had gone
To America in his youth,
Today he would be on the
Cover of *Time* magazine. But
He would never have written the
Poem about the midinette
And the camel, or the song
About the nuns who got drunk.
If only poverty was not
Killing him. I write an address.
"You can mail those plans to Detroit.
I am sure they would give you
A job. But like M'sieu le berger,
You would not like America."
When we leave the card is crumpled
On the floor. It is the law
Of the falling rate of profit.
I ask Léontine where she got
Her name. "Ah, but Kennet', you are
A poet and philosopher –
It was the name of the great
Courtesan, the mistress of
The philosophe Epicure."
At first I am too tipsy to
Appreciate this statement.
Then the full force of it hits me.
Here I am, living Landor's

Best piece of prose, more beautiful
Than anything in English
Outside of Gibbon, but not
In just the way he wrote it.
It is getting late. Signor
Picelli invites us to his house
For minestrone. He explains
His name. "Picelli – almost like the
Pope. I almost became Pope,
But alas, everyone knew my wife."
He stands in his loft, erect
In his slumping body, surrounded by
Dead white replicas of all
The sculpture of the ages,
And talks about aesthetics,
In English, French, and Italian.
Then he takes me aside and asks
If Marthe is broadminded.
I assure him she is and he
Shows us a series of little
Erotic sculptures, lovers in
All sorts of tangled embraces.
"All I can do now. My hand
Is gone. Dépourvu d'esprit –
Les plaisirs de mon vieux sang –
Et par la paresse." I am too
Stupid and polite to buy one.
"Mon vieux sang," Vitalis' words
The night he froze to death, over
Which I shuddered as a child.
As we are singing over the
Minestrone, he has a fit,
And the party breaks up.
We come out, back of the Gare
Montparnasse into the narrow
Alley, like a stage set in the
Dense November fog. Its name
Is the Passage du Départ.

A community of love is
A community of mutual
Indwelling, in which each member
Realizes his total
Liability for the whole.
A collectivity is like
A cancer disorganizing the
Organism which produced it.
The healthy organism
Itself, responds instantly,
As a whole, to the injury
To the slightest of its parts.
Those who by function, or the chance
Of historical accident,
Have mercifully been shut off
From the ravages of social
Paranoia and cancer
Still possess the remnants of
Community, and can begin
To widen and extend it.
This class, unfortunately,
Includes few white Americans.
Where it survives, community
Can transcend history only
By becoming self conscious,
And its first step must be the
Stopping of the insanity
Of commodity production,
And the substitution of free
Satisfaction of human needs.

Bienheureux sont les débonnaires
Car ils hériteront la terre.

O Paris, ses faubourgs anonymes!
O Paris, ses avenues disparues!
Paris, où la pauvreté était toujours la vertu.
Paris, où la Révolution vint et attend.

Paris, que vous n'auriez pas trouvé autour de la rue Scribe.
Le soleil qui s'couche dans les ruelles bornées derrière
Clignancourt.
Belleville, la brune d'hiver, les lumières faibles.
Place République ténébreuse, les filles perdues se répandent
invisiblement.
Rue de la Chapelle dans la bagarre de minuit.
Midi d'été, l'Avenue de l'Ouest bouillant avec les pauvres;
Ici on achète le boudin, le cheval, les fruits sales, les pièces des
vélos.
Les andouillettes de la rue des Rosiers, où je retrouve mon
Yiddish.
Avenue du Maine, "Bikini," le Dancing Nègre, le rhum punch.
Saint Germain de Charonne garde un aspect villageois au milieu
de son petit cimetière en terrasse où repose Magloire Bègue,
secrétaire de Robespierre et amateur de roses.
Le lion en pantoufles défend les souterrains à Denfert-Rochereau.
Villette, la nuit étoilée, vide comme le Nevada.
Stalingrad, les escargots, la bière, le billard.
Vercingétorix, le poiré et le tric-trac.
Rue Daguerre, le calvados et les échecs.
Saint Denis, les oursins et la Saintonge avec
Un vieillard qui avait connu Louise Michel.
Rue Vieille-du-Temple, Gazelle chantant "Le Pont Mirabeau,"
Son dos une cicatrice solide, grâce aux camps de concentration.
Paris, de l'Internationale du sang et du chair.

Milosz' "Symphonie de Novembre":
"It will be exactly like this life. The same room.
Yes, my child, the same. At dawn the bird of time in the foliage,
Pale as a corpse. Then the servants will get up,
And you will hear the frozen noises, in the hollow basins

"Of the fountains. O terrible, terrible youth! O empty heart!
It will be exactly like this life. There will be
The poor voices, the voices of Winter in old slums,
The glass mender singing his own duet,

"The broken grandmother under a dirty bonnet
Crying out the names of fish, the man with the blue apron,
Who spits into a hand worn by the wheelbarrow,
And yells nobody knows what, like the Angel of Judgment."

Lamarck's four laws. Carnot's three laws.
The organic composition
Of capital. The law of
The falling rate of profit.

Organization at the
Point of production.
Abolition of the wage system.

Once they made war with swords,
Now they make it by withholding,
Now here, now there, bread which a good
Father would deny to no one.

Under the somber Autumn sky
We walk in the deserted
Jardin des Plantes. All the plants
Wear straw pelisses for Winter.
Evening comes on, smoky
And blue, and then cold fine rain.
A sign:

AVIS
LES JEUX
SONT
INTERDITS
DANS LE
LABYRINTHE

The maigre November rain
Is falling on the Boulevard
Montparnasse. The streets are dark

Blue and dim. Tiny weak lights
Of bicycles wobble past,
Of men going to work before
Daylight. Garbage collectors
Bang cans, vegetable men
Make deliveries in a
Few open shops. The neon
Bar ornament glows through the
Steaming windows of the Dôme.
No breakfast, they are just cleaning up.
The beautiful monument
By the Closerie des Lilas
On the Avenue Observatoire
Is barely visible,
Glistening in the cold first dawn.
Morning comes up Port Royal,
Wet, and biting to the bone.
This is our last sight of the
Crowded little shops of Paris,
Tall houses leaning back from the
Narrow streets and the cold grey
Façades of the Boulevards,
And then the river, silken
In the rain, the coal and gravel
Barges whispering through the rain.
Gare d'Austerlitz exactly
Like all Monet's portraits of it.

It clears before noon. Let Autumn
Golden on the golden Loire,
On the land, rich and beautiful,
Like Italy, like America.

Most men present themselves as parts
Of some malignant collection,
And, as such, are evidently

Bent on their own extinction.
Only a tiny handful
Appear as conscious members of
A community, as persons.
Therefore, either men are
Incapable of love and damned,
Or most men are illusions.
But the term "most men" refers
To nothing more real than any
Contingent aspect of the world.
The quantified collection
Is unreal. There are no most men,
As there are no most trees or stars.
Behind the collection stands,
One by one, a person. And
Unless I can touch that person,
I am only making a mistake
In grades of illusion, as one
Who thinks the shadow of a rope
Is a snake. When I offer love
And receive injury or hate,
I have not dealt with a person,
But with a projection of myself.

The associations of
Paris confuse the issue.
Here where Tourney had a free hand
In his home town, royal
Boulevard architecture
Stands revealed in all its sterile
Provincial grandeur. Even
The age of Boucher could not
Equal one Roman piazza
Let alone Florence or Venice.
Louis Quinze architects were
Best at boudoirs.

There are two Bordeaux, one a
Port for the North Atlantic,
The other for Spain and Africa.
So the best people in town
Were the black feline Negroes
Working the docks or studying
At the university,
And the Sephardic Jews. The
Negroes are still there. The Jews –
Beyond the tomb of Montaigne,
At the end of a narrow
Street, is one of the best
Examples of Louis Quinze
Architecture. From a distance
The gable looks odd, crowned with
Two little bumps; nearer they
Become the curved tops of the
Tablets of the Law. In the
Forecourt is another tablet.
Five hundred names are arranged by
Families: Moses Cohen,
Rebecca Cohen, Samuel
Cohen, Sarah Cohen, Saul
Texeira, Ruth Texeira,
Leah Texeira, David Texeira –
The Nazis locked the entire
Jewish population in this
Small building, kept them without
Food and water for a few days,
Machine gunned them through the windows.
When they heard of such things, the
Pogrom loving Poles and the
Ukrainians revolted,
The Italians fought like tigers,
The French and Negro workers
Made Bordeaux industrially
Worthless to the Nazis. But

The citoyens did nothing.
Ribbentrop was once a wine
Salesman. Business was better
Than usual.

Bordeaux with its
Pencil stub towers – a bit of
France that is forever England.
The center of Protestantism,
The bailiwick of the country
Gentlemen and merchants who
Died such pathetic deaths, struggling
To introduce the ghost of
William of Orange, that morose,
Homosexual, progressive
Millionaire, to the France of
Marat, Hébert, Jacques Roux.
The poules become tarts, the arcade
Where they hustle looks like Soho,
And their faces are bitter
With guilt. The churches are neuter
Gothic and sadly jumbled,
But it must be admitted
The detached towers are an
Unforgettable sensation.
Sainte-Croix, our last sight of the
Beautiful Langue d'Oc Romanesque,
Like all of them, lovingly
Rebuilt by Abadie.
We load up on Château Ausone
And our little French freighter
Crawls moaning through the fog down the
Gironde, and out into the
Invisible Atlantic.
Behind us in the Bordeaux
Museum, Delacroix's *Greece Dying*
At Missolonghi, ivory

And gold, burning and charred, the
Perfect farewell of France, the
Symbol of how many
Revolutions betrayed.

Midnight, the swollen half moon,
Setting in the warm seas, the wake
Seething with stars and nebulae
Of living phosphorescence.

"What is evil?" said Pilate.
This is the blood of Rahab,
Lifted upon high on the
Riven wood of the tree of
Paradise for the confounding
Of all nations.

Boehme's flagrat, the cross on
Which being turns to meaning,
And water turns back to wine.

Love who moves the sun and other stars.

V

New York a grey haze with flights of
Pigeons wheeling above Harlem
As the boys on the rooftops
Whirl long poles and call them home.
The skyscrapers vanish quickly
Away and away forever.
As the observation car
Crosses the Harlem River
Past the tall red brick Berlinese-
Looking Negro housing projects,
The lights turn red, closing the way.
The Hudson sinks deeper and

Deeper into the blue until
Nothing is left but the black
Outline of the Catskills, the lights
Of the other shore, the soaring
Bridge over the long water
Wan in the end of evening.

Through direct knowledge of the
Dual, indirect knowledge of
All the others, the manifold
Of all the possible, passes
Toward the critical point where
It vanishes to reappear
As a growing kernel of
Direct knowledge of the others.

Toledo late in the night,
The factories roaring. Elkhart
Before dawn, a few street signs
Still blazing, the lights of lonely
Cars waiting at the crossings.
Gary, the red fires and purple
Fires of the mills in the red
And purple Winter sunrise.

Being alternates with non-being.
For millions of years Shiva sleeps,
For millions of years he dances.
The world flows from the void, the void
Drinks up the world. We assume
That this is a period
Of being, action, creation,
A time of Shiva's dancing.

My favorite painting in Chicago,
A little Cazin – October day,
A rising field, withered grass,

A dull sky, a pink roof, coral
And silver, grey green and ashes
Of roses. And Corot's Roman
Paintings. Society is
Immoral and immortal.
The fragments that survive can
Always laugh at the dead. But
A young man has only one
Chance and brief time to seize it.
Shang bronzes. What endures, what
Perishes. In the vacant
Lots where we built trenches after
One war, now there are foxholes.

The evidence for full direct
Knowledge, not of the dual,
But of the manifold other,
Under conditions known to us,
Is slight and sporadic and
Difficult to class as knowledge.
However, this may be due to
Its unanalyzable
Character in terms of a
Pattern of experience
Which for discursive knowledge
Of the world of consequence
We have made mechanically
Analytic. Certainly some
Knowledge of the other is
The universal content of
All mystical experience
And of much that is not so called.

We walk in the silver and grey
Afternoon along the Midway
And visit the neighborhood
Where I grew up and pass my old

Grammar school, now all Negro
Children. On the frosty air
From the northwest comes faintly
The odor of the stockyards,
Decadent now, and hardly
Perceptible, not the old-
Time rich stench. We walk back through
Washington Park in the windy
Early night, lights among the
Bare trees, the air thick with frost.
Dinner in one of the last
Good restaurants in America –
The Red Star Inn, the menu,
As the cooking, unchanged as
The highchair I used to sit in,
Still there in its corner.
The blissful Buddha face of
Sweets Williams driving the piano
Like a locomotive over
The stumblebum squalor of
The cheapest North Clark Street bar.
The entranced sadistic face
Of one girl who does the
Most cunnilingual strip in
The business, the customers
Like yawning hippopotami,
Not a dry fly in the house.
No other city deserves
North Clark Street, the B girls and
Dice girls in glen plaid suits and
Tailored blouses, the only
Sign of vice the fetishistic
Castled hair like Fuseli's tarts,
Spike heels and black net stocking.
"You look lonely, I am lonely too.
Would you enjoy a drink with me?"
The management prefers girls

With a college education.
The dice girl has a new boyfriend
From Hell's Kitchen who regales
Her with stories of the wonders
Of New York, and how tough he is.
At 3 AM he says, "Hey,
Tomato, what do you say
To coppin' a mo'?" She says,
"Yes, darling, I am awfully tired,
I think it would be nice to leave."
Tonight she has taken any
Number of customers and
Primed and fingered three suckers
And sent them to meet her in
The dark hallway of her supposed
Apartment, where they met a
Sock full of sand. The B girls
Never bother with tea, but
Quickly toss off "triple gins,"
Three dollars worth of water.

V. I. T. R. I. O. L.
Visita interiora terrae
Rectificando invenies
Occultem lapidem. Seek
In the interior of
The earth, rectify, and you
Will discover the hidden stone.

In K.C. everyone, even
The whores and an appreciable
Number of Negroes, looks like
Truman. I go out with a
Black, deep bosomed, aquiline nosed
Girl like a Sudanese – no
Public place possible in
Kansas City, so we go

To the house of a friend, who
Turns out to be my train porter,
Drink beer and dance to records.
A city uninhabited
Except for a few Negroes
And some good Chinese paintings.

Calvinist and Liberal
Both strive to reduce moral
Action to the range of the
Objectively guaranteed.
The essential character
Of the moral act is its lack
Of objective guarantee.

In Kansas even the horses
Look like Landon, ugly parched
Faces like religious turtles,
The original scissorbills.

Augustine, Luther, Kierkegaard,
The pragmatic leap in the dark.
Act loses reality,
Reality is equated
With mechanical stability,
Masochistic decision
Becomes hallucination,
A blind plunge out of being,
Sacrifice its own value –
The Nibelungen Spirit.

West from Newton a dust storm,
The air whirling and smothering,
All the bare trees painted with
Pale grey dust, a flock of crows
Crying through the dust, over
The stubble and young fall wheat

Grey with dust, the edge of the flock
Invisible in the dust.
The decline and fall of the
Capitalist system, born
In blood in the Thirty Years' War.

A ruined country and a
Ruining people, the world
Would be better if Kansas
Were not in it. Dodge City,
Nearing the West, the air has changed,
Migrating ducks fly across
The full moon, a warm wind
Before a storm blows down the
Long continental slope from
The Rockies. Before Trinidad
It starts to snow, the high plains
Stretch away to the first mountains,
A thin wash of white under
The obscure moon, the air full of
Wandering snowflakes, saturated
With moonlight. Out at 3 AM,
Raton, a full blast of blizzard,
Impossible to stand up,
I sleep on a station bench.

"Early in the morning of
The next day, looking along
The horizon before us,
We saw that at one point it
Was faintly marked with pale
Indentations like the teeth
Of a saw. The distant lodges
Of the Arapahoes rising
Between us and the sky caused
This singular appearance."
Parkman, a boy on the

Oregon Trail, before he was
Terrified by the libidos
Of the Indians and turned to
His fourteen-volume epic
Of the triumph of anal
Over oral sexuality.

South of Raton by a small bus
To Taos, the dry grass with
Snow blowing through it looks like
Opossum fur. As the clouds
Scatter and the just-risen sun
Breaks out and lights up the mountains,
The landscape turns blue and silver
And pale wintry gold, with tatters
Of clouds hurrying to the
Edges of the sky. I am
Back home. This is my country.
All that back there is illusion.
The sign says Taos 86,
Cimarron 26, and all
The sick and liberated
Writresses and fairies vanish
Into the great abysm
Of pain and commodities
That is civilization.
The mountains come nearer and nearer,
Two punchers get on I knew once
On a ranch in Montana.
The bus radio plays cowboy
Songs, I read a novel by
Ernest Haycox, so much better than
The continued story about
The Jewish boy who doesn't
Want to get a job, and the
Serial about Henry James,
And the serial about Kafka

In each issue of the leading
Reviews. The moon just past full
Is setting in the cold western
Sky of early morning over
The headwaters of the Cimarron,
Over hills brushed with snow and
Junipers storm-encrusted
With new snow. The bus driver
Stops and waits. Everybody
Discusses some deer tracks on the
Road. Finally we go back
And dig out a car we were
Leading out of Eagle Nest.

Comet tails and sunspots suffice
To account for all history.

Taos mostly gone, pavements, neon,
Four times as many houses.
The natives, at least the Spanish,
Still friendly and hospitable.
Most of the people newcomers,
New Yorkers and Chicagoans,
Everyone a shady customer
Of some kind, spreading an air
Of fake over the whole town.
The Lawrence set like the surly
Aging employees of a mausoleum,
All still hating each other.
Frieda gone for the Winter
The Indian girls on the street
Still look as hot as ever.
Andrew Dasburg, one of the
Old masters of modern art,
Comes to my lecture and we
Talk of fine nights of drunken
Argument twenty years gone.

Black night, bright moon, Orion
Vast over Lawrence's ashes.

The white race approaches the end of
Its tether, withers on its frontiers.
Vulvas of flame open in the sun.
The glaciers grow, the cyclones move south,
A black Thales falls into a well.
The morning brilliant, the fields
Blazing with snow, a pile of
Perfumed fresh lumber, a shaggy
Black horse breathing steam into the
Glare.

It is likely that even
The most etherialized
Vision of the mystic is
Knowledge much as an amoeba
Might be said to know a man.

Back to Raton and north, past the
Long Sangre de Cristo chain
Running off to the southwest.
Night shuts over the Rockies,
Gloomy and thick. Over Kansas
Furious blizzards are raging.
Next day traffic is all bound up.
I go back to Pueblo and cross
By the Royal Gorge on the
Only train through. Skurries of
Snow under heavy sky, the
Mountain somber to the west,
The continent falling away
On my left. Suddenly the sun
Breaks out and shines through driving snow.
Two long-tailed magpies, black and white,
Fly past, dipping through the storm.

Up from the Industrial Age,
Forward to the Atomic Age,
Man moves from the clinamen
Of Newton's apple, towards
The catastrophe of the Kant-
Laplace hypothesis. Descartes's
Angels fall from their bicycles.

Royal Gorge, across the stream
On the red cliff face runs a flume
Which has leaked and festooned itself
And the grass and rocks with twelve-foot
Icicles. In the daycoach
Eleven baby hillbillies,
California bound, all crying
At once. Steam from the curving train,
Clouds, snow, snow-covered mountains,
Emerge and merge. At the summit
The sky clears as the sun sets
And the peaks stand out as huge
As Kanchenjunga in the
Early twilight – a plain two
To three miles across and ten
Miles long, then the forested
Lower slopes, then three thousand
Feet of snow-covered massif –
In the plain, bunch grass sticking
Out of the snow, and shaggy
Horses walking delicately
In the wind, cutting the snow crust
With sharp steps like deer. Smoke, snow,
And the winding headlight. I stand
On the platform in the storm,
At my feet west-running water.
At Grand Junction a great
Monadnock with a narrow
Streamer of cloud across it

Near the top. The moon at the
Tail of the train, through orchards,
Past the lights of houses
In the zero night. I worked here
Once, it was all range country then.
Provo, first dawn, thick snow on
The ground, low clouds, the obscure moon
High in the sky, neat compact
Mormon houses, the breakfast
Lights coming up in them. Lombardy
Poplars bare in the white fields.
The lives of men beginning
Again, remote in the dawn.

Complete direct knowledge of
The others as the self, of
All the others, of all selves
As self knowledge, would cause the
Knower to vanish from our world.
Of course the disciples of
The founders of religions
Make exactly this claim for
Their masters, Christ's Ascension
And Buddha's Parinirvana.

Salt Lake City, the Lion
On the Lion House watches
Thick flakes of wet snow falling
Between the old locust trees.
The people on the calm streets
Look healthy and happy. Here
America reached its finest
Expression, in the most peaceful
City in the country, maybe
Now in the world. The strong power
Of communion still blesses it,
Brigham Young's peace, carved with a sword.

The clear water running in
The gutters, the white and cream
Brick houses with green shutters,
The home-going crowds and the snow
Falling through windless air in
The wide streets, at the heart
Of all this are calm bygone
Men with eighteen wives.

Since in the act of love the
Others are known in the other
As loved by him, jealousy
Destroys the meaning of the
Love relationship, corrodes it,
At last makes it impossible.
This means literal destruction
Of being and is the only
Real Hell. Jealousy objects
To love because it arises
From its opposite, hate, the
Desire to exploit the other
For purposes of ignorance
And grasping. Of course, as in most
Things, what this civilization
Calls love is its opposite.
Its love is an endless struggle
For flashy commodities, rare
Frigid fucking for frigidaires.

Night across Utah, to the south-
West snowy pyramids speckled
With junipers going by like
White mammoths as I fall asleep.
At noon the next day rolling
Down the long grade through Joshua
Trees I see a highway sign
And realize I am in California.

The mountains ahead of me
Are the tail end of the
Panamints, beyond them the high
Arid White Mountains, the desert
Valley, and the Sierra
Nevadas with their long trails
Through illusion and vision.

The good and evil of the world
Are the reflections of the will
Of the owner of that world.
Contemplation can multiply
Illusion until consequence
Is utterly exhausted.
All matter is redeemed by man,
Hence in poisonous medicines
It is the sick themselves who are
The doctors and heal the poisons.

I come back to the cottage in
Santa Monica Canyon where
Andrée and I were poor and
Happy together. Sometimes we
Were hungry and stole vegetables
From the neighbors' gardens.
Sometimes we went out and gathered
Cigarette butts by flashlight.
But we went swimming every day,
All year round. We had a dog
Called Proclus, a vast yellow
Mongrel, and a white cat named
Cyprian. We had our first
Joint art show, and they began
To publish my poems in Paris.
We worked under the low umbrella
Of the acacia in the dooryard.
Now I get out of the car

And stand before the house in the dusk.
The acacia blossoms powder the walk
With little pills of gold wool.
The odor is drowsy and thick
In the early evening.
The tree has grown twice as high
As the roof. Inside, an old man
And woman sit in the lamplight.
I go back and drive away
To Malibu Beach and sit
With a grey-haired childhood friend and
Watch the full moon rise over the
Long rollers wrinkling the dark bay.

"It is those who are married
Who should live the contemplative
Life together. In the world
There is the long day of
Destruction to go by. But
Let those who are single, man
Torn from woman, woman from
Man, man altogether, woman
Altogether, separate
Deathly fragments, each returning
And adhering to its own kind,
The body of life torn in two,
Let these finish the day of
Destruction, and those who have
United go into the
Wilderness to know a new
Heaven and a new earth."

There are those who spend all their lives
Whirling in the love and hate
Of the deities they create.

Contemplation is direct
Knowledge, beyond consequence,
Ignorance, appetite, grasping
Of possibility. The
Contemplative knows himself
As the focus of the others,
And he knows the other, the
Dual, as the mirror of
Himself and all the others,
The others as the mirror
Of himself and the dual.

Christmas Eve, unseasonably cold,
I walk in Golden Gate Park.
The Winter twilight thickens.
The park grows dusky before
The usual hour. The sky
Sinks close to the shadowy
Trees, and sky and trees mingle
In receding planes of vagueness.
The wet pebbles on the path
Wear little frills of ice like
Minute, transparent fungus.
Suddenly the air is full
Of snowflakes – cold, white, downy
Feathers that do not seem to
Come from the sky but crystallize
Out of the air. The snow is
Unendurably beautiful,
Falling in the breathless lake,
Floating in the yellow rushes.
I cannot feel the motion
Of the air, but it makes a sound
In the rushes, and the snow
Falling through their weaving blades
Makes another sound. I stand still,

Breathing as gently as I can,
And listen to these two sounds,
And watch the web of frail wavering
Motion until it is almost night.
I walk back along the lake path
Pure white with the new snow. Far out
Into the dusk the unmoving
Water is drinking the snow.
Out of the thicket of Winter
Cattails, almost at my feet,
Thundering and stamping his wings,
A huge white swan plunges away.
He breaks out of the tangle,
And floats suspended on gloom.
Only his invisible
Black feet move in the cold water.
He floats away into the dark,
Until he is a white blur
Like a face lost in the night,
And then he is gone. All the world
Is quiet and motionless
Except for the fall and whisper
Of snow. There is nothing but night,
And the snow and the odor
Of the frosty water.

The contemplative begins
By putting aside as far
As he can all appetite,
All wish to reap consequence
From possibility, and then
Cultivates disinterested
Knowledge of himself and of
The simplest things, knowing them
As really perspectives into
The others. By this means he
Rises to the first direct

Acquaintance with another,
With the dual as a person,
And more and more perfectly
Knowing the dual, rises
Towards the direct knowledge of
All the others, the infinite,
Absolute society.

The beginning of truth is
Wonder. He who wonders shall
Reign and he who reigns shall rest.

Seven days now, in the midst
Of the rainy season, the
Weather has been dry and bright,
In the evening the air
Is hazy with exhalations
Of the drying forest. Night
And morning the dewfall
Is tremendous, and there is
Frost on the bottoms and in
The open glades. New Year's night,
I walk in the moonlight. In the
Immaculate night the moonbeams
Are like needles. Great bars of
Moonhaze buttress the redwoods.
As I cross the meadow little
Pannicles of ice on the grass
Tinkle against my shoes.
There is a glory around
The head of my shadow, a soft,
Phosphorescent, lunar rainbow.
Over the vast downs, between
The redwoods and the sea, a few
Cattle and sheep move slowly
Or not at all. Then nothing moves.
No light is visible nearer

Than the moon and the stars. Far off,
The world falls like a bomb towards
Its own destruction. I have
Ceased to hear it. I no longer
Have any theories about it.
I no longer have any
Philosophy. All of my
Capacity for tragedy
Is exhausted. I tread softly,
Listening to the earth in the
Moonlight. Peace flows without stopping.
The peace is illimitable.
The clear glory is without end.

The contemplative heart, and
Reciprocally the other,
Rise above the levels of
Consequence, appetite, and
Discursive knowledge, with their
Limitations of time and space,
Coming to be and passing away,
And come to know each other
More and more directly. The
Fullness of being is the
Direct knowledge of all the
Others with its love and joy.

When abandoned by Zeus, the
Body of Leda's swan was
Murdered by jealous Electra.

Under the second moon the
Salmon come, up Tomales
Bay, up Papermill Creek, up
The narrow gorge to their spawning
Beds in Devil's Gulch. Although

I expect them, I walk by the
Stream and hear them splashing and
Discover them each year with
A start. When they are frightened
They charge the shallows, their immense
Red and blue bodies thrashing
Out of the water over
The cobbles; undisturbed, they
Lie in the pools. The struggling
Males poise and dart and recoil.
The females lie quiet, pulsing
With birth. Soon all of them will
Be dead, their handsome bodies
Ragged and putrid, half the flesh
Battered away by their great
Lust. I sit for a long time
In the chilly sunlight by
The pool below my cabin
And think of my own life – so much
Wasted, so much lost, all the
Pain, all the deaths and dead ends,
So very little gained after
It all. Late in the night I
Come down for a drink. I hear
Them rushing at one another
In the dark. The surface of
The pool rocks. The half moon throbs
On the broken water. I
Touch the water. It is black,
Frosty. Frail blades of ice form
On the edges. In the cold
Night the stream flows away, out
Of the mountain, towards the bay,
Bound on its long recurrent
Cycle from the sky to the sea.

The road which can be travelled is
Not the right road. The word which can
Be spoken is not the true word.

Most often God has been the name
Given to the most powerfully
Known person behind all the
Perspectives into all the
Others. Each contemplative
Has, usually, his own god
Whom he has come to know because
That person, however remote,
Has responded directly
To him. Theoretically
All the universe could be
The conversation of one
Person, the god of mystical
Monotheism. (The Sufi,
For instance, not of course
The orthodox Christian, who
Is not a monotheist.)
It seems, from the testimony
Of all religious experience,
That there are as many gods
As there are persons. When the
Object of contemplation
Is a person whom we know
Also as another like
Ourselves in the universe of
Possibility and consequence,
We do not customarily
Think of that person as a
God. But this is merely a
Convention of terminology.

Li Po and I both like to
Look at waterfalls. Deep in

The mountains, I turn my skis
And pause where black and white water
Breaks through the snow. All about
My feet are loose crystals of ice
Formed by the mist, as big as hands.
After a long time I turn
And drop into the valley,
Maneuvering swiftly over
Tumbled avalanche cones and snow
Covered rocks and through sparse thickets
Of dwarf maples, their trunks not
Much thicker than my thumb and pale
Silver grey. Their winged samaras
Still cling to them, a paler,
Silver yellow. Each twig
Is tipped with buds, deep crimson,
Overlaid with fine black lines
Like drops of congealing blood.
Here and there on the snow is
A skeleton of a leaf, thin
And frail as an x-ray picture,
Its flesh eaten by Winter.

Striving to perpetuate
Itself endlessly, illusion
Endures only an instant;
In the face of contemplation
It vanishes in not-being.
Appetite, the struggle of
Form and formlessness; desire,
The reversal of the waste
Of the historic process.

Love is the subjective
Aspect of contemplation.
Sexual love is one of
The most perfect forms of

Contemplation, as far as it
Is without ignorance, grasping,
And appetite. As far as it
Attempts to use the dual to
Manipulate the changing
Relations of consequence
And possibility, it
Is not love but hate.

There are hardly any blossoms
Left on the apple and pear trees
In the broken orchard where I
Have walked so many Springs.
I did not see them this year, white
And splendid under the full moon.
Now in the evening as the fog
Comes in across the new moon,
I bury my face in one last
Cluster of blossom and remember
The mockingbirds in the South,
That sang all through the brilliant
Night, as we lay arm in arm.

Knowledge of the others through
The dual is probably not
The only method of knowing
In the sense that all men must
Have a monogamous lover
Or a monotheistic god.
Some persons seem to be linked
Like atoms of oxygen,
Others not. But the nature
Of reality would seem to
Demand that in each specific
Act of love there be one other.
Duality is a condition
Of direct knowledge. However,

The dual can be found in the
Void of the one or in the
Fullness of all the others,
Just as they are found in it.

The afternoon ends with red
Patches of light on the leaves
On the northeast canyon wall.
My tame owl sits serenely
On his dead branch. A foolish
Jay squalls and plunges at him.
He is ignored. The owl yawns
And stretches his wings. The jay
Flies away screaming with fright.
My king snake lies in inert
Curves over books and papers.
Even his tongue is still, but
His yellow eyes are judicial.
The mice move delicately
In the walls. Beyond the hills
The moon is up, and the sky
Turns to crystal before it.
The canyon blurs in half light.
An invisible palace
Of glass, full of transparent
People, settles around me.
Over the dim waterfall
The intense promise of light
Grows above the canyon's cleft.
A nude girl enters my hut,
With white feet, and swaying hips,
And fragrant sex.

Although they might
In theory all emanate
From the contemplative himself,
We assume the others as real.

In a sense all persons are
Emanations of each other.
Reality is like a
Magnetic field with an infinite
Number of poles. We can know
At least the dual directly
And the others through the dual.
This is a fact of experience.
Like all experience, it is
Not subject to proof since proof
Is discursive description
Of consequence. In the dual
Each appears to the other
As his power, as the sum
Total of all the possible.

The reason why the illusion
Of consequence can exert
Its influence is to be found
In the laws of the rhythm
Of being; action is always
Followed by rest, as the labor
Of the day by sleep. As the
Contemplative drowses, the
Five daughters of illusion
Appear. The world of limited
Experience is the dream
Of being. We think of this
As the time of Shiva's dancing.
It is not. What we call being
Is illusion, the dream of Shiva.
It is an instant or a million
Times a million years before he wakes.

Two years since I have been in
The Fillmore District. I go down
And walk around aimlessly.

As I pass the house where ——
Used to work, she appears at the
Window, very excited.
I go in, she kisses me
And seems delighted to see me.
She says, "I'll knock off for an hour
And we'll go get a drink."
As a matter of fact we go
To lunch. I tell her I have
Been away, and she says, "Oh,
So have I – so we didn't
Miss each other. Where've you been?
I thought of you a lot."
"Europe." "Gee, swell, you must
Tell me all about it. I have
Been having a baby." "That's fine.
I didn't know you had an
Old man." "I don't." "Who's the father?"
"I don't know, some customer.
But he's a swell baby, I guess
I pulled the lever just right and
Hit the jackpot. Anyway,
He's white. I wanted to nurse him,
So I turned square for a while."
She is all excited and
Elated, laughing, eyes glistening,
Full of happiness about
Her baby. "What do you do
With him while you're working?"
"My mother takes care of him,
You see, I've got another one,
A three year old boy, he's a
Regular Dempsey." (——
Is about twenty-five, the
Legend still lives.) "You ought to see
Him." "I'd like to." "Would you honest?"
"Sure." "Honest? Look, how about

Coming to dinner tomorrow.
I'd like you to meet my mother,
Too." "Fine." "OK, I've got to
Get back to work now. Gee, you'll
Like the oldest guy. I got
Him out of the grab bag, too."

The leading philosopher
Of the University
Of California asks me,
"Why do you poets charge so much
Money?" "I beg your pardon.
What was that?" "Why do poets charge
So much? I would read poetry
If it wasn't so expensive.
The other day I was in
Sather Gate Bookshop and picked up
A book of poetry. You
Wouldn't believe it, but the price
Was two dollars and it contained
Less than a hundred pages!"
The logical positivist –
Life's answers are vended by
Slot machines. Just drop a nickel.
The magical Weltanschauung
Of the Australian bushman.
My lamp is small and bright
In the darkness of the night.

Said Pilate, "What is proof?" and washed
His hands before the multitude.

The age drives mad its saviors,
Courtesan and beggar turn
Bolshevik agitators.
Insanity is the crippling
Of the organ of reciprocity.

Off from the climbing road fall
Away folded shadows of
Mountains, range on moony range.
Under the waning moon the great
Valley like a hazy sea,
The town like the riding lights
Of fishing boats. The mountain
Peaks white and indistinct, their
Congruent tops merged in a high
Undulant horizon. Faint
Bells come up from the meadows.

The insecurity and
Ambiguity of modern
Culture is a reflection
Of the instability
Of the love relationship.
Art provides instruments of
Contemplation. Contemplation
Is the satisfaction of fulfilled
Love relationships, union with
The beloved object. If love is
Invalided, the whole fabric
Of the world culture crumbles.

Little Blue Lake – violet
Green swallows skimming above
Their reflections and dipping
To sip the water from their
Imaged beaks. Deep, deep and still,
Black and grey cliffs and white snow,
And the pale pure blue drowned ice.

Tara, the Power of Buddha;
Kali, the Power of Shiva;
Artemis, Apollo's sister;
The Wisdom of the Lord; the

Shekinah, Jehovah's Glory;
Mary the Mother of God;
Magdalene, the Bride of Christ;
Act and power, the twin lovers;
Each reflects the other like
The two chambers of the heart.

The lavabo of Pilate
Was the Graal of the Passover.

Once more we climb up the long
Gentle grade to Chagoopa
Plateau and look back, through the
Twisted foxtail pines growing
In the white talus, at the
Vast trough of Big Arroyo.
Again as always the Clark
Nutcrackers, grey, black and white,
Caw in the trees. Life repeats
Itself. We have camped here so
Many times by the shores of
Moraine Lake, the beautiful
Kaweah Peaks reflected
In the water, blue damsel
Flies on all the rushes.
In the evening, nighthawks
Will cry and dart through the air,
Dive, turn and swoop up again,
The twisting blades of their wings
Making a special growling roar
Like no other sound at all.
We will swim night and morning,
Catch golden trout in the creek,
See the water ouzel's nest
In the waterfall. Bear will
Bounce away from us as we
Wander between the open

Columns of the arid forest
Through the blue and white dwarf lupins.
In Sky Parlor Meadow there
Will be dozens of deer. The
Antlers of the bucks will look
Like dead branches above the
Tall rushes in the little lost
Marsh. The crimson bryanthus
And white Labrador tea will
Bloom by the lake as always.
In the evening crossing
The great meadow the sunset
On the water in the sedge
Will look like green and citron
Brocade, shot with copper and
Gold and blue – and the killdeer
Crying around us. And as
We come near camp, the nighthawks,
Those happy, happy birds,
Plunging over the lake again.
So the nighthawks cried over me
As I walked through smoky saffron
Twilights in the parks and long
Streets of Chicago in my
Entranced childhood. It is
Wise to keep the pattern of
Life clear and simple and filled
With beautiful and real things.
The round may be narrow enough.
The rounds of the world are narrower.

A truly radical, naïve,
Religious empiricism
Would describe all experience
In terms of its central fact.
The workings of the mind, the
Will, the physical and the

Transcendental worlds, would be seen
From the viewpoint of the
Contemplative immersed in
Contemplation. Reality
In a concourse of contemplatives.

Big Horn Plateau – four ravens,
Two hawks, one sandpiper, foxes
Barking in the rocks, the wool
Of wild sheep clinging to dead trees.
The voices of the thunder, all
The supernatural voices
Of the world, lightning striking
Continuously against the
Kaweahs, then the Kings-Kern peaks.
Here high above timberline,
Busy animalcules swim
In the cold volatile water.
In the frosty moonlight the
Burro is restless. Coyotes
Howl close to camp all night long.

At the center of every
Universe, which flows from him
And back to him again is a
Contemplator; there are millions
Of universes, each with its
Contemplator, in a grain of sand.
Every entity, real or
Imagined, dust mote or hero
Of fiction, is one face of a
Contemplative – reality,
Their infinite conversation.

At twelve thousand feet, the perfume
Of the phlox is like a drug.
Far off, the foxtail forest
On Big Horn Plateau is orange

And black-green stubble. Clouds are
Rising in the distance beyond
Milestone and Thunder Mountains.
I glissade down the long snow bank
Of penitents to the shores
Of Tulainyo Lake, barren
As the moon. I break the thin
Crust of bubbly white ice and
Drink the black tasteless water.
I climb to the final ridge
And look out of the windows
In the fourteen thousand foot
Arête. At my feet are the
Bluest polemonium and
The most crimson primrose, and far
Away, the russet Inyo
Mountains rise through grey desert heat.
In the evening by the flaring
Campfire of timberline wood,
Full of pitch and incense, I read
Buddha's farewell to his harem
And watch the storm move in the night,
The lightning burning a fire
From peak to peak, far below me.

Christ – the good people are the
Bad people and the bad people
Are the good people. The world
Is going to be destroyed
Any minute now, so live.
And Buddha – at the center
Of being is the act of
Contemplation, unqualified,
Unique, unpredictable.

As long as we are lost
In the world of purpose
We are not free. I sit

In my ten foot square hut.
The birds sing. The bees hum.
The leaves sway. The water
Murmurs over the rocks.
The canyon shuts me in.
If I moved, Bashō's frog
Would splash in the pool.
All summer long the gold
Laurel leaves fell through space.
Today I was aware
Of a maple leaf floating
On the pool. In the night
I stare into the fire.
Once I saw fire cities,
Towns, palaces, wars,
Heroic adventures,
In the campfires of youth.
Now I see only fire.
My breath moves quietly.
The stars move overhead.
In the clear darkness
Only a small red glow
Is left in the ashes.
On the table lies a cast
Snakeskin and an uncut stone.

There is no need to assume
The existence of a god
Behind the community
Of persons, the community
Is the absolute. There is no
Future life because there is
No future. Reality
Is not conditioned by time,
Space, ignorance, grasping.
The shift from possibility
To consequence gives rise to

The convention of time. At
The heart of being is the act of
Contemplation, it is timeless.

Since Isis and Osiris
Many gods and goddesses
Have ridden the boats of
The sun and the moon. I stand
On the hill above my hut
And watch the sun set in the
Fog bank over the distant
Ocean. Shortly afterward
The moon rises, transparent
In the twilight above the
Mountain. There is nobody
In them this evening. I
Am sure they are empty, that
I am alone in the great
Void, where they journey, empty
Through the darkness and the light.

Deep in myself arise the rays
Called Artemis and Apollo,
Helios, Luna, Sun and Moon,
Flowing forever out into
The void, towards the unknown others.

The heavens and hells of man,
The gods and demons, the ghosts of
Superstition, are crude attempts;
The systems of philosophers,
The visions of religion,
Are more or less successful
Mythological descriptions
Of knowing, acting, loving –
You are Shiva, but you dream.

It is the dark of the moon.
Late at night, the end of Summer,
The Autumn constellations
Glow in the arid heaven.
The air smells of cattle, hay,
And dust. In the old orchard
The pears are ripe. The trees
Have sprouted from old rootstocks
And the fruit is inedible.
As I pass them I hear something
Rustling and grunting and turn
My light into the branches.
Two raccoons with acrid pear
Juice and saliva drooling
From their mouths, stare back at me,
Their eyes deep sponges of light.
They know me and do not run
Away. Coming up the road
Through the black oak shadows, I
See ahead of me, glinting
Everywhere from the dusty
Gravel, tiny points of cold
Blue light, like the sparkle of
Iron snow. I suspect what it is,
And kneel to see. Under each
Pebble and oak leaf is a
Spider, her eyes shining at
Me with my reflected light
Across immeasurable distance.

IN DEFENSE OF THE EARTH (1956)

For my daughters
Mary and Katharine

THE REFLECTING TREES OF BEING AND NOT BEING

In my childhood when I first
Saw myself unfolded in
The triple mirrors, in my
Youth, when I pursued myself
Wandering on wandering
Nightbound roads like a roving
Masterless dog, when I met
Myself on sharp peaks of ice,
And tasted myself dissolved
In the lulling heavy sea,
In the talking night, in the
Spiraling stars, what did I
Know? What do I know now,
Of myself, of the others?
Blood flows out to the fleeing
Nebulae, and flows back, red
With all the worn space of space,
Old with all the time of time.
It is my blood. I cannot
Taste in it as it leaves me
More of myself than on its
Return. I can see in it
Trees of silence and fire.
In the mirrors on its waves
I can see faces. Mostly
They are your face. On its streams
I can see the soft moonlight
On the Canal du Midi.
I can see the leaf shadows
Of the plane tree on the deep
Fluids of your eyes, and the
Golden fires and lamps of years.

SHE IS AWAY

All night I lay awake beside you,
Leaning on my elbow, watching your
Sleeping face, that face whose purity
Never ceases to astonish me.
I could not sleep. But I did not want
Sleep nor miss it. Against my body,
Your body lay like a warm soft star.
How many nights I have waked and watched
You, in how many places. Who knows?
This night might be the last one of all.
As on so many nights, once more I
Drank from your sleeping flesh the deep still
Communion I am not always strong
Enough to take from you waking, the peace of love.
Foggy lights moved over the ceiling
Of our room, so like the rooms of France
And Italy, rooms of honeymoon,
And gave your face an ever changing
Speech, the secret communication
Of untellable love. I knew then,
As your secret spoke, my secret self,
The blind bird, hardly visible in
An endless web of lies. And I knew
The web too, its every knot and strand,
The hidden crippled bird, the terrible web.
Towards the end of night, as trucks rumbled
In the streets, you stirred, cuddled to me,
And spoke my name. Your voice was the voice
Of a girl who had never known loss
Of love, betrayal, mistrust, or lie.
And later you turned again and clutched
My hand and pressed it to your body.
Now I know surely and forever,
However much I have blotted our
Waking love, its memory is still

There. And I know the web, the net,
The blind and crippled bird. For then, for
One brief instant it was not blind, nor
Trapped, nor crippled. For one heart beat the
Heart was free and moved itself. O love,
I who am lost and damned with words,
Whose words are a business and an art,
I have no words. These words, this poem, this
Is all confusion and ignorance.
But I know that coached by your sweet heart,
My heart beat one free beat and sent
Through all my flesh the blood of truth.

MOCKING BIRDS

In mid-March in the heart of
The night, in the center of
The sterile city, in the
Midst of miles of asphalt and
Stone, alone and frustrated,
Wakeful on my narrow bed,
My brain spinning with worry,
There came to me, slipping through
The interstices of the
Blowing darkness, the living,
Almost imperceptible,
Faint, persistent, recurrent
Song of a single tree toad –
A voice sweeter than most birds.
Seven years ago we lay
Naked and moist, making love
Under the Easter full moon,
The thick fragrant light shaking
With the songs of mocking birds.

LONELINESS

To think of you surcharged with
Loneliness. To hear your voice
Over the recorder say,
"Loneliness." The word, the voice,
So full of it, and I, with
You away, so lost in it –
Lost in loneliness and pain.
Black and unendurable,
Thinking of you with every
Corpuscle of my flesh, in
Every instant of night
And day. O, my love, the times
We have forgotten love, and
Sat lonely beside each other.
We have eaten together,
Lonely behind our plates, we
Have hidden behind children,
We have slept together in
A lonely bed. Now my heart
Turns towards you, awake at last,
Penitent, lost in the last
Loneliness. Speak to me. Talk
To me. Break the black silence.
Speak of a tree full of leaves,
Of a flying bird, the new
Moon in the sunset, a poem,
A book, a person – all the
Casual healing speech
Of your resonant, quiet voice.
The word freedom. The word peace.

You, because you love me, hold
Fast to me, caress me, be
Quiet and kind, comfort me
With stillness, say nothing at all.
You, because I love you, I
Am strong for you, I uphold
You. The water is alive
Around us. Living water
Runs in the cut earth between
Us. You, my bride, your voice speaks
Over the water to me.
Your hands, your solemn arms,
Cross the water and hold me.
Your body is beautiful.
It speaks across the water.
Bride, sweeter than honey, glad
Of heart, our hearts beat across
The bridge of our arms. Our speech
Is speech of joy in the night
Of gladness. Our words live.
Our words are children dancing
Forth from us like stars on water.
My bride, my well beloved,
Sweeter than honey, than ripe fruit,
Solemn, grave, a flying bird,
Hold me. Be quiet and kind.
I love you. Be good to me.
I am strong for you. I uphold
You. The dawn of ten thousand
Dawns is afire in the sky.
The water flows in the earth.
The children laugh in the air.

GROWING

Who are you? Who am I? Haunted
By the dead, by the dead and the past and the
Falling inertia of unreal, dead
Men and things. Haunted by the threat
Of the impersonal, that which
Never will admit the person,
The closed world of things. Who are
You? Coming up out of the
Mineral earth, one pale leaf
Unlike any other unfolding,
And then another, strange, new,
Utterly different, nothing
I ever expected, growing
Up out of my warm heart's blood.
All new, all strange, all different.
You own leaf pattern, your own
Flower and fruit, but fed from
One root, the root of our fused flesh.
I and thou, from the one to
The dual, from the dual
To the other, the wonderful,
Unending, unfathomable
Process of becoming each
Our selves for the other.

A LIVING PEARL

At sixteen I came West, riding
Freights on the Chicago, Milwaukee
And St. Paul, the Great Northern,
The Northern Pacific. I got
A job as helper to a man
Who gathered wild horses in the

Mass drives in the Okanogan
And Horse Heaven country. The best
We culled out as part profit from
The drive, the rest went for chicken
And dog feed. We took thirty head
Up the Methow, up the Twisp,
Across the headwaters of Lake
Chelan, down the Skagit to
The Puget Sound country. I
Did the cooking and camp work.
In a couple of weeks I
Could handle the stock pretty well.
Every day we saddled and rode
A new horse. Next day we put a
Packsaddle on him. By the
Time we reached Marblemount
We considered them well broken.
The scissorbills who bought them
Considered them untamed mustangs
Of the desert. In a few weeks
They were peacefully pulling
Milk wagons in Sedro-Wooley.
We made three trips a season
And did well enough for the
Post-war depression.
Tonight,
Thirty years later, I walk
Out of the deserted miner's
Cabin in Mono Pass, under
The full moon and the few large stars.
The sidehills are piebald with snow.
The midnight air is suffused
With moonlight. As Dante says,
"It is as though a cloud enclosed
Me, lucid, dense, solid, polished,
Like a diamond forged by the sun.
We entered the eternal pearl,

Which took us as water takes
A ray of light, itself uncleft."
Fifteen years ago, in this place,
I wrote a poem called, "Toward
An Organic Philosophy."
Everything is still the same,
And it differs very little
From the first mountain pass I
Crossed so long ago with the
Pintos and zebra duns and
Gunmetal roans and buckskins,
And splattered lallapaloosas,
The stocky wild ponies whose
Ancestors came with Coronado.
There are no horse bells tonight,
Only the singing of frogs
In the snow-wet meadows, the shrill
Single bark of a mountain
Fox, high in the rocks where the
Wild sheep move silently through the
Crystal moonlight. The same feelings
Come back. Once more all the awe
Of a boy from the prairies where
Lanterns move through the comfortable
Dark, along a fence, through a field,
Home; all the thrill of youth
Suddenly come from the flat
Geometrical streets of
Chicago, into the illimitable
And inhuman waste places
Of the Far West, where the mind finds
Again the forms Pythagoras
Sought, the organic relations
Of stone and cloud and flower
And moving planet and falling
Water. Marthe and Mary sleep
In their down bags, cocoons of

Mutual love. Half my life has
Been passed in the West, much of it
On the ground beside lonely fires
Under the summer stars, and in
Cabins where the snow drifted through
The pines and over the roof.
I will not camp here as often
As I have before. Thirty years
Will never come for me again.
"Our campfire dies out in the
Lonely mountains. The transparent
Moonlight stretches a thousand miles.
The clear peace is without end."
My daughter's deep blue eyes sleep
In the moon shadow. Next week
She will be one year old.

FIFTY

Rainy skies, misty mountains,
The old year ended in storms.
The new year starts the same way.
All day, from far out at sea,
Long winged birds soared in the
Rushing sky. Midnight breaks with
Driving clouds and plunging moon,
Rare vasts of endless stars.
My fiftieth year has come.

THE LIGHTS IN THE SKY ARE STARS

for Mary

HALLEY'S COMET

When in your middle years
The great comet comes again
Remember me, a child,
Awake in the summer night,
Standing in my crib and
Watching that long-haired star
So many years ago.
Go out in the dark and see
Its plume over water
Dribbling on the liquid night,
And think that life and glory
Flickered on the rushing
Bloodstream for me once, and for
All who have gone before me,
Vessels of the billion-year-long
River that flows now in your veins.

THE GREAT NEBULA OF ANDROMEDA

We get into camp after
Dark, high on an open ridge
Looking out over five thousand
Feet of mountains and mile
Beyond mile of valley and sea.
In the star-filled dark we cook
Our macaroni and eat
By lantern light. Stars cluster
Around our table like fireflies.
After supper we go straight

To bed. The night is windy
And clear. The moon is three days
Short of full. We lie in bed
And watch the stars and the turning
Moon through our little telescope.
Late at night the horses stumble
Around camp and I awake.
I lie on my elbow watching
Your beautiful sleeping face
Like a jewel in the moonlight.
If you are lucky and the
Nations let you, you will live
Far into the twenty-first
Century. I pick up the glass
And watch the Great Nebula
Of Andromeda swim like
A phosphorescent amoeba
Slowly around the Pole. Far
Away in distant cities
Fat-hearted men are planning
To murder you while you sleep.

THE HEART OF HERAKLES

Lying under the stars,
In the summer night,
Late, while the autumn
Constellations climb the sky,
As the Cluster of Hercules
Falls down the west
I put the telescope by
And watch Deneb
Move towards the zenith.
My body is asleep. Only
My eyes and brain are awake.
The stars stand around me

Like gold eyes. I can no longer
Tell where I begin and leave off.
The faint breeze in the dark pines,
And the invisible grass,
The tipping earth, the swarming stars
Have an eye that sees itself.

A MAZE OF SPARKS OF GOLD

Spring – the rain goes by, the stars
Shine pale beside the Easter
Moon. Scudding clouds, tossing leaves,
Whirl overhead. Blossoms fall
In the dark from the fragrant
Madrone trees. You lie beside
Me, luminous and still in sleep.
Overhead bees sleep in their
Tree. Beyond them the bees in
The Beehive in the Crab drift
Slowly past, a maze of points
Of fire. I've had ten times your
Years. Time holds us both fixed fast
Under the bright wasting stars.

A SWORD IN A CLOUD OF LIGHT

Your hand in mine, we walk out
To watch the Christmas Eve crowds
On Fillmore Street, the Negro
District. The night is thick with
Frost. The people hurry, wreathed
In their smoky breaths. Before
The shop windows the children
Jump up and down with spangled
Eyes. Santa Clauses ring bells,

Cars stall and honk. Streetcars clang.
Loud speakers on the lampposts
Sing carols, on juke boxes
In the bars Louis Armstrong
Plays "White Christmas." In the joints
The girls strip and grind and bump
To "Jingle Bells." Overhead
The neon signs scribble and
Erase and scribble again
Messages of avarice,
Joy, fear, hygiene, and the proud
Names of the middle classes.
The moon beams like a pudding.
We stop at the main corner
And look up, diagonally
Across, at the rising moon,
And the solemn, orderly
Vast winter constellations.
You say, "There's Orion!"
The most beautiful object
Either of us will ever
Know in the world or in life
Stands in the moonlit empty
Heavens, over the swarming
Men, women, and children, black
And white, joyous and greedy,
Evil and good, buyer and
Seller, master and victim,
Like some immense theorem,
Which, if once solved would forever
Solve the mystery and pain
Under the bells and spangles.
There he is, the man of the
Night before Christmas, spread out
On the sky like a true god
In whom it would only be
Necessary to believe

A little. I am fifty
And you are five. It would do
No good to say this and it
May do no good to write it.
Believe in Orion. Believe
In the night, the moon, the crowded
Earth. Believe in Christmas and
Birthdays and Easter rabbits.
Believe in all those fugitive
Compounds of nature, all doomed
To waste away and go out.
Always be true to these things.
They are all there is. Never
Give up this savage religion
For the blood-drenched civilized
Abstractions of the rascals
Who live by killing you and me.

PROTOPLASM OF LIGHT

How long ago
Frances and I took the subway
To Van Cortlandt Park. The people
All excited, small boys and
Cripples selling dark glasses.
We rushed to the open hills
North of the station as though
We'd be too late, and stood there
Hand in hand, waiting. Under
The trees the sun made little
Lunes of light through the bare branches
On the snow. The sky turned gray
And very empty. One by
One the stars came out. At last
The sun was only a thin
Crescent in our glasses with the

Bright planets nearby like watchers.
Then the great cold amoeba
Of crystal light sprang out
On the sky. The wind passed like
A silent crowd. The crowd sobbed
Like a passing wind. All the dogs
Howled. The silent protoplasm
Of light stood still in the black sky,
In its bowels, ringed with ruby
Fire, its stone-black nucleus.
Mercury, cold and dark like a
Fleck of iron, stood silent by it.
That was long ago.
Mary and I stand on the
Seashore and watch the sun sink
In the windy ocean. Layers
Of air break up the disc. It looks
Like a vast copper pagoda.
Spume blows past our faces, jellyfish
Pulse in the standing water,
Sprawl on the wet sand at our feet.
Twilight comes and all of the
Visible planets come out.
Venus first, and then Jupiter,
Mars and Saturn and finally
Mercury once more. Seals bark
On the rocks. I tell Mary
How Kepler never saw Mercury,
How, as he lay dying it shone
In his window, too late for him
To see. The mysterious
Cone of light leans up from the
Horizon into the pale sky.
I say, "Nobody knows what
It is or even where it is.
Maybe it is the great cloud
Of gas around the sun which

You will see some day if you
Are lucky. It stands out only
During an eclipse. I saw it
Long ago."

BLOOD ON A DEAD WORLD

A blowing night in late fall,
The moon rises with a nick
In it. All day Mary has
Been talking about the eclipse.
Every once in a while I
Go out and report on the
Progress of the earth's shadow.
When it is passing the half,
Marthe and Mary come out
And we stand on the corner
In the first wisps of chilling
Fog and watch the light go out.
Streamers of fog reach the moon,
But never quite cover it.
We have explained with an orange,
A grapefruit, and a lamp, not
That we expect a four
Year old child to understand –
Just as a sort of ritual
Duty. But we are surprised.
"The earth's shadow is like blood,"
She says. I tell her the Indians
Called an eclipse blood on the moon.
"Is it all the blood on the earth
Makes the shadow that color?"
She asks. I do not answer.

QUIETLY

Lying here quietly beside you,
My cheek against your firm, quiet thighs,
The calm music of Boccherini
Washing over us in the quiet,
As the sun leaves the housetops and goes
Out over the Pacific, quiet –
So quiet the sun moves beyond us,
So quiet as the sun always goes,
So quiet, our bodies, worn with the
Times and the penances of love, our
Brains curled, quiet in their shells, dormant,
Our hearts slow, quiet, reliable
In their interlocked rhythms, the pulse
In your thigh caressing my cheek. Quiet.

FOR ELI JACOBSON

December 1952

There are few of us now, soon
There will be none. We were comrades
Together, we believed we
Would see with our own eyes the new
World where man was no longer
Wolf to man, but men and women
Were all brothers and lovers
Together. We will not see it.
We will not see it, none of us.
It is farther off than we thought.
In our young days we believed
That as we grew old and fell
Out of rank, new recruits, young
And with the wisdom of youth,

Would take our places and they
Surely would grow old in the
Golden Age. They have not come.
They will not come. There are not
Many of us left. Once we
Marched in closed ranks, today each
Of us fights off the enemy,
A lonely isolated guerrilla.
All this has happened before,
Many times. It does not matter.
We were comrades together,
Life was good for us. It is
Good to be brave – nothing is
Better. Food tastes better. Wine
Is more brilliant. Girls are more
Beautiful. The sky is bluer
For the brave – for the brave and
Happy comrades and for the
Lonely brave retreating warriors.
You had a good life. Even all
Its sorrows and defeats and
Disillusionments were good,
Met with courage and a gay heart.
You are gone and we are that
Much more alone. We are one fewer,
Soon we shall be none. We know now
We have failed for a long time.
And we do not care. We few will
Remember as long as we can,
Our children may remember,
Some day the world will remember.
Then they will say, "They lived in
The days of the good comrades.
It must have been wonderful
To have been alive then, though it
Is very beautiful now."
We will be remembered, all

Of us, always, by all men,
In the good days now so far away.
If the good days never come,
We will not know. We will not care.
Our lives were the best. We were the
Happiest men alive in our day.

ON A FLYLEAF OF *RIME* – GASPARA STAMPA

bought in the Libreria Serenissima
Venice, June 14, 1949

While the light of Canaletto
And Guardi turns to the light of
Turner, and the domes of the Saluta
Begin to take on the evening,
I drink chocolate and Vecchia
Romagna, that estimable
Brandy, on the terrace of
The Café International,
And read these twisting,
Burning pages. Love was
An agony for you, too, signora,
And came to no good end after
All the terrible price.
Enveloped in the evening
Sussura of this quiet city,
Where the loudest human sound
Is a footfall, I sit alone
With my own life. Last night I took
A gondola, out past the Giudecca,
Straight into the moonlight.
Coming back the monks
Were singing matins in San Giorgio
Maggiore. I wonder if it is possible

To be more alone than in a gondola
In Venice under the full moon
Of June. All I have for company
Are the two halves of my heart.

TIME IS THE MERCY OF ETERNITY

Time is divided into
Seconds, minutes, hours, years,
And centuries. Take any
One of them and add up its
Content, all the world over.
One division contains much
The same as any other.
What can you say in a poem?
Past forty, you've said it all.
The dwarf black oak grows out of
The cliff below my feet. It
May be two hundred years old,
Yet its trunk is no bigger
Than my wrist, its crown does not
Come to my shoulder. The late
Afternoon sun behind it
Fills its leaves with light like
A gem tree, like the wishing
Tree of jewels in the Eastern
Stories. Below it the cliff
Falls sheer away five hundred
Feet to a single burnt pine,
And then another thousand
Feet to a river, noisy
In spate. Off beyond it stretches
Shimmering space, then fold on
Dimmer fold of wooded hills,
Then, hardly visible in

The pulsating heat, the flat
Lands of the San Joaquin Valley,
Boiling with life and trouble.
The pale new green leaves twinkle
In the rising air. A blue
Black, sharp-beaked, sharp-crested jay
Rests for a moment amongst
Them and then plunges off, down
Through the hazy June afternoon.
Far away the writhing city
Burns in a fire of transcendence
And commodities. The bowels
Of men are wrung between the poles
Of meaningless antithesis.
The holiness of the real
Is always there, accessible
In total immanence. The nodes
Of transcendence coagulate
In you, the experiencer,
And in the other, the lover.
When the first blooms come on the
Apple trees, and the spring moon
Swims in immeasurable
Clear deeps of palpable light,
I sit by the waterfall.
The owls call, one beyond the
Other, indefinitely
Away into the warm night.
The moist black rocks gleam faintly.
The curling moss smells of wet life.
The waterfall is a rope
Of music, a black and white
Spotted snake in the moonlit
Forest. The thighs of the goddess
Close me in. The moon lifts into
The cleft of the mountains and a
Cloud of light pours around me like

Blazing perfume. When the moon has
Passed on and the owls are loud in
My ears again, I kneel and drink
The cold, sweet, twisting water.

All day clouds drift up the canyon.
By noon the high peaks are hidden.
Thunder mutters in the distance.
Suddenly the canyon is gone.
My camp on its narrow ledge is
Isolated in swirling mist.
Even the nearby pines grow dim,
And recede into the grayness.
Yellow lightning bursts, like fire through
Smoke, and sets all the mist aglow.
Thunder explodes under my feet.
The rain pours hissing through the
Pine needles. White hailstones fall
Awry between the red pine trunks.
They rattle on my tent. I catch
Some and watch them melt in my hand.
As evening comes, birds ruffle
Their feathers, and fly gingerly
From branch to branch, and sing a few
Notes, while through the orange twilight
Fall green, widely spaced drops of rain.

For three days the clouds have piled up,
And rain has circled the mountains.
For a while it will fall over
Black Rock Pass, and then move across
To the red Kaweahs, and then
On to the white Whitney Range. But
Here by the lake it does not fall,
And the air grows more oppressive.
I swim lazily. Even the
Water seems to be heavier.

The air is full of mosquitoes.
After a listless lunch, I sit
On the bank reading the wise poems
Of Charles Cros. Suddenly the wind
Rises. The tent flaps noisily.
Twigs and dust and pine needles fly
In all directions. Then the wind
Drops and the rain falls on the lake.
The drops chime against the ripples
Like the Japanese glass wind bells
I loved so much as a child.
The rain is gone in an hour.
In the clear evening freshness,
I hear the bell on my donkey,
In his meadow, a mile away.
Nighthawks cry overhead and dive,
Thrumming their wings as they turn.
A deer comes down to the water.
The high passes are closed with snow.
I am the first person in this season.
No one comes by. I am alone
In the midst of a hundred mountains.

Five o'clock, mid-August evening,
The long sunlight is golden
On the deep green grass and bright
Red flowers of the meadow.
I stop where a meander
Of the brook forms a deep pool.
The water is greenish brown,
But perfectly transparent.
A small dense cloud of hundreds
Of midges, no bigger than
My head, hovers over it.
On the bank are two small frogs.
In the water are beetles,
Hydras, water bugs, larvae

Of several insects. On
The surface are water boatmen.
I realize that the color
Of the water itself is
Due to millions of active
Green flecks of life. It is like
Peering into an inkspot,
And finding yourself staring
Out into the Milky Way.
The deep reverberation
Of my identity with
All this plenitude of life
Leaves me shaken and giddy.
I step softly across the
Meadows as the deer lift their
Antlers and idly watch me.

Here on this high plateau where
No one ever comes, beside
This lake filled with mirrored mountains,
The hours and days and weeks
Go by without variation.
Even the rare storms pass over
And empty themselves on the peaks.
There are no fish in the water.
There are few deer or bear in the woods.
Only the bright blue damsel flies
On the reeds in the daytime,
And the nighthawks overhead
In the evening. Suspended
In absolutely transparent
Air and water and time, I
Take on a kind of crystalline
Being. In this translucent
Immense here and now, if ever,
The form of the person should be
Visible, its geometry,

Its crystallography, and
Its astronomy. The good
And evil of my history
Go by. I can see them and
Weigh them. They go first, with all
The other personal facts,
And sensations, and desires.
At last there is nothing left
But knowledge, itself a vast
Crystal encompassing the
Limitless crystal of air
And rock and water. And the
Two crystals are perfectly
Silent. There is nothing to
Say about them. Nothing at all.

A SINGING VOICE

Once, camping on a high bluff
Above the Fox River, when
I was about fourteen years
Old, on a full moonlit night
Crowded with whip-poor-wills and
Frogs, I lay awake long past
Midnight watching the moon move
Through the half drowned stars. Suddenly
I heard, far away on the warm
Air a high clear soprano,
Purer than the purest boy's
Voice, singing, "Tuck me to sleep
In my old 'Tucky home."
She was in an open car
Speeding along the winding
Dipping highway beneath me.
A few seconds later

An old touring car full of
Boys and girls rushed by under
Me, the soprano rising
Full and clear and now close by
I could hear the others singing
Softly behind her voice. Then
Rising and falling with the
Twisting road the song closed, soft
In the night. Over thirty
Years have gone by but I have
Never forgotten. Again
And again, driving on a
Lonely moonlit road, or waking
In a warm murmurous night,
I hear that voice singing that
Common song like an
Angelic memory.

OUR HOME IS IN THE ROCKS

for Richard Eberhart

Breasted, beginning his lectures,
"The development of religion
And thought in ancient Egypt" says,
"In going up to the daily
Task on some neighboring temple
In Nubia, I was not
Infrequently obliged to pass
Through the corner of a graveyard
Where the feet of a dead man,
Buried in a shallow grave
Were uncovered and extended
Directly across my path.
They were precisely like the rough

And calloused feet of the workmen
In our excavations. How old
The grave was I do not know, but
Anyone familiar with
The cemeteries of Egypt,
Ancient and modern, has found
Numerous bodies or portions
Of bodies, indefinitely
Old, which seemed about as well
Preserved as those of the living."

We went to call on a lady,
Whose father has seen the lifted
Ear of corn at Eleusis,
Her mother, a well tempered poetess,
Her brother was killed in Spain,
For his own epitaph he wrote,
"Thought shall be the harder,
Heart the keener,
Mood shall be the more
As our might lessens."
Hige sceal the heardra
Heorte the cenre
Mod sceal the mare
The ure maegan lythlath.
Which happens also to be the
Epigraph of Toynbee's sermon.
She too will be moderately immortal.

And now
I sit looking out of the cabin
At the rain falling through the green
Under-water gloom of the narrow
Gulch, listening to the counterpoint
Of rain and waterfall and leaf.
Somewhere in his wanderings
Today, my dog has rolled in

A spatched cock or flattened cat,
And the faint effluvium
Of dry death clings to his foolish
And frolicking body.

I think
Of Lucretius and Socrates
And the actor on the *Titanic*.
I suppose you can hear the leathery
Sibilant voice of death speaking
Behind their unbelievable
Plausibility.

Do I fear death?
As far as I can make out I
Feel towards death as Rochefoucauld
Must have felt, though I don't recall
He ever mentioned it.

The dead
Cow that stunk in the hemlock thicket
Three years ago is now only
Bright white bones on the bright green
Grass by day. When I walk out
Late at night they glimmer like pearls
By the waning moonlight, nodes of
Light in the amorphous dimness.
It is spring again and I am
Back from Europe. The frogs' children
Sing in the wet meadow. The green
Pronged fires burst from the buckeye
Again. Again the rosy web
Of alder twigs catches the moon.
Again the small hazel flowers
Put forth their crimson serpent tongues.
Perched on his rock the aplodontia,
The mountain beaver, with the face

Of an overfed angel, eyes me
With his black jewels of ultimate
Innocence. Of far feebler folk
Than the Scripture's coney, he dies
If touched, so quietly you can't
Believe he is dead, as he lies
So still in your hand, breathless, with
Dulling eyes.

XMAS COMING

November night. Waning moon
Cold after rain. Ferns of ice
Form on the puddles. Dead leaves
Are crisp with cold. Deer bound past,
Their eyes green in my lamplight.
The children grunt in their sleep.
Mary dreams of Christmas trees.
Baby Katharine of secrets,
The jolly secrets she can't tell.

MY HEART'S AS GAY AS A YOUNG SUNFLOWER

Oh, who will shoe your pretty little foot,
    And who will glove your hand,
And who will kiss your cherry red lips,
    When I'm gone to the foreign land?

My pappy'll shoe my pretty little foot,
    And my mammy'll glove my hand,
And there's plenty of boys'll kiss my cherry red lips
    When you're gone to the foreign land.

Oh, who will comb your golden hair
　　With the brand new turtle comb,
And who will kiss your satin neck,
　　When I'm gone across the foam?

Oh, my sis will comb my golden hair
　　With the dark red turtle comb;
And I'll find them'll kiss my neck,
　　Before ever you come home.

The doves fly off to the woods from the cote,
　　But at night they all come home;
And my heart will turn like that to you,
　　No matter how far I may roam.

Oh, the wild birds fly all day in the woods,
　　From tree to tree they roam;
My heart's like the birds that have no cote,
　　Wherever they roost is their home.

Oh, the crow is the bird with the blackest wing,
　　And it turns to a purple hue;
If ever I loose this love that I hold,
　　Let my body waste like the dew.

On top of the church is a bird that sits,
　　And he turns with the winds as they blow;
My heart's not ready to hold to a man,
　　So why do you plague me so?

My heart's as clear as a pane of glass,
　　Your name's carved there in gold;
It'll stay right there till the day I die,
　　For all men to behold.

THE MIRROR IN THE WOODS

A mirror hung on the broken
Walls of an old summerhouse
Deep in the dark woods. Nothing
Ever moved in it but the
Undersea shadows of ferns,
Rhododendrons and redwoods.
Moss covered the frame. One day
The gold and glue gave way and
The mirror slipped to the floor.
For many more years it stood
On the shattered boards. Once in
A long time a wood rat would
Pass it by without ever
Looking in. At last we came,
Breaking the sagging door and
Letting in a narrow wedge
Of sunlight. We took the mirror
Away and hung it in my
Daughter's room with a barre before
It. Now it reflects ronds, écartés,
Relevés, and arabesques.
In the old house the shadows,
The wood rats and moss work unseen.

THE BAD OLD DAYS

The summer of nineteen eighteen
I read *The Jungle* and *The*
Research Magnificent. That fall
My father died and my aunt
Took me to Chicago to live.
The first thing I did was to take
A streetcar to the stockyards.

In the winter afternoon,
Gritty and fetid, I walked
Through the filthy snow, through the
Squalid streets, looking shyly
Into the people's faces,
Those who were home in the daytime.
Debauched and exhausted faces,
Starved and looted brains, faces
Like the faces in the senile
And insane wards of charity
Hospitals. Predatory
Faces of little children.
Then as the soiled twilight darkened,
Under the green gas lamps, and the
Sputtering purple arc lamps,
The faces of the men coming
Home from work, some still alive with
The last pulse of hope or courage,
Some sly and bitter, some smart and
Silly, most of them already
Broken and empty, no life,
Only blinding tiredness, worse
Than any tired animal.
The sour smells of a thousand
Suppers of fried potatoes and
Fried cabbage bled into the street.
I was giddy and sick, and out
Of my misery I felt rising
A terrible anger and out
Of the anger, an absolute vow.
Today the evil is clean
And prosperous, but it is
Everywhere, you don't have to
Take a streetcar to find it,
And it is the same evil.
And the misery, and the
Anger, and the vow are the same.

A DIALOGUE OF WATCHING

Let me celebrate you. I
Have never known anyone
More beautiful than you. I
Walking beside you, watching
You move beside me, watching
That still grace of hand and thigh,
Watching your face change with words
You do not say, watching your
Solemn eyes as they turn to me,
Or turn inward, full of knowing,
Slow or quick, watching your full
Lips part and smile or turn grave,
Watching your narrow waist, your
Proud buttocks in their grace, like
A sailing swan, an animal,
Free, your own, and never
To be subjugated, but
Abandoned, as I am to you,
Overhearing your perfect
Speech of motion, of love and
Trust and security as
You feed or play with our children.
I have never known any
One more beautiful than you.

MARY AND THE SEASONS

DRY AUTUMN

In the evening, just before
Sunset, while we were cooking
Supper, we heard dogs, high on

The west ridge, running a deer.
With unbelievable speed
They quartered down the hillside,
Crossed the gulch, climbed the east ridge
And circled back above us.
As they rushed down again, I
Ran to catch them. The barking
Stopped when they reached the creek bed.
As I came near I could hear
The last terrified bleating
Of a fawn. By the time I
Got there it was already dead.
When the dogs caught sight of me,
They scurried guiltily away.
The fawn was not torn. It had
Died of fear and exhaustion.

My dearest, although you are
Still too young to understand,
At this moment horrible
Black dogs with eyes of fire and
Long white teeth and slavering
Tongues are hunting you in the dark
Mountains to eat your tender heart.

SPRING RAIN

The smoke of our campfire lowers
And coagulates under
The redwoods, like low-lying
Clouds. Fine mist fills the air. Drops
Rattle down from all the leaves.
As the evening comes on
The treetops vanish in fog.
Two saw-whet owls utter their
Metallic sobbing cries high

Overhead. As it gets dark
The mist turns to rain. We are
All alone in the forest.
No one is near us for miles.
In the firelight mice scurry
Hunting crumbs. Tree toads cry like
Tiny owls. Deer snort in the
Underbrush. Their eyes are green
In the firelight like balls of
Foxfire. This morning I read
Mei Yao Chen's poems, all afternoon
We walked along the stream through
Woods and meadows full of June
Flowers. We chased frogs in the
Pools and played with newts and young
Grass snakes. I picked a wild rose
For your hair. You brought
New flowers for me to name.
Now it is night and our fire
Is a red throat open in
The profound blackness, full of
The throb and hiss of the rain.

AUTUMN RAIN

Two days ago the sky was
Full of mares' tails. Yesterday
Wind came, bringing low cigar
Shaped clouds. At midnight the rain
Began, the first fine, still rain
Of autumn. Before the rain
The night was warm, the sky hazy.
We lay in the field and watched
The glowing October stars,
Vega, Deneb, Altair, high,
Hercules and the Crown setting,

The Great Nebula distinct
Through the haze. Every owl
In the world called and made love
And scolded. Once in a while
We would see one on the sky,
Cruising, on wings more silent
Than silence itself, low over
The meadow. The air thickened.
The stars grew dim and went out.
The owls stopped crying in the wood.
Then the rain came, falling so
Gently on the tent we did
Not notice until a slight
Breeze blew it in on our faces.
At dawn it was still raining.
It cleared as we cooked breakfast.
We climbed through tatters of cloud
To the east ridge and walked through
The dripping, sparkling fir forest.
In the meadow at the summit
We ate lunch in the pale sun,
Ever so slightly cooler,
And watched the same long autumn
Mares' tails and came back down the
Steep rocks through the soaking ferns.

CLEAR AUTUMN

This small flat clearing is not
Much bigger than a large room
In the steep narrow canyon.
On every side the slender
Laurel trunks shut us in close.
High on the southern sidehill
Patches of sunlight filter
Through the fir trees. But the sun

Will not come back here until
Winter is past. New-fallen
Leaves shine like light on the floor.
The air hums with low-flying
Insects, too weakened to rise.
The stream has stopped. Underground,
A trickle seeps from pool to pool.
All the summer birds have gone.
Only woodpeckers and jays
And juncos have stayed behind.
Soon the rains will start, and then
Fine, silent, varied thrushes
Will come from the dark rain forests
Of the Northwest, but not yet.
We climb to the long west ridge
That looks out on the ocean
And eat lunch at a high spring
Under the rocks at the top.
Holstein calves cluster around
And watch us impassively.
No wind moves in the dry grass.
The sky and the distant sea,
The yellow hills, stretching away,
Seem seen in a clouded mirror.
Buzzards on the rising air
Float without moving a wing.
Jet bombers play at killing
So high overhead only
Long white scrawls can be seen, the
Graffiti of genocide.
The planes are invisible.
Away from the sun the air
Glitters with millions of glass
Needles, falling from the zenith.
It is as though oxygen
And nitrogen were being
Penetrated and replaced

By some shining chemical.
It is the silk of a swarm
Of ballooning spiders, flashes
Of tinsel and drifting crystal
In the vast rising autumn air.
When we get back everything
Is linked with everything else
By fine bright strands of spun glass,
The golden floor of October,
Brilliant under a gauze of light.

SNOW

Low clouds hang on the mountain.
The forest is filled with fog.
A short distance away the
Giant trees recede and grow
Dim. Two hundred paces and
They are invisible. All
Day the fog curdles and drifts.
The cries of the birds are loud.
They sound frightened and cold. Hour
By hour it grows colder.
Just before sunset the clouds
Drop down the mountainside. Long
Shreds and tatters of fog flow
Swiftly away between the
Trees. Now the valley below
Is filled with clouds like clotted
Cream and over them the sun
Sets, yellow in a sky full
Of purple feathers. After dark
A wind rises and breaks branches
From the trees and howls in the
Treetops and then suddenly
Is still. Late at night I wake

And look out of the tent. The
Clouds are rushing across the
Sky and through them is tumbling
The thin waning moon. Later
All is quiet except for
A faint whispering. I look
Out. Great flakes of wet snow are
Falling. Snowflakes are falling
Into the dark flames of the
Dying fire. In the morning the
Pine boughs are sagging with snow,
And the dogwood blossoms are
Frozen, and the tender young
Purple and citron oak leaves.

ANOTHER TWILIGHT

Far out across the Great Valley
The sun sets behind the Coast Range.
The distant mountains mingle
With the haze of the valley,
Purple folded into purple.
Over them the evening
Turns orange and green, the white fire
Of Venus and the transparent
Crescent moon. Venus is caught
In the Crab's claws, the moon creeps
Between the Virgin's open thighs.
Bats dodge and squeak between the trees.
A velvety, chocolate-colored
Bear comes and begs for food. Two
Gray and orange foxes quarter
Over the ground below camp,
Searching for scraps. Their cubs
Peek out from the manzanita.

THE ORPHIC SOUL

As I walk slowly along
The sun flecked wood road, a large
Fritillary comes to rest
On my naked shoulder, then
Flies in a little spiral
And comes back again and
Again to my shoulders and
Arms, fluttering over me
Like the souls on Orphic tombs.
This never happened to me
Before, and I feel my flesh
Has suddenly become sweet
With a metamorphosis
Kept secret even from myself.

HUMAN, AVIAN, VEGETABLE, BLOOD

Today, three days before Christmas,
I had planned to cut some berries
From the toyon bush in the yard.
For three years it has not done well.
This is the first year it produced
A decent crop. But this morning
A flock of thirty migrating
Robins appeared, and before noon
Every berry had been eaten.
This year we will buy our foliage
As usual, and the symbols
Of incarnate flesh we tended
All year will be flying, mingled
With pale hot bird blood, high over
The barren Mexican mountains.

THOU SHALT NOT KILL

a memorial for Dylan Thomas

I

They are murdering all the young men.
For half a century now, every day,
They have hunted them down and killed them.
They are killing them now,
At this minute, all over the world,
They are killing the young men.
They know ten thousand ways to kill them.
Every year they invent new ones.
In the jungles of Africa,
In the marshes of Asia,
In the deserts of Asia,
In the slave pens of Siberia,
In the slums of Europe,
In the nightclubs of America,
The murderers are at work.

They are stoning Stephen,
They are casting him forth from every city in the world.
Under the Welcome sign,
Under the Rotary emblem,
On the highway in the suburbs,
His body lies under the hurling stones.
He was full of faith and power.
He did great wonders among the people.
They could not stand against his wisdom.
They could not bear the spirit with which he spoke.
He cried out in the name
Of the tabernacle of witness in the wilderness.
They were cut to the heart.
They gnashed against him with their teeth.

They cried out with a loud voice.
They stopped their ears.
They ran on him with one accord.
They cast him out of the city and stoned him.
The witnesses laid down their clothes
At the feet of a man whose name was your name –
You.

You are the murderer.
You are killing the young men.
You are broiling Lawrence on his gridiron.
When you demanded he divulge
The hidden treasures of the spirit,
He showed you the poor.
You set your heart against him.
You seized him and bound him with rage.
You roasted him on a slow fire.
His fat dripped and spurted in the flame.
The smell was sweet to your nose.
He cried out,
"I am cooked on this side,
Turn me over and eat,
You
Eat of my flesh."

You are murdering the young men.
You are shooting Sebastian with arrows.
He kept the faithful steadfast under persecution.
First you shot him with arrows.
Then you beat him with rods.
Then you threw him in a sewer.
You fear nothing more than courage.
You who turn away your eyes
At the bravery of the young men.

You,
The hyena with polished face and bow tie,

In the office of a billion dollar
Corporation devoted to service;
The vulture dripping with carrion,
Carefully and carelessly robed in imported tweeds,
Lecturing on the Age of Abundance;
The jackal in double-breasted gabardine,
Barking by remote control,
In the United Nations;
The vampire bat seated at the couch head,
Notebook in hand, toying with his decerebrator;
The autonomous, ambulatory cancer,
The Superego in a thousand uniforms;
You, the finger man of behemoth,
The murderer of the young men.

II

What happened to Robinson,
Who used to stagger down Eighth Street,
Dizzy with solitary gin?
Where is Masters, who crouched in
His law office for ruinous decades?
Where is Leonard who thought he was
A locomotive? And Lindsay,
Wise as a dove, innocent
As a serpent, where is he?
      Timor mortis conturbat me.

What became of Jim Oppenheim?
Lola Ridge alone in an
Icy furnished room? Orrick Johns,
Hopping into the surf on his
One leg? Elinor Wylie
Who leaped like Kierkegaard?
Sara Teasdale, where is she?
      Timor mortis conturbat me.

Where is George Sterling, that tame fawn?
Phelps Putnam who stole away?
Jack Wheelwright who couldn't cross the bridge?
Donald Evans with his cane and
Monocle, where is he?
    Timor mortis conturbat me.

John Gould Fletcher who could not
Unbreak his powerful heart?
Bodenheim butchered in stinking
Squalor? Edna Millay who took
Her last straight whiskey? Genevieve
Who loved so much; where is she?
    Timor mortis conturbat me.

Harry who didn't care at all?
Hart who went back to the sea?
    Timor mortis conturbat me.

Where is Sol Funaroff?
What happened to Potamkin?
Isidor Schneider? Claude McKay?
Countee Cullen? Clarence Weinstock?
Who animates their corpses today?
    Timor mortis conturbat me.

Where is Ezra, that noisy man?
Where is Larsson whose poems were prayers?
Where is Charles Snider, that gentle
Bitter boy? Carnevali,
What became of him?
Carol who was so beautiful, where is she?
    Timor mortis conturbat me.

III

Was their end noble and tragic,
Like the mask of a tyrant?
Like Agamemnon's secret golden face?
Indeed it was not. Up all night
In the fo'c'sle, bemused and beaten,
Bleeding at the rectum, in his
Pocket a review by the one
Colleague he respected, "If he
Really means what these poems
Pretend to say, he has only
One way out –." Into the
Hot acrid Caribbean sun,
Into the acrid, transparent,
Smoky sea. Or another, lice in his
Armpits and crotch, garbage littered
On the floor, gray greasy rags on
The bed. "I killed them because they
Were dirty, stinking Communists.
I should get a medal." Again,
Another, Simenon foretold,
His end at a glance. "I dare you
To pull the trigger." She shut her eyes
And spilled gin over her dress.
The pistol wobbled in his hand.
It took them hours to die.
Another threw herself downstairs,
And broke her back. It took her years.
Two put their heads under water
In the bath and filled their lungs.
Another threw himself under
The traffic of a crowded bridge.
Another, drunk, jumped from a
Balcony and broke her neck.
Another soaked herself in

Gasoline and ran blazing
Into the street and lived on
In custody. One made love
Only once with a beggar woman.
He died years later of syphilis
Of the brain and spine. Fifteen
Years of pain and poverty,
While his mind leaked away.
One tried three times in twenty years
To drown himself. The last time
He succeeded. One turned on the gas
When she had no more food, no more
Money, and only half a lung.
One went up to Harlem, took on
Thirty men, came home and
Cut her throat. One sat up all night
Talking to H.L. Mencken and
Drowned himself in the morning.
How many stopped writing at thirty?
How many went to work for *Time*?
How many died of prefrontal
Lobotomies in the Communist Party?
How many are lost in the back wards
Of provincial madhouses?
How many on the advice of
Their psychoanalysts, decided
A business career was best after all?
How many are hopeless alcoholics?
René Crevel!
Jacques Rigaud!
Antonin Artaud!
Mayakofsky!
Essenin!
Robert Desnos!
Saint Pol Roux!
Max Jacob!
All over the world

The same disembodied hand
Strikes us down.
Here is a mountain of death.
A hill of heads like the Khans piled up.
The first-born of a century
Slaughtered by Herod.
Three generations of infants
Stuffed down the maw of Moloch.

IV

He is dead.
The bird of Rhiannon.
He is dead.
In the winter of the heart.
He is Dead.
In the canyons of death,
They found him dumb at last,
In the blizzard of lies.
He never spoke again.
He died.
He is dead.
In their antiseptic hands,
He is dead.
The little spellbinder of Cader Idris.
He is dead.
The sparrow of Cardiff.
He is dead.
The canary of Swansea.
Who killed him?
Who killed the bright-headed bird?
You did, you son of a bitch.
You drowned him in your cocktail brain.
He fell down and died in your synthetic heart.
You killed him,
Oppenheimer the Million-Killer,
You killed him,

Einstein the Gray Eminence.
You killed him,
Havanahavana, with your Nobel Prize.
You killed him, General,
Through the proper channels.
You strangled him, Le Mouton,
With your *mains étendues.*
He confessed in open court to a pince-nezed skull.
You shot him in the back of the head
As he stumbled in the last cellar.
You killed him,
Benign Lady on the postage stamp.
He was found dead at a Liberal Weekly luncheon.
He was found dead on the cutting room floor.
He was found dead at a *Time* policy conference.
Henry Luce killed him with a telegram to the Pope.
Mademoiselle strangled him with a padded brassiere.
Old Possum sprinkled him with a tea ball.
After the wolves were done, the vaticides
Crawled off with his bowels to their classrooms and quarterlies.
When the news came over the radio
You personally rose up shouting, "Give us Barabbas!"
In your lonely crowd you swept over him.
Your custom-built brogans and your ballet slippers
Pummeled him to death in the gritty street.
You hit him with an album of Hindemith.
You stabbed him with stainless steel by Isamu Noguchi,
He is dead.
He is Dead.
Like Ignacio the bullfighter,
At four o'clock in the afternoon.
At precisely four o'clock.
I too do not want to hear it.
I too do not want to know it.
I want to run into the street,
Shouting, "Remember Vanzetti!"
I want to pour gasoline down your chimneys.

I want to blow up your galleries.
I want to burn down your editorial offices.
I want to slit the bellies of your frigid women.
I want to sink your sailboats and launches.
I want to strangle your children at their finger paintings.
I want to poison your Afghans and poodles.
He is dead, the little drunken cherub.
He is dead,
The effulgent tub thumper.
He is Dead.
The ever living birds are not singing
To the head of Bran.
The sea birds are still
Over Bardsey of Ten Thousand Saints.
The underground men are not singing
On their way to work.
There is a smell of blood
In the smell of the turf smoke.
They have struck him down,
The son of David ap Gwilym.
They have murdered him,
The Baby of Taliessin.
There he lies dead,
By the Iceberg of the United Nations.
There he lies sandbagged,
At the foot of the Statue of Liberty.
The Gulf Stream smells of blood
As it breaks on the sand of Iona
And the blue rocks of Canarvon.
And all the birds of the deep sea rise up
Over the luxury liners and scream,
"You killed him! You killed him.
In your God damned Brooks Brothers suit,
You son of a bitch."

THE AMERICAN CENTURY

Blackbirds whistle over the young
Willow leaves, pale celadon green,
In the cleft of the emerald hills.
My daughter is twenty-one months old.
Already she knows the names of
Many birds and flowers and all
The animals of barnyard and zoo.
She paddles in the stream, chasing
Tiny bright green frogs. She wants
To catch them and kiss them. Now she
Runs to me with a tuft of rose
Gray owl's clover. "What's that? Oh! What's that?"
She hoots like an owl and caresses
The flower when I tell her its name.
Overhead in the deep sky
Of May Day jet bombers cut long
White slashes of smoke. The blackbird
Sings and the baby laughs, midway
In the century of horror.

A BESTIARY

for my daughters, Mary and Katharine

Aardvark

The man who found the aardvark
Was laughed out of the meeting
Of the Dutch Academy.
Nobody would believe him.
The aardvark had its revenge –
It returned in dreams, in smoke,

In anonymous letters.
One day somebody found out
It was in Hieronymus
Bosch all the time. From there it
Had sneaked off to Africa.

Ant

Achilles, Aesop, Mark Twain,
Stalin, went to the ant.
Your odds are one to three if
You decide to ignore it.
The aardvark, he eats them up,
And frightens all the people.

Bear

When the world is white with snow,
The bear sleeps in his darkness.
When the people are asleep,
The bear comes with glowing eyes
And steals their bacon and eggs.
He can follow the bees from
Point to point for their honey.
The bees sting but he never
Pays them any attention.
Tame bears in zoos beg for buns.
Two philosophies of life:
Honey is better for you
Than buns; but zoo tricks are cute
And make everybody laugh.

Cat

There are too many poems
About cats. Beware of cat
Lovers, they have a hidden

Frustration somewhere and will
Stick you with it if they can.

Coney

Coneys are a feeble folk,
But their home is in the rocks.
If you've only got one rock
There are better things to do
With it than make a home of it.

Cow

The contented cow gives milk.
When they ask, "Do you give milk?"
As they surely will, say "No."

Deer

Deer are gentle and graceful
And they have beautiful eyes.
They hurt no one but themselves,
The males, and only for love.
Men have invented several
Thousand ways of killing them.

Eagle

The eagle is very proud.
He stays alone, by himself,
Up in the top of the sky.
Only brave men find his home.
Few telescopes are sharper
Than his eyes. I think it's fine
To be proud, but remember
That all the rest goes with it.

There is another kind of
Eagle on flags and money.

Fox

The fox is very clever.
In England people dress up
Like a movie star's servants
And chase the fox on horses.
Rather, they let dogs chase him,
And they come along behind.
When the dogs have torn the fox
To pieces they rub his blood
On the faces of young girls.
If you are clever do not
Let anybody know it,
But especially Englishmen.

Goat

G stands for goat and also
For genius. If you are one,
Learn from the other, for he
Combines domestication,
Venery, and independence.

Herring

The herring is prolific.
There are plenty of herrings.
Some herrings are eaten raw.
Many are dried and pickled.
But most are used for manure.
See if you can apply this
To your history lessons.

Horse

It is fun to ride the horse.
If you give him some sugar
He will love you. But even
The best horses kick sometimes.
A rag blowing in the wind
Can cause him to kill you. These
Characteristics he shares
With the body politic.

I

Take care of this. It's all there is.
You will never get another.

Jackal

The jackal's name is often
Used as a term of contempt.
This is because he follows
The lion around and lives
On the leavings of his kill.
Lions terrify most men
Who buy meat at the butcher's.

Kangaroo

As you know, the kangaroo
Has a pocket, but all she
Puts in it is her baby.
Never keep a purse if all
You can find to put in it
Is additional expense.
(The reception of these words
Will also serve to warn you:
NEVER MAKE FUN OF BABIES!)

Lion

The lion is called the king
Of beasts. Nowadays there are
Almost as many lions
In cages as out of them.
If offered a crown, refuse.

Man

Someday, if you are lucky,
You'll each have one for your own.
Try it before you pick it.
Some kinds are made of soybeans.
Give it lots to eat and sleep.
Treat it nicely and it will
Always do just what you want.

Mantis

In South Africa, among
The Bushmen, the mantis is
A god. A predatory
And cannibalistic bug,
But one of the nicer gods.

Monkey

Monkeys are our relatives.
On observing their habits
Some are ashamed of monkeys,
Some deny the relation,
Some are ashamed of themselves.
They throw coconuts at us.

N

N is for nothing. There is
Much more of it than something.

Okapi

The okapi is extinct.
The reason is under "N."

Possum

When in danger the possum
Plays dead. The State when dying
Plays danger. With the possum
This trick works; sometimes
He escapes. But when the State
Plays with death, it really dies.

Quagga

The quagga is extinct also.
If it hadn't been for the quagga
We'd be short a beast for *Q*.
I can't think of one, can you?

Raccoon

The raccoon wears a black mask,
And he washes everything
Before he eats it. If you
Give him a cube of sugar,
He'll wash it away and weep.
Some of life's sweetest pleasures
Can be enjoyed only if
You don't mind a little dirt.
Here a false face won't help you.

Scarecrow

A hex was put on you at birth.
Society certified your
Existence and claimed you as
A citizen. Don't let it
Scare you. Learn to cope with a world
Which is built entirely of fake,
And in which, if you find a truth
Instead of a lie, it is due
To somebody's oversight.
These stuffed old rags are harmless,
Unless you show them the fear
Which they can never warrant,
Or reveal the contempt which
Of course is all they deserve.
If you do, they'll come to life,
And do their best to kill you.

Seal

The seal when in the water
Is a slippery customer
To catch. But when he makes love
He goes on dry land and men
Kill him with clubs.
To have a happy love life,
Control your environment.

Trout

The trout is taken when he
Bites an artificial fly.
Confronted with fraud, keep your
Mouth shut and don't volunteer.

Uncle Sam

Like the unicorn, Uncle
Sam is what is called a myth.
Plato wrote a book which is
An occult conspiracy
Of gentlemen pederasts.
In it he said ideas
Are more nobly real than
Reality, and that myths
Help keep people in their place.
Since you will never become,
Under any circumstances,
Gentlemen pederasts, you'd
Best leave these blood-soaked notions
To those who find them useful.

Unicorn

The unicorn is supposed
To seek a virgin, lay
His head in her lap, and weep,
Whereupon she steals his horn.
Virginity is what is
Known as a privation. It is
Very difficult to find
Any justification for
Something that doesn't exist.
However, in your young days
You might meet a unicorn.
There are not many better
Things than a unicorn horn.

Vulture

St. Thomas Aquinas thought
That vultures were lesbians
And fertilized by the wind.
If you seek the facts of life,
Papist intellectuals
Can be very misleading.

Wolf

Never believe all you hear.
Wolves are not as bad as lambs.
I've been a wolf all my life,
And have two lovely daughters
To show for it, while I could
Tell you sickening tales of
Lambs who got their just deserts.

You

Let *Y* stand for you who says,
"Very clever, but surely
These were not written for your
Children?" Let *Y* stand for yes.

Zebra

Clothes do not make the zebra.
Better wear a convict's stripes
Free on the lonely savannah
Than the panoplied harness
Of a queen on Rotten Row,
Or a thief's colors at Ascot.

Do not pick my rosemary.
Do not pick my rue.
I am saving up my sorrow,
And I have none for you.

I expect to meet a lover
Who will break my heart.
He will be a nobleman.
His folks will make us part.

When my heart is broken
I will jump in the sea.
You can take the herbs of sorrow
And throw them after me.

Hidden in the briar bush
The ogre masturbates.
High in her tower,
The lady sits and waits.
She sends him an apple
By her little foot page.
He cannot eat the apple
For a heart sick with rage.
Here come the posse
And set the bush on fire.
The lady in the tower
Knows she is a liar.
Take the ogre's ashes,
Cast them in the sea.
There they will mingle
With a billion ladies' pee.

Last night I saw in the moon
Three little rabbits
Eating a prune.
Pipe in the mouth,
Glass in the hand,
Listening to the music
Of Dead Men's Band.
Missus, Mister,
Have some wine!
No thank you, bunnies,
I'll drink mine.

A gold and silver bird
Is flying in the meadow.
Gold and silver scissors
Are cutting in the shadow.
Come home and eat your clabber.
Your mother cries, "Come home!"
Mice have dabbled in your clabber,
These two hours gone.
Come home! Come home!

I came into the kitchen.
Death was cooking meat.
I sneaked up behind him,
And seized his hands and feet.
I held him up above me,
And threw him in the stew.
The sun turned yellow,
The sky turned blue.
The pot boiled over.
The stove blew up.
Death escaped up the chimney,
And left just a cup.
I drank the cup down quickly,

And now I'll never die.
But there'll be no yellow sun
And no more blue sky.

This is the way we plant our feet.
À la mode. Deep. Deep. Deep.
This is the way we plant our hands.
À la mode. Damned. Damned. Damned.
This is the way we plant our hearts.
À la mode. Smart. Smart. Smart.
This is the way we plant our heads.
À la mode. Dead. Dead. Dead.

Disemboweled babies
Drift in the sky.
Exploded mothers
Waft gently by.
Hear all the voices
Give a mighty shout
When the fathers find out
They are wrong side out.

Once there was a nightingale
Sang above their bed.
A jolly nightingale,
The night they were wed.
A nightingale of ashes.
The nightingale is dead.
A nightingale of dust.
The nightingale is dead.
And the world turns away.
The world turns,
And echoes in the head.

Hide the white stone
In the left fist.
Hide the white stone
In the right fist.
I am your secret brother.
Where is the white stone?
You've swallowed it.
You dirty bastard.

Jeanette Brunette
Had a wooden leg.
Her mother beat her,
And set her to beg.
She begged for meat,
She begged for bread.
They gave her swine's feet
And a spoiled cabbage head.
She begged for gold.
They gave her a nail.
The nail made her bold.
She hid it in a pail.
When her mother was asleep
She drove it in her head.
She didn't cry a bit
When her mother lay dead.

An old faggot who's lost his class,
A gray-haired valet with a sagging ass,
Hanging on the well rope,
Without love, faith, or hope.
Put pansies and lilies in a mustard pot
On his unkempt grave. Forget the old sot.

Ram. Damn. Slicker Sam,
Stole the crown
And away he ran.
The bishops cursed.
The generals swore.
Sam gave the crown
To his hot whore.
The ladies wept.
The lords all cried.
The queen slept
By Sam's side.

Diane de Poitiers, Josephine and Pompadour
Were doing something ugly all over the floor.
In came a white kitten with a green skull,
Said, "Ladies, don't you know we are all in Hell?"

This is the gallows that hung the maid.
This is the carpenter
Who built the gallows
That hung the maid.
These are the dogs
Who tore the carpenter
Who built the gallows
That hung the maid.
This is the hangman
Who bought the dogs
Who tore the carpenter
Who built the gallows
That hung the maid.
This is the gold
That paid the hangman
Who bought the dogs
Who tore the carpenter
Who built the gallows

That hung the maid.
This is the prince
Who gave the gold
That paid the hangman
Who bought the dogs
Who tore the carpenter
Who built the gallows
That hung the maid.
This is the maid
Who loved the prince
Who gave the gold
That paid the hangman
Who bought the dogs
That tore the carpenter
Who built the gallows
That hung the maid.
This is the carpenter
Who loved the maid
Who loved the prince
Who gave the gold
That paid the hangman
Who bought the dogs
That tore the carpenter
Who built the gallows
That hung the maid.

Marborough went to the war.
Cavendish stayed to home.
Marborough died of a pox,
Cavendish of a bomb.
Serves the stinkers jolly well right.

The heart is bitten.
The bone is broken.
The words are written.

The curse is spoken.
The cannibal frogs,
With bloody jaws,
Climb the blazing logs,
And write the laws.

Ibbitty, Bibbitty, Sibbitty, Sab.
Ibbitty, Bibbitty, Kanaba.
The Queen's name is Mad Mab.
The King's name is Baba.

Ibbitty, Bibbitty, Sibbitty, Sab.
Ibbitty, Bibbitty, Kanaba.
Where is the knave in the taxi cab,
Who kidnapped our King Baba?

Ibbitty, Bibbitty, Sibbitty, Sab.
Ibbitty, Bibbitty, Kanaba.
Into the bloody ditch with Mab!
We've fried the liver of Baba!

Ibbitty, Bibbitty, Sibbitty, Sab.
Ibbitty, Bibbitty, Kanaba.
The King's name is Fat Dab.
The Queen's name is Raba.

The red wind blew.
The black wind blew.
At last there blew the blue.
Said the last naked devil
To the last naked angel,
"Girl, I think we're through."

ON A MILITARY GRAVEYARD

Stranger, when you come to Washington
Tell them that we lie here
Obedient to their orders.

after Simonides

SURVIVAL OF THE FITTEST

I realize as I
Cast out over the lake
At thirteen thousand feet –
I don't know where you are.
It has been years since we
Married and had children
By people neither of
Us knew in the old days.
But I still catch fish with flies
Made from your blonde pubic hair.

REVOLT

Outside of the movies
I have seen a monocle
On the eye of a living man
Only three times in my life,
On a Hollywood producer,
On a German officer,
And on a speaker at the
London Anarchist Group.

AFTER SAPPHO

I loved you, Leslie, long ago,
In the flower of your youth,
When I was just an ungainly boy.

LOST ETC.

The expatriates of the
Twenties and their leader Pound
Were those who, in an age of
World revolt found nothing more
Important to revolt against
Than the Eighteenth Amendment.

NEATNESS IS ALL

Out of Ptolemy's principle
Of economy and Occam's
Razor have come all the great
Omnivorous, rectangular
Immortal cosmophages.

SENSE OF PROPORTION

The old lion hunter and I
Exchange goodbyes. "See you again
Someday in the woods." The last
Time I saw him was on the
Santa Lucia Ridge in
Nineteen twenty-nine. It isn't
Likely. He is seventy-three
And I am forty-eight. Someday
Will never come round again.

A BREAD AND BUTTER LETTER

Although it was not my home
The first cold plum blossom by
The window smelled just the same.

METEMPSYCHOSIS

Two months old, already
Across my daughter's face
Pass faces long past and dead.

ON THE POST OFFICE

Have you ever forgotten
The first time, in the evil
Boiling cauldron of New York,
You saw, high in the carven stone,
That noble sentence of
Herodotus?

AFTER SA'ADI

I said, "I do not fear the
Day when we shall part, I shall
Be strong." But when the day came,
Strength failed me.

FACT

Chirotherium tracks occur
Mainly in the Middle Bunter.

FROM THE PERSIAN (1)

Naked out of the dark we came.
Naked into the dark we go.
Come to my arms, naked in the dark.

ILLUSION

When we were young, because we
Were older than the heroes
And heroines of fiction,
We thought we were middle-aged.

FROM THE PERSIAN (2)

You are like the moon except
For your dark hair. You are like
Venus, except for your lips,
Crimson and perfumed, and like
The sun except that you are
Most splendid naked, at night.

VALUTA

Have you ever noticed how, the
World over, fairy princesses
Delight to give themselves to louts
And cowherds whom they enrich past
Belief? With all the privilege
And wealth of fairy land, the hot
Sweat of mortality gives off
A warmth more precious than all the
Illimitable bounties of
Deathlessness.

—— lives in the woods,
Where she languidly enjoys
A dim-witted lover, Nature,
Endometriosis,
Exophthalmia, marasmus,
Too much money. She has moments
She Does Things With Her Hands, Lovely
Things, with an exquisite sense of
Chic. I saw her last at cocktails
In her town studio in
1937. Everybody
Was there, e.g., all the leading
Fairies and/or WPA
Officials. The smell of tweeds,
Blue Boar, and carbon paper
Was overpowering. The din
Of Phi Beta Kappa keys
Was deafening. There were an
Indeterminate number
Of spaniels pissing on their
Masters' Scotch brogans, and on
Other people's shoes. They were
Drinking the boys on the Ebro
Out of the trenches by Christmas.
A novelist who had been
In Spain spoke. Recently I hear
She has been entertaining
The leading male whore of Paris,
France, that pimp with the face of a
Poisoned Irish setter, who has
Been had by all the sexes of
Six continents. They say he has
Converted her to Anarchism,
A fascinating new theory
Which is sweeping England, and

Is the rage with all the really
Rafinée modistes and parfumistes.
Isn't that exciting?
KEEP OFF MY BANDWAGON YOU SOW!

PORTRAIT OF THE AUTHOR AS A YOUNG ANARCHIST

1917–18–19,
While things were going on in Europe,
Our most used term of scorn or abuse
Was "bushwa." We employed it correctly,
But we thought it was French for "bullshit."
I lived in Toledo, Ohio,
On Delaware Avenue, the line
Between the rich and poor neighborhoods.
We played in the jungles by Ten Mile Creek,
And along the golf course in Ottawa Park.
There were two classes of kids, and they
Had nothing in common: the rich kids
Who worked as caddies, and the poor kids
Who snitched golf balls. I belonged to the
Saving group of exceptionalists
Who, after dark, and on rainy days,
Stole out and shat in the golf holes.

AFTER THE ANTHOLOGY

Artemis, more passionate
Than Aphrodite, at sunset
Your light rose in the east, and
All night was a fire in
The trees over us. Now alone
You hang, pale and splendid above
The dim sea while the first glow
Runs round the fringe of the mountains.

Go and inflame the pulses
Of the stolid Chinese. Leave us
To sleep exhausted till you return.

THEY SAY THIS ISN'T A POEM

I

All that is is a harmony,
Otherwise it would not endure.
Harmony of the parts with the whole
Is the definition of goodness.
Therefore all that is is good.
Man is part of all that is, so
He is part of its harmony.
Therefore he is by nature good.
Insofar as he knows what is,
He knows it because he is
Within himself a harmony
Of parts in a whole, of the same
Kind as all that is. Therefore,
The harmony of all that is
Without man can unite with
The harmony of all that is
Within man as a knowable
Good, an inner moral good.
But if this good is known within
By one party, man, it must
Also be known by the other
Party, All That Is, hence he who
Is in perfect accord with All
That Is can act upon It
Without effort, with a kind
Of reciprocity, like acts

Of the mutual love of friends.
How beautiful and specious
And how stinking with the blood
Of wars and crucifixions.

II

The order of the universe
Is only a reflection
Of the human will and reason.
All being is contingent,
No being is self-subsistent.
All objects are moved by others.
No object moves itself.
All beings are caused by others.
No being is its own cause.
There is no perfect being.
Being has no economy.
Entities are multiplied
Without necessity. They
Have no sufficient reason.
The only order of nature
Is the orderly relation
Of one person to another.
Non-personal relations
Are by nature chaotic.
Personal relations are
The pattern through which we see
Nature as systematic.
Homer, and all sensible
Men since, have told us again
And again, the universe –
The great principles and forces
That move the world – have order
Only as a reflection
Of the courage, loyalty,
Love, and honesty of men.

By themselves they are cruel
And utterly frivolous.
The man who yields to them goes mad,
Kills his child, his wife or friend
And dies in the bloody dust,
Having destroyed the treasured
Labor of other men's hands.
He who outwits them survives
To grow old in his own home.

CODICIL

Most of the world's poetry
Is artifice, construction.
No one reads it but scholars.
After a generation
It has grown so overcooked,
It cannot be digested.
There is little I haven't
Read, and dreary stuff it was.
Lamartine – Gower – Tasso –
Or the metaphysicals
Of Cambridge, ancient or modern,
And their American apes.
Of course for years the ruling
Class of English poetry
Has held that that is just what
Poetry is, impersonal
Construction, where personal
Pronouns are never permitted.
If rigorously enough
Applied, such a theory
Produces in practice its
Opposite. The poetry
Of Eliot and Valéry,

Like that of Pope, isn't just
Personal, it is intense,
Subjective revery as
Intimate and revealing,
Embarrassing if you will,
As the indiscretions of
The psychoanalyst's couch.
There is always sufficient
Reason for a horror of
The use of the pronoun, "I."

NATURAL NUMBERS (1964)

For my daughters
Mary and Katharine

A LEMMA BY CONSTANCE REID

There is a square for every
Natural number. If we
Divide the squares into even
And odd, we find that we can
Place the natural numbers
And the two sets of even
And odd squares in one to one
Correspondence.
We will never
Run out of squares. But neither
Will we run out of even
Or odd squares. Rest assured, though
Squares are inexhaustible, and
Problems concerning squares are
Also inexhaustible,
So are natural numbers.

Glitter of Nausicaä's
Embroideries, flashing arms,
And heavy hung maiden hair;
Doing the laundry, the wind
Brisk in the bright air
Of the Mediterranean day.
Odysseus, hollow cheeked,
Wild eyed, bursts from the bushes.
Mary sits by the falling
Water reading Homer while
I fish for mottled brook trout
In the sun mottled riffles.
They are small and elusive.
The stream is almost fished out.
Water falls through shimmering
Panelled light between the red
Sequoias, over granite
And limestone, under green ferns
And purple lupin. Time was
I caught huge old trout in these
Pools and eddies. These are three
Years old at the very most.
Mary is seven. Homer
Is her favorite author.
It took me a lifetime of
Shames and wastes to understand
Homer. She says, "Aren't those gods
Terrible? All they do is
Fight like those angels in Milton,
And play tricks on the poor Greeks
And Trojans. I like Aias
And Odysseus best. They are
Lots better than those silly
Gods." Like the ability
To paint, she will probably

Outgrow this wisdom. It too
Will wither away as she
Matures and a whole lifetime
Will be spent getting it back.
Now she teaches Katharine
The profound wisdom of seven
And Katharine responds with
The profound nonsense of three.
Grey-haired in granite mountains,
I catch baby fish. Ten fish,
And Homer, and two little
Girls pose for a picture by
The twenty foot wide, cinnamon
Red trunk of a sequoia.
As I snap the camera,
It occurs to me that this
Tree was as big as the pines
Of Olympus, not just before
Homer sang, but before Troy
Ever fell or Odysseus
Ever sailed from home.

FISH PEDDLER AND COBBLER

Always for thirty years now
I am in the mountains in
August. For thirty Augusts
Your ghosts have stood up over
The mountains. That was nineteen
Twenty-seven. Now it is
Nineteen fifty-seven. Once
More after thirty years I
Am back in the mountains of
Youth, back in the Gros Ventres,
The broad park-like valleys and

The tremendous cubical
Peaks of the Rockies. I learned
To shave hereabouts, working
As cookee and night wrangler.
Nineteen twenty-two, the years
Of revolutionary
Hope that came to an end as
The iron fist began to close.
No one electrocuted me.
Nothing happened. Time passed.
Something invisible was gone.
We thought then that we were the men
Of the years of the great change,
That we were the forerunners
Of the normal life of mankind.
We thought that soon all things would
Be changed, not just economic
And social relationships, but
Painting, poetry, music, dance,
Architecture, even the food
We ate and the clothes we wore
Would be ennobled. It will take
Longer than we expected.
These mountains are unchanged since
I was a boy wandering
Over the West, picking up
Odd jobs. If anything they are
Wilder. A moose cow blunders
Into camp. Beavers slap their tails
On their sedgy pond as we fish
From on top of their lodge in the
Twilight. The horses feed on bright grass
In meadows full of purple gentian,
And stumble through silver dew
In the full moonlight.
The fish taste of meadow water.
In the morning on far grass ridges

Above the red rim rock wild sheep
Bound like rubber balls over the
Horizon as the noise of camp
Begins. I catch and saddle
Mary's little golden horse,
And pack the first Decker saddles
I've seen in thirty years. Even
The horse bells have a different sound
From the ones in California.
Canada jays fight over
The last scraps of our pancakes.
On the long sandy pass we ride
Through fields of lavender primrose
While lightning explodes around us.
For lunch Mary catches a two pound
Grayling in the whispering river.
No fourteen thousand foot peaks
Are named Sacco and Vanzetti.
Not yet. The clothes I wear
Are as unchanged as the Decker
Saddles on the pack horses.
America grows rich on the threat of death.
Nobody bothers anarchists anymore.
Coming back we lay over
In Ogden for ten hours.
The courthouse square was full
Of miners and lumberjacks and
Harvest hands and gandy dancers
With broken hands and broken
Faces sleeping off cheap wine drunks
In the scorching heat, while tired
Savage eyed whores paraded the street.

PROUST'S MADELEINE

Somebody has given my
Baby daughter a box of
Old poker chips to play with.
Today she hands me one while
I am sitting with my tired
Brain at my desk. It is red.
On it is a picture of
An elk's head and the letters
B.P.O.E. – a chip from
A small town Elks Club. I flip
It idly in the air and
Catch it and do a coin trick
To amuse my little girl.
Suddenly everything slips aside.
I see my father
Doing the very same thing,
Whistling "Beautiful Dreamer,"
His breath smelling richly
Of whiskey and cigars. I can
Hear him coming home drunk
From the Elks Club in Elkhart,
Indiana, bumping the
Chairs in the dark. I can see
Him dying of cirrhosis
Of the liver and stomach
Ulcers and pneumonia,
Or, as he said on his deathbed, of
Crooked cards and straight whiskey,
Slow horses and fast women.

AIX-EN-PROVENCE

AUTUMN

The children have colds and snore
In the night. The rain falls on
All autumn Provence, the gold
And orange and green and purple
Hidden in rustling darkness.
At my feet under the stove
Pierre Lapin sleeps and purrs.
I open the door and walk
Down the garden path towards
The ghostly statue of Flora.
Behind the clouds the moon is full.
The night is like a sea cave
At noon, and a wet owl flies
By me, silent as a fish.
The wind is shifting, the pines
On the opposite hill have
Begun to murmur like water.
Here it is still except for
The slow sweep of massive rain.
Heavy rain soaked gold leaves drop
From the plane trees through the dark.

CHRISTMAS

The biggest tree in Provence.
A milky faïence barber's bowl.
A merde d'oie velvet waistcoat.
Medieval poetry.
A most bouffant cretonne skirt.
A merde d'oie sweater. A mantilla.
Six copper pots. A brass nameplate.

Dolls. A crèche with santons.
Boules. Nine-pins. Dresses. Dozens
Of packages from the States.
A goose with prunes and almonds.
Champagne, Château Simon, cognac.
Outside the ruts are frozen.
Cézanne's pines are steely gray.
Mont Sainte Victoire is not blue
Or lavender in the sky,
It is pure bright limestone gray.
It is two weeks since the sound
Of the mines at Gardanne came
Over the hill on the South wind.
The girls sing songs from *Mireille*
And the "Pastourelle Maurel,"
And act out the parts, turn about.
Pierre Lapin purrs under
The smoky poêle. A cloud
Of frost hangs under the bare
Plane trees on Cour Mirabeau.
We drink grog in the Deux Garçons.
We visit two friends from the States.
We visit a heroine
Of the Resistance. At Mass,
As the Bishop passed our row,
He gave his ring to our girls
To kiss. But the professors
And the Gaullist intellectuals
Still snub us on the street.
We visit the bazaar for
The home for the aged infirm.
On the festooned arch it says,
"Les souvenirs des jours
Heureux sont terribles
A ceux qui souffrent
Et qui sont seuls."
Midnight, the Spring stars rise up

Over Mont Sainte Victoire standing
Like a crystal of smoky quartz
In the sky at the road's end.

SPRING

There are no images here
In the solitude, only
The night and its stars which are
Relationships rather than
Images. Shifting darkness,
Strains of feeling, lines of force,
Webs of thoughts, no images,
Only night and time aging
The night in its darkness, just
Motion in space in the dark.
It is a night full of darkness,
And space, and stars, and the hours
Going by, and time going by,
And the night growing old, and all
The webs, and nets, of relationships
Changing, and it is Spring night
In Provence, here where I am,
And under the half moon the almond
Buds are ready to burst. Before noon
The blossoms will open, here by
This peach colored house amongst
The steel gray pines and the gray
Limestone cliffs. Now the buds
Are round and tight in the dim
Moonlight, in the night that
Stretches on forever, that had
No beginning, and that will
Never end, and it doesn't mean
Anything. It isn't an image of
Something. It isn't a symbol of

Something else. It is just an
Almond tree, in the night, by
The house, in the woods, by
A vineyard, under the setting
Half moon, in Provence, in the
Beginning of another Spring.

SPRING

In the morning all the almond trees
Are blooming all over Provence like
They were blooming in a popular song.
Everywhere in the uplands in the woods
Where the old trees have shattered the
Ancient walls, everywhere by the pale
Ochre ruined houses, the almond trees
Are blooming. In the dry bright February,
All day I walk in the lifeless forest.
Nothing moves. Once in a great while
Some magpies rustle and cry, off in the
Trees somewhere. Once in a great while
I smell a hidden polecat or a deserted
Badger hole. Every few hundred meters,
There is a high wall of dry laid stone,
Stretching away out of sight through
The forest, fencing ruin from ruin.
Roofless houses, broken walls, dry
Canals, roads that go nowhere now. Even
The shooting blinds are abandoned.
Everywhere there are almond trees
Just out in bloom this morning,
And black jagged dead olives
With silver green shoots coming
Up around them. No sound. Only
The movement of leaves and stones.

SPRING

Wind in almond blossoms.
Ants on limestone mountains.
Cézanne's bones in red earth.
Countless vines on red earth.
Black wine on oak tables.
They drink love or hate as
The old plane trees blossom.
They drink coffee or pastis
Under the blowing young leaves.
Under feathery pines,
On red and gray hillsides,
Hidden from the mistral,
Two by two they make love.
In red sand pits, squad by squad,
Soldiers shoot at paper men.

ON THE EVE OF THE PLEBISCITE

The mistral blows, the plane leaves
Parachute to earth. The Cour
Mirabeau turns from submarine
Green to blue gray and old gold.
When the wind drops it is warm
And drowsy. Glace or pastis
In a sunny chair, the Aixois
Decline to winter. Civic
Calm, the contemplative heart
Of Mediterranean
Civilization throbs with
Its slow, all governing pulse.
Tricolor posters, surcharged
OUI or NON flicker and battle
Like broken film on the screen
Of a malodorous cinema.

The Jeunesse Dorée of the
Law School hunt a sensitive
Overcivilized Algerian
Fellow student between the
Parked cars, around the plane trees,
Like an exhausted fox.
Horror tightens its steel bands
On this land and on every
Heart. Lewd sycophancy and
Brutalized indifference
Rule the highbrow terrasses
And the once militant slums.
Clowns and torturers and cheap
Literary adventurers
Parade like obscene dolls. This
Is no country I ever knew.
And who tightens the screws?
And who pulls these puppets' wires?
Oh, how well I remember
Listening to Chancellor
Bruening's last appeal. Late night,
By the cold green eye of the short-
Wave radio. "You have raised up
Forces from the bottom of
Society. You think they
Will be your willing tools. I
Tell you they will betray you
And destroy you. I beseech
You, bethink yourselves before
It is too late." To whom did
He speak? To the State Department,
The Foreign Office, National City,
Chase, The Bank of England,
Shell, Standard Oil, Krupp, US Steel,
Vickers, Dupont, the same ones
Who are still there – "reducing the heart
Of Europe to the status of a barbaric

Colony." And behind them – to you
By whose indifferent consent they rule.

ELEGY ON ENCOUNTERING THE TROUBLE OF THE WORLD

Young, in Spring, I gathered
Flowers on the mountain.
Old, in Autumn, I pick
Sedges by the river.
Positive – negative.
Negative – positive.
Ordinary people
Never understand me.
As long as I have lovely
Children I have nothing
To be sorry about.

Geese out of Sweden cry,
Going past in the night.
Under the yellowing
Plane trees, over the walled
Pond, the swallows circle
For the last times. They swarm,
High in the bright Fall air
In the evenings. Then
One day they are all gone.
The great leaves float down like
Golden crumpled letters,
Fill the pond and cover the
Avenue in Cézanne's village.
On warm days ballooning
Spiders fill the air with
Threads and spicules of light.

Spring comes back. Trees blossom
In order: almond, plum,

Cherry, peach, last, apple.
Green gold maple tassels,
Rosy alder, yellow
Poplar catkins, and then
Great pompoms of chestnuts,
White and rose. One day
One swallow flies above
Flooded river meadows.
Next week they are all back.

Winter, children learn the stars.
Spring, children gather wild
Jonquils, violets, orchids.

Springs and Autumns gone by
I know by their record,
But I can no longer
Keep track of them
In my own memory.

My girls are eight and four.
Their hearts beat systole
And diastole. Their young
Legs twinkle in the deep
Meadow amongst flowers.

poems at L'Atelier, Route Tholonet

VICENZA

ROGATION DAYS

Under the orchards, under
The tree strung vines, little blue

Figures are making hay, high
On the steep hillsides above
Palladio's drowsy villas
And Tiepolo's swirling walls.
On the highest field they are
Still cutting with swinging scythes;
Down below they are tossing
The long swathes of hay to cure
In the sun; further down they
Are cocking it, or carrying
It off in two-wheeled donkey carts.
The Venetian plain vanishes
In haze. The nearby Alps are
Indefinite blue smudges,
Capped with faint streaks of orange
Snow. Clouds of perfume roll up
The hillside in waves. All the birds
Sing. All the flowers bloom. Here
At a stone table like this,
On a little hill like this,
In a circle of cypress
And olive like this, the infinite
Visited Leopardi,
And ravished him and carried
Him off in the deep summer.
It would carry me off, too,
If I knew where I wanted
To go, or if I just wanted
To go nowhere at all.

ASCENSION NIGHT

I take a bath enveloped
In the essential odor of
Mediterranean civilization.
The ceiling high copper heater

At the foot of the tub
Is fired with sarments –
Prunings of vine and olive.
Down below the blossoming
Cherry trees full of nightingales
An electronic voice calls the trains
As they go through sleeping Vicenza
Bound for Paris, Belgrade, Munich.
Downstairs in the chapel,
The sisters are saying compline.
Next door in the bedroom,
My girls are all asleep.
The last penny rocket
Rises from the street fair.
Moonlight over the Alps
In a stormy sky.

poems at Casa San Rafaelle, Monte Berico

VENICE

May Day

Once more it is early summer,
Like an opal, in Venice.
I listen to the monks sing
Vespers in San Giorgio Maggiore.
Ten years have gone by. I am
No longer alone. My little
Daughter and I sit hand in hand,
As the falling sunlight rises
Up Palladio's noble aisles
And shimmers in the incense.
The incense billows over
The altar. The Magnificat

Of May Day surges through the incense.
Six years ago, another May Day,
Mary played in a meadow stream,
And caught emerald green baby frogs.
Overhead then, dive bombers wrote
Monograms of death in the sky.
They are still there. Now they have
A new trick. At "He has put down
The mighty from their seat," one
Of them breaks the sound barrier
With a shuddering belch of hate,
One omnipresent sound in
The sky of Tiepolo.
The same shave jowled apes sit at
The same round mahogany tables,
Just across those pretty mountains.
They are pushing all this pretty
Planet, Venice, and Palladio,
And you and me, and the golden
Sun, nearer and nearer to
Total death. Nothing can stop them.
Soon it will be over. But
This music, and the incense,
And the solemn columned thought,
And the poem of a virgin,
And you and me, and Venice
In the May Day evening on the
Fiery waters, we have our own
Eternity, so fleeting that they
Can never touch it, or even
Know that it has passed them by.

from poems at Casa Paganelli, Campo San Zaccaria

ROSE COLORED GLASSES

Ten years, and it's still on the
Radio. "La Vie en rose"
Spills out of a dozen windows
Onto the canal. A woman
And her son in a vegetable
Barge sing it. A man polishing
The prow of his gondola
Sings it while his dog wags its tail.
Children playing hopscotch sing it.
Grimy half washed clothes hang overhead.
Garbage floats in the narrow canal.
More radios join in. Across
The canal, beyond the iron windows
Of the Women's Prison, a hundred
Pure voices of pickpockets
And prostitutes start to sing it.
It is just like being in church.
The next number is "Ciao, ciao, bambina."

OBSERVATIONS IN A CORNISH TEASHOP

How can they write or paint
In a country where it
Would be nicer to be
Fed intravenously?

EIGHT FOR ORNETTE'S MUSIC

if the pain is greater
than the difference
as the bird in the night
or the perfumes in the moon
oh witch of question
oh lips of submission
in the flesh of summer
the silver slipper
in the sleeping forest
if hope surpasses the question
by the mossy spring
in the noon of harvest
between the pillars of silk
in the luminous difference
oh tongue of music
oh teacher of splendor
if the meat of the heart
if the fluid of the wing
as love
if birth
or trust as
love as love

is it dreaming falling in
the tangling light
calls the light
the small sharp wafers
in the whirlpool
on white plume
floating

in the sky the blades
nibbling the breasts
new trembling
discover honey
kiss kiss

She didn't say where

nobody home
they all left
lipstick letters stockings
torn
a star
on the sooty pane
deep in the far off forest
initials and hearts entwined
nobody ever comes back
night planes
over village sky rockets
the most wonderful one
we ever had
darling
in the drawer
the chambermaid
found 1000
counterfeit
$10 bills

then the waning
moon in young leaves
do you think of the old wounds
it is like Mykenai
with those terrible
dead kings with gold foil
over their faces

no animal or vegetable
anywhere
another landscape
with some people in a boat
sewn with needles or with thread
birds with dry human voices

who issues certificates
to whom it may concern:
the bearer is alive
turn on the sky
take off your dress
saw down the tree
climb the mountain
kiss the lips
close the eyes
speak low
open
come

time turns like tables
the indifferent and blissful Spring
saves all souls and seeds and slaves asleep
dark Spring
in the dark whispering human will
words spoken by two kissing tongues
hissing union
Eve's snake
stars come on
two naked bodies tumble
through bodiless Christmas trees
blazing like bees and rosebuds
fire turns to falling powder
lips relax and smile and sleep
fire sweeps

the hearth of the blood
on far off red double stars
they probate their own tied wills

Blues

the sea will be deep
the eye will be deep
the last bell has been deep

the iceberg has been cold
the nail has been cold
the hungry whore was cold

the jungle was fierce
the tooth was fierce
the poor bum's woman is fierce

the plate of tripe is shallow
the omelette in the pan is shallow
shallow as the wisdom of the ages

the hawk in the zenith knows
the mole under the spade knows
the curly brain knows too

don't you forget it

Blues

grey as the arctic
grey as the sea
grey as the heart
grey as the bird in the tree

red as the sun
red as the robin
red as the heart
red as the axe in the tree

blue as the star
blue as the gull
blue as the heart
blue as the air in the tree

black as the tongue
black as the vulture
black as the heart
black as the hanged girl in the tree

TWO FOR BREW AND DICK

State and 32nd, Cold Morning Blues

A girl in a torn chemise
Weeps by a dirty window.
Jaws are punched in the street.

A cat is sick in the gutter.
Dogs bark up nightbound alleys.
There's nothing like the sorrow

Of the jukeboxes at dawn.
Dice girls going home.
Whores eating chop suey.

Pimps eat chile mac.
Drowsy flatfeet, ham and eggs.
Dawn of labor, dawn of life.

The awakening noises
Of the old sacrifices.
The snow blows down the bare street

Ahead of the first streetcar.
The lovers light cigarettes,
And part with burning eyes,

And go off in the daylight.

Married Blues

I didn't want it, you wanted it.
Now you've got it you don't like it.
You can't get out of it now.

Pork and beans, diapers to wash,
Too poor for the movies, too tired to love.
There's nothing we can do.

Hot stenographers on the subway.
The grocery boy's got a big one.
We can't do anything about it.

You're only young once.
You've got to go when your time comes.
That's how it is. Nobody can change it.

Guys in big cars whistle.
Freight trains moan in the night.
We can't get away with it.

That's the way life is.
Everybody's in the same fix.
It will never be any different.

THIS NIGHT ONLY

[*Erik Satie: "Gymnopédie #1"*]

Moonlight   now   on Malibu
The winter night   the few stars
Far away   millions   of miles
The sea   going on   and on
Forever   around   the earth
Far   and   far   as your lips   are near
Filled   with the same light   as your eyes
Darling   darling   darling
The future   is long gone by
And the past   will never happen
We have   only this
Our one forever
So small   so infinite
So brief   so vast
Immortal   as our hands that touch
Deathless   as the firelit wine we drink
Almighty   as this single kiss
That has no beginning
That will never
Never
End

AT LEAST THAT ABANDON

As I watch at the long window
Crowds of travelers hurry
Behind me, rainy darkness
Blows before me, and the great plane
Circles, taxis to the runway,

Waits, and then roars off into
The thick night. I follow it
As it rises through the clouds
And levels off under the stars.
Stars, darkness, a row of lights,
Moaning engines, thrumming wings,
A silver plane over a sea
Of starlit clouds and rain bound
Sea. What I am following
Is a rosy, glowing coal
Shaped like the body of a
Woman – rushing southward a
Meteor afire with the
Same fire that burns me unseen
Here on the whirling earth amongst
Bright, busy, incurious
Faces of hundreds of people
Who pass me, unaware of
The blazing astrophysics
Of the end of a weekend.

AN EASY SONG

It's rained every day since you
Went away. I've been lonely.
Lonely, empty, tenderness –
Longing to kiss the corners
Of your mouth as you smile
Your special, inward, sensual,
And ironic smile I love
Because I know it means you
Are content – *content* in French –
A special, inward, sensual,
And ironic state of bliss.
Tu es contente, ma chérie?
I am, even if lonely,

Because I can call to mind
Your body in a warm room,
In the rainy winter night,
A rose on the hearth of winter,
A rose cloud standing naked,
In the perfume of your flesh.
Moi aussi, je suis content.

COMING

You are driving to the airport
Along the glittering highway
Through the warm night,
Humming to yourself.
The yellow rose buds that stood
On the commode faded and fell
Two days ago. Last night the
Petals dropped from the tulips
On the dresser. The signs of
Your presence are leaving the
House one by one. Being without
You was almost more than I
Could bear. Now the work is squared
Away. All the arrangements
Have been made. All the delays
Are past and I am thirty
Thousand feet in the air over
A dark lustrous sea, under
A low half moon that makes the wings
Gleam like fish under water –
Rushing south four hundred miles
Down the California coast
To your curving lips and your
Ivory thighs.

PACIFIC BEACH

This is the sea called peaceful,
And tonight it is quiet
As sleeping flesh under
The October waning moon.
Late night, not a moving car
On all the moonlit Coast Highway.
No sound but the offshore bells
And the long, recurrent hiss
Of windless surf. "Sophocles
Long ago heard it by the
Aegean." I drive eighty
Miles an hour through the still,
Moonfilled air. The surf withdraws,
Returns, and brings into my
Mind the turgid ebb and flow
Of human loyalty –
The myriad ruined voices
That have said, "Ah, love, let us
Be true to one another."
The moon lured voyagers sleep
In all the voiceless city.
Far out on the horizon
The lights of the albacore
Fleet gleam like a golden town
In another country.

MAROON BELLS

How can I love you more than
The silver whistle of the
Coney in the rocks loves you?
How can I love you better
Than the blue of the bluebells
By the waterfall loves you?

Eater of moonlight, drinker
Of brightness, feet of jewels
On the mountain, velvet feet
In the meadow grass, darkness
Braided with wild roses, wild
Mare of all the horizons…
A far away tongue speaks in
The time that fills me like a
Tongue in a bell falling
Out of all the towers of space.
Eyes wide, nostrils distended,
We drown in secret happy
Oceans we trade in broad daylight.
O my girl, mistress of all
Illuminations and all
Commonplaces, I love you
Like the air and the water
And the earth and the fire and
The light love you and love you.

ASPEN MEADOWS

Look. Listen. They are lighting
The moon. Be still. I don't want
To hear again that wistful
Kyriale of husbands and lovers.
Stop questioning me
About my women. You are
Not a schoolgirl nor I a
Lecturing paleobotanist.
It's enough that the green glow
Runs through the down on your arms
Like a grass fire and your eyes
Are fogs of the same endless light.
Let the folds and divisions
Of your anatomy envelop

All horizons. O my sweet
Topology and delusion,
You may be arrogant and feral
But no clock can measure
How long ago you fell asleep
In my arms in the midst of
Sliding doors, parting curtains,
Electric fishes and candy lotuses
And the warm wet moonlight.

LIKE QUEEN CHRISTINA

Orange and blue and then grey
The frosty twilight comes down
Through the thin trees. The fresh snow
Holds the light longer than the sky.
Skaters on the pond vanish
In dusk, but their voices stay,
Calling and laughing, and birds
Twitter and cry in the reeds.
Indoors as night fills the white rooms,
You stand in the candle light
Laughing like a splendid jewel.

GÖDEL'S PROOF (1965)

"A self-contained system is a contradiction of terms. QED*"*

For my daughters
Mary and Katharine
and for Carol, these new poems.

When the nightingale cries
All night and all day,
I have my sweetheart
Under the flower
Till the watch from the tower
Cries, "Lovers, rise!
The dawn comes and the bright day."
– Anonymous Provençal

ANDROMEDA CHAINED TO HER ROCK THE GREAT NEBULA IN HER HEART

I

The ache
The heart is never well
The incurable pain
The iron warp of time
The shrinking web of life
The grey unquiet ocean
Under uninhabited fog
The roar which always begins
And is never still
Which nothing will ever stop
In the grey
In the white
In the bitter throat
Against the concave wall
The little pile of soiled bones
Nails will never glitter
Brain will never ooze
Gulf will no longer open
O heart
O charred heart
O broken eye

II

Anguish and form and prayer
No excuse no betrayal
No dimension in space or time
Without caution without consequence without motion
The many blades of the revolving razors
The many tears of the breaking sorrow
The fear of the bear the ghost of the bear

The gear of care that is always here
When the cross of words spells zero
There are trees in the sea
There are red columns on the horizon
And fear everywhere
And every year no word at all for all her pain
And she said I want just what you want she said
Just a big box full of old veils
And the shears were always cutting at night
Always far away or always near cutting
Move the cube at right angles to everywhere
At right angles to itself
Lips to lips and eyes to eyes move
At right angles
Hands on hands edges
Spin in light beams
In the rattleflake of brightness
Gone
Call
Kindred
Keep
Coinage

III

O fire around fire in fire of fire with fire
By fire alone
Fire pointed fire the star in star
And the self falls in god shimmer
The visionary shipwreck
The kidnapped ecstasy
The copulation of the lightning and the lighthouse
A skirt lifts its tent of perfume
A woman's frail veiled sight moved stirred
Stirred the virgin in the womb of the man
Ishtar the tree of fiery stars
The eye wraps itself up in its retina

The old dark transmigrating eye
A boat of oak sails
Under a tree of silver
Under a crown of thorns
Gold spring blue autumn purple winter
Song alone
Or the harp in a crystal room
Snow falling ever more heavily
The room growing steadily darker
Bones like white wires cry out in their dream

IV

Eyes in moss
Salt in mouth
Stone in heart
An owl rings the changes of silence
Torn head
Crow's wings
Black eyeballs
Poison seeps through the parabolic sand
The rock on fire
Ice falls towards the sun
The hurled axe
Lost in the future
Of an automatic and anonymous dream
The brazen serpent
In the desert of hallucination
Manna is the excrement of vermin
What is the shadow
Crawling on the eggshell
What chorale
Flees in the sea shell
The bite of the gods
In the wilderness
Metamorphosing the demigods
Thunder lost in shadow

The arc with its unknown spectrum
Of colors never seen before
Infants falling
In the web of sudden geometries
And caution awry
In the power of these hearts
O tower in the dark
Chord in perfume
Day of wrath
Morning of delusion
The iron crow wings
Bear away the torn head
Into the fragile sky
Into the rapture of the depths
Where the blood runs cold

TRAVELERS IN EREWHON

You open your
Dress on the dusty
Bed where no one
Has slept for years
An owl moans on the roof
You say
My dear my
Dear
In the smoky light of the old
Oil lamp your shoulders
Belly breasts buttocks
Are all like peach blossoms
Huge stars far away far apart
Outside the cracked window pane
Immense immortal animals
Each one only an eye
Watch

You open your body
No end to the night
No end to the forest
House abandoned for a lifetime
In the forest in the night
No one will ever come
To the house
Alone
In the black world
In the country of eyes

OAXACA 1925

You were a beautiful child
With troubled face, green eyelids
And black lace stockings
We met in a filthy bar
You said
"My name is Nada
I don't want anything from you
I will not take from you
I will give you nothing"
I took you home down alleys
Splattered with moonlight and garbage and cats
To your desolate disheveled room
Your feet were dirty
The lacquer was chipped on your fingernails
We spent a week hand in hand
Wandering entranced together
Through a sweltering summer
Of guitars and gunfire and tropical leaves
And black shadows in the moonlight
A lifetime ago

GRADUALISM

We slept naked
On top of the covers and woke
In the chilly dawn and crept
Between the warm sheets and made love
In the morning you said
"It snowed last night on the mountain"
High up on the blue black diorite
Faint orange streaks of snow
In the ruddy dawn
I said
"It has been snowing for months
All over Canada and Alaska
And Minnesota and Michigan
Right now wet snow is falling
In the morning streets of Chicago
Bit by bit they are making over the world
Even in Mexico even for us"

OPEN THE BLIND

Nests in the caves stir in the dawn
Ephemeral as our peace
Morning prayer
Grace before food
I understand
The endless sky the small earth
The shadow cone
Your shining
Lips and eyes
Your thighs drenched with the sea
A telescope full of fireflies
Innumerable nebulae all departing
Ten billion years before we ever met

HIGH PROVENCE

Every evening at seven o'clock
We met under the soaring swallows
In the dense shade of the ancient plane trees
At the same café table
On a little square of golden limestone houses
Dry grass and gravel
Where a fountain spoke softly
The language of the dwellers
In the center of the earth
Rose and green gold and blue
Smoke of olive and wine twigs
From the supper stoves
High up swallows
Laced the immense sky
We kissed in the perfumed evening
And walked off hand in hand
Along a winding road
Over a Roman bridge
Each bucket of the mossy mill wheel
That revolved so slowly
Through the vanishing water
From the dark underground
To the twilit sky
Held an aquarium
Full of brilliant fish
No one had ever seen before
We sat on the hillside and looked back
Over the town and counted the bells
And the new stars
Hazy hair flesh like a plume
Did you watch this half moon
Ten hours ago when it went by
The end of your steep street
Swimming over the Mediterranean

CAMARGUE

Green moon blaze
Over violet dancers
Shadow heads catch fire
Forget forget
Forget awake aware dropping in the well
Where the nightingale sings
In the blooming pomegranate
You beside me
Like a colt swimming slowly in kelp
In the nude sea
Where ten thousand birds
Move like a waved scarf
On the long surge of sleep

AMONG THE CYPRESSES AT THE END OF THE WAY OF THE CROSS

Will you eat water melon
Or drink lemonade
Beside San Miniato
This hot twilight
Arno blurring in its white dry cobbled bed
Wine honey olive oil
Fill the air with their secret vapors
And a black potter
Treads treads treads
Her wheel shaping a pot
With a template cut from your flesh
Lovers whimper in the dusk
We are lost do you hear
We are all lost
As the hundred bells break
And the stars speak

SOTTOPORTICO SAN ZACCARIA

It rains on the roofs
As it rains in my poems
Under the thunder
We fit together like parts
Of a magic puzzle
Twelve winds beat the gulls from the sky
And tear the curtains
And lightning glisters
On your sweating breasts
Your face topples into dark
And the wind sounds like an army
Breaking through dry reeds
We spread our aching bodies in the window
And I can smell the odor of hay
In the female smell of Venice

LEAVING L'ATELIER – AIX-EN-PROVENCE

Bare trees
Smoky lavender twigs
All the world
Receding horizontal grey blue panels
Ochre walls
Piebald pink tile roofs
Black jagged olive trees killed in the winter of great cold
Everywhere feathers of silver green new olive sprouts
Everywhere red brown plowed fields
Stubs of waiting vines
Hoarfrost on the dark purple plum buds
A black white and green magpie
In wavy flight
Under the morning moon

TIME IS AN INCLUSION SERIES SAID McTAGGART

Five Poems on This Subject

I

In just a minute we will say goodbye
I will drive away and see you
Cross the boulevard in the rear view mirror
Maybe you will make out the back of my head
Disappearing in the traffic
And then we will never see one another ever again
It will happen in just another minute now

II

Willow Street
Street of bitter leaves
Three generations of whores in the windows
Mother daughter granddaughter
Whose fox are you
Nobody's fox I'm a lone fox
A lone black fox a lone blue fox
Blue fox that's me
The best head on Willow Street
She's dead Helen is dead Dolores is dead
Willow Street is only an embayment
In a ten-story housing project
Willow Street is gone along with
The street of bad boys the street of bad girls
The street where the heart rests
Will they leave even a tiny alley
To name after me

III

Talk in a dark room
Birds fly into the clouded mirror
And never come back
The mirror wears out

IV

For a very long time now
I have been following a black vine
I cannot find the root
I cannot find the tip
There is a high wall of thorns
There is a thick wall of thorns
Around an unknown castle
The thorns are covered with flowers
Each flower is different
But their odor is the perfume
Of a body I have lost

V

Thousands of white scattered
Petals on the waters of hours
Moonlight music surging sea
Commonplace sentiments
Heartbreaks and kisses
Singing voices and voices
Far down the misty beach
By the driftwood fires
Singing forever forever

PHAEDO

After Midnight Mass
In the first black subzero hour of Christmas
I take a twig and white piece of paper
And show you the fragile shadow of Sirius
The Dog Star guarding the Manger
Sleeping at the foot of the Cross

PARK IN THE PUBLIC'S
OR IN THE PUBLIC, PARKS

for Parks Hitchcock's magazine KYACK

Cessible
Inack
Cessibleinack
In Nyack
Inaccessible the evidence is
They are all intransitive
You can't get Through
You can't get Anyplace
Not with them Zeno knew it
You know Zeno
Zenon Cruel Zenon D'Elée
M. Zenon
Cessible
Inack
On the Isle of Dogs
In the Horse Latitudes
Gentlemen by the Bowels of Christ I regret that I have
    only one fox to feed for my country that is what
    Bishop Latimore said as he was being bit and et
        in the Horse Latitudes

Cessible cessible
In Nyack
N.Y.

Attached to their harpoons by long rawhide cords were
inflated whole seal skins a couple of seals of air to each
harpoon they came as close as possible and rammed
home the harpoons by main force the whale dove but the
floats of sealskin pulled him back to the surface again
and then they would ram in another harpoon and finally
when he was worn out the leader would come directly
up to his snout and stab him through the eye into the
brain

You wouldn't think Eskimos could do that would you
The whale is comparatively inaccessible to Stone Age Man
And the Eskimos unless they tempt Fate are inaccessible to the
whale

In Nyack
N.Y.

Cessible
Inack

Not in a
Kyack

SONG FOR A DANCER

I dream my love goes riding out
Upon a coal black mare.
A cloud of dark all about
Her – her floating hair.

She wears a short green velvet coat.
Her blouse is of red silk,
Open to her swan like throat,
Her breasts white as milk.

Her skirt is of green velvet, too,
And shows her silken thigh,
Purple leather for her shoe,
Dark as her blue eye.

From her saddle grows a rose.
She rides in scented shade.
Silver birds sing as she goes
This song that she made:

"My father was a nightingale,
My mother was a mermaid.
Honeyed notes that never fail
Upon my lips they laid."

OTTFFSSENTE

twelve
a dozen
a docent
a hundred does in the zendo
does
1905
down on Victoria Nyazi
The African Princess by Erasmus B. Black
The Lady or the Tiger by Claude Balls
does
dozing sing do
oh do
from dark to full fill filled and fully factual
does
there is at least an entity *a*
there is at least an entity not *a* called *b*
fundamental to the assumption of duality
is the assumption that the class of classes

is itself a class
that's what *b* is
don't you see
A B C D
goldfish
out of order springs the multifarious world
out of order
oh do
everything going joyfully everywhere
in all the gleaming myriad dimensions of space
do do
oh do
to the mathematically mature it is well known that there
is no such thing as the correct missing number in any
specified sequence. It is possible to insert any number whatever
and find a formula which will justify the sequence term for term
but the does were missing
from the zendo garden
a dozen does
and the singular literate goldfish
from the crystal deep
said the knowing
docent to the dozen
unknowing
dozing
Africans
who said
oh do
sing
so the Princess
the lady
Claude
and the Tiger
all sang
do.

CINQUE TERRE

A voice sobs on colored sand
Where colored horses run
Athwart the surf
Us alone in the universe
Where griefs move like the sea
Of the love lost
Under the morning star
Creeping down the sky
Into pale blind water
And we make love
At the very edge of the cliff
Where the vineyards end
In a fringe of ancient
Silver olive trees

TOOK

take it bright day first hour
single chime clear water one thought
nobody has it
take age
take again
take anger
take anguish
point take point
or yellow collars question
take and take
nobody
nobody rode the sheep and has it
take nobody and got away nobody
so bright and salty
so bright and blue
young nobody has it

take girlish
and fans and blades
and glittering scales
take time
and mark it
dogged dogged
but what dogged
makes merry
takes and calves answers
each each
when the bears are polar
it all goes round and round
and rockets and rackets
take time take time
the time nobody ever had
take it all away take it far away
                                        and
                                        hide
it somewhere under the fine sand filled with shards of pots shaped
    like the torsos of splendor where everything is hidden and
    never will be deciphered and all the camels will die before
    anybody gets there and not one of the angels will ever come
    back
as
took

A FLUTE OVERHEARD

Grey summer
Low tide the sea in the air
A flute song
In a neighboring house
Forty years ago
Socrates on death
The pages turn

The clear voice
Sea fog in the cypress
My daughter calls
From the next room
After forty years
A girl's candid face
Above my desk
Twenty-five years dead
Grey summer fog
And the smell of the living sea
A voice on the moving air
Reading Socrates on death

THE WHEEL REVOLVES

You were a girl of satin and gauze
Now you are my mountain and waterfall companion.
Long ago I read those lines of Po Chü-i
Written in his middle age.
Young as I was they touched me.
I never thought in my own middle age
I would have a beautiful young dancer
To wander with me by falling crystal waters,
Among mountains of snow and granite,
Least of all that unlike Po's girl
She would be my very daughter.

The earth turns towards the sun.
Summer comes to the mountains.
Blue grouse drum in the red fir woods
All the bright long days.
You put blue jay and flicker feathers
In your hair.
Two and two violet green swallows
Play over the lake.

The blue birds have come back
To nest on the little island.
The swallows sip water on the wing
And play at love and dodge and swoop
Just like the swallows that swirl
Under and over the Ponte Vecchio.
Light rain crosses the lake
Hissing faintly. After the rain
There are giant puffballs with tortoise shell backs
At the edge of the meadow.
Snows of a thousand winters
Melt in the sun of one summer.
Wild cyclamen bloom by the stream.
Trout veer in the transparent current.
In the evening marmots bark in the rocks.
The Scorpion curls over the glimmering ice field.
A white crowned night sparrow sings as the moon sets.
Thunder growls far off.
Our campfire is a single light
Amongst a hundred peaks and waterfalls.
The manifold voices of falling water
Talk all night.
Wrapped in your down bag
Starlight on your cheeks and eyelids
Your breath comes and goes
In a tiny cloud in the frosty night.
Ten thousand birds sing in the sunrise.
Ten thousand years revolve without change.
All this will never be again.

ORGANIZATION MEN IN AFFLUENT SOCIETY

It is deep twilight, my wife
And girls are fixing supper
In the kitchen. I turn out

The reading lamp and rest my eyes.
Outside the window the snow
Has turned deep blue. *Antony
and Cleopatra* after a trying day. I think of
Those vigorous rachitic
Men and women taking off
Their clothes of lace and velvet
And gold brocade and climbing
Naked into bed together
Lice in their stinking perfumed
Armpits, the bed full of bugs.

THE HANGED MAN

Storm lifts from Wales
And blows dark over England,
And over my head
As I stand above the Teme,
And look out across Ludlow and the dark castle,
And the ringing church tower.
Clear bells on the storm,
And grey rain on the river,
And me where I will not come again,
And pain I doubt that formal poet ever knew
Who wrote "This is me"
Anent the page of one too cowardly to love.
Ache and hunger fill the lives
Of those who dare not give or take.
Misery is all the lot of the unlovable ones,
And of rejected lovers,
But not one of these knows the empty horror
Of the slow conquering, long fought off,
Realization that love assumed and trusted
Through years of mutual life
Had never been there at all.

The bells of St. Lawrence
Sprinkle their music over the town.
Silver drops, gathered in Bermuda,
Shimmer and are lost in the brown English water.
It is all just like the poet said.

YIN AND YANG

It is spring once more in the Coast Range
Warm, perfumed, under the Easter moon.
The flowers are back in their places.
The birds back in their usual trees.
The winter stars set in the ocean.
The summer stars rise from the mountains.
The air is filled with atoms of quicksilver.
Resurrection envelops the earth.
Geometrical, blazing, deathless,
Animals and men march through heaven,
Pacing their secret ceremony.
The Lion gives the moon to the Virgin.
She stands at the crossroads of heaven,
Holding the full moon in her right hand,
A glittering wheat ear in her left.
The climax of the rite of rebirth
Has ascended from the underworld
Is proclaimed in light from the zenith.
In the underworld the sun swims
Between the fish called Yes and No.

THE HEART'S GARDEN, THE GARDEN'S HEART (1967)

For
Mary
Katharine
Carol

THE HEART'S GARDEN, THE GARDEN'S HEART

I

Young rice plants are just being
Transplanted. Tea bushes are
Low and compact. Eggplants are
Still under their little tents.
K'oto meadows, samisen
Lakes, mountain drums; water flutes
Falling all night in moonlight.
Migrating birds twitter on
The roofs. Azaleas bloom.
Summer opens. A man of
Sixty years, still wandering
Through wooded hills, gathering
Mushrooms, bracken fiddle necks,
And bamboo shoots, listening
Deep in his mind to music
Lost far off in space and time.
The valley's soul is deathless.
It is called the dark woman.
The dark woman is the gate
To the root of heaven and earth.
If you draw her out like floss
She is inexhaustible.
She is possessed without effort.
It was a green jacket, a green
Jacket with a yellow lining.
When will the heartbreak stop?
It was a green jacket, a green
Jacket with a yellow skirt.
When will the heartbreak go?
The evergreen pines grow more
Green as Spring draws to an end.
Yellow rice blades in blue water.

II

Pausing in my sixth decade
At the end of a journey
Around the earth – where am I?
I am sitting on a rock
Close beside a waterfall
Above Kurama Hot Springs
In the hills above Kyoto.
So I have sat by hundreds,
In the Adirondacks and
The Green Mountains of Vermont,
In the Massif Central, Alps,
Cascades, Rockies, Sierras,
Even Niagara long, long
Ago in a night of snow.
The water speaks the same language.
It should have told me something
All these years, all these places,
Always saying the same thing.
I should have learned more than I did,
My wit ought to have been more.
I am now older than I was,
In Winters and in lore.
What can I see before me
In the water's smoke and mist?
I should have learned something. "Who
Am I? What can I do? What can I
Hope?" Kant on Euler's bridges
Of dilemma in Koenigsberg.
Somewhere in some topology
The knots untie themselves,
The bridges are all connected.
Is that true? How do you know?
"What is love?" said jesting Pilate
And would not stay for an answer.
I have asked many idle

Questions since the day I could speak.
Now I have many Winters
But very few answers.
Age has me bestolen on
Ere I it wist.
Ne might I see before me
For smoke nor for mist. The smoke
And mist of the waterfall
Shifts and billows. The double
Rainbow remains constant.
There are more years behind me
Than years ahead, and have been
For a very long time. What
Remains in either pan of
The unstable balances of time?
Childbirth, love, and ecstasy
Activate nerves otherwise
Never used and so are hard
To recall, and visions are
The measure of the defect
Of vision. I loved. I saw.
All the way down to Kyoto,
And high above me on all
The ridges are temples full of
Buddhas. This village of stone
Carvers and woodcutters is
Its own illimitable Buddha world.
The illuminated live
Always in light and so do
Not know it is there as fishes
Do not know they live in water.
Under the giant cypresses
Amongst the mossy stones and
Bamboo grass there are white stars
Of dwarf iris everywhere.
The forest is filled with incense.
Boys' Day, the giant wind carp

Float in the breeze of early
Summer over all the houses
Of this mountain village.
The light, cheap, paper ones do.
The more durable cloth ones
Hardly lift and sway at all.
There are rocks on the earth
More durable than the
Constellations of heaven.
Gold leaves of feather bamboo
Fall through the warm wind of May
On to the white rectangle
Of raked gravel in the temple
Garden. Why does the bamboo shed
Its leaves at this time of year?
Smoky, oppressively hot,
The evening comes to an end.
An uguisu sings in the gnarled pine.
The cuckoos call in the ginko trees,
Just like they do in the old poems.
Swallows mate on the telephone wires.
A wood pigeon, speckled like
A quail, drinks from the dew basin.
The new leaves are just coming in.
The bamboos look like green gold smoke.
In the weavers' quarter
Beyond the temple walls,
As the noises of the day cease
I can hear the throb and clack
Of thousands of home looms.
Nishikigi – but no ghosts rise.
Gold fish swim in the moat, red
As fire, they burn in the brown
Water. The moat guards the scriptures
From fire, but the Buddha word
Is burning like the dry grass on
The Indian hills and like the stars.

How easy it is for men
To do right – the submarine
Green of young maple leaves on moss,
Fourteen trees and some earth bare
Of all but moss, and the light
Like Cours Mirabeau in Aix
Before greed destroyed it.
The turtle is the symbol
Of obscenity, but all
The moats that guard the scriptures
Are planted with honorable
Turtles. Turtle-san, protect
The Three Jewels, as the lewd
Pigeons in the air protect
The Great Void. When they rut and beg
In the gravel garden, they fill
Their craws with uncut stones.
"Vectors of reticulation."
We are defined by the webs
Of ten thousand lines of force.
Rocks surrounded by currents
Of raked gravel. Stripes of tigers
Playing in the bamboo shade.
Lichens on ruined dragon stones.
"When I see the wild chrysanthemum
Blooming in the crannies
Of the cliff, I try to forget
The glories of the capital."
The water ouzel walks on
The bottom under the torrent
And builds her nest behind the
Waterfall. Kurama River,
Kaweah River, it is
The same water ouzel although
It is a different species.

III

Gathering early morning
Mushrooms, the music of the
Waterfall washes my ears.
Jumbled rocks clog the clear stream
But the trout love the whirlpools
And riffles. K'ao P'an Tsai Kien.
Two thousand years ago that was
A synonym for happiness –
"Find a hut by a mountain stream."
Hard as stone, water glitters
Like a diamond, and makes a huge
Mountain towering into
The clouds, and carves out canyons
Ten thousand feet deep, and caps
The poles. The same water is
An invisible vapor
Which materializes
When it comes near the mountain.
Here, where bones and mud piled up
And turned to stone and made this
Mountain, the sea once stretched from
Horizon to horizon.
Deep under the shallow sea,
And in the monk's rosary
Amber remembers the pine.
Millions of pearls in the mist
Of the waterfall added
Together make a rainbow.
Deep in the heart one pearl glows
With ten million rainbows.
Weary of the twin seas of
Being and not-being, I
Long for the mountain of bliss
Untouched by the changing tides.
Deep in the mountain wilderness

Where nobody ever comes,
Only once in a while something
Like the sound of a far off voice,
The low rays of the sun slip
Through the dark forest and gleam
In pools on the shadowy moss.
Wild flowers and grass grow on
The ancient ceremonial
Stairs. The sun sinks between the
Forested mountains. The swallows
Who nested once in the painted
Eaves of the palaces of
The young prince are flying
This evening between the homes
Of woodcutters and quarrymen.
More ancient by far than the stairs
Are the cyclopean walls
Of immense, dry laid stones covered
With moss and ferns. If you approach
Quietly and imitate their
Voices, you can converse all day
With the tree frogs who live there.
Peach petals float on the stream
Past the rubbish of the village.
Twilight gathers in the mountain
Village. Peach petals scatter
On the stream at the boom of
The evening bell. All past and
Future sounds can be heard in
A temple bell. The mountain
Goes on being a mountain,
And the sea, a sea, but life
Is frail as a petal in
A world like an insect's shell.
I sit in the hot spring and
Wash my body, spotless from
Its creation, in radiant

Waters, virgin and electric
From the earth womb, pillowed on
Water, a pebble in my mouth.
Tired of the twin peaks of plus
And minus, I float in the
Unruffled sea.

IV

Water is always the same –
Obedient to the laws
That move the sun and the other
Stars. In Japan as in
California it falls
Through the steep mountain valleys
Towards the sea. Waterfalls drop
Long musical ribbons from
The high rocks where temples perch.
Ayu in the current poise
And shift between the stones
At the edge of the bubbles.
White dwarf iris heavy with
Perfume hang over the brink.
Cedars and cypresses climb
The hillsides. Something else climbs.
Something moves reciprocally
To the tumbling water.
It ascends the rapids,
The torrents, the waterfalls,
To the last high springs.
It disperses and climbs the rain.
You cannot see it or feel it.
But if you sit by the pool
Below the waterfall, full
Of calling voices all chanting
In a turmoil of peace,
It communicates itself.

It speaks in the molecules
Of your blood, in the pauses
Between your breathing. Water
Flows around and over all
Obstacles, always seeking
The lowest place. Equal and
Opposite, action and reaction,
An invisible light swarms
Upward without effort. But
Nothing can stop it. No one
Can see it. Over and around
Whatever stands in the way,
Blazing infinitesimals –
Up and out – a radiation
Into the empty darkness
Between the stars.

V

The water in a bottle
Has a bottle shape. A girl
In a dress has a girl shape.
The girl contains the dress.
The stone alone on the ground
Makes a sound like a sound.
The carp in the temple pool
Of the vegetarians
Grow forever. Where no waves
Wash the myriad sands
The thousand birds do not come.
Forty million school children
Sightseeing. Forty thousand
Old ladies praying. The prayer
Gong never stops ringing. Around
The corner past the formal
Garden, nobody climbs the
Mountain path to the waterfalls,

Where a ninety year old woman
Worships the Earth Womb,
Singing in a loud falsetto,
And clapping her hands,
As the waterspout splashes
On her thin white hair
And withered breasts.
After a long time walking
Up and down the long hall
And looking at the thousand
Kwannons through the incense smoke
And candle light I realize
That each one looks different.
The curve of the lips, the regard
Of the eye, is never quite
The same, never exactly the same
Gesture of the blessing hands.
He who hears the world's cry.
Thirty-three thousand thirty-three
Heads, each with a hundred arms
And eleven faces.
Unalike.
Chidori, chidori, crying
Kannon, Kannon, Kannon, Kannon.
Each sandpiper has a thousand
Wings. The birds of midocean
Leave the deep sea only to breed.
Japan is an island empire
With twenty million women
Each with ten thousand giggles
Every day. But consider
This heavy-eyed art student
With hair to her knees
On the lawn of the museum.
She has just finished smoking
A marijuana cigarette.
Now she is being tickled

By her lover.
As my horse's hooves
Splashed through the clear water
Of the ford at Sado the
Ten thousand birds rose crying
About us.
Chidori, chidori,
Kannon, Kannon,
Each bird with
Ten thousand wings.
He who hears
The crying of all the worlds.
At the end of an avenue
Of boars, like a line of sphinxes,
Is the temple of Marichi,
Patroness of geisha and whores,
And goddess of the dawn. The girl
Beside me tells me she was
A great Indian prostitute
Who was really an incarnate
Bodhisattva. The girl herself
Turned out to be a Communist.
I will not enter Nirvana
Until all sentient creatures are saved.
There is a street fair around
The Shinto shrine across the street
And its booths have overwhelmed
The precincts of Marichi.
It is their annual children's festival.
In the long warm evening
The mountains unfold above
Kamo River like a fan
Of wet silk dipped in thin ink.
At Daisenji the abbot's
Garden consists of two cones
Of gravel heaped to the angle
Of repose, surrounded by

A herring bone sea of raked
Gravel. Between the cones
Devadatta has thrown an empty
Film box, red and yellow,
The colors of fire. We meet
And touch and pass on, as log
Meets log in midocean.
On the screen in the guest house
Is a fan with a cock quail
Crying out alone amongst
Snow bound reeds. Deep evening
I walk home and see
The greatest of the gravel
Gardens of enlightenment,
A tire tracked gas station yard
With seven empty oil cans,
And a rack of used tires, and
A painting of an imbecile
Tiger in red and yellow fire.
The spread of the ripples
Is not due to its size
But is proportionate
To the hidden power
In the stone thrown in the pool.
The waves of the sea have
A number, the sands of the
Shores have a number, the birds
Of the air have a number.
There is no number for the
Saviors of the universes.

VI

The Eve of Ch'ing Ming – Clear Bright,
A quail's breast sky and smoky hills,
The great bronze gong booms in the
Russet sunset. Late tonight

It will rain. Tomorrow will
Be clear and cool once more. One more
Clear, bright day in this floating life.
The slopes of Mt. Hiei are veiled
In haze for the last day of Spring.
Spring mist turns to Summer haze
And hides the distant mountains,
But the first evening breeze
Brings the scent of their flowers.
I say a few words and the haze
Lifts from Mt. Hiei and trees
And temples and climbing people
Stand out as sharp as glass.
Three red pigeons on the sunbaked
Gravel, murmuring like the
Far off voices of people
I loved once. The turtles sleep
On the surface of the moat.
If belief and anxiety,
Covetousness and grasping,
Be banished from experience
Of any object whatever,
Only its essence remains,
Only its ultimate being.
He who lives without grasping
Lives always in experience
Of the immediate as the
Ultimate. The solution
Of the problem of knowing
And being is ethical.
Epistemology is moral.
The rutting cock pigeons fill
Their craws with cob from the wall.
Each has his territory,
Where, already this season,
He has dug a hole as big
As a tea cup. They defend

The holes against intrusion
Like they quarrel over the hens.
The knot tied without a rope
Cannot be untied. The seven
Bridges of Koenigsberg cannot
Be crossed but you can always
Go for a swim in the river.
The lower leaves of the trees
Tangle the sunset in dusk.
Awe perfumes the warm twilight.
St. John of the Cross said it,
The desire for vision is
The sin of gluttony.
The bush warbler sings in the
Ancient white pine by the temple
Of the Buddha of Healing.

VII

Tea drinking, garden viewing,
The voices of Japanese
Women are like happy birds.
A calico cat rolls in
The sun on the silky moss.
At the end of the branches
The youngest maple leaves are
As red as they will be again
This Autumn when they are old.
Another cat, brown as a mink.
Most Japanese don't like cats.
The monks at this temple are
Eccentrics. However in
The daytime their cats wear bells.
Birds are nesting in the maples.
The women are admiring
The iris and waterlilies.
Beyond the wall – Nishikigi –

The click of the looms –
In all this quarter they are
Weaving obis.
                                        "All day I
Work in the click of the looms.
At night I go out and play
Pachinko amidst the clinks
Of a hundred pinball machines."
The goddess of mercy has
A hundred arms. The steel balls
Fall from heaven to hell,
Bouncing through the wickets
Of circumstance. On the field
Of Law? On the field of chance.
Where Krishna drove, Arjuna fought.
All over Japan pinballs fall
Like the myriad gonads of the
Human race through history.
The clicks of the looms, the clinks
Of the wickets, are the random
Ticking of organic time.
Shizu, shizu, shizu, yo –
Bobbins whisper through the threads,
Endlessly repeating, "If
Only I could somehow make
Yesterday today."
Currite ducentes subtegmina currite fusi.
Two black swallow tailed butterflies
Hover over the two cats.
They are too old and wise to mind.
A cicada cries in the heat
Of late afternoon and then
A telephone bell answers him.
Is this right? Should Buddhist monks
Have telephones? Who hears
The worlds cry out in pain?
A young man with immense teeth

And stiff hair is working himself
Into a lather explaining
The contemplative mysteries
Of the garden to five
Remarkably beautiful
Young women. He sees neither
Garden nor girls. He sounds like
A cheerleader. A baby
Breaks away from its mother,
The lady who sells tickets,
And runs across the limitless sea
Of raked gravel, just where
The film box was yesterday.
Life is unruly in the
Zendo. What is the secret,
The reward of right contemplation?
The revelation that it is all
Gravel and moss and rocks and clipped
Shrubbery. That it doesn't
Symbolize anything at all.
The birds are quite aware
Of its meaning. They ignore
Monastery walls and are
Furiously mating everywhere
In the hot perfumed sunlight.
The secret of the moss garden
Is sprinkling it just enough,
Depending on the weather,
And sweeping it twice a day
So lightly the leaves are removed,
And the moss is stimulated.
Except for the ancient masterpiece
That hangs in the kakemono
The best calligraphy in this
Monastery is a white strip
Of plain typing paper, on it
In straightforward clerk's hand:

"These examples of cloud writing
By our saintly Zen Master
Are for sale for fifteen thousand yen each."
I am startled to discover
The *Papilio indra*
Has gone as the day grew cool
And the smaller black butterfly
I had thought was still him
Is one of the rarest that flies,
Found only in Kyoto.
Like the owl of Minerva
He is still flying as the sunset
Makes long patches of
Ruddy gold on moss and lichened
Maple trunks and the gongs
Ring for evening prayers
All about us, temple calling
To temple, and the doves in
The eaves murmur sleepily,
And the swallows fly one last
Circuit, and the bats come out
Under the half moon. I walk
Slowly away through the outer
Garden as the sounds of night,
Both of city and forest,
Grow around me. Outside the
Monastery workmen have
Been repairing the wall and
Have left three neat piles of rubbish.
Red earth, white gravel, yellow
Wet clay and straw. A little
Further along is a neat
Stack of cobbles. The ground is
Carefully swept between the
Four mounds and around a pine tree
And a stump cut off at ground
Level. The strokes of the broom

Make interlocked spirals in the dust.
On the other side of the wall
Is the famous garden, a long
Rectangle of white raked gravel
Separated from another
Equal rectangle of moss
With two standing rocks, a spreading
Pine, and some azalea bushes.
The bushes echo the shapes
Of the vast distant mountains.
The sea is placid. The forest
Drowses in the sunset. Far
Away the Himalayas
Guard the world from all trouble.
The hands move from gesture to
Gesture. "Peace to the earth."
"I protect you from evil."
"I am the source of power."
"I turn the orbits of the planets."
"The mind rests in the clear void."

VIII

The dust of man's trouble rises
And makes the sunset's rosy glow.
The full moon appears on the
Horizon above the temple
Of Dainichi as an
Immense, incomprehensible
Silence overwhelming the world,
The orb of wonder, not moving,
But growing like an obsession.
The salvation of Amida
Has enraptured both the monk
And the householder, but the
Prostitute worships in her
Own way all through the white night.

The promise of the vow of
The Bodhisattva is so
Powerful the stormy ocean of
Karma turns to an unruffled mirror.
The guardians of the gates
Of life cannot sleep for the
Cries of the winged bundles
Of consequence that fly from
Life to life, never finding bliss.
Chidori, chidori,
The looms and pachinko balls
Echo each other and the nightjar
Cries in the incense scented
Garden as the moon shadows move.
The rising of the real moon brings
No light, its setting no darkness.
Ecstasy is luxury.
The crystal mirror of man's affairs
Hangs in the star thinned heaven,
Transparent; nothing is reflected
In it. Only the ghosts of
Grasping, the imaginary
Permanent residents, are
Visible, a rabbit pounding
Bitter herbs, a toad, and a
Dancing virgin, an exiled thief.
Where is the three legged crow?
He is flying across the
Solar system to the moon –
The mascot of Dainichi.
My heart is not a mirror.
I cannot see myself in it.
If thee does not turn to the
Inner Light, where will thee turn?
Night deepens. In the corner of
The ceiling a black centipede
With fiery red feet lurks by the

Web of a terrified spider.
I rise from my book and fetch
A broom and save the spider.
Altair and Vega climb heaven.
Across the Milky Way the Eagle
Plays the Lyre with his rays.

IX

Under the full moon strange birds
Call in the ancient cedars
Behind the high temple walls.
Or perhaps they are tree toads,
Or the high clear notes come from
The clappers of watchmen monks.
They converse all the warm night.
Toak. tolk. tock. toak. toik. tok. tok.
The bamboos are like plumes of
Incense in the dim moonlight.
The branches of the cedars
Are like great black clouds. The moon
Travels from one to another
As we walk slowly under them.
Owls come and go without sound.
If the full moon is the symbol
Of Amida, who is the half moon?
The half moon is the embrace
Of Shaka and Tara.
Midnight.
The clatter of the looms
Is louder than when other
People are working. They are
Weaving a kimono with
Colors like the fluctuant
Ocean and an obi of
Flowers amongst rocks at the
Edge of the snow on a summer

Mountain. The owls stop flying
And cry from garden to garden.
A huge red moth flies around
The lantern. The butterflies
Sleep. So do the swallows.
So do the pigeons. So even
Do the bats. The air is sweet
With the scents of a May night,
And the faint smell of incense
At each temple gate. A bell.
And then gongs sound from every
Compound, and temple by temple,
The chanting of the monks.
The looms go on as they have always done.
    Click clack click click clack click
Cho Cho
    Click clack click click clack click
Cho Cho.

x

The sound of gongs, the songs of birds,
The chanting of men, floating wisps
Of incense, drifting pine smoke,
Perfume of the death of Spring –
The warm breeze clouds the mirror
With the pollen of the pines,
And thrums the strings of the lute.
Higher in the mountains the
Wild cherry is still blooming.
The driving mist tears away
And scatters the last petals,
And tears the human heart. Altair
And Vega climb to the zenith.
A long whistling wail on the flute,
The drummer makes a strangling cry.
And to the clacking of the sticks,

The weaving girl dances for
Her cowboy far across the
Cloudy River. Wings waver
And break. Pine boughs sigh in the
Dark. The water of life runs
Quick through dry reeds.
Under the full moon, a piercing
Fragrance spreads through the white night
Like the perfume of new snow.
An unknown tree has blossomed
Outside my cabin window.
In the warm night cold air drains
Down the mountain stream and fills
The summer valley with the
Incense of early Spring. I
Remember a grass hut on
A rainy night, dreaming of
The past, and my tears starting
At the cry of a mountain cuckoo.
Her bracelets tinkle, her anklets
Clink. She sways at her clattering
Loom. She hurries to have a new
Obi ready when he comes –
On the seventh day of the seventh
Month when the pachinko balls
Fall like meteor swarms.
        Click clack click click clack click
Cho Cho
        Click clack click click clack click
Cho Cho
        Toak. tolk. tock. toak. toik. tok. tok.
Chidori. Chidori.
Kannon. Kannon.
The great hawk went down the river
In the twilight. The belling owl
Went up the river in the
Moonlight. He returns to

Penelope, the wanderer
Of many devices, to
The final woman who weaves,
And unweaves, and weaves again.
In the moon drenched night the floating
Bridge of dreams breaks off. The clouds
Banked against the mountain peak
Dissipate in the clear sky.

Kyoto, 1967

A SONG AT THE WINEPRESSES

for Gary Snyder

It is the end of the grape
Harvest. How amiable
Thy dwellings, the little huts
Of branches in the vineyards
Where the grape pickers rested.
Adieu, paniers, vendanges sont faites.
Five months have passed. Here am I –
Another monastery
Garden, another waterfall,
And another religion,
Perched on the mountain's shoulder,
Looking out over fogbound
Santa Barbara. Cactus
And stone make up the garden,
At its heart a heavy cross.
Off behind the monastery,
Deep in the canyon, a cascade
Of living water, green and white,
Breaks the arid cliffs, twisting
Through yellow sandstone boulders,

Sycamores, canyon oaks, laurels,
Toyonberries, maples, pines.
Buzzards dream on the wing, high
On the rising morning air.
A canyon wren sings on a dead
Yucca stem. Over a high rock
Across the stream, a bobcat
Peeks at me for a moment.
A panting doe comes down to drink.
And then the same water ouzel
I just saw above Kyoto.
Passing through the dry valley
Of gum trees, they make it a place
Of springs, and the pools are filled
With water. Deep calls to deep
In the voice of the cataracts.
Loving kindness watches over
Me in the daytime and a song
Guards me all through the starlit night.
Altair and Vega are at
The zenith in the evening.
The cowboy has gone back
Across the Cloudy River.
The weaving girl is pregnant
With another year. The magpie
Wing bridge of dreams has dissolved.
The new wine dreams in the vat.
Low over the drowsy sea,
The sea goat moves towards the sun.
Richard of St. Victor says,
"Contemplation is a power
That coordinates the vast
Variety of perception
Into one all embracing
Insight, fixed in wonder on
Divine things – admiration,

Awe, joy, gratitude – singular,
Insuperable, but at rest."
The sparrow has found her a home,
The swallow a nest for herself,
Where she may raise her brood.
When we have tea in the loggia,
Rusty brown California towhees
Pick up crumbs around our feet.
The towhees were pets of the Indians.
They are still to be found on
The sites of old rancherías,
Waiting for the children to
Come and feed them acorn cakes.
Just so the swallows still nest
In the eaves of all the buildings
On the site of the vanished
Temple in Jerusalem.
Above us from the rafters
Of the loggia hang two wooden
Mexican angels; on their rumps
Are birds' nests. The Autumn sun
Is a shield of gold in heaven.
The hills wait for the early rain
To clothe them in blessings of flowers.
It is the feast of Raphael
The archangel, and Tobit
And the faithful dog.

Mt. Calvary, Santa Barbara, 1967

THE SPARK IN THE TINDER OF KNOWING

for James Laughlin

Profound stillness in the greystone
Romanesque chapel, the rush
Of wheels beyond the door only
Underlines the silence. The wheels
Of life turn ceaselessly.
Their hiss and clank is
The noiseless turning of the Wheel
Of the Law, that turns without
Moving, from zenith to nadir,
From plus to minus, from black to white.
Love turns the uncountable,
Interlocking wheels of the stars.
The earth turns. The sun sets.
A bolt of iron all on fire
Falls into the turning city.
Love turns the heart to an unknown
Substance, fire of its fire.
Not by flesh, but by love, man
Comes into the world, lost in
The illimitable ocean
Of which there is no shore.
The sea of circumstance where
The heart drowns is the sea of love.
The heart drinks it and it drinks
The heart – transubstantiation
In which the One drinks the Other
And the Other drinks the One.
The sea of fire that lights all being
Becomes the human heart.
No place. No place.
Moon. Sun. Stars. Planets.
Water. Rivers. Lakes. Ocean.
Fish in them. The swimming air.

Birds and their flying.
All turn to jewels of fire,
And then to one burning jewel.
The feathered heart flies upward
Out of this universe.
The broken heart loses its plumes
And hides in the earth until
It can learn to swim in the sea.
Empty the heart and peace will fill it.
Peace will raise it until it floats
Into the empyrean.
It is love that produces
Peace amongst men and calm
On the sea. The winds stop. Repose
And sleep come even in pain.
Peace and windlessness and great
Silence arise in midheaven.
That which appears as extant
Does not really exist,
So high above is that which truly is –
Reality enclosed in the heart,
I and not I, the One
In the Other, the Other
In the One, the Holy Wedding.
Innumerable are the arrows
In love's quiver and their flight
Defines my being, the ballistics
Of my person in time.

Cowley Fathers, Cambridge, 1968

LOVE IS AN ART OF TIME (1974)

For Carol

NOW THE STARLIT MOONLESS SPRING

Now the starlit moonless Spring
Night stands over the Fontaine
De Medicis, and the gold
Fish swim in the cold, starlit
Water. Yesterday, in the
New sunshine, lovers sat by
The water, and talked, and fed
The goldfish, and kissed each other.
I am in California
And evening is coming on.
Now it is morning in Paris
By the Fontaine de Medicis.
And the lovers will come today,
And talk and kiss, and feed the fish,
After they have had their coffee.

THE FAMILY

Late night
Coming back to Melbourne
From a party on the Kangaroo Plains,
We stop the car by a black pool.
The air is immobile, crystalline.
I get out, light a match,
And study my star map.
I blow out the match,
And overhead and before and below me,
Doubled in the unmoving water,
The million stars come on
That I have never seen before
And will never see again.
And there are the two
Daughter universes of my universe,

The Magellanic Clouds –
Two phosphorescent amoebas overhead,
And two in the bottomless water.

NO WORD

The trees hang silent
In the heat.....

Undo your heart
Tell me your thoughts
What you were
And what you are.....

Like bells no one
Has ever rung.

SCHATTEN KÜSSE, SCHATTEN LIEBE

after Heine

Shadow kisses, shadow love,
There is nothing else left now –
Faint electric traces
In the nerve cells of two brains.

The rain falls in the deep night –
Black streets, a distant city –
Far away, too far away –
Yes? Too far away from where?

Too far from time which passes?
Too far from flesh breaking change?

Too far from happiness
Which would not wait an instant?

Two heads alone in dark rooms,
Far apart in rainy night,
Shelter sparks of memory,
Lamps once blazing with kisses.

HAPAX

The Same Poem Over and Over

Holy Week. Once more the full moon
Blooms in deep heaven
Like a crystal flower of ice.
The wide winter constellations
Set in fog brimming over
The seaward hills. Out beyond them,
In the endless dark, uncounted
Minute clots of light go by,
Billions of light years away,
Billions of universes,
Full of stars and their planets
With creatures on them swarming
Like all the living cells on the earth.
They have a number, and I hold
Their being and their number
In one suety speck of jelly
Inside my skull. I have seen them
Swimming in the midst of rushing
Infinite space, through a lens of glass
Through a lens of flesh, on a cup of nerves.
The question is not
Does being have meaning,

But does meaning have being.
What is happening?
All day I walk over ridges
And beside cascades and pools
Deep into the Spring hills.
Mushrooms come up in the same spot
In the abandoned clearing.
Trillium and adder's tongue
Are in place by the waterfall.

A heron lifts from a pool
As I come near, as it has done
For forty years, and flies off
Through the same gap in the trees.
The same rush and lift of flapping wings,
The same cry, how many
Generations of herons?
The same red tailed hawks court each other
High on the same rising air
Above a grassy steep. Squirrels leap
In the same oaks. Back at my cabin
In the twilight an owl on the same
Limb moans in his ancient language.
Billions and billions of worlds
Full of beings larger than dinosaurs
And smaller than viruses, each
In its place, the ecology
Of infinity.
I look at the rising Easter moon.
The flowering madrone gleams in the moonlight.
The bees in the cabin wall
Are awake. The night is full
Of flowers and perfume and honey.
I can see the bees in the moonlight
Flying to the hole under the window,
Glowing faintly like the flying universes.
What does it mean. This is not a question, but
    an exclamation.

CONFUSION OF THE SENSES

Moonlight fills the laurels
Like music. The moonlit
Air does not move. Your white
Face moves towards my face.
Voluptuous sorrow
Holds us like a cobweb
Like a song, a perfume, the moonlight.
Your hair falls and holds our faces.
Your lips curl into mine.
Your tongue enters my mouth.
A bat flies through the moonlight.
The moonlight fills your eyes
They have neither iris nor pupil
They are only globes of cold fire
Like the deers' eyes that go by us
Through the empty forest.
Your slender body quivers
And smells of seaweed.
We lie together listening
To each other breathing in the moonlight.
Do you hear? We are breathing. We are alive.

BLUE SUNDAY

Chestnut flowers are falling
In the empty street that smells
Of hospitals and cooking.
The radio is breaking
Somebody's heart somewhere
In a dirty bedroom. Nobody
Is listening. For ten miles
In either direction
The houses are all empty.

Nobody lives in this city.
Outside the city limits
Are green and white cemeteries.
Nobody is in the graves.
At very long intervals
The broken cast iron fountain
In the courtyard sneezes and spurts.
In the dirty bedroom
Three young whores are shooting dice.
At very long intervals
One of them speaks to the dice.
Otherwise they are silent.
After the chestnut blossoms
Have all fallen the yellow
Sun will set and stars shine
Over the empty city
And papers blow down the street.

I DREAM OF LESLIE

You entered my sleep,
Come with your immense,
Luminous eyes,
And light brown hair,
Across fifty years,
To sing for me again that song
Of Campion's we loved so once.
I kissed your quivering throat.
There was no hint in the dream
That you were long, long since
A new arrivéd guest,
With blithe Helen, white Iope and the rest –
Only the peace
Of late afternoon
In a compassionate autumn

In youth.
And I forgot
That I was old and you a shade.

EDUCATION

Now to the dry hillside,
Terraced with crumbling limestone,
Where there were vineyards long ago,
Evening comes cool and violet
Under the olive trees, and only
The almond blossoms and the first stars
Are alight. Your fine lean hand
Like a spindle of light
Moves as you talk, as if
You were conducting a slow music.
What are you talking about?
You are explaining everything to me –
The abandoned olive grove,
The walls older than the Romans,
The flowering almond tree,
And the twilight darkening
Around the stars and around
Your speaking lips and moving hand.

PRIVACY

Dense fog shuts down
Between the hills.
I step out of my cabin.
You'd never know
It was in the midst of a forest.
Fog curls in the lighted doorway like smoke.

I hear the raccoon rustling
In the invisible thicket.
The cool dampness creeps under my clothes.
I thought I heard a car
Come up the road below me.
I walk cautiously through the fog
To the edge of the cutting.
I can see nothing.
Suddenly I hear
Beneath my feet
A man and a woman cry out with love.

PARITY

My uncle believed he had
A double in another
Universe right here at hand
Whose life was the opposite
Of his in all things – the man
On the other side of zero.
Sometimes they would change places.
Not in dreams, but for a moment
In waking, when my uncle
Would smile a certain sly smile
And pause or stagger slightly
And go about his business.

IT IS A GERMAN HONEYMOON

They are stalking humming birds
The jewels of the new world
The rufous hummingbird dives
Along his parabola

Of pure ether. We forgot –
An imponderable and
Invisible elastic
Crystal is the womb of space.
They wait with poised cameras
Focused telescopic lens
Beyond the crimson trumpet vine.
He returns squealing against
The sky deeper than six billion
Light years, and plunges through sun
Blaze to the blood red flower womb.
A whirling note in the lens of space.
"Birds are devas," says Morris
Graves. "They live in a world
Without Karma." No grasping,
No consequence, only the
Grace of the vectors that form
The lattices of the unending
Imponderable crystal.
The blond and handsome young man
And woman are happy, they
Love each other, when they have
Gone around the world they will
Sit in the Grunewald and
Look at a picture of a
California hummingbird.
Nobody can swim across
The Great River. Turn your back
And study the spotted wall.
Turn around on the farther shore.
Nine dice roll out, one by one.
The mouse eats them. They never were.
The hundred flowers put their
Heads together, yellow stamens and
Swelling pistils. Between them
In midspace they generate
A single seed. You cannot

Find it in a telescope.
Found, you could not see it in
An electron microscope.

BEI WANNSEE

Evening twirling
In a thousand thanks
The spindle glows
Pale water
Copper flows
Swans
Sails cluster and part again
Ripples
Mouths kiss and suck and part
The sun breaks in bands of haze
A silent exclamation
A white bird
A naked joy
A thousand thanks
The water becomes imaginary
The swans go
The lights come
Paler than water
The perfume of the bed of stock
Billows down the lawn and out
Over the water
Past the motionless scarves of weeping willow
And up from the glittering boat
A flute spirals and says quietly
Like a waving light

A blonde

Come

A thousand thanks
A waving light.

RED MAPLE LEAVES

The maple leaves are brilliant
Over the tree lined streets.
The deep shade is filled
With soft ruddy light.
Soon the leaves will all have fallen.
The pale winter sunlight
Will gleam on snow covered lawns.
Here we were young together
And loved each other
Wise beyond our years.
Two lifetimes have gone by.
Only we two are left from those days.
All the others have gone with the years.
We have never seen each other since.
This is the first time I have ever come back.
I drive slowly past your home,
Around the block again and once again.
Beyond the deep pillared porch
Someone is sitting at the window.
I drive down by the river
And watch a boy fishing from the bridge
In the clear water amongst
Falling and floating leaves.
And then I drive West into the smoky sunset.

IT TURNS OVER

The lightning does not go out
But stays on in the sky all night
A waterfall of solid white fire
Red hands speak
In deaf and dumb language
Their green shadows
Projected on the orange sky
All the worms come out
All the eggs hatch
All the clouds boil away
Only Orion all alone in the zenith
Of midsummer midnight.

STAR AND CRESCENT

The air has the late summer
Evening smell of ripe foliage
And dew cooled dust. The last long
Rays of sunset have gone from
The sky. In the greying light
The last birds twitter in the leaves.
Far away through the trees, someone
Is pounding something. The new
Moon is pale and thin as a
Flake of ice. Venus glows warm
Beside it. In the abode
Of peace, a bell calls for
Evening meditation.
As the twilight deepens
A voice speaks in the silence.

LA VIE EN ROSE

Fog fills the little square
Between Avenue du Maine
And the Gaîté Montparnasse.
I walk around and around,
Waiting for my girl.
My footsteps echo
From the walls
Of the second storeys.
Deep in the future
My ghost follows me,
Around and around.

VOID ONLY

Time like glass
Space like glass
I sit quiet
Anywhere Anything
Happens
Quiet loud still turbulent
The serpent coils
On itself
All things are translucent
Then transparent
Then gone
Only emptiness
No limits
Only the infinitely faint
Song
Of the coiling mind
Only.

SUCHNESS

In the theosophy of light,
The logical universal
Ceases to be anything more
Than the dead body of an angel.
What is substance? Our substance
Is whatever we feed our angel.
The perfect incense for worship
Is camphor, whose flames leave no ashes.

LATE HALF MOON

Late half moon
High over head.
Shaka merges with Tara.
The dark bride possesses her lover.
Two moaning owls fly from the
Pine to the cypress.
The largest telescope
Reveals more nebulae
Outside our galaxy
Than stars within it –
There are more cells
In a single brain.
The sands of all the seas
Have a number.
The red shift –
The mortal soul
In its immortal body.
Light tires and wears out,
Travelling through space.
The owls mate
In the moonfilled dawn.

YOUR BIRTHDAY IN THE CALIFORNIA MOUNTAINS

A broken moon on the cold water,
And wild geese crying high overhead,
The smoke of the campfire rises
Toward the geometry of heaven –
Points of light in the infinite blackness.
I watch across the narrow inlet
Your dark figure comes and goes before the fire.
A loon cries out on the night bound lake.
Then all the world is silent with the
Silence of autumn waiting for
The coming of winter. I enter
The ring of firelight, bringing to you
A string of trout for our dinner.
As we eat by the whispering lake,
I say, "Many years from now we will
Remember this night and talk of it."
Many years have gone by since then, and
Many years again. I remember
That night as though it was last night,
But you have been dead for thirty years.

THE FLOWER SUTRA

Deep drowsy shade under the broad leaves,
The dusty plain far below dim with haze,
Picking flowers – bush clover, gold banded lily,
Bell flower, wild pink, while a mountain cuckoo
Flutters about, watching me and crying,
"Kegonkyo."

EARTH SKY SEA
TREES BIRDS
HOUSE
BEASTS FLOWERS

"COLD BEFORE DAWN"

Cold before dawn,
Off in the misty night,
Under the gibbous moon,
The peacocks cry to each other,
As if in pain.

"A COTTAGE IN THE MIDST"

A cottage in the midst
Of a miniature forest.
The only events are the distant
Cries of peacocks, the barking
Of more distant dogs
And high over head
The flight of cawing crows.

"PAST AND FUTURE FALL AWAY"

Past and future fall away.
There is only the rose and blue
Shimmer of the illimitable
Sea surface.
No place.
No time.

"Slowly the moon rises"

Slowly the moon rises
Over the quiet sea.
Slowly the face of my beloved
Forms in my mind.

"Moonless night"

Moonless night.
In the black heavens
The eye goes ten million miles.
Melancholy fills the heart.

"Spring puddles give way"

Spring puddles give way
To young grass.
In the garden, willow catkins
Change to singing birds.

"A dawn in a tree of birds"

A dawn in a tree of birds.
Another.
And then another.

“PAST MIDNIGHT”

Past midnight,
In the dark,
Under the winter stars,
Tendrils of ice
Creep through the duckweed.

“AS THE YEARS PASS”

As the years pass,
The generations of birds pass too.
But you must watch carefully.
The same towhees and jays
Seem to have been in the same places
To thousands of generations of men.

“IN THE DARK FOREST THE WHISPER”

In the dark forest the whisper
Of a million leaves.
On the deep sea the sigh
Of a million waves.

“A LONG LIFETIME”

A long lifetime
Peoples and places
And the crisis of mankind –
What survives is the crystal –
Infinitely small –
Infinitely large –

THE CITY OF THE MOON

for Kimiko Nakazawa

I

The sun sets as the moon
Rises. The red maple leaves
Fade to the color
Of an aging heart.

II

In the fine warm rain
Falling over the late turning
Maple leaves, an uguisu
Sings as if in Spring.

III

The East Wind brings clouds
And rain. In the ruffled pond
Happy goldfish play.
But it is the end
Of the eleventh month, warm,
Unseasonably.

IV

Although I am far from home
The red maple leaves
Over the old pond
Of the temple garden
Are falling with the
Plum leaves by my own window.

V

No, I did not say a word.
It is useless to
Pretend that the sound of rain
Is a human voice.

I shall have the banana
Trees by my window destroyed.
The pattering of
The rain sounds like the weeping
Of all the spirits
Of the air, and the
Wind tearing the leaves sounds like
The sound of ripped silk.

VI

In a waking dream,
A princess of the old time
Comes to me over
The twisting foot bridge,
Through the midst of the marsh
Of yellow iris
And lightly touches my lips.
The delicate sensation
Of utter intimacy
Lingers as the light goes out,
And the leaves of the iris
Murmur and rustle
In the twilight wind.

VII

Although the great plane
Flies away toward the sun,

The morning raven
Will still perch on the balcony
Of the Ueno Park of the heart.

VIII

The New Year

Midnight passes –
A new year – Orion strides
Into the warm waves
Westward to Yamashina
Where the red and gold
Of a glorious Autumn
Lie under the snow.

IX

Ichō

The plane rises through
Snowing clouds. Far beneath two
Autumn ginkos blaze,
Burning gold in the harsh
Night lights of Tokyo.

X

Buddha took some Autumn leaves
In his hand and asked
Ananda if these were all
The red leaves there were.
Ananda answered that it
Was Autumn and leaves
Were falling all about them,
More than could ever

Be numbered. So Buddha said,
"I have given you
A handful of truths. Besides
These there are many
Thousands of other truths, more
Than can ever be numbered."

XI

Clouds are the thoughts of
Heaven. It is difficult
To read the thoughts of
Other people, but you can
Always read those of heaven.

Kyoto
November 1972

IMITATIONS OF THE CHINESE

for Ling

THE FALL OF CH'OU

Jade pendants chime before the dawn audience.
Peach blossoms drown in the swollen stream.
Barbarian fires overwhelm the guards.
Together two skylarks rise towards heaven.
Two hearts singing like chiming jade.

ERINNERUNG

At the door of my thatched hut,
Buried deep in the forested mountains,
The wind in the ancient ginko tree
Sounds like the rustle of brocaded silk.

LOST LOVE

Geese fly from North to South
You are far away in
The East. The West wind will carry
A message to the East, but
Here in the Far West, the East
Wind never blows.

THE MORNING STAR (1979)

To Carol

THE LOVE POEMS OF MARICHIKO

To Marichiko
Kenneth Rexroth

To Kenneth Rexroth
Marichiko

I

I sit at my desk.
What can I write to you?
Sick with love,
I long to see you in the flesh.
I can write only,
"I love you. I love you. I love you."
Love cuts through my heart
And tears my vitals.
Spasms of longing suffocate me
And will not stop.

II

If I thought I could get away
And come to you,
Ten thousand miles would be like one mile.
But we are both in the same city
And I dare not see you,
And a mile is longer than a million miles.

III

Oh the anguish of these secret meetings
In the depth of night,
I wait with the shoji open.
You come late, and I see your shadow
Move through the foliage
At the bottom of the garden.
We embrace – hidden from my family.
I weep into my hands.
My sleeves are already damp.
We make love, and suddenly
The fire watch loom up
With clappers and lantern.
How cruel they are
To appear at such a moment.
Upset by their apparition,
I babble nonsense
And can't stop talking
Words with no connection.

IV

You ask me what I thought about
Before we were lovers.
The answer is easy.
Before I met you
I didn't have anything to think about.

V

Autumn covers all the world
With Chinese old brocade.
The crickets cry, "We mend old clothes."
They are more thrifty than I am.

VI

Just us.
In our little house
Far from everybody,
Far from the world,
Only the sound of water over stone.
And then I say to you,
"Listen. Hear the wind in the trees."

VII

Making love with you
Is like drinking sea water.
The more I drink
The thirstier I become,
Until nothing can slake my thirst
But to drink the entire sea.

VIII

A single ray in the dawn,
The bliss of our love
Is incomprehensible.
No sun shines there, no
Moon, no stars, no lightning flash,
Not even lamplight.
All things are incandescent
With love which lights up all the world.

IX

You wake me,
Part my thighs, and kiss me.
I give you the dew
Of the first morning of the world.

X

Frost covers the reeds of the marsh.
A fine haze blows through them,
Crackling the long leaves.
My full heart throbs with bliss.

XI

Uguisu sing in the blossoming trees.
Frogs sing in the green rushes.
Everywhere the same call
Of being to being.
Somber clouds waver in the void.
Fishing boats waver in the tide.
Their sails carry them out.
But ropes, as of old, woven
With the hair of their women,
Pull them back
Over their reflections on the green depths,
To the ports of love.

XII

Come to me, as you come
Softly to the rose bed of coals
Of my fireplace
Glowing through the night-bound forest.

XIII

Lying in the meadow, open to you
Under the noon sun,
Hazy smoke half hides
My rose petals.

XIV

On the bridges
And along the banks
Of Kamo River, the crowds
Watch the character "Great"
Burst into red fire on the mountain
And at last die out.
Your arm about me,
I burn with passion.
Suddenly I realize –
It is life I am burning with.
These hands burn,
Your arm about me burns,
And look at the others,
All about us in the crowd, thousands,
They are all burning –
Into embers and then into darkness.
I am happy.
Nothing of mine is burning.

XV

Because I dream
Of you every night,
My lonely days
Are only dreams.

XVI

Scorched with love, the cicada
Cries out. Silent as the firefly,
My flesh is consumed with love.

XVII

Let us sleep together here tonight.
Tomorrow, who knows where we will sleep?
Maybe tomorrow we will lie in the fields,
Our heads on the rocks.

XVIII

Fires
Burn in my heart.
No smoke rises.
No one knows.

XIX

I pass the day tense, day-
Dreaming of you. I relax with joy
When in the twilight I hear
The evening bells ring from temple to temple.

XX

Who is there? Me.
Me who? I am me. You are you.
You take my pronoun,
And we are us.

XXI

The full moon of Spring
Rises from the Void,
And pushes aside the net
Of stars, a pure crystal ball
On pale velvet, set with gems.

XXII

This Spring, Mercury
Is farthest from the sun and
Burns, a ray of light,
In the glow of dawn
Over the uncountable
Sands and waves of the
Illimitable ocean.

XXIII

I wish I could be
Kannon of eleven heads
To kiss you, Kannon
Of the thousand arms,
To embrace you forever.

XXIV

I scream as you bite
My nipples, and orgasm
Drains my body, as if I
Had been cut in two.

XXV

Your tongue thrums and moves
Into me, and I become
Hollow and blaze with
Whirling light, like the inside
Of a vast expanding pearl.

XXVI

It is the time when
The wild geese return. Between
The setting sun and
The rising moon, a line of
Brant write the character "heart."

XXVII

As I came from the
Hot bath, you took me before
The horizontal mirror
Beside the low bed, while my
Breasts quivered in your hands, my
Buttocks shivered against you.

XXVIII

Spring is early this year.
Laurel, plums, peaches,
Almonds, mimosa,
All bloom at once. Under the
Moon, night smells like your body.

XXIX

Love me. At this moment we
Are the happiest
People in the world.

XXX

Nothing in the world is worth
One sixteenth part of the love
Which sets free our hearts.
Just as the Morning Star in
The dark before dawn
Lights up the world with its ray,
So love shines in our hearts and
Fills us with glory.

XXXI

Some day in six inches of
Ashes will be all
That's left of our passionate minds,
Of all the world created
By our love, its origin
And passing away.

XXXII

I hold your head tight between
My thighs, and press against your
Mouth, and float away
Forever, in an orchid
Boat on the River of Heaven.

XXXIII

I cannot forget
The perfumed dusk inside the
Tent of my black hair,
As we awoke to make love
After a long night of love.

XXXIV

Every morning, I
Wake alone, dreaming my
Arm is your sweet flesh
Pressing my lips.

XXXV

The uguisu sleeps in the bamboo grove,
One night a man traps her in a bamboo trap,
Now she sleeps in a bamboo cage.

XXXVI

I am sad this morning.
The fog was so dense,

I could not see your shadow
As you passed my shoji.

XXXVII

Is it just the wind
In the bamboo grass,
Or are you coming?
At the least sound
My heart skips a beat.
I try to suppress my torment
And get a little sleep,
But I only become more restless.

XXXVIII

I waited all night.
By midnight I was on fire.
In the dawn, hoping
To find a dream of you,
I laid my weary head
On my folded arms,
But the songs of the waking
Birds tormented me.

XXXIX

Because I can't stop,
Even for a moment's rest from
Thinking of you,
The obi which wound around me twice,
Now goes around me three times.

XL

As the wheel follows the hoof
Of the ox that pulls the cart,
My sorrow follows your footsteps,
As you leave me in the dawn.

XLI

On the mountain,
Tiring to the feet,
Lost in the fog, the pheasant
Cries out, seeking her mate.

XLII

How many lives ago
I first entered the torrent of love,
At last to discover
There is no further shore.
Yet I know I will enter again and again.

XLIII

Two flowers in a letter.
The moon sinks into the far off hills.
Dew drenches the bamboo grass.
I wait.
Crickets sing all night in the pine tree.
At midnight the temple bells ring.
Wild geese cry overhead.
Nothing else.

XLIV

The disorder of my hair
Is due to my lonely sleepless pillow.
My hollow eyes and gaunt cheeks
Are your fault.

XLV

When in the Noh theater
We watched Shizuka Gozen
Trapped in the snow,
I enjoyed the tragedy,
For I thought,
Nothing like this
Will ever happen to me.

XLVI

Emitting a flood of light,
Flooded with light within,
Our love was dimmed by
Forces which came from without.

XLVII

How long, long ago.
By the bridge at Uji,
In our little boat,
We swept through clouds of fireflies.

XLVIII

Now the fireflies of our youth
Are all gone,
Thanks to the efficient insecticides
Of our middle age.

XLIX

Once again I hear
The first frogs sing in the pond.
I am overwhelmed by the past.

L

In the park a crow awakes
And cries out under the full moon,
And I awake and sob
For the years that are gone.

LI

Did you take me because you loved me?
Did you take me without love?
Or did you just take me
To experiment on my heart?

LII

Once I shone afar like a
Snow-covered mountain.
Now I am lost like
An arrow shot in the dark.

He is gone and I must learn
To live alone and
Sleep alone like a hermit
Buried deep in the jungle.
I shall learn to go
Alone, like the unicorn.

LIII

Without me you can only
Live at random like
A falling pachinko ball.
I am your wisdom.

LIV

Did a cuckoo cry?
I look out, but there is only dawn and
The moon in its final night.
Did the moon cry out
Horobirete! Horobirete!
Perishing! Perishing!

LV

The night is too long to the sleepless.
The road is too long to the footsore.
Life is too long to a woman
Made foolish by passion.
Why did I find a crooked guide
On the twisted paths of love?

LVI

This flesh you have loved
Is fragile, unstable by nature
As a boat adrift.
The fires of the cormorant fishers
Flare in the night.
My heart flares with this agony.
Do you understand?
My life is going out.
Do you understand?
My life.
Vanishing like the stakes
That hold the nets against the current
In Uji River, the current and the mist
Are taking me.

LVII

Night without end. Loneliness.
The wind has driven a maple leaf
Against the shoji. I wait, as in the old days,
In our secret place, under the full moon.
The last bell crickets sing.
I found your old love letters,
Full of poems you never published.
Did it matter? They were only for me.

LVIII

Half in a dream
I become aware
That the voices of the crickets
Grow faint with the growing Autumn.

I mourn for this lonely
Year that is passing
And my own being
Grows fainter and fades away.

LIX

I hate this shadow of a ghost
Under the full moon.
I run my fingers through my greying hair,
And wonder, have I grown so thin?

LX

Chilled through, I wake up
With the first light. Outside my window
A red maple leaf floats silently down.
What am I to believe?
Indifference?
Malice?
I hate the sight of coming day
Since that morning when
Your insensitive gaze turned me to ice
Like the pale moon in the dawn.

THE SILVER SWAN

poems and translations
written in Kyoto, 1974–1978

I

for Ruth Stephan

Twilit snow,
The last time I saw it
Was with you.
Now you are dead
By your own hand
After great pain.
Twilit snow.

II

As the full moon rises
The swan sings
In sleep
On the lake of the mind.

III

Orange and silver
Twilight over Yoshino.
Then the frosty stars,
Moving like crystals against
The wind from Siberia.

IV

Under the half moon
The field crickets are silent.
Only the cricket
Of the hearth still sings, louder
Still, behind the gas heater.

V

Late night, under the
Low, waning eleventh month
Moon, wild frosted kaki
On the bare branches gleam like
Pearls. Tomorrow they
Will be sweet as the
Honey of Summer.

VI

Asagumori

On the forest path
The leaves fall. In the withered
Grass the crickets sing
Their last songs. Through dew and dusk
I walk the paths you once walked,
My sleeves wet with memory.

VII

Void Only

I cannot escape from you.
When I think I am alone,
I awake to discover
I am lost in the jungle
Of your love, in its darkness
Jewelled with the eyes of unknown
Beasts. I awake to discover
I am a forest ascetic
In the impenetrable
Void only, the single thought
Of which nothing can be said.

VIII

Seven Seven

Can I come to you
When the cowboy comes to the
Weaving girl? No sea is as
Wide as the River of Heaven.

IX

The new moon has reached
The half. It is utterly
Incredible. One
Month ago we were strangers.

X

After Akiko – "Yoru no cho ni"

for Yasuyo

In your frost white kimono
Embroidered with bare branches
I walk you home New Year's Eve.
As we pass a street lamp
A few tiny bright feathers
Float in the air. Stars form on
Your wind blown hair and you cry,
"The first snow!"

XI

Late Spring.
Before he goes, the uguisu
Says over and over again
The simple lesson no man
Knows, because
No man can ever learn.

XII

Bride and groom,
The moon shines
Above the typhoon.

XIII

Only the sea mist,
Void only.
Only the rising
Full moon,
Void only.

XIV

Hototogisu – horobirete

The cuckoo's call, though
Sweet in itself, is hard to
Bear, for it cries,
"Perishing! Perishing!"
Against the Spring.

XV

Tsukutsukuboshi

In the month of great heat
The first bell cricket cries.
"It is time to leave."

XVI

New Year

The full moon shines on
The first plum blossoms and opens
The Year of the Dragon.
May happy Dragons
Attend you with gifts of joy.

XVII

An hour before sunrise,
The moon low in the East,
Soon it will pass the sun.
The Morning Star hangs like a
Lamp, beside the crescent,
Above the greying horizon.
The air warm, perfumed,
An unseasonably warm,
Rainy Autumn, nevertheless
The leaves turn color, contour
By contour down the mountains.
I watch the wavering,
Coiling of the smoke of a
Stick of temple incense in
The rays of my reading lamp.
Moonlight appears on my wall
As though I raised it by
Incantation. I go out
Into the wooded garden
And walk, nude, except for my
Sandals, through light and dark banded
Like a field of sleeping tigers.
Our raccoons watch me from the
Walnut tree, the opossums
Glide out of sight under the
Woodpile. My dog Ch'ing is asleep.
So is the cat. I am alone
In the stillness before the
First birds wake. The night creatures
Have all gone to sleep. Blackness
Looms at the end of the garden,
An impenetrable cube.
A ray of the Morning Star
Pierces a shaft of moon-filled mist.
A naked girl takes form
And comes toward me – translucent,

Her body made of infinite
Whirling points of light, each one
A galaxy, like clouds of
Fireflies beyond numbering.
Through them, star and moon
Still glisten faintly. She comes
To me on imperceptibly
Drifting air, and touches me
On the shoulder with a hand
Softer than silk. She says,
"Lover, do you know what Heart
You have possessed?"
Before I can answer, her
Body flows into mine, each
Corpuscle of light merges
With a corpuscle of blood or flesh.
As we become one the world
Vanishes. My self vanishes.
I am dispossessed, only
An abyss without limits.
Only dark oblivion
Of sense and mind in an
Illimitable Void.
Infinitely away burns
A minute red point to which
I move or which moves to me.
Time fades away. Motion is
Not motion. Space becomes Void.
A ruby fire fills all being.
It opens, not like a gate,
Like hands in prayer that unclasp
And close around me.
Then nothing. All senses ceased.
No awareness, nothing,
Only another kind of knowing
Of an all encompassing
Love that has consumed all being.

Time has had a stop.
Space is gone.
Grasping and consequence
Never existed.
The aeons have fallen away.

Suddenly I am standing
In my garden, nude, bathed in
The hot brilliance of the new
Risen sun – star and crescent gone into light.

XVIII

Midnight, the waning moon
Of midsummer glows
From the raindrops on
The first flowers of Autumn.

XIX

The drowned moon plunges
Through a towering surf
Of storm clouds, and momently
The wet leaves glitter.
Moment by moment an owl cries.
Rodents scurry, building
Their winter nests, in the moments of dark.

XX

Plovers cry in the
Dark over the high moorland,
The overtones of the sea,
Calling deep into the land.

XXI

Long past midnight, I walk out
In the garden after a
Hot bath, in yukata
And clogs. I feel no cold.
But the leaves have all fallen
From the fruit trees and the
Kaki hang there alone
Filled with frosty moonlight.
Suddenly I am aware
There is no sound
Not of insects nor of frogs nor of birds
Only the slow pulse of
An owl marking time for the silence.

XXII

Bright in the East
The morrow pure and pale
This hour, this is our last hourglass.
The parting forever of lovers
Is a double suicide
Of the consciousness.
By tens and thousands the stars go out.

XXIII

All This to Pass Never to Be Again

for Christina, Carol, and Kenneth

We feed the blue jays
Peanuts from our hands.
As the sun sets, the quarter moon
Shows pale as snow in the orange sky.

While we eat our high cuisine,
The moon, deep in the sky
Moves again in the pool,
And makes it deep as the sky
Where Scorpio moves with it,
Past the South. The crossroads
Of heaven glimmer with billions
Of worlds. The night cools.
We go indoors and talk
Of the wisdom and the
Insoluble problems of India.
Late in the night,
After the moon is down,
Coyotes sing on the hills.
How easy it is to put together
A poem of life lived
Simply and beautifully.
How steadily, as the age grows old,
The opportunity to do so narrows.

XXIV

Flowers sleep by the window.
The lamp holds fast the light.
Carelessly the window holds back the darkness outside.
The empty picture frames exhibit their contents,
And reflect the motionless flies on the walls.

The flowers hold themselves up against the night.
The lamp spins the night.
The cat in the corner spins the wool of sleep.
On the fire now and then the coffeepot snores with content.
Silent children play with words on the ground.

Set the white table. Wait for someone
Whose footsteps will never come up the stairs.

A train bores through the distant silence,
Never revealing the secret of things.
Destiny counts the clock ticks in decimals.

Gunnar Ekelof

XXV

October Mirror

Nerves grind quietly in the twilight
That flows grey and quiet past the window,
When red flowers fade quiet in the twilight
And the lamp sings to itself in the corner.

Silence drinks the quiet Autumn rain
Which no longer means anything to the harvest.
The hands warm their knuckles.
The eyes gaze quiet at the fading embers.

Gunnar Ekelof

XXVI

Equation

Only truth can explain your eyes
That sow stars in the vault of heaven,
Where the clouds float through a field of tones

(The flowers which are born out of nothing,
When your eyes make fate so simple,

And the stars fly away from the hive
In the blue-green waiting room of heaven)

And explain your rapport with destiny.

Gunnar Ekelof

XXVII

I look around,
No cherry blossoms,
No maple leaves,
Only a narrow inlet,
A thatched hut,
In the Autumn evening.

Fujiwara no Teika

XXVIII

I wonder if you can know
In the island of
Your heart, deprived of
Food, unable to escape,
How utterly banished I am.

Yosano Akiko

ON FLOWER WREATH HILL

for Yasuyo Morita

I

An aging pilgrim on a
Darkening path walks through the
Fallen and falling leaves, through
A forest grown over the
Hilltop tumulus of a
Long dead princess, as the
Moonlight grows and the daylight
Fades and the Western Hills turn
Dim in the distance and the
Lights come on, pale green
In the streets of the hazy city.

II

Who was this princess under
This mound overgrown with trees
Now almost bare of leaves?
Only the pine and cypress
Are still green. Scattered through the
Dusk are orange wild kaki on
Bare branches. Darkness, an owl
Answers the temple bell. The
Sun has passed the crossroads of
Heaven.

            There are more leaves on
The ground than grew on the trees.
I can no longer see the
Path; I find my way without

Stumbling; my heavy heart has
Gone this way before. Until
Life goes out memory will
Not vanish, but grow stronger
Night by night.
                    Aching nostalgia –
In the darkness every moment
Grows longer and longer, and
I feel as timeless as the
Two thousand year old cypress.

III

The full moon rises over
Blue Mount Hiei as the orange
Twilight gives way to dusk.
Kamo River is full with
The first rains of Autumn, the
Water crowded with colored
Leaves, red maple, yellow ginko,
On dark water, like Chinese
Old brocade. The Autumn haze
Deepens until only the
Lights of the city remain.

IV

No leaf stirs. I am alone
In the midst of a hundred
Empty mountains. Cicadas,
Locusts, katydids, crickets,
Have fallen still, one after
Another. Even the wind
Bells hang motionless. In the

Blue dusk, widely spaced snowflakes
Fall in perfect verticals.
Yet, under my cabin porch,
The thin, clear Autumn water
Rustles softly like fine silk.

V

This world of ours, before we
Can know its fleeting sorrows,
We enter it through tears.
Do the reverberations
Of the evening bell of
The mountain temple ever
Totally die away?
Memory echoes and reechoes
Always reinforcing itself.
No wave motion ever dies.
The white waves of the wake of
The boat that rows away into
The dawn, spread and lap on the
Sands of the shores of all the world.

VI

Clustered in the forest around
The royal tumulus are
Tumbled and shattered gravestones
Of people no one left in
The world remembers. For the
New Year the newer ones have all been cleaned
And straightened and each has
Flowers or at least a spray
Of bamboo and pine.
It is a great pleasure to

Walk through fallen leaves, but
Remember, you are alive,
As they were two months ago.

VII

Night shuts down the misty mountains
With fine rain. The seventh day
Of my seventieth year,
Seven-Seven-Ten, my own
Tanabata, and my own
Great Purification. Who
Crosses in midwinter from
Altair to Vega, from the
Eagle to the Swan, under the earth,
Against the sun? Orion,
My guardian king, stands on
Kegonkyoyama.
So many of these ancient
Tombs are the graves of heroes
Who died young. The combinations
Of the world are unstable
By nature. Take it easy.
Nirvana.
Change rules the world forever.
And man but a little while.

VIII

Oborozuki,
Drowned Moon,
The half moon is drowned in mist
Its hazy light gleams on leaves
Drenched with warm mist. The world
Is alive tonight. I am

Immersed in living protoplasm,
That stretches away over
Continents and seas. I float
Like a child in the womb. Each
Cell of my body is
Penetrated by a
Strange electric life. I glow
In the dark with the moon drenched
Leaves, myself a globe
Of St. Elmo's fire.

I move silently on the
Wet forest path that circles
The shattered tumulus.
The path is invisible.
I am only a dim glow
Like the tumbled and broken
Gravestones of forgotten men
And women that mark the way.
I sit for a while on one
Tumbled sotoba and listen
To the conversations of
Owls and nightjars and tree frogs.
As my eyes adjust to the
Denser darkness I can see
That my seat is a cube and
All around me are scattered
Earth, water, air, fire, ether.
Of these five elements
The moon, the mist, the world, man
Are only fleeting compounds
Varying in power, and
Power is only insight
Into the void – the single
Thought that illuminates the heart.
The heart's mirror hangs in the void.

Do there still rest in the broken
Tumulus ashes and charred
Bones thrown in a corner by
Grave robbers, now just as dead?
She was once a shining flower
With eyebrows like the first night's moon,
Her white face, her brocaded
Robes perfumed with cypress and
Sandalwood; she sang in the Court
Before the Emperor, songs
Of China and Turkestan.
She served him wine in a cup
Of silver and pearls, that gleamed
Like the moonlight on her sleeves.
A young girl with black hair
Longer than her white body –
Who never grew old. Now owls
And nightjars sing in a mist
Of silver and pearls.

The wheel
Swings and turns counterclockwise.
The old graspings live again
In the new consequences.
Yet, still, I walk this same path
Above my cabin in warm
Moonlit mist, in rain, in
Autumn wind and rain of maple
Leaves, in spring rain of cherry
Blossoms, in new snow deeper
Than my clogs. And tonight in
Midsummer, a night enclosed
In an infinite pearl.
Ninety-nine nights over
Yamashina Pass, and the
Hundredth night and the first night
Are the same night. The night

Known prior to consciousness,
Night of ecstasy, night of
Illumination so complete
It cannot be called perceptible.

Winter, the flowers sleep on
The branches. Spring, they awake
And open to probing bees.
Summer, unborn flowers sleep
In the young seeds ripening
In the fruit. The mountain pool
Is invisible in the
Glowing mist. But the mist-drowned
Moon overhead is visible
Drowned in the invisible water.

Mist-drenched, moonlit, the sculpture
Of an orb spider glitters
Across the path. I walk around
Through the bamboo grass. The mist
Dissolves everything else, the
Living and the dead, except
This occult mathematics of light.
Nothing moves. The wind that blows
Down the mountain slope from
The pass and scatters the spring
Blossoms and the Autumn leaves
Is still tonight. Even the
Spider's net of jewels has ceased
To tremble. I look back at
An architecture of pearls
And silver wire. Each minute
Droplet reflects a moon, as
Once did the waterpails of
Matsukaze and Murasame.

And I realize that this
Transcendent architecture
Lost in the forest where no one passes
Is itself the Net of Indra,
The compound infinities of infinities,
The Flower Wreath,
Each universe reflecting
Every other, reflecting
Itself from every other,
And the moon the single thought
That populates the Void.
The night grows still more still. No
Sound at all, only a flute
Playing soundlessly in the
Circle of dancing gopis.

ABOUT THE AUTHOR

KENNETH REXROTH (1905–1982) was one of the twentieth century's great literary minds, the author of fifty-four volumes of poetry, essays, and translations from a dozen languages. All of the important details of his life are discussed in his celebrated and controversial autobiography. *The Complete Poems* collects all of the original poetry he is known to have written, including early work that appeared in revolutionary magazines and a few later uncollected poems. Rexroth's poems of nature and protest are remarkable for their erudition and biting social and political commentary; his love poems are renowned for their incandescent eroticism and clarity of emotion; and his poems of transcendent wisdom bridge Eastern and Western traditions. Born in Indiana, he came of age in Chicago in the 1920s, and lived most of his life in San Francisco, where he was a central figure in the San Francisco Renaissance of the 1950s. He spent his last years in Santa Barbara, translating Chinese and Japanese women poets and promoting young women poets in America and Japan. While all the other graves in the Santa Barbara cemetery where he is buried face the continent, Rexroth's alone faces the Pacific.

ABOUT THE EDITORS

SAM HAMILL is the author of a dozen volumes of original poetry (including *Destination Zero: Poems 1970–1995*, *Gratitude*, and *Dumb Luck*); three collections of essays; and two dozen volumes translated from ancient Greek, Latin, Estonian, Japanese, and Chinese, including *Crossing the Yellow River: Three Hundred Poems from the Chinese*; *The Essential Chuang Tzu*; Bashō's *Narrow Road to the Interior & Other Writings*; and *The Erotic Spirit*. He has been the recipient of fellowships from the National Endowment for the Arts, the Guggenheim Foundation, the Lila Wallace–Reader's Digest Fund, the U.S.–Japan Friendship Commission, and the Andrew Mellon Fund, and of two Washington Governor's Arts Awards. He is director of the Port Townsend Writers' Conference and Founding Editor of Copper Canyon Press.

BRADFORD MORROW's novels include *Come Sunday*, *The Almanac Branch*, *Trinity Fields*, *Giovanni's Gift*, and most recently *Ariel's Crossing* (Viking). He founded and edits the literary journal *Conjunctions*. As Kenneth Rexroth's literary executor he has edited *The Selected Poems of Kenneth Rexroth*, *World Outside the Window: The Selected Essays of Kenneth Rexroth*, *Classics Revisited*, and *More Classics Revisited* (all New Directions). In 1998, the American Academy of Arts and Letters presented him with the Academy Award in Literature. He is a professor of literature at Bard College, and lives in New York.

A NOTE ON THE TEXT

Kenneth Rexroth varied spellings, often shifting between British and American spellings such as "grey" and "gray" or "color" and "colour." Sometimes such variant spellings imply political overtones, and at other times reflect the poet's extensive travels overseas. Rexroth was above all an internationalist, and the editors have in nearly all cases followed the poet's original text, assuming all spellings were intentional. In cases in which the transliteration of foreign words and names has changed over the years, such as "Mayakovsky" to "Mayakovski," we have retained the poet's spellings as representative of his time. "Kwannon" is a variant spelling of the Japanese incarnation of Avalokitesvara, "Kannon," or the Chinese "Kuan Yin," the bodhisattva of compassion; the added "w" represents an earlier transliteration, as found in the work of James Legge and Lafcadio Hearn, two translators with whose work Rexroth was intimately familiar. Here too, we have retained the poet's spelling as indicative of his working tradition.

"A Lantern and a Shadow" may well have been the intended title of an early collection of poems. The poems are clearly very early Rexroth, and he confirmed his authorship with Bradford Morrow, but the dates of composition and use of the title remain uncertain.

Many hands have contributed to this book in no small way, and foremost among them was Art Hanlon, who came to Rexroth's poetry while serving an internship at Copper Canyon Press and who worked indefatigably to track down and organize materials. Thanks also to Ken Knabb, whose scholarship contributed in many ways, including helping with the formidable challenge of proof reading. And special thanks to New Directions, Rexroth's primary publisher for many years, and without whose cooperation this book would not be possible.

APPENDIX

Following are Kenneth Rexroth's notes for the volume *The Morning Star* (New Directions, 1974).

THE LOVE POEMS OF MARICHIKO

Marichiko is the pen name of a contemporary young woman who lives near the temple of Marishi-ben in Kyoto.

Marishi-ben is an Indian, pre-Aryan, goddess of the dawn who is a bodhisattva in Buddhism and patron of geisha, prostitutes, women in childbirth, and lovers, and, in another aspect, once of samurai. Few temples or shrines to her or even statues exist in Japan, but her presence is indicated by statues, often in avenues like sphinxes, of wild boars, who also draw her chariot. She has three faces: the front of compassion; one side, a sow; the other a woman in ecstasy. She is a popular, though hidden, deity of tantric, Tachigawa Shingon. As the Ray of Light, the Shakti, or Prajna, the Power or Wisdom of Vairocana (the primordial Buddha, Dainichi Nyorai), she is seated on his lap in sexual bliss, Myōjō – the Morning Star.

Marichiko writes me, now that I am doing so many of her poems, in reference to the note on her in my *One Hundred More Poems from the Japanese*, "Although Marichi is the Shakti, or power, of the Indian god of the sun, she is the Prajna, or wisdom, of Dainichi Nyorai. Dainichi means Great Sun, but he is that only in a metaphorical sense, the Illuminator of the compound infinity of infinities of universes. The Buddhas and Bodhisattvas of Mahayana do not have Shaktis as consorts, for the simple reason that there is no such thing as power in Buddhism. Power is ignorance and grasping. With illumination, it turns into wisdom."

Notice, that like the English seventeenth-century poet Rochester, many of her poems turn religious verse into erotic, and she also turns traditional geisha songs into visionary poems. They therefore bear comparison with Persian Sufi poets, Hafidh, Attar, Sa'adi, and others, and with the Arab, Ibn el Arabi – with all of whom she is familiar in translation.

The series of poems, as should be obvious, form a sort of little novel and recall the famous *Diary of Izumi Shikibu* without the connecting prose. Notice that the sex of the lover is ambiguous.

Poem IV. Echoes Fujiwara no Atsutada, "Ai minto no."

Poem V. Narihira compares the leaf covered water of Tatsuta River to Chinese old brocade.

Poem VI. Echoes several "honeymoon houses," the modern one by Yosano Akiko.

Poem VII. Echoes a passage in the *Katha Upanishad.*

Poem VIII. Echoes a passage in the *Katha Upanishad.*

Poem XI. The uguisu, often translated "nightingale," is not a nightingale and does not sing at night. It is the Japanese bush warbler, *Horeites cantans cantans*, or *Cettia diphone.*

Poem XIV. Refers to the Festival, Daimonji Okuribi, sending of the dead back to heaven, when huge bonfires in the shape of characters are lit on the mountain sides around Kyoto. There is a paraphrase of Buddha's Fire Sermon and a paraphrase of Rilke's paraphrase of that.

Poem XVI. Based on a geisha song in many forms.

Poem XVII. Either the poem on Hitomaro's (Japan's greatest poet – b.?–d. 739) death or his own poem on a friend's death.

Poem XX. This poem, though syntactically barely possible, would be inconceivable in classical Japanese.

Poem XXI. There is an implied reference to the doctrine of Void Only and then to the Avatamsaka Sutra (Kegongyo) as the Net of Indra.

Poem XXII. The ray of light of the Morning Star – Marishiten – Myōjō.

Poem XXIII. Both forms of Kannon (Avalokitesvara) are common statues. Sanjusangendo, across from the Kyoto Art Museum, is a hall of over a thousand such, each very slightly different.

Poem XXVI. Brant, *Branta bernicia* is Japanese Koku-gan, are small, dark geese, who winter in the north of Honshu, the main island. Unlike many birds of the family, they do not fly in arrow formations, but in an irregular line.

Poem XXVII. The horizontal mirror is a narrow mirror, closed by sliding panels, alongside the bed in many Japanese inns (ryokan). Shunga erotic woodblock prints, representing them, are usually called "seen through the slats of a bamboo screen" by Westerners – Japanese until recent times had nothing resembling our venetian blinds.

Poem XXX. Echoes the Buddhist sutra Itivuttaka, III, 7.

Poem XXXI. Echoes the Buddhist sutra, Samyutta Nikaya, II, 3, 8.

Poem XXXII. "Orchid boat" is a metaphor for the female sexual organ.

Poem XXXIII. Echoes Yosano Akiko.

Poem XXXVI. Shoji – sliding doors or windows with "panes" of paper.

Poem XXXVIII. Ono no Komachi (834–880) is certainly Japan's greatest woman poet. Marichiko echoes her most famous poem – "Hito no awan / Tsuki no naki ni wa / Omoiokite / Mune hashibiri ni / Kokoro yakeori."

Poem XL. Echoes the first lines of the Dhammapada, the ancient popular exposition of Theravada Buddhism.

Poem XLI. Echoes an anonymous poem usually attributed to Hitomaro.

Poem XLII. Echoes a Buddhist sutra.

Poem XLIV. There are a great many midaregami, "tangled hair" poems, from an exchange between Mikata and his wife in the *Manyoshu* – eighth century – to the first great book of Yosano Akiko, called *Midaregami*, the early twentieth-century woman poet and still the unequalled poet of modern verse in classical (tanka) form.

Poem XLV. Shizuka Gozen (twelfth century) was a white dress dancer of spectacular beauty who became the lover of Minamoto no Yoshitsune, the tragic hero of the epic of the war between the Taira and Minamoto, which brought to an end the great years of early Japanese civilization. He was the principal general of his brother Yoritomo, and broke the power of the Taira in a series of battles. After Yoritomo outlawed his brother, Shizuka was captured fleeing through the snowbound wilderness on Mt. Yoshino. When Yorimoto and his courtiers were worshipping at the Tsuruga-Oka Shrine at Kamakura, he commanded Shizuka to perform her most famous dance. She refused but was finally forced to dance. Shortly after, she gave birth to Yoshitsune's son, whom Yoritomo murdered. She then became a Buddhist nun and lived to an old age, long after Yoshitsune had been destroyed in his refuge in the far North. She is not a great poet but, with Yoshitsune, one of the tragic figures of Japanese history. Her dance occurs in several Noh plays.

Poem XLVI. Echoes a Buddhist sutra, but also refers to herself as Marichi – Ray of Light – and Dainichi (Vairocana) – The Transcendent Sun.

Poems XLVII–XLVIII. These two poems are factual – DDT exterminated most of the fireflies of Japan, and the Hotaru Matsuri – Firefly Festivals – are no longer held, or even remembered by the younger generation.

Poem LII. Echoes a Buddhist sutra, the poems of Yokobue and her lover in the *Heike Monogatori*, and finally Buddha's Unicorn (often called "Rhinoceros") Sermon.

Poem LIII. Pachinko is a form of vertical pinball – and immense pachinko parlors, crowded with hypnotized players, litter Japan. It is a symbol of total immersion in the world of illusion, ignorance, suffering, and grasping. Wisdom is Prajna – the female consort of a Buddha in esoteric Shingon Buddhism, corresponding to the Shakti, power, the consort of a Hindu god. Note that Prajna is, in a sense, the contradictory of Shakti.

Poem LIV. The first cuckoo in the dawn poem probably dates back before the *Kokinshu*, the second Imperial Anthology. There are many geisha songs that essentially repeat it. But Marichiko says, "was it the moon itself that cried out?" a completely novel last line. The hototogisu does not say "cuckoo," but something like the five syllables of its name, or "horobirete," perishing. It is *Cuculus poliocephalus.*

Poem LV. Echoes a Buddhist sutra.

Poem LVII. The bell cricket is the Tsukutsuku boshi, *Cosmopsal tria colorata.*

As I finish these notes, I realize that, whereas Westerners, alienated from their own culture, embrace Zen Buddhism, most young Japanese consider it reactionary, the religion of the officer caste, the great rich, and foreign hippies. There is however a growing movement of appreciation of Theravada (Hinayana) Buddhism, hitherto hardly known except to scholars in Japan. Marichiko's poems are deeply influenced by Theravada suttas, Tachigawa Shingon, folksongs, Yosano Akiko, and the great women poets of Heian Japan – Ono no Komachi, Murasaki Shikibu, and Izumi Shikibu.

ON FLOWER WREATH HILL

In 1974–75, we lived in Kyoto in an embayment of Higashiyama, the Eastern Hills, in a seven hundred year old farm house.

The range, which rises directly above the easternmost long street of the city, culminates in Mt. Hiei. It is almost entirely forest and wildlife reserve because scattered all through it are temples and tombs and cemeteries. Our street led up to Yamashina Pass and across the street from our house a shoulder of the range rose abruptly to a little plateau on which long ago had been built the tumulus of a princess which now is only an irregular heap of low mounds covered with trees. Behind it is the complex of Shingon Temples called Sennuji, which includes a large building in which are stored the ashes of former emperors. The Japanese seldom bury the dead, and the tumulus age was of very short duration at the beginning of Japanese history, although it resulted in immense keyhole shaped mounds, one of them of greater bulk than the Great Pyramid of Gizeh, keyhole shaped and surrounded by a moat. The one mentioned in the poem had been a far more modest structure. Mt. Hiei is the site of the founding temples of Tendai and once, before they were all slaughtered by Nobunaga, contained sixty thousand monks at least. Today there are still many monasteries – but also an amusement park. Kamo River flows close to the edge of the mountains.

The second and third verses of Part II are a conflation of well-known classic Japanese poems, and Part V is entirely so.

Tanabata is Seven-Seven, the seventh day of the seventh month, when the Cowboy, Altair, crosses the Milky Way to lie for one night only with the Weaving Girl, Vega. Magpies link wings and form a bridge for him to cross, but there are many Chinese and Japanese dawn poems which would indicate that he rowed himself back.

Kegonkyo (Flower Wreath Sutra) is the Avatamsaka Sutra, by far the most profound and the most mystical of the sutras of Mahayana.

Before he entered Parinirvana, Buddha said, "The combinations of the world are unstable by nature. Monks, strive without ceasing."

St. Elmo's fires are the glowing balls of atmospheric electricity that usually appear as tips of light on the extremities of pointed objects such as church towers or airplane wings during stormy weather.

Important Japanese graves or family burial plots (only the ashes are buried) are often marked by a stupa (Japanese: *sotoba*) consisting of four and sometimes five stones, a cube, a sphere, a lune, a triangle, and sometimes a little shape on top of the triangle. Amongst other things, they symbolize the elements: earth, water, air, fire, and what we used to call ether. Unstable by nature, they do not take many decades to fall apart. There is a Mahayana doctrine, Sunyata, that ultimate reality is Void Only and what seems like reality are only fleeting compounds.

The third verse paragraph of Part VIII begins the possession by Ono no Komachi continued in the next paragraph, and there are many echoes of the three great Noh plays on Komachi, the greatest Japanese woman poet.

The fifth paragraph opens with an echo of a commentary on the Lotus Sutra; but with the orb spider's net, it becomes a poem of the Flower Wreath Sutra, known in Hinduism as the Net of Indra. Matsukaze and Murasame were two lovers of a prince exiled to the shore of Suma. They were salt girls who evaporated sea water over burning dried seaweed and driftwood, and who saw the moon one night after the prince had left, each in her own water pail or pails. There is a very beautiful Noh play on the subject, and they are common dolls. As dolls, they each carry two pails on a yoke and the classic dance with the yoked pails is one of the most beautiful.

The gopis are the nineteen thousand milkmaids who dance to Krishna's flute. His flute music connects true reality and the gopis, who dance and become Real. Music is being, but behind being is Ishvara, what Western philosophy would call the Absolute behind all absolutes. Kabbalah calls it the Ayn Soph and Buddhism the Adi-buddha. As the music enters her, and she enters the dance, each gopi knows that she is Radha, the beloved of Krishna, his Shakti, his Power, or his Prajna, his Wisdom. He is the avatar of Vishnu, and power and wisdom are the same. The Vishnulila, the play of Vishnu with the world of illusion.

Modern stuffy Indian pundits say that Krishna didn't really make love to nineteen thousand milkmaids. He knew by heart 19,000 slokas of the Vedas.

Flower Wreath Hill is also a Chinese and Japanese euphemism for a cemetery.

Copper Canyon Press wishes to acknowledge the support of Lannan Foundation in funding the publication and distribution of exceptional literary works.

LANNAN LITERARY SELECTIONS 2004

Marvin Bell, *Rampant*

Cyrus Cassells, *More Than Peace and Cypresses*

Ben Lerner, *The Lichtenberg Figures*

Joseph Stroud, *Country of Light*

Eleanor Rand Wilner, *The Girl with Bees in Her Hair*

LANNAN LITERARY SELECTIONS 2000–2003

John Balaban, *Spring Essence: The Poetry of Hồ Xuân Hương*

Hayden Carruth, *Doctor Jazz*

Norman Dubie, *The Mercy Seat: Collected & New Poems, 1967–2001*

Sascha Feinstein, *Misterioso*

James Galvin, *X: Poems*

Jim Harrison, *The Shape of the Journey: New and Collected Poems*

Maxine Kumin, *Always Beginning: Essays on a Life in Poetry*

Antonio Machado, *Border of a Dream: Selected Poems,* translated by Willis Barnstone

W.S. Merwin, *The First Four Books of Poems*

Cesare Pavese, *Disaffections: Complete Poems 1930–1950,* translated by Geoffrey Brock

Antonio Porchia, *Voices,* translated by W.S. Merwin

Kenneth Rexroth, *The Complete Poems of Kenneth Rexroth,* edited by Sam Hamill and Bradford Morrow

Alberto Ríos, *The Smallest Muscle in the Human Body*

Theodore Roethke, *On Poetry & Craft*

Ann Stanford, *Holding Our Own: The Selected Poems of Ann Stanford,* edited by Maxine Scates and David Trinidad

Ruth Stone, *In the Next Galaxy*

Rabindranath Tagore, *The Lover of God,* translated by Tony K. Stewart and Chase Twichell

Reversible Monuments: Contemporary Mexican Poetry, edited by Mónica de la Torre and Michael Wiegers

César Vallejo, *The Black Heralds,* translated by Rebecca Seiferle

C.D. Wright, *Steal Away: Selected and New Poems*

For more on the Lannan Literary Selections, visit:

www.coppercanyonpress.org

The Chinese character for poetry is made up of two parts: "word" and "temple." It also serves as pressmark for Copper Canyon Press.

Founded in 1972, Copper Canyon Press remains dedicated to publishing poetry exclusively, from Nobel laureates to new and emerging authors. The Press thrives with the generous patronage of readers, writers, booksellers, librarians, teachers, students, and funders – everyone who shares the conviction that poetry invigorates the language and sharpens our appreciation of the world.

PUBLISHERS' CIRCLE

The Allen Foundation for the Arts
Lannan Foundation
Lila Wallace–Reader's Digest Fund
National Endowment for the Arts

EDITORS' CIRCLE

Thatcher Bailey
The Breneman Jaech Foundation
Cynthia Hartwig and Tom Booster
Port Townsend Paper Company
Target Stores
Emily Warn and Daj Oberg
Washington State Arts Commission

CONTRIBUTING EDITORS' CIRCLE

Anonymous
Mimi Gardner Gates
Carolyn and Robert Hedin Fund of the Saint Paul Foundation
Jeanne Marie and Rhoady Lee
Wright Family Fund

For information and catalogs:
Copper Canyon Press
Post Office Box 271
Port Townsend, Washington 98368
360/385-4925
www.coppercanyonpress.org

BOOK DESIGN & composition by John D. Berry, using Adobe InDesign 1.5 on a Macintosh PowerBook G3. The typeface is Minion Pro, designed by Robert Slimbach as part of the Adobe Originals type library. Minion is based on typefaces of the later Renaissance, but is derived from no single source. Slimbach designed Minion in 1990, expanded it in 1992 to become a multiple master font (the first to include a size axis for optical scaling), and in 2000 turned it into an OpenType font that includes Greek and Cyrillic versions. *Printed by McNaughton & Gunn.*

www.ingramcontent.com/pod-product-compliance
Lightning Source LLC
LaVergne TN
LVHW090428230725
816804LV00022B/762